Slander and Sedition in Elizabethan Law, Speech, and Writing

Slander and Sedition

in Elizabethan Law, Speech, and Writing

Steven Veerapen

Peter Lang
Oxford • Bern • Berlin • Bruxelles • New York • Wien

Bibliographic information published by Die Deutsche Nationalbibliothek
Die Deutsche Nationalbibliothek lists this publication in the Deutsche Nationalbibliografie; detailed bibliographic data is available on the Internet at http://dnb.d-nb.de.

A catalogue record for this book is available from the British Library.

A CIP catalog record for this book has been applied for at the Library of Congress.

ISBN 978-1-78997-673-1 (print) • ISBN 978-1-78997-680-9 (ePDF)
ISBN 978-1-78997-681-9 (ePub) • ISBN 978-1-78997-682-9 (mobi)

Cover design by Peter Lang Ltd.

Published by Peter Lang Ltd, International Academic Publishers,
52 St Giles, Oxford, OX1 3LU, United Kingdom
oxford@peterlang.com, www.peterlang.com

This publication has been peer reviewed.

Contents

INTRODUCTION

Slander, Sedition and Libel: An Elizabethan Cerberus

In 1640, an illegal, handwritten poem which boldly proclaimed itself 'A Libell upon William Lord, Archbishop of Canterbury, in Parliament-time' was produced and circulated in manuscript.[1] The fact that the anonymous poet was unashamed in his recognition of his work as libellous is worthy of consideration, as Kevin Sharpe notes the 'multiple negative associations' of what remains a pejorative term.[2] What might have prompted a poet to associate his work with the much-criticised practice of defamation? The scene – literate readers passing handwritten verses full of vituperative comments about a dead political figure – calls to mind images of Ancient Romans gathered in shadowed corners on the Palatine Hill doing much the same, as much as it anticipates sniggering Georgians sharing satirical drawings. It is probably due to the former association that so much has been written on the verse libel's classical antecedents. It has been well recognised, certainly, in the work of David Colclough, who traces the history of poetic means of 'dispraise.'[3] More recently, the Early Stuart Libels website has opened up study of seventeenth-century libellous verses by providing an online database of surviving verses along with excellent commentaries.[4]

1 For discussion of the various manuscript miscellanies which included verses proclaiming themselves to be libels, see Marotti, *Manuscript, Print and the English Renaissance Lyric*, pp. 92–4. This particular libel can be found in the Bodleian Library's Rawlinson manuscript collection (Bod. MS Rawl. Poet. 26).

2 Sharpe, *Culture and Politics in Early Stuart England*, p. 286.

3 Colclough, 'Verse Libels and the Epideictic Tradition in Early Stuart England,' pp. 15–30.

4 Over 350 Stuart verse libels have now been published on this innovative open-access website, available at: <http://www.earlystuartlibels.net/htdocs/index.html>.

This form of attack was not suddenly born – or reborn – in the Stuart period, despite the seventeenth century witnessing its most celebrated examples. Indeed, Steven W. May's edited collection of fifty-two sixteenth-century verse libels with accompanying scholarly commentary provides a glimpse into earlier uses of the genre. In examining the earlier period, it becomes obvious that libelling was a lively if subversive pastime. As Alan Bryson puts it,

> the scurrilous, sometimes seditious, nature of verse libel made it immensely popular in Elizabethan England, although, while also restricting it mainly to manuscript circulation. Few examples found their way into print, rendering the genre largely invisible until today. Despite this, verse libel was one of the most pervasive forms of the period, nurtured with imagination and verve by a broad range of poets. Poems were passed – and not necessarily secretively – from one person to the next, they were cast into pulpits and public places, scattered about the streets, posted on walls. Some were even sung to popular tunes, the better to humiliate their victims while also introducing the genre to the illiterate (and thus broadening the public debate contained within them beyond the elite). Libellous verse was part of everyday life decades before scholars have thought; its impact largely unknown today.[5]

Here we have a vivid picture of the living libel – a word which having meant 'little book' had come to mean written attack – playing a role in sixteenth-century public discourse. The historical record attests to this, replete as it is with notorious cases such as that of the Dutch libel fixed upon a church wall in 1593, which drew on Marlowe's *Tamburlaine* and appropriated policy by telling immigrants to go home and threatening riots if they did not; the libellous writings which appeared daubed on Robert Cecil's home in London, calling him a toad; and, even earlier, the 1561 libellous writings thrown in the streets at Westchester following the fire at St Paul's cathedral.[6] Crucially, in these cases, the texts did not declare themselves 'libels': the state did that with the aim of condemning them. But then, 'the state' was itself in a process of formation, with overlapping jurisdictions, personal and idiosyncratic government in various areas, and

5 Bryson, 'Elizabethan Verse Libel,' p. 477.

6 Libellous epigrams and notes were thus evidently in use prior to the Stuart period, but their appearances were sporadic.

a legal system which, based as it was on precedent, was continually being written. Further, defamatory words were not only sung to popular tunes but, once those tunes had acquired scurrility via association, their apparently innocuous original versions could be sung and retain dangerous traces of malicious intent.[7] Despite their illegality, it is clear that written invectives played a role in public life, albeit one that authorities would like to see snuffed out, throughout the sixteenth century. But why?

The conventional answer lies in the name we have given the period: the renaissance. In this heady era, classical texts, writers, and modes of expression were reborn and, in England as across Europe, educated people rushed to adopt them. Hence Clare Bucknell notes that

> satiric poetry has existed in some form since the Ancient Greek period, but the Romans were the first to categorize it as a genre in its own right. The 1st-century rhetorician Quintilian claimed that satire was a distinctively Roman achievement, originating in the verse satires of Lucilius and becoming progressively refined by the poets Horace, Persius, and Juvenal. From the Renaissance to the Romantic period, satirists and commentators continued to look to the classical heritage of the genre in order to provide an authoritative basis for their enterprise. Elizabethan writers on satire argued that the genre was rough, wild, and vituperative, originating in the misanthropic 'satyr' figure of Greek drama. This image suited the group of angry young men who wrote verse satires in English in the 1590s, modelling their attitudes on the 'biting' satiric rage of Juvenal and Persius.[8]

There are problems here. On the one hand, it is tempting to imagine that renegade classicists sought to sharpen their political claws on a genre condemned by their peers as an embarrassing vice of the writers of antiquity; on the other, it is evident that verse libels were utilised prior to the much-examined 1590s, and, further, that neither the 1590s wits nor other libellers made overt or serious attempts to bring the genre into a higher degree of repute. Libel, as a mode of expression, remained murky, often funny, eminently creative, and perpetually underground. The classical associations of the verse libel as genre were more a justification, and an admittedly sophisticated dressing up, of transgressive language than a cause.

7 Veerapen, 'Slanderisation and Censure-ship.'
8 Bucknell, 'Verse Satire from the Renaissance to the Romantic Period.'

If we are to discover why the genre exploded in the seventeenth century, it will be necessary to gain a fuller understanding of how it developed in the earlier period not just as a toy of 'angry young men' (often educated and aristocratic) but as a living, breathing genre which, though unashamed, never did gain absolute respectability. Throughout the early modern period, such poems continued to be traduced as 'slanderous' and 'seditious' by opponents and victims – terms which were used interchangeably with 'libellous' and helped those using them condemn condemnatory writings.

It will be the purpose of this study to examine the conditions which led to libellous poetry being produced in such volume, in addition to tracing the writing practices, cultural movement and resistance to official methods of censorship and regulation which resulted in the popularity of seventeenth-century libellous writing. In order to do so, it will focus not on the explosive politics of the mid-1600s, but rather the operations, failings and negotiations of the Elizabethan and early Jacobean regimes in asserting control and authority over speech and writing. What will be revealed is a state which sought to regulate language through multiple institutions, legal and religious, and yet lacked the resources and machinery to combat increasingly muscular dissidents; which faced attacks on several fronts; was riven by internal competition for jurisdiction; relied on idiosyncratic offices; and was hampered by fierce debates about whether state authorities or literary figures ought to be the masters of language. As will be seen, 'slander' and 'sedition' were terms which, though possessed of legal definitions, were apt to be used with a degree of latitude in neighbourly disputes, in religious and political debates, on the stage, and against playwrights. To understand what slander and sedition actually were, how they came to be used so loosely, and how poets could appropriate them as political tools, it will be necessary to look across the courts, the church, and the burgeoning dramatic sphere.

At the heart of this book will not only be the ways in which slander and sedition were defined and deployed as accusations by the state and its various arms (and its various manifestations), but the ways in which such accusations were negotiated and resisted. As such, different approaches to slanderous speech and writing will be considered, in addition to such defences as the justification of truth, parliamentary privilege, the rhetoric of counsel, counter-accusations of defamation, artistic satire, anonymity, the use of manuscripts and secret presses and, ultimately, the embracement of the term 'libel' as an artistic (and often political) written endeavour used at variance with less well-regarded (and more easily caught) forms of slanderous speech.

That the Elizabethan period coincided with a rise in cases of defamation is well recognised, with M. Lindsay Kaplan noting the increase in libels, defamatory ballads, epigrams and other forms of speech as well as the consequent linguistic and material obstacles faced by the law in its attempts to control and regulate transgressive language.[9] Further, as Debora Shuger has astutely recognised, academic research has in recent years begun to critically reconsider the ways in which state power was revealed by the clashes between authoritarian, regulatory censorship, and the individual capacity for resistance.[10] This trend in scholarship has repercussions for any critical study of slander: an offence which itself crossed the thresholds of tort law, criminal law, seditious libel and ecclesiastical misconduct.

At root, a slander represents a malicious imputation against an individual's title, morals, reputation or, in early modern parlance, fame and honour. Common slanders therefore typically centred on allegations of bastardy, cuckoldry, and whoredom. The slanderer's danger lay in his or her ability to use defamation in order to breach social hierarchies and destabilise existing, civil social orders. So it was with libel. As Hickson and Ruck recognise, modern libel denotes written defamation whilst slander refers only to the spoken word.[11] In the Elizabethan period, however, the precedent-based common law courts drew only a faint line between libel and slander – a notion certainly borne out by the various contemporary proclamations which decry 'slanderous libelling' and forbid 'bookes sclanderous to the state.'[12] Spoken or written, harmful language was harmful. Whether they used the word 'slander' or 'libel,' to a great many Elizabethan minds, it

9 Kaplan, *The Culture of Slander*, p. 2.

10 Shuger, *Censorship and Cultural Sensibility*, p. 6.

11 Hickson and Carter-Ruck, *The Law of Libel and Slander*, p. 1.

12 Dean, *Law Making and Society in Elizabethan England: The Parliament of England, 1584–1601*, p. 71; Clegg, *Press Censorship in Elizabethan England*, p. 31.

was a pervasive and mischievous force, with ecclesiastical and common law court jurisdictions embroiled in suits aimed at punishing slanderers as malefactors or seeking religious restitution or civil damages for individuals whose reputations and honour were maligned. Few would support the circulation of slanderous material for the simple reason that if laws against it were to be relaxed, any neighbour might freely attack the reputation of another without consequence or recourse on the part of the defamed. Worth bearing in mind throughout are the triple pillars on which slander lay, any of which authorities might choose to rest cases against: intent (whether words were maliciously spoken or written); audience (did people of sufficiently good credit – or people likely to breach the peace as a result – hear or read those words?); and effect (did someone suffer or might a tumult or disorder have arisen?).

The modern distinction between slander and libel has its roots in a particular judicial body which flourished under Elizabeth – that of the prerogative court of Star Chamber, the motives of which were 'not those of private law, or of the compensation of injury, but of criminal law.'[13] In short, it was the prerogative of the Star Chamber to 'repress [dis]order and disaffection.' Providing legal muscle in the pursuit of certain slanders as criminal, the statute of *Scandalum Magnatum* – which can be traced to 1275, and provided for the punishment of those who spread defamatory rumours about important personages of the state – was re-enacted with changes in the second year of Elizabeth's reign.[14] Prior to Elizabeth's accession, it had been reissued by Mary I, and it never lost its political associations (its perennial intent being to prevent rebellions and the spread of popular disaffection, rumour, false prophecy, and untrue stories which might provoke civil disobedience). As the common law did not outlaw slander, but rather treated it as a civil wrong, a heavy burden fell on the statute: it was often invoked to deal with those whose words attacked public figures.

13 Milsom, *Historical Foundations of the Common Law*, p. 388.

14 Baker (*An Introduction to Legal History, 4th Edition*, p. 437) notes that the statute was designed to prevent discord between classes, 'but the purpose of an action on the statute was clearly to vindicate the magnate's name by recovering damages.'

That the statute was utilised during the Elizabethan period is telling, suggesting as it does a contemporary preoccupation with the dangers inherent in political dissent voiced through the slander of public figures. It is here that one finds the origins of a doctrine which was to bloom with vexatious speed in the seventeenth century – that of sedition – or words of such potentially provocative and explosive import that they might have resulted in a breach of the peace.[15] Throughout the reign of Elizabeth, the severity with which one might expect to be treated for slander varied wildly depending on the nature and form of the words spoken, the target of calumny, the political climate and the region in which the words were investigated. Such variety could prove useful in exercising clemency. The blurred line between slander and sedition certainly ensured that the state, in certain cases, could charge malfeasants with slander rather than the more serious crimes of sedition or treason, thus sparing them more serious penalties – treason, especially, being the ultimate crime and carrying the ultimate penalty.[16]

So, in this welter of developing legal thought, political tumult, and experimental poetic expression, what exactly was slanderous, what was seditious, and how did people know? How, too, could transgressive language be reclaimed and the accusations of slanderer and libeller turned on the state? The answers lurk in various aspects of Elizabethan daily life, from its network of law courts, secular and religious, to its reformed faith, which sought to govern language whilst fending off attacks from Catholics and non-conformists, to the stage, which became a locus for exploring the power relations inherent in the use of language.

15 Sedition, as Manning ('The Origins of the Doctrine of Sedition,' p. 101) recognises, came to be glossed as 'words that fell short of treason and did not directly involve – although they might lead to – acts of violence.'

16 The laws on treason were themselves amended throughout the sixteenth century and often reactively so. The 1571 Act, for example, made it illegal to bring foreigners into the country. See: Bellamy, *The Tudor Law of Treason*, p. 1397.

Models of Censorship

Attempts at controlling slanderous discourses, whether handwritten or printed, are inextricably linked with censorship and press control. It is therefore unsurprising to note that 'the Star Chamber, assisted by statute, quickly assumed a strict control over all printed matter,' rigorously punishing slanderers whose words fell under its jurisdiction on the basis that they constituted a threat to the security of the state.[17] In recent years, a variety of models of censorship have been proposed by scholars, with M. Lindsay Kaplan providing a critique of the most well-known. In *The Culture of Slander in Early Modern England* (1997), Kaplan explores slander as a 'model for the analysis of power relations between poet and state'; she recognises the dynamism inherent in state attempts to control slander whilst tracing the government's own employment of slanderous activity in humiliating, defaming and discrediting its enemies. In advancing this argument, Kaplan further recognises the limitations of such influential critics as Annabel Patterson, whose *Censorship and Interpretation* (1984) is held to lack historical perspective.[18]

Similarly, Janet Clare's *Art Made Tongue Tied by Authority* (1999), though recognised for its meticulous scholarship, is held to be overly speculative and presumes to suggest that the thoughts of writers were actively controlled by all-powerful state mechanisms. Richard Dutton, in his *Mastering the Revels* (1991), is considered to have tacitly revealed connections between the structures of defamation and censorship and it is here that Kaplan explicates a notion critical to any study of slander: that the state's overt concern with suppressing and censoring seditious printed works (especially at times of political turbulence), is symptomatic of a wider concern with a range of transgressive and unlawful discourse. The problem here is that if we accept that the Elizabethan government deplored dangerous speech and writing, it must have been remarkably ineffective at doing anything about it. Much material seems to have reached readerships (and listeners),

17 Hickson and Carter-Ruck, *The Law of Libel and Slander*, p. 15.
18 Kaplan, *The Culture of Slander*, pp. 2–3.

leaving the state to hunt down those it called slanderers after their words had got into circulation.

Naturally, given the aims and objectives of Kaplan and those she critiques, focus is placed on literary and theatrical censorship. This, unfortunately, reduces the scope of study to the relationship between poets, playwrights and the state, despite the fact that legal bills were intermittently issued which, rather than focusing on dramatic or literary work, recognised the need to curtail and, where necessary, destroy all 'slanders against the present government of the realme in causes eyther Ecclesiasticall or Temporall' as well as 'against Slanderous Books and Libels.'[19] The commercial stage comprised only a small, London-centric – though obviously important – part of the relationship between slanderous language and the state.

As Cyndia Clegg notes, press control in Elizabethan England hardly corresponded to the 'overwhelming systemization' identified by such scholars as Annabel Patterson.[20] Instead, she argues, it comprised a

> pragmatic response to an extraordinary variety of particular events ... government enactments affecting printing, as well as practices in the printing trade, were contradictory and idiosyncratic: a crazy quilt of proclamations, patents, trade regulations, judicial decrees, and privy council and parliamentary actions patched together by the sometimes common and sometimes competing threads of religious, economic, political and private interests.

Clegg's perception of the ways in which slanderous printed material was repressed is suggestive of a government which responded to events rather than pre-emptively sought to control them. In essence, she provides a dynamic view of press control akin to Kaplan's understanding of literary censorship. To Shuger, the similarity is obvious, with censorship (whilst retaining the potential to be viciously repressive) 'apt to be hijacked in all manner of directions.'[21] If instances of censorship – be they of dramatic, literary, printed or religious complexion – suggest the state's anxiety over

19 Dean, *Law Making and Society in Elizabethan England: The Parliament of England, 1584–1601*, pp. 58, 72.

20 Clegg, *Press Censorship in Elizabethan England*, p. 5.

21 Shuger, *Censorship and Cultural Regulation*, p. 7.

suppressing disorder, it is also worth considering the difficulties faced by the government in dealing with a society which still retained a thriving manuscript culture.

Attempting to address the question of why calls for a free press were relatively unheard of prior to Milton's *Areopagatica* (1644), Shuger has in many ways refreshed the study of censorship with a convincing new model which holds that English censorship differed significantly from the ideological war on heresy and thought common in Papal Europe. Instead, she argues, the regulation of language in Tudor England centred on the prevention of defamation and hate speech. Rather than controlling ideas, Shuger's model posits a system which did not seek to ban ideas, but rather attempted to avoid giving official approval to unlicensed and inflammatory words. Excavating the rich, intertwined and complex Roman and common law roots of English law, it is Shuger's ultimate contention that the English remedy for defamation and slander (as it developed in the common law) was especially derived from the Roman concept of *iniuria* – a concept which held that verbal attacks carried the same weight as physical assault.[22] In this she is undoubtedly correct. However, she goes a little far. The implication of her model is that slanderers and libellers were roundly viewed as transgressors, with the law a protective force geared towards safeguarding reputation and righting wrongs, at least on the surface. It certainly could be. Yet it could also be a monstrous and autocratic beast with a number of legal tools at its disposal, including much-used statutory laws popular with the Tudor monarchs. Which it would use the slanderer could never be entirely sure.

Nevertheless, Shuger's argument is not only rooted in legal history but presents an important understanding of why Elizabethans did not call for a free press (such calls being tantamount to calling for the removal of protection from verbal attack) and hence why severe repression of texts was relatively rare. As will be seen, several texts labelled 'slanderous' by the state, both literary and religious, escaped the authoritarian retribution inflicted on John Stubbs for his *Discoverie of a Gaping Gvlf*. The state, it will be seen, was more adept at refuting and answering charges of slander than

22 Shuger, *Censorship and Cultural Regulation*, p. 66.

it was at cracking down on dissenting voices. Further, the legal recourses to which the Elizabethan government could turn were legion. Indeed, it is probably more useful to consider the laws which were used by the state (in its various ecclesiastical and secular courts) than the courts themselves. Shuger usefully provides five main, substantive legal categories available to those charged with punishing slanderers:

I. Ecclesiastical law (spiritual defamation);
II. Civil law (the common law action on the case for words, i.e. civil defamation);
III. Criminal law (scandalous libel);
IV. Statutes (in particular, those concerning religion, treason and sedition);
V. Royal proclamations.

The first was the domain of the Church courts, which had a long history of power over defamation, and which ostensibly sought community harmony. The second was a branch of the common law: it was the province of the secular courts and focused on righting civil wrongs, basing its rulings on precedent. The third is problematic; under the precedent-based common law system, slander and libel would not be adequately addressed until 1605, when 'seditious libel' entered the law books. This did not mean, however, that the Tudors did not prosecute as criminals those who spoke (and wrote) words considered dangerous. Prior to 1605, the crime-focused Star Chamber did (arguably mis-)use the existing law of libel to fine and punish people whose slanderous words were held to provoke unrest, though the law itself was intended to allow redress to private individuals. This was useful in extorting fines, with the state as the injured party, but it put jurists on less secure ground in maiming and imprisoning malfeasants as criminals. More reliably, the fourth, statutory law, provided a number of legislative means of doing so. Royal proclamations followed suit, often outlawing specific texts and behaviours.

Not only were the laws against slanderous discourse divided between a hive of law courts, but they were further presided over by a vast array of officials, from judges to Masters of the Revels, High Commissioners and Privy

Counsellors. Still further were they complicated by a multitude of minor rules and legal precepts which were applied with varying severity regionally and according to fluctuations in the number of cases tried throughout the period, as English law absorbed and engaged two aspects of the Roman law of defamation: *mala carmina* (which protected a person's name) and *mala calumnia* (which aimed to protect people from false accusations which put them in danger of the courts). Shuger's study, whilst providing a convincing and welcome new model of censorship which foregrounds slander and defamation law as pivotal is nevertheless troublesome. Though the fusing of law, literature, libels, and consensual cultural practice sheds a new light on censorship as it likely worked in practice, whilst moving away from the conjectural and extrapolated, case-specific models previously noted, it may be argued that the presentation of any 'model' of censorship remains constricting. Furthermore, as Joad Raymond recognises, Shuger's 'cultural case' precludes a close look at the procedural.[23] The two were necessarily intertwined, with cultural attempts by state bodies to answer slanderous attacks frequently following the procedures of the law courts. This we should expect. The Elizabethan law courts were well used to dealing with slander, and the path involved a tedious back-and-forth of answer, rejoinder, and surrejoinder between plaintiff and defendant. When the state itself played the plaintiff, a similar dance followed.

As has been noted, slander was a significant problem not only for the law courts, but for dramatic and literary production as well as press control and censorship. Myriad questions, however, remain. How did the law respond to slander and in what ways did it construct the image of the slanderous figure? In what ways were legal developments and the patchy and reactive developments in censorship related? Quite why slanderers were of such persistent concern to the state is obvious – indulging in slander implied a disregard for social hierarchies, with popular allegations such as bastardy, licentiousness or whoredom impinging not only on the lower orders, but peers of the realm and the sovereign herself. Whilst censorship, suppression, control, and legal redress might mitigate the effects of slanderous discourse, it remains true that the state was hampered not only

23 Raymond, 'Review of *Censorship and Cultural Sensibility*,' p. 1605.

by shifting political circumstances, but by religious invectives and dissent from abroad and at home; the inability (in either resources or intent) of state institutions to sustain a monolithic system of censorship; and the invidious reality of manuscript proliferation negotiating its way around state-operated printing presses. Further, the rise in the common law courts of slander suits and countersuits fought between members of an increasingly litigious populace is also worthy of consideration in examining precisely how the state maintained a role as arbiter and governor of language.

Methods of Resistance

In a world of frowning state institutions overseeing a web of laws and law courts each geared towards stopping slanderous speech and writing, one wonders how those bent on defamation set about it. What could the man or woman determined to speak or write proscribed (or even just unneighbourly) speech do? Simply speaking out of turn could, after all, have dire consequences. In April 1585, Jeremy Vanhill was sentenced to hang for saying, 'shite upon your queen, I would she were dead that I might shit on her face.'[24] In 1598 the Catholic Thomas Cholcroft was examined for saying, 'they that hated not the queen, I would they were hanged.'[25] The Sessions at Newgate, too, hanged a lawyer's clerk named Waterhouse at Smithfield in 1601 'for making libels' (this as part of what the government's had declared the Earl of Essex's 'rebellion').[26] These unfortunates were either unaware of the risks of what they said and did or uncaring. More likely is that they lacked the skill of voicing dissent in ways that might offer hope of evasion and, further, were doubly unfortunate in speaking out during periods of unrest. What is clear, though, is that people, then as now, wished to speak out. But for authorities, disgruntled words and

24 The preceding cases of slanderous speeches made against Elizabeth are drawn from Cressy, *Dangerous Talk*, pp. 76–7.

25 Questier, *Catholicism and Community*, p. 41.

26 *CSP, Domestic, Elizabeth* – Vol. CCLXXXI.

writings could easily herald the outbreak of treasonous activity, popular disaffection, riots, revolts, or coups.

A variety of options were available, and each, as will be seen, was tested and found to be of lesser or greater efficacy. We might start with one of the key tenets of the legal principle – that of the justification of truth. In the civil courts, defendants accused of slander and/or libel were at liberty to plead the truth of their words and thus impute that they had not constituted slander. Cases could be lost and won on the grounds of words being successfully or unsuccessfully justified as true. Naturally, this presented a problem for authorities, who at various times sought to crack down with some force on any and all language which was scurrilous, fractious, and sowed societal discord and division. Hence, the law took a somewhat schizophrenic view of the truth of defamatory language, and in cases prosecuted under statutory laws, they were at pains to demonstrate the malicious and seditious intent of speakers and writers. Depending on the nature of words spoken and the quality of the person at whom they were directed, justifications of truth were treated with varying degrees of tolerance. In cases in which libellous words were considered criminal, truth was no defence at all.[27] Thus, poor Thomas Cholcroft could hardly mount a defence that it was true indeed that he wished all who did not hate the Queen were dead (nor that he imputed no specific crimes to the Queen in his words against her); his words were in breach of felony statutes and thus a criminal act in themselves.

As Hamburger, notes, 'it was one matter for a judge to denounce a common law defamation as false, but quite another for a defendant to have a statutory right to defend his crime on the ground of its truth.'[28] Indeed, during the early years of the Jacobean age, the justification of truth was to part company entirely from criminal law, remaining only a defence for slanderous accusations brought in civil suits. Ultimately, therefore, we must view the justification of truth as a particularly dangerous strategy during Elizabeth's reign. Alleged slanderers who invited the wrath of the

27 Habermann, *Staging Slander and Gender*, pp. 46–7.

28 Hamburger, 'The Development of the Law of Seditious Libel and the Control of the Press,' pp. 668–9.

state and who were prosecuted under statutes which expressly allowed for pleadings of truth (the wording of the statutes explicitly requiring the falsity of the words spoken or written) were vulnerable to barbarous punishment regardless.

Those who wished to express potentially slanderous sentiment had another quiver to their bow. Appropriation of the term 'slander' was a common theme of slanderous language, particularly that which was written. Texts denounced as 'libellous' by the state were apt to engage in a public dialogue, deploying counter accusations of slander and scurrility and suggesting that the state itself was the slanderer. Such was certainly the case in several celebrated religious controversies – notably that involving the mysterious Martin Marprelate, who libelled leading Church figures with gusto whilst maintaining that they themselves were the slanderers. A similar strategy was involved in the back-and-forth witnessed in Doleman episode, which was begun by the Jesuit Robert Parsons penning *A Conference About the Next Succession to the Crown of England* (1594), which made its way to Britain from Douai. Touching on the unsecured and forbidden succession question, his text jabbed indirectly at the Elizabethan government, noting that 'election, which is subject to great and continual dangers of ambition, emulation, division, sedition and contention, which do bring with them evident peril of universal destruction and desolation of the whole Body, and this at every change of the Prince, which change on the other side is much assured by Succession.'[29] Queen Elizabeth, in other words, was the cause of sedition through her refusal to name an heir. Response came in the form of Sir Thomas Craig's *The Right of Succession to the Kingdom of England*, which immediately castigated Persons ('who assum'd the counterfeit name of Doleman') for seeking 'to kindle the flames of Sedition.' The counter accusation lacked the punch and effect of the original – the original seditionist was more adept than the state-authorised response. Yet the point is that it was made at all. As Lake, in his recent overview of the libellous invectives poured out by the Elizabethan government and its enemies, notes,

29 Parsons, *A Conference About the Next Succession to the Crown of England*, p. 102.

> each side thus cited the other's activities as a licence for their own. In particular, each cited the other's side resort to various sorts of appeals to the public or opinion in order to justify their own equally libellous, malign, and illegitimate resort to the same claims and methods. Quite remarkable is the eerie resemblance between each side's account of the other's sinister manipulation of news and rumour and of the nature of the arena of discourse and debate, of rumour and opinion, to which both were appealing and indeed seeking to bend their own version of events.[30]

This is textbook courtroom stuff. Either side was engaged in a process of claiming authority of whichever narrative was in question (the succession; religion; the Queen's reputation) and denounce the other as malicious slanderers full of gall and lacking in authority. It was the plaintiff's counsel forming a narrative denigrating the defendant's, and the defendant's rubbishing the plaintiff's writ large.

Popular recognition of this mode of negotiation is attested to by contemporary dramatic production, which frequently recognised the role of the state in employing slanderous rhetoric against its enemies. Such figures as Ben Jonson and Shakespeare were to be vocal in their recognition, with the latter, in particular, identifying in slander its power not only to defame its victim, but to redound on the authorities charged with punishing the alleged slanderer. However, this too was a problematic method of negotiation. For one, those who were either caught slandering the state (however much they counter-accused it) were liable to be punished, and so counter slander alone could not hope to protect or justify those who were, in effect, subject to a state armed with the power to make laws, proscribe language and offer official alternatives to illicit discourse. It was a dangerous game. It is telling that both Marprelate and Doleman were pseudonyms; the writers behind them could not count on calling out the government as the real troublemaker as a protective strategy.

For dramatists and poets, the late Elizabethan period's engagement with libel and slander was not just one which invited theatrical representation. Instead, it was a topic of lively debate, with a vogue for satirical expression becoming a problem for authorities, who were to be stirred to anger by such satirical – and therefore, in the law's eyes, slanderous – plays

30 Lake, *Bad Queen Bess*, p. 37.

as Jonson's *Isle of Dogs* and *Eastward Ho*. As Michelle O'Callaghan suggests, poets in particular were to engage directly in recovering classical ideas of the satire and testing the limits of satirical decorum.[31] The reaction of the authorities was to introduce a 'partially successful 1599 ban on printed satire.'[32] Indulging in public satire, whilst evidently a desirable mode of expression, was evidently not a successful means of avoiding charges of slander or sedition. Indeed, producing such matter for the stage was instead likely to invite such accusations, demonstrating as it did a willingness to expose dangerous language to third parties. As will be seen, however, satirists were not to abandon satire; instead, they were simply obliged to find alternative methods of sidestepping legal censure.

Another key method – the limits of which were particularly tested in Elizabeth's reign – by which potential slanderers attempted to defend their work was the adoption of the rhetoric of counsel. To John Guy, the period coincided with significant debates about what could be publicly broached by active citizens who wished to engage in affairs of state. Traditionally the privilege of nobles and legitimate counsellors who were duty-bound tender honest opinions, 'which the ruler received in a spirit of likeness and equality,' this humanist-classical model was appropriated by those who sought to advise the Queen on political matters without the benefit of noble birth or access to the inner workings of the state.[33] Such individuals, invariably, were deemed to be nothing more than upstart slanderers. As Natalie Mears has recognised, however, rigid acceptance of the humanist-classical model was not universal; some subjects were to misunderstand (wilfully or otherwise) counsel as 'socially inclusive and essential to queenship.'[34] To their misfortune, Elizabeth was to 'explicitly reject the view that subjects, beyond those she specially appointed, had any right, duty or responsibility

31 O'Callaghan, *The English Wits*, p. 38.

32 Bellany, 'Railing Rhymes Revisited: Libels, Scandals, and Early Stuart Politics,' p. 1143.

33 Guy, 'The rhetoric of counsel,' pp. 292–4.

34 Mears, 'Counsel, public debate and queenship: John Stubbs' "The Discoverie of a Gaping Gulf",' p. 646.

to contribute to the policy-making process.'[35] Such was certainly the case in the prosecution of John Stubbs' *The Discoverie of a Gaping Gvlf* (1579): a text which openly sought to counsel the Queen, but came from an upstart Inns of Court lawyer and, rather than keeping its advice private, sought to open it up to public deliberation.

Peter Mack has, however, widened the recognisable scope of rhetorical counsel beyond the Queen's specially appointed counsellors.[36] The Elizabethan parliament, he suggests, exercised not inconsiderable powers of counsel (much to the chagrin of the Privy Council itself). For the study of slander and sedition, this is particularly interesting. As Peter Lake notes, parliament was traditionally considered a privileged sounding board which could forestall accusations of slander (due to the privilege of speech there inherent) whilst appealing to and manipulating public opinion.[37] Yet the use of parliamentary counsel in advancing opinions did not, in the Elizabethan period, grant freedom of speech. Indeed, particularly slanderous MPs (such as the Wentworth brothers) were arrested for taking their vitriolic speeches too far, even as they were delivering them.[38] Furthermore, texts which played on the notion of the deliberative, privileged site of parliament (such as the first and second *Admonitions to Parliament* [1572–3]) whilst appealing to the public were also to come in for state censure and, rather expectedly, to be condemned as slanderous libels. Thus, the adoption of the rhetoric of counsel, whether by subjects, parliamentarians, or those seeking to appropriate the perceived privileges of parliament, simply invited the ignominy of accusations of slander (and, at worst, violent legal retribution).

Thus far, the methods of navigation by which potential slanderers could air their views and circumvent the law have been problematic. It is therefore necessary to consider the various media available to facilitate avoidance of punishment and censorship (if not accusations of libel itself which, as we have seen, were ultimately to be embraced). Notable in many of the

35 Mears, 'Counsel, public debate and queenship: John Stubbs' "The Discoverie of a Gaping Gulf"', p. 649.

36 Mack, *Elizabethan Rhetoric*, pp. 239–45.

37 Lake, 'The Politics of Popularity,' p. 78.

38 Mack, *Elizabethan Rhetoric*, p. 241.

methods of circumvention previously discussed is the identification of the slanderer: either by virtue of policing or due to the simple fact that figures such as Stubbs, Jonson and Wentworth made no attempt to conceal their identities when producing material which was to be deemed slanderous. Those who spoke slanderous words were, of course, easily identified. Those who wrote them down, via printing press or pen, had potential recourse to anonymity and were to thus prove more elusive.

There are several important cases in which manuscript and print intersect. In particular, one might consider *The Copy of a Letter Written by a Master of Art of Cambridge to His Friend in London* (1584), commonly titled *Leicester's Commonwealth*. Framed by a letter ostensibly written by a Cambridge scholar, the text presents itself as a true account of a conversation between the scholar, a Protestant gentleman, and a Catholic lawyer, which interweaves comic vilification of Elizabeth I's perennial favourite, the Earl of Leicester. Given the state's intolerance of attacks on leading members of the nobility (as underpinned by the statute of *Scandalum Magnatum*), it is unsurprising that every effort was made to recover and destroy all extant printed copies. Nevertheless, numerous manuscript copies were made and circulated.[39] It is a fact which betrays not only the popularity of the libel (Leicester being unpopular with the public), but displays neatly the limitations of repressing the printed word in a society which retained the ability to reproduce and disseminate handwritten material in a subversive and alternative way.

Naturally, however, the scribally produced word had its own drawbacks. Private letters (including those containing impressions of slander cases and seditious material noted by ambassadors) could transmit the details of slander – and, hence, the slanderous accusations themselves. As a consequence, manuscript copies of transgressive writing brought material considerations and required technologies of early modern espionage. James Daybell has, for example, identified the strategies available to those bent on committing words of slanderous or seditious import to paper. Whether using codes, ciphers, invisible ink or name substitution, 'secret forms of letters-writing crowd the archives of state papers foreign and domestic.'[40]

39 Raymond, *Pamphlets and Pamphleteering*, p. 22.
40 Daybell, *The Material Letter*, p. 149.

It is perhaps for this reason that Shuger claims that manuscript writing was unregulated. This is, however, a claim which requires a broader scope of critical thought, as well as a more liberal view of regulation. As Daybell further recognises, 'mechanisms by which hundreds of manuscript copies of letters were scribally circulated from the late-Elizabethan period onwards were broadly similar to other texts such as libels.'[41] Libels, of course, were anathema to the state (despite their increasing popularity and circulation). Whilst not formally regulated by official censors or state authorities, slanderous manuscripts were subject to searches and punitive laws which could inspire self-censorship (as will be seen in the case of Fulke Greville's 1600–1 *Antony and Cleopatra*). Further, they could cause writers to employ covert writing techniques. It is certainly difficult to reconcile Shuger's claim with such evasive strategies. In fact, it may be argued that manuscripts were not unregulated, but simply that the relatively poor regulation which attended them made slanderous handwritten texts (often circulated amongst small groups of kin, friends and neighbours) less likely to be caught.[42] To claim that manuscripts were unregulated is to claim that speech was unregulated, when of course speech was open to being reported, used too freely, or otherwise brought to the attention of authorities and, if deemed slanderous, subject to slander and libel law (which allowed fewer legal avenues of escape by presuming that the act of writing constituted evidence of malicious intent whereas speakers might plead innocence of intent; thus the law sought to make up for the reality that speakers were potentially easier to catch than manuscript-writers). We must, therefore, not conflate a lack of regulation with relatively weak and inefficient regulation.

A particularly important facet of scribal publication is not just its ability to allow slanderers a route of anonymous publication, but its tendency to produce material directed at high-ranking, public figures. The boon of anonymity, argues Harold Love held a great attraction for those who wished to abuse the great, albeit it was largely limited, for obvious reasons, to people willing and able to write down their slanders rather than speaking them.[43] Attacks on the great personages of the realm were, of

41 Daybell, *The Material Letter*, p. 190.

42 Bellany, 'Railing Rhymes Revisited,' p. 1148.

43 Love, *Scribal Publication*, p. 189.

course, to be discouraged. Unsurprisingly, however, the illicit manuscript writings 'which achieved the widest currency were those associated with monarchs, well-known politicians and public figures.'[44] Throughout the period, a range of legal mechanisms were used to proceed against those who dared write, print or speak ill of the great personages of state. It is understandable that slanderous accusations made against the Queen herself were subject to the most rigorous legal penalties.[45] Illustrating this point is the fact that slandering or defaming Elizabeth – which Clegg equates with attacking her authority – constituted high treason. However, Clegg further notes that possessing books which did this 'often became evidence rather than the cause itself in treason trials.' Further, 'writing, publishing or printing texts with rumours, libels, or slanders against the Queen' were felonies which invoked increasingly rigorous sanctions.[46]

It is therefore worth considering the treatment afforded *An Admonition to the Nobility and People of England and Ireland* (1588): a pamphlet of doubtful authorship attributed to Catholic Cardinal William Allen. Famously, the Queen was not only attacked due to her 'unjuste tyrannicall statutes' and 'Antichristian and unnaturall proude challenge of supremacy,' but on a personal level she was considered 'an incestuous bastard, begotten and born in sin, of an infamous courtesan Anne Bullen.'[47] The invitation was therefore made to refuse to recognise Elizabeth's claim to the throne and consider her deposition. Similarly of threat to the existing social order was the sharp criticism of the Queen's ministers, with allegations made that she had suppressed the rightful Catholic nobility for the purpose of elevating lesser men such as Burghley and Leicester, with the latter's credit once more impugned by slanderous claims that he had forged himself a particularly murderous career. Whatever the true authorship of the *Admonition*, it provides an example of the anti-Elizabethan propaganda

44 Daybell, *The Material Letter*, p. 191.
45 Hamburger ('The Development of the Law of Seditious Libel and the Control of the Press,' p. 670–1) lists the various felony statutes introduced to protect the Queen and her ministers from libellous attack. The series of statutes provide ratification of Daybell's claim that the famous were likely to come under attack.
46 Clegg, *Press Censorship in Elizabethan England*, pp. 32–3.
47 Allen, *An Admonition to the Nobility and People of England and Ireland*, pp. 8, 6.

which flared up at various times during Elizabeth's reign and led to a wave of 'polarized rhetoric' found in later proclamations which advocated 'loving subjects ... to inquire and search for all such bulls, transcripts, libels, books and pamphlets, and for all such persons whatsoever as shall bring in, publish, disperse or utter any of the same.'[48] It is therefore no surprise that the pro-Catholic voices which rose in opposition to the Elizabethan state were deeply invested in constructing a highly personalised enemy. Not only Elizabeth, but the Cecils, father and son, were lambasted as the crooked and corrupt hands on the English tiller. In some ways these Catholic attacks, which posited a *regnum cecilianum*, played into the hands of authorities, who could point out those making them as slanderers and seditionists. According to the polemicists, the Cecils had engineered a degraded state that promoted new and unworthy men, and it was the Catholics who were the voice of traditional authority. Yet the attacks proved annoyingly popular; indeed, Elizabeth's last favourite, Essex, would prove as much an opponent of Cecilian pre-eminence as the Catholics had been, and in much the same fashion. And, typically, Essex would respond to attacks that he was engaging in slander by counter-accusing Cecil and others as 'frantic libellers.'[49]

It became the prerogative of the government not merely to suppress especially slanderous texts, but to respond to them by constructing slanderous enemies in order to delegitimise and counter-slander them. In return, the accused slanderer might well repay the state in the same coin. Equally worthy of consideration, however, are the added difficulties faced by the government in controlling material which originated on the continent. Indeed, it seems mostly a matter of luck that the full textual edition of the *Admonition* was likely lost amongst the cargo of the Armada galleons, as the dangers of continental slanders, from anonymous or counterfeit sources, finding their way into England continued to present a source of anxiety to the state.[50] The problem was that the importation of anonymous

48 Clegg, *Press Censorship in Elizabethan England*, p. 70.

49 Hiscock, 'Achilles Alter,' p. 120.

50 Orwell and Reynolds, *British Pamphleteers*, p. 45.

material, like homegrown material produced anonymously, often confounded authorities.

Given the relative success of anonymity (as it was increasingly recognised by those who wished to engage in slanderous discourse), it is possible to reconsider the 1640 poem which proclaimed itself unashamedly slanderous. As noted, as an art form verse libels were to increase in frequency following the reign of Elizabeth. Throughout the early modern period, however, they were often marked by anonymity, which Pauline Croft recognises as 'a useful form of protection.'[51] Various theories have been proposed to account for the growth in their popularity. For Croft, as for Bucknell, it was the result of the growth in factionalism in the 1590s – a factionalism which has been disputed, at least prior to the late 1590s, by Paul E. J. Hammer.[52] For David Colclough, they achieved popularity due to the shortcomings of the humanist-classical model of counsel and the awareness of writers of the place of the libel in a civic, humanist tradition, which viewed them as a legitimate means of counsel – despite the prevailing attitude of the state contending that 'libels were not an acceptable vehicle for moral rebuke or counsel.'[53] In an overview of the development of academic study of Stuart verse libels, Alastair Bellany recognised, however, that 'our understanding of the verse libel's genealogy is hazier than it should be.'[54] This is because they popped up not as a full-fledged poetic genre but as intermittent thorns in the side of the body politic: amalgamations of various tried-and-tested methods of resistance to the state. In part, this study will argue that verse libels did not just gain popularity and political cachet due to the failure of humanist-classical counsel or growing factional tensions in the Elizabethan court (although both played a part). Instead, it will pursue the rather elastic, haphazard and occasionally barbarous ways in which the Elizabethan state accused and fought slanderous discourses, in addition to examining the ways in those who sought to engage in such discourses either satirically,

51 Croft, 'Libels, popular literacy and public opinion,' p. 273.

52 Croft, 'The Reputation of Robert Cecil,' p. 63; Hammer, *The Polarisation of Elizabethan Politics*, pp. 359–61.

53 Colclough, 'Verse Libels and the Epideictic Tradition,' pp. 27–30; Bellany, 'The embarrassment of libels,' p. 151.

54 Bellany, 'Railing Rhymes Revisited,' p. 1165.

artistically or for personal, political or religious purposes attempted to negotiate and mitigate accusations of slander. Ultimately, it will be argued, the proud verse libel was born out of lessons learned in Elizabeth's reign, which led not to the stifling of libellous material, but the appropriation of it as a mode of expression which was to part company with spoken, civil disputation and develop as a discrete literary genre which, depending on the quality of the individual poem, had the power to fascinate and engage contemporaries.[55]

Sites and Sources of Slander and Sedition

In the pursuit of a wider understanding of Elizabethan slander and sedition, the term 'Elizabethan' must be treated with some laxity. Given that many legal developments had their roots in previous eras and reached their peak in the opening years of the Jacobean regime, there was a certain degree of overlap between operations before and shortly after the period of Elizabeth's reign. Broadly, this study will follow a legal and cultural rather than a regnal narrative, bearing in mind James Daybell's assertion that 'cultural and social practices … are rarely constrained by precise dates.'[56] Elizabeth's death did not mark an absolute end of the period to which we ascribe her name. Rather, the golden age of Elizabeth drew to a close in the 1580s, and thereafter rose in prominence many of the great Jacobean figures; as Elizabeth aged and her closest associates died off, she became something of a relic in her own realm. Aside from the regnal name affixed to legal documentation, little else changed in terms of the law, at least until James I began drawing up his own diktats (perhaps most relevantly his rules governing what might be permissible on the stage – an area which during Elizabeth's reign had been uncodified and mutable). One of the chief roles of the early modern English monarch was

55 Bellany 'The embarrassment of libels,' p. 161.
56 Daybell, *The Material Letter*, p. 19.

guardianship of the law and oversight of the dispensing of justice rather than wholesale rewriting of the law books. Consequently, this study will begin with an examination of slander as it was applied in the legal sense, with an analysis of law cases in which slander was fought as a civil tort as well as those in which slanderous speech and writing were tried in the criminal courts using, predominantly, statutory law.

Here, questions of the representativeness of available cases must be addressed. A debt of gratitude is particularly owed to the antiquarian efforts of legal scholars such as R. H. Helmholz, whose compilation of translated Elizabethan defamation suits in the common law courts has proven especially useful.[57] Nevertheless, although they provide an excellent insight into how justice was administered according to precedent and the rule of law, this approach has its problems. For one, the rank of litigants is not always known with certainty, and the cases recounted do not include full details of witness statements and deliberation. This problem is somewhat mitigated by archival use of the records of the Star Chamber, as they comprise interrogatories, preliminary statements and – usually – details of the outcome of cases. Yet Star Chamber records are incomplete and disorganised. Furthermore, for the period in which this study is most concerned – the reign of Elizabeth – surviving Star Chamber manuscripts are catalogued only by the names of plaintiffs rather than by offence. One is therefore reliant on finding the names of litigants embroiled in criminal cases in the Star Chamber via alternative channels: particularly the nineteenth-century examination of the court's proceedings compiled by John Southerden Burn (1870). Equally useful has been the compilation of Star Chamber records preserved in John Hawarde's reports, the *Reportes del cases in Camera Stellata, 1593 to 1609: from the original ms. of John Hawarde* (1894). Hawarde's reports, however, are problematic in their temporal scope, focusing as they do on the latter years of the Elizabethan regime.

57 It will be noted that the records of the common law courts held in the National Archives are difficult to navigate because there are relatively few finding-aids to their contents (there are no indexes at all to the files, and very few to the rolls after 1250), and some of them are not yet completely sorted or catalogued. More problematically, they are written in abbreviated Latin.

Caveats must therefore be made concerning not just the representativeness of the suits that will be studied, but acknowledgement of the likelihood of their having been the subject of previous study by scholars interested in slander and sedition. The difficulty in finding relevant sources from across the spectrum of royal courts requires, therefore, a qualitative rather than a quantitative analysis. Nevertheless, it must be pointed out that such an analysis is useful in allowing us to see the options which were available to those brought before the courts under slander charges.

To build a wider picture of the operation of slander and sedition in the period, it is necessary to keep in mind Andrew Gordon's assertion that 'too rigid an emphasis on the legal records may blind us to the preconditions of prosecution for libel, which necessitate both an aggrieved party and an accused individual.'[58] With this in mind, the study will turn from the legal records of the Star Chamber to the breeding ground of the lawyers who played a central role in constructing judicial narratives: the Inns of Court. It was there that lawyers were trained, in part, through dramatic conceit and theatrical performance, and the Inns themselves produced drama which mused on the limits of counsel that were visibly pushed beyond acceptability by John Stubbs. In addition to well-known Inns of Court drama, consideration will also be given to the semi-private dramas staged during the traditional Christmas Revels. Particularly useful here is the publication of a wealth of material relating to the Inns. Nelson and Elliott's 2011 three-volume edition of dramatic records surviving from the Inns of Court includes material from manuscripts and printed books from the archives and libraries of all four Inns, as well as from The National Archives, the British Library, the Folger Shakespeare Library and other repositories. This has proved to be an invaluable resource and allows for an examination of the way in which semi-private stages 'performed' and understood slander and sedition as legal concepts.

Given that the Inns enjoyed a degree of liberty in performance, consideration will move to those sites in which slander was both deployed (sometimes unwittingly) and represented privately. Closet dramas will therefore come under scrutiny, although problems with such a study are obvious.

58 Gordon, 'The Act of Libel,' p. 385.

Whilst examination of representations of slander (and slanderers) is fairly straightforward, closet dramas which were themselves deemed slanderous will perforce have to be studied in terms of the reaction they provoked, and what this tells us about regulation of non-commercial material. This is a consequence, quite simply, of many such plays not surviving. 'Slanderous' plays do, however, survive from the commercial stage, to which attention will subsequently be turned. Attention will be focused on the transmission and performance of slander (and the requirements needed before it could be so accused) in semi-private and public playing spaces. Particularly useful here is the examination and criticism of existing models of censorship, in addition to consideration of the evident vogue for satire by playwrights who lacked the means and ability to express themselves freely without inviting accusations of slander.

The deficiencies of free expression highlighted in this section will lead into the religious sphere, with an examination of the ways in which the Church – which played a traditional role in combatting defamation – exercised control and sought dominance in the regulation of language through both the ecclesiastical courts and the often desultory efforts of the High Commission. Study here will begin with the Church courts, drawing primarily on the printed trascriptions produced by Helmholz, Essex ecclesiastical court records recounted by F. G. Emmison, and Public Record Office cases compiled by Paul Hair. As in earlier work on the common law courts, it will be noted that questions of representativeness again arise, with an acknowledgement of Laura Gowing's warning that urban and rural areas evinced differing levels of defamation litigation, likely due to the close quarters of urban life.[59] Questions also arise at to the differences in legal engagement over defamation according to gender, with women evincing significantly higher levels of engagement, perhaps due to litigation offering them a platform by which to publicly seek redress for grievances. Mitigation of the issue of representativeness will here be met by secondary material which allows for a wider scope of defamatory activity – particularly the work of Martin Ingram (1987). Emphasis, however, will be placed not only on the operation of the Church courts, but the ways in which religious

59 Gowing, *Domestic Dangers*, p. 20.

officials were granted increased powers of press control – a fact which led not only to resistance by illicit press users, but ultimately a recognition of the power of anonymous libel which could preclude the possibility of legal repercussions. Remaining a constant will be the term 'slander,' its various permutations, the necessities of invoking it as an accusation, and the benefits and drawbacks of the state's attempts to maintain authority over an intrinsically unstable, slippery and potentially dangerous category of language which could circulate via loose or malicious speech, the output of the press and potentially poisonous pens.

PART I

Slander in the Elizabethan Courts

CHAPTER 1

Elizabethan Slander and Sedition in Law and the Law Courts

One would like to think that, even in the Elizabethan period, the law provided clarity in its pursuit of justice. To do so would, unfortunately, be to embrace idealism. Based on precedent, English common law was an amorphous beast, constantly evolving as cases arose; and, in terms of slander, arose they did – with alarming frequency. To illustrate something of the complexity of slander suits, it is instructive to consider a number of potential scenarios:

1. John says to Robert, privately, 'you are a thief.' As the two men are alone, no third party is present to create the conditions necessary for a successful slander suit. If Robert sought restitution, his lawyer would have to prove that the words, which undoubtedly imputed a crime, reached a wider audience and negatively affected his income. Otherwise the words are liable to be dismissed as pure insult. The whole matter is civil.
2. John says to Robert, 'your wife, Alice, is a thief.' Alice is accordingly defamed before Robert, the third party. Robert and his wife have a case, if they can demonstrate that their income has been negatively affected. In this scenario, John's counsel must prove that Alice is indeed a thief. The whole matter is civil.
3. John writes, 'Robert is a thief.' Whether the note is passed around or kept close, the act of writing puts John past all justification of truth, and Robert might sue him as a slanderer in the secular courts (an attractive proposition given its powers of ordering recompense from a guilty defendant).
4. John says to Robert, 'the Queen is a thief.' Here, Robert is third party to a slander against the Queen. This is potentially treasonous

and certainly criminal, and therefore it will likely be prosecuted under statutory rather than common law. The Queen and therefore the state are the plaintiffs and John, if found guilty, might face any number of punishments.

5. John writes, 'the Queen is a thief.' Again, John has passed all justification and has committed an undoubtedly criminal offence. But what punishment might he expect? That rather depends on the political climate, the court which tries him, and the exact legislation invoked against him.
6. John says to Robert, 'you are a thief and a whoremaster.' If the words are spoken between the two men, Robert's lawyers would struggle to make a case. If others hear, he might sue John; but where? The accusation of thievery warrants the secular courts, whilst the accusation of whoremastery warrants the ecclesiastical courts. Wrangling might well ensue.
7. John says to Robert, 'you are a cuckold.' Again, the matter is dubious and rests on whether anyone else heard the words. If they did not, the dispute is likely to be written off as private insult; if they did, the nature of the accusation warrants a hearing in the spiritual courts due to the nature of the word 'cuckold.'
8. John says to Robert, 'you are a fool and worse' in a tavern. The word was heard before a third party – a number of people, in fact – but is the word 'fool' actionable at law? Or is it pure insult? A good lawyer might press the case in the civil courts, but the courts might be less amenable to taking on a matter arguably frivolous.

Even the consideration of these manifold scenarios is problematic. What if the nefarious John was of a far lower rank than Robert? What if he was of a higher rank? What if, in the scenarios involving words against the Queen, he spoke them during a heated political climate, or wrote them and circulated them under a pseudonym? Further, depending on the courtroom in which he found himself and the laws or legislation under which he was tried he might find himself defending or mitigating the words he expressed; the intent behind them; the situation in which he expressed them; the real-world effects of them claimed by his accusers; or he might be denied defence completely. Intent, audience, and effect were determined by trial or prior investigation, again depending on the court involved – and which of the three would be given the most attention depended on the laws under which the alleged slanderer was tried. The clarity we like to associate with legal process suddenly becomes rather clouded. And yet scenarios similar to each of those above abounded. The law had to deal with them and, in so doing, it had to take into account all variables germane to any given case. The nature of the court in which the alleged victim – the plaintiff – might have his day itself rested on the ability to pay, the nature of the words spoken, the volume of litigation that the court had to deal with, and a number of other factors.

As has been noted, slander represented an enormously problematic offence throughout the sixteenth and early seventeenth centuries, due in no small part to its perceived capacity to subvert existing social hierarchies. Naturally, the growth in litigation during Elizabeth's reign had repercussions for the ways in which the law and, hence, the law courts, dealt with slander suits. The period coincided with a great deal of contemporary debate which questioned both the ethics of increased litigation (viewed as it occasionally was as symptomatic of an increasingly contentious society) and the propriety of increasing public access to legal machinery.[1] It has, indeed, been argued that the proliferation of lawyers and litigation indicates a more legally literate society than ever before. This is, however, a hazardous supposition. Many Elizabethans were certainly quite willing to go to the law with little provocation, but the idea that they understood it is belied by the need for so many trained lawyers. An apt metaphor might be that more people than ever were willing to travel through increasingly thorny forests, but they had less idea than ever of how to make their way; hence, more and better guides were required to prevent them getting lost.

Any consideration of the legal means by which litigants sought to sue, repress and punish slanderers requires recognition of the fact that English jurists of the sixteenth and early seventeenth centuries 'maintained that legal relief for defamatory words depended not only on the nature of the

1 Brooks, *Lawyers, Litigation and English Society Since 1450*, pp. 23–4.

words themselves, but also on the quality of the person of whom the words were spoken.'[2] By the Elizabethan period, this notion had a curious provenance; during the period of Thomas Cromwell's ascendancy and Henry VIII's break with Rome, the 1534 Treason Act had promised punishment for those who

> do maliciously wish, will or desire by words or writing, or by craft imagine, invent, practise, or attempt any bodily harm to be done or committed to the king's most royal person, the queen's or the heirs apparent, or to deprive them of any of their dignity, title or name of their royal estates, or slanderously and maliciously publish and pronounce, by express writing or words, that the king should be heretic, schismatic, tyrant, infidel or usurper of the crown.[3]

The word 'maliciously' is noteworthy, focusing attention as it does on the intent behind speech – an intent to be determined by the state. It is a rather clumsy attempt to stifle words prejudicial to the monarchy and its religious pretensions, but what is more interesting is that it was found necessary. The indication is that people were slandering their superiors. The Act did not eradicate this. Under it, people such as Margaret Cowpland were arrested for calling Anne Boleyn a 'strong whore' and Henry VIII an 'extortioner and knave.'[4] Under the second Tudor monarch, it became illegal to speak treasonable words rather than just committing or encouraging treasonable acts, as had been the case under earlier Acts.[5] It is sometimes claimed that, for the first time, speaking ill of governors out of sheer discontent was illegal, where once prosecution for dangerous talk rested on its being proven to action rebellious or seditious deeds. However, this is overstatement. In fact, during the reigns of Henry IV and Henry VI, there had been executions carried out against people whose treason had been to be heard speaking against the monarch.[6] What Henry VIII, with the help of his minister, Thomas Cromwell, did was

2 Lassiter, 'Defamation of Peers: The Rise and Decline of the Action for *Scandalum Magnatum*,' p. 216.

3 Baker, *The Oxford History of the Laws of England Volume VI*, p. 586.

4 Marshall, *Heretics and Believers: A History of the English Reformation*, p. 214.

5 Bird, *Press and Speech Under Assault*, p. 145.

6 van Patten, 'Magic, Prophecy, and the Law of Treason,' pp. 5–6.

to reactivate and codify laws against speech which had hitherto been invoked at times of unrest and which, in likelihood, no one then living had seen enacted until the episode of 'the King's Great Matter.'

The Boleyn marriage had, however, another important effect in that it also gave new energy to the swirl of rumour and prophecy which had been a feature of mediaeval life. Rumours, for example, could be notoriously difficult to trace due to the speed and scope of their spread. In 1527 rumours surrounding the pulling down of churches were popular and required laborious investigations.[7] Prophecies were just as dangerous – more so, perhaps, because they anticipated and encouraged future action rather than simply spreading stories of what had or was happening. So it was that the infamous Elizabeth Barton was executed for her prophecies against the King's separation from Catherine of Aragon and remarriage to Anne Boleyn prior to the tightening up of the Treasons Act (1534). Though Barton's prophecies did not rhyme, they coincided with a wider renaissance of prophetic rhyming, which led Henry VIII's council to examine and execute 'the so-called prophets who had uttered rhyming predictions filled with topical references to people and events.'[8] This has led Marcus Harmes and Gillian Colclough to collapse the words spoken against Henry's ministers with those later spoken against Elizabeth's: both are considered examples of the resurrection of the mediaeval practice of prophetic rhyming. This is only partially fair. The practice of libelling, though it bore a resemblance to rhyming prophecy, was more of a great-grandchild than a sibling, with later sixteenth-century (and early Stuart) libels being less political attacks shrouded in mysticism and religion and more political attacks nakedly direct and insulting. One finds more in common between the 1484 epigram, nailed to the door of St Paul's, which read, 'the cat, the rat, and Lovel the Dog / rule all England under a Hog' and 'A Libell upon William Lord, Archbishop of Canterbury, in Parliament-time' than between the former and the following popular verse (reworked from a ballad dating from the reign of Henry VI) against Cromwell:

7 Elton, *Policy and Police*, p. 47.
8 Harmes and Colclough, 'Proverbs and Princes,' p. 312.

Much ill cometh of a small note,
As Crum well set in a man's throat,
That shall put many other to pain, God wote;
But when Crumwell is brought a-low,
And we rede out the Christ Cross rowe,
To R. L. and M. then shall we know news.[9]

The style of the 1484 epigram and the anti-Cromwell verse are manifestly different, though they share the common goal of criticism and both represent ancestors of the more famous, later verse libels. Under Henry VIII and his descendants, though, the weapons used to combat religious, secular, mystical, and personally insulting speech and writing were blunt. Statutory law cared less about the style of words attacking the state than finding those behind them. Nevertheless, there was a great deal of turbulent artistic and legal water between 1484 and 1640.

In the first year of the reign of Edward VI, all forms of treason were abolished except those contained in the new 1547 Act, those in the original 1351 Act, and treasons consisting of counterfeiting coinage or forging the King's seals. Yet prophecies denigrating the government – caused by religious alteration and economic woes – were 'buoyant.'[10] Although Henry VIII's legislation against false prophecies spoken even during private conversations was repealed, Edward's government felt it necessary to issue 'a less severe one against fond and fantastical prophecies.'[11] After his death, Mary I again underscored the 1351 Act's provisions, complaining of 'vain prophecies' which 'caused tumults and disorders,' relying also on a reissue of statute law (notably *Scandalum Magnatum*, of which much more later) to suppress dangerous speech.[12] Elizabeth would follow suit, with felony statutes and proclamations also sporadically issued and aimed at protecting defamation of her person and outlawing specific texts. It is fair to say, therefore, that the sixteenth century was one of shifting laws designed to

9 Wright, *Political Poems and Songs, Vol. II*, p. 221.

10 Goodbody, *The Spoken Word*, p. 153.

11 Wickins, *Victoria Protestantism and Bloody Mary*, p. 261.

12 Ibid. See also: Loades, *The Reign of Mary Tudor*, pp. 116–17 for the difficulty of catching Marian rumour mongers.

regulate what people could safely say and write, and the government was predominantly interested in what they said and wrote about their ostensible betters. Whether people were legally permitted to say and write things, of course, hardly tells us whether they were more or less inclined to do so. Indeed, the fact that Tudor-era authorities saw fit to tinker quite so much with language laws suggests that people were exercising their tongues and pens with alacrity. One might draw a modern parallel with, for example, piracy of copyrighted content: the multiplicity of laws against piracy suggests not that people are under the cosh of legal oppression and frightened to pirate music and films, but rather that a significant number of people are doing exactly that.

Yet again, one must consider the issue of rank (when it can be determined), and the consequences it had for the defendants, plaintiffs, and even the type of court employed in slander suits. In so doing, it is necessary to consider the various activities of such disparate jurisdictions as the common law courts, which were capable of dealing with slander using the civil law of tort as well as criminal law; the ecclesiastical courts, which operated on the principle of public penance, without a view to pecuniary compensation of the victim; and the Star Chamber, which centred its jurisdiction on the protection or punishment of high-ranking individuals.

Early modern England's network of law courts often had overlapping jurisdictions.[13] The wheels of justice turned with varying degrees of speed and efficacy in such varied courtrooms as that of the travelling Assizes, the Quarter Sessions, the Court of Chancery, manorial courts, the Common Pleas, the King's Bench and the Star Chamber. Those that are of particular interest in the study of slander suits and the legal status of defamation, however, are undoubtedly the latter three, due not only to the availability of surviving legal manuscripts, but to the issues raised by the courtrooms'

13 Habermann (*Staging Slander and Gender*, p. 54) notes the overlapping of jurisdictions particularly concerning defamation law. It is, she argues, 'not surprising that defamation law should frequently have been a bone of contention in power struggles between different branches of jurisdiction. The nature of the offence necessitates deliberations about the force and meaning of words which may be difficult to maintain since they are likely to have repercussions on the process of deliberation itself.'

separate, though not entirely unrelated, jurisdictions. Both the court of Common Pleas and the King's Bench, for example, were linked by their focus on cases fought at the level of the common law. Further, both made use of juries and publicly produced witnesses, with the sentence being read by a judge. In his 1583 overview of the commonwealth, Sir Thomas Smith usefully distinguishes between the justices of the two courts, with the 'Chiefe Justice' leading the King's Bench and the 'other chiefe Justice of the common place' hearing predominantly civil matters 'where the pleading is for money, or land or possession, part by writing, part by declaration and altercation of the advocates the one with thother, [so] it doeth so proceede before them till it doe come to the issue.'[14] The key differences of note between the two common law courts lie in their jurisdictions and legal costs. The Common Pleas held sway only over matters that were purely civil in nature whereas the more expensive services of the King's Bench could be appealed to in matters both civil (that is, with financial restitution sought from plaintiffs) and criminal (which meant, during Elizabeth's reign, that the court might try defendants using statutory legislation, royal proclamations, or even the woolly laws of libel designed not for criminal but private, civil suits).

The prerogative court of Star Chamber may be differentiated, at least nominally, by its common affiliation with, in the age of Elizabeth, exclusively prosecuting criminal cases. Defamation charges could be brought in the Star Chamber against any individual who threatened the security of the state through immoderate speech, writing or print, and was thus deemed to have allegedly committed a crime. As opposed to the courts of common law, the Star Chamber retains a certain notoriety for its composition. Judgements were made entirely by privy counsellors, who proceeded on handwritten depositions and pre-digested evidence (or occasionally on verbal confessions), and only summoned the accused before the bar in the final stage of the trial. As will be seen, the records of all three courts, despite their disparity in legal jurisdiction, display a number of similarities in authoritarian and legal concern. It will also be seen that the interplay between spoken, handwritten and printed slander gave rise to varying judicial

14 Smith, *De republica Anglorum*, p. 30.

punishments across the three courts, with the perceived role of slanderer a fluid one, capable of exercising tongue, pen or printing press with varying, but invariably malicious and damaging intent.

In his comprehensive overview of the development of the law of seditious libel (defined in the common law in 1605 as slanderous discourses against the state or its governors: itself a criminal matter rather than a civil one), Philip Hamburger adumbrates the various legal methods by which the Crown could prosecute the authors, producers and distributors of printed libel.[15] However, it is worth remembering that no sharp line was drawn between spoken slander and written libel.[16] The danger was not simply in the content, but the form; writing and print were merely representations of the spoken word, and all writing carried with it the implicit danger of being spoken.[17] Furthermore, it remained a keenly felt concern that texts which could not be legally printed could nevertheless enter circulation via manuscripts, in foreign or clandestine imprints or via word of mouth.

As Hamburger notes, it was the prerogative of the Crown to control the dissemination of slanderous material by the laws of treason, heresy, the law of libel, felony statutes (including *Scandalum Magnatum*), defamation (in the Church courts) or licensing. Treason, Hamburger argues, provided certain procedural advantages (for one, the defendant was afforded no defence); however, it risked public outrage and represented too harsh a punishment for men whom the authorities rather wished to control than eliminate.[18] Consequently, Elizabethan cases of high treason for defamatory speech (such as the 1577 burning of Mary Cleere of Ingateston, for declaring the Queen to be 'base born and not born to the crown') or for the spread of seditious, illicitly printed material (as in the 1581 execution of

15 Hamburger, 'The Development of the Law of Seditious Libel and the Control of the Press,' pp. 661–765.

16 Hickson and Carter-Ruck, *The Law of Libel and Slander*, p. 16.

17 Bellany ('Railing Rhymes Revisited: Libels, Scandals, and Early Stuart Politics,' p. 1146) has identified in libellous writings their particular propensity to work in ways even beyond their original author's intent. In other cases, such as that of the work of Martin Marprelate, material lent itself well to oral recitation.

18 Hamburger, 'The Development of the Law of Seditious Libel and the Control of the Press,' pp. 667–8.

the Jesuit, Edmund Campion) were relatively rare. Still rarer were heresy trials, with Catholics spared a method of punishment – burning – reserved for Anabaptists.[19]

Rather more effective was the statute of *Scandalum Magnatum*, refined under Elizabeth, which had 'created a statutory offence of defamation … making it illegal to invent or spread either spoken or written false news or tales concerning the King, prelates, dukes, earls, barons and other nobles and great men … and also of the Chancellor, Treasurer, Clerk of the Privy Seal, Steward of the King's house, Justices … and of other great officers of the realm.'[20] Crucially, slanders indicted under the statute were prosecuted on the basis that they were known untruths, with the alleged slanderer permitted, during the court proceedings, to defend his words or writings on the grounds of their veracity.[21] As a criminal court, the Star Chamber was keen to stress the dangerous effects of such words or writings, which put them beyond justification; unless tried under specific felony statutes, it was not what people said or did which was the crime, but what their words caused, intended, or invited. In this it borrowed from the proceedings of the non-criminal common law of libel, which relied on the real-world effects of language in the form of lost earnings – but in criminal prosecutions effects were investigated as potentially (or demonstrably) seditious. Other, more specific, statutes, such as that passed in 1581 which held that any printed or handwritten defamation of the Queen that was not already treasonous was to become a felony; that introduced in 1585 which made slander of the government in print or manuscript a felony; that which made slander of the established religion a *praemunire*; and that which subjected a slanderer of the Queen's council to imprisonment and fine at her pleasure all served, Hamburger argues, to shore up laws on licensing which were only tightened with the widening of the powers of the Star Chamber and High Commission over printing presses later in the reign.

19 Mortimer, *The Time Traveller's Guide to Elizabethan England*, p. 92.

20 Cressy, *Dangerous Talk*, p. 29.

21 Hamburger, 'The Development of the Law of Seditious Libel and the Control of the Press,' p. 669.

The law of libel, which, in the Elizabethan period, included handwritten and printed as well as spoken defamation (the modern distinction between written libel and spoken slander not being made until 1660), constituted a further method of repressing slander.[22] Crucially, Hamburger notes that

> criminal prosecutions for written defamations parted company with other actions and prosecutions for defamation after 1521, when a new rule in King's Bench allowed some unprivileged defamations to be justified as true. This new rule apparently applied to all actions on the case for defamation and perhaps, at least in the early seventeenth century, to some criminal prosecutions for spoken defamations. In prosecutions for written defamations, however, the defendant could never justify his words as true.[23]

Here, prosecution was contingent on the fact that defamations 'had been made known or published to a person other than the defamed.' That is, words affecting the honour or reputation of any individual were only deemed injurious if they occurred before a third party and caused financial or reputational losses. To Hamburger, however, the laws of licensing provided authorities with rather more advantages: notably that they 'provided the crown with censorship prior to publication and easy conviction of offenders.'[24]

The multiplicity of methods recognised as potential avenues of prosecution for language routinely deemed 'slanderous,' however, suggests that licensing was an imperfect system of language regulation. Texts considered slanderous by the state might (as will later be seen) have achieved licence via lax censorship, or even bypassed government censors entirely through the use of illegal presses or manuscript. As Shuger notes, such texts as Campion's *Rationes Decem* (1581) were even legally published in England as a preamble to Anglican William Whitaker's denunciatory response.[25] Here we arrive at an apparent paradox of accusations of 'slander' and the

22 Baker, *An Introduction to Legal History, 4th Edition*, p. 445.

23 'Privilege' is here used in the legal sense acknowledged – that is, that there was an appropriate reason for the words being spoken.

24 Hamburger, 'The Development of the Law of Seditious Libel and the Control of the Press,' p. 673.

25 Shuger, *Censorship and Cultural Regulation*, p. 15.

practice of censorship. In order to be deemed slanderous (and therefore publicly censured), material must reach a third party. As such, it is arguable that licence may have been given to texts such as the *Rationes Decem* as an exercise in the re-establishment of state authority, which intended not to stifle all debate, but to provide its own, sanctioned answer. Licensing, at any rate, was a method of proactive censorship which neither achieved nor attempted the wholesale curtailment of inflammatory print – and had no jurisdiction over speech or manuscript.

Naturally, issues therefore arise concerning the form of slanderous material, as well as its intended audience. Painter recognises that printed material lends itself well to publication and distribution in the trade sense, whilst identifying the legal notion of 'republication' as a term encompassing the repetition of defamation in any form.[26] Nevertheless, it must be noted that Elizabethan prosecutions for handwritten and printed defamation did not allow for the justification of truth. Interesting questions remain as to the ways in which handwritten (or printed) inflammatory material was viewed in relation to its spoken counterpart. That truth could provide a defence for spoken defamation but not written suggests, certainly, a demarcation; and yet scholars have been quick to recognise the lack of distinction between 'slander' and 'libel' in the period. Nomenclature aside, however, several reasons for the variance in legal treatment may be suggested. Primarily, it was an issue of pragmatism. William Hudson's *Treatise of the Court of Star Chamber* reflects that he who put 'a slander in writing, [put it] past any justification, for then the manner [i.e. the fact of publication] is examinable and not the matter.'[27] In essence, the act of writing a libel with the intent of publication allowed that act to be examined, the truth of the words notwithstanding. The intent, it was argued, was to cause division and discord, and harm the reputation of an individual or group before a third party. Writing involved premeditation; speech could be heated or even meant innocuously.

Perhaps more interesting, however, is the relatively recent suggestion in cultural studies of the early modern hierarchical view of speech and

26 Painter, 'Republication Problems in the Law of Defamation,' p. 1131.

27 Hudson, *Treatise of the Court of Star Chamber*, pp. 100–4.

writing. With speech once removed from thought, writing provided only a 'dull, dumb and gross' representation of the purer breath of the voice.[28] Still further, and in addition to such cultural prejudices, the frequent fact of anonymity was to be a problem little provided for by existing laws and statutes – at least insofar as it made prosecution difficult. Listing the various ways in which anonymity provided an elusive (and subsequently troublesome) mode of expression, Joad Raymond posits the possibilities of 'neministic' anonymity (which actively sought to avoid prosecution); 'pseudonymity' (to conceal identity or appeal to a selective audience); and the simple loss of the author's name, in addition to a host of others.[29] All, of course, may have been deployed either purposefully or accidentally in the production of slanderous written works, making the authoritarian capture of culprits a more difficult proposition than of those who wagged their tongues in the presence of witnesses. The act of writing slander (true or otherwise), therefore, became a potential problem which required greater intolerance lest it spread. It is likely for this reason that, by the Stuart period, libel investigations 'blurred the lines between authors, distributors, and even readers.'[30]

At any rate, sixteenth-century authorities relied on punishing libel as a tort at the level of common law; a crime in the Star Chamber (whose presiding council frequently had to use rather bog-standard libel laws, statutes, and laws against sedition to convict, but with disputes as to justification); treason when the monarch or crown was brought into disrepute; or – in the case of defamed magnates – under an action for *Scandalum Magnatum*. In all matters of spoken slander, however, truth remained a thorny issue; even *Scandalum Magnatum* allowed for the technically admissible, legal justification of truth – despite the fact that, to the authoritarian Tudor regime, it was believed that 'if the facts alleged were true, the offence was worse, since a true slander was more likely to cause a breach

28 Slander, interestingly, offered a potential exception to the rule: defamatory words being 'but wind' in comparison to more dangerous illicit writing. See Habermann, *Staging Slander and Gender*, p. 57; Hope, *Shakespeare and Language: Reason, Eloquence and Artifice in the Renaissance*, p. 38.

29 Raymond, *Pamphlets and Pamphleteering*, pp. 64–5.

30 North, 'Anonymity in Early Modern Manuscript Culture: Finding a Purposeful Convention in a Ubiquitous Condition,' p. 27.

of the peace than a false one.'[31] In terms of the common law, however, the notion of 'seditious libel' (or libel likely to cause a breach of the peace) as punishable regardless of truth, did not make its first appearance until 1605, and was then utilised as a means of combatting predominantly handwritten seditious material.[32]

It was not until his post-Elizabethan survey, *de Libellis Famosis* (1605), that celebrated lawyer Edward Coke proved pivotal in establishing the lack of the defence of truth in common law cases of seditious libel, whilst further arguing that libel 'could be committed not only by means of written or spoken words, but even in a private letter.'[33] In tracing the development of judicial punishment for sedition, Hamburger perceives the hitherto unappreciated role of scribal production in the development of Coke's legal doctrine of 'seditious libel' as a separate common law crime.[34] Recognising the failure of existing laws (from the statute *Scandalum Magnatum*, with its focus on 'false' news, to licensing laws, which sought to keep abreast of burgeoning print), it is evident that 'none of the traditional options seemed suitable for use against manuscripts.' He continues,

> As it existed in the late sixteenth century, it [the law of libel] was not yet a suitable means of prosecuting manuscripts that defamed officials (let alone those that more generally criticised the government) … Thus, in the late sixteenth century, the Attorney General could use libel law to bring a criminal action against someone who defamed an official in manuscript, but he could do so only with a libel law that had been developed to punish defamations of mere private individuals. He [Coke] needed a law especially designed to deal with attacks on officials.[35]

Hitherto, it had been a felony under statutory law to defame the Queen in speech and writing and to spread (loosely defined) false news or

31 Manning, 'The Origins of the Doctrine of Sedition,' pp. 100–1.

32 Hamburger, 'The Development of the Law of Seditious Libel and the Control of the Press,' p. 665.

33 Manning, 'The Origins of the Doctrine of Sedition,' p. 121.

34 Hamburger, 'The Development of the Law of Seditious Libel and the Control of the Press,' p. 692.

35 Hamburger, 'The Development of the Law of Seditious Libel and the Control of the Press,' p. 692–3.

proscribed texts. Coke determined to extend the severity of the law to afford similar protection to the reputations of others in high office, guarding them against spoken and written defamation. Here one also might return to Shuger's claim that scribally published material was free from regulation. Evidently, there was an anxiety about the ways in which those spreading slanderous manuscripts could be punished – but it is arguable that even unsuitable methods of control (such as the threat of prosecution for libel, with no recourse to pleading truth) constituted a form of regulation, albeit one without the formal rigour of licensing or official, pre-publication censorship. Furthermore, Hamburger's acknowledgement that the 1605 law of seditious libel was employed primarily to prosecute those who circulated illegal manuscript writings cannot be ignored.[36] Such intolerance of (and the apparently rising need to legislate against) handwritten material is, in itself, indicative of what Loades recognises as a hierarchical society often conceptualised in organic terms: a body, the component parts of which were believed to 'exist in a foreordained and permanent relationship with the rest.'[37] Consequently, such material evidence of social disharmony as handwritten or printed slander (especially when it voiced sedition) exposed discord, and, whether true or not, constituted both a crime and an offence against God's divinely ordered social hierarchy. Furthermore, it is no great deductive leap to suppose that written slander, in addition to its potential for widespread circulation, was far more likely to be directed at high-ranking and well-known individuals – another compelling reason for the law's unfavourable disposition towards it.[38] Hamburger further notes that various

36 Hamburger, 'The Development of the Law of Seditious Libel and the Control of the Press,' p. 665.

37 Loades, 'The Theory and Practice of Censorship,' p. 141.

38 In particular, slanderous material circulated in manuscript was apt to be directed at great personages of the state (Daybell, *The Material Letter*, p. 191). Love (*Scribal Publication*, pp. 37–8, 189) also provides a useful discussion of the ways in which scribal and print publication differed – chiefly noting that, whilst 'scribally circulated texts would have had a much more restricted availability than the average printed text … [but], operating at lower volumes and under more restrictive conditions of availability than print publication, it was still able to sustain the currency of

(unsuccessful) felony statutes which defined certain types of dissent as criminal also arose. Whilst *Scandalum Magnatum* and libel 'looked solely to the defamatory and therefore fractious consequences of language … the Tudor felony statutes punished the expression of seditious opinion as a crime in itself.'[39]

It was under such felony statutes that the Queen herself sought restitution in the remarkable case of John Stubbs' seditious *The Discoverie of a Gaping Gvlf*. As Hamburger notes, it was the Queen's desire that Stubbs be hanged for what she considered felonious and injurious writing; however, the Grand Jury refused to indict, leaving justice to be sought as a criminal matter under the auspices of a 'seditious libel' statute of *Scandalum Magnatum* in the court of King's Bench (which, it will be remembered, could act as both civil and criminal court).[40] Consideration of the work itself, however, provides a useful exercise in determining the nature of anti-establishment views which stirred the ire of the Crown and led to the book's reputation as a 'heap of slanders and reproaches of the said Prince (Alençon), bolstered up with manifest lies … and therewith also seditiously and rebelliously stirring up all estates of her Majesty's subjects.'[41]

The Dangers of Counsel: *The Discoverie of a Gaping Gvlf*

Published in 1579, *The Discoverie* touched on a matter peculiarly personal to Queen Elizabeth: her proposed marriage with the French Prince, the Catholic Duke of Alençon. A divisive prospect amongst the Queen's counsellors and a deeply unpopular match amongst her infamously

popular texts for very long periods and bring them to the attention of considerable bodies of readers.'

39 Hamburger, 'The Development of the Law of Seditious Libel and the Control of the Press,' p. 671.

40 It is a quirk of history that Elizabeth did not have the court renamed the 'Queen's Bench' during her reign.

41 Clegg, *Press Censorship in Elizabethan England*, p. 123.

xenophobic subjects, it was nevertheless Elizabeth's desire – as well as her custom – to nurture negotiations as long as possible, neither committing to nor jeopardising the possibility of an alliance.[42] Although it is impossible to know with any certainty whether or not the Queen had any real intention of marrying the Duke, their continuing amity after the marriage negotiations had foundered and until Alençon's death indicate, at least, that he was a useful tool of foreign policy.

Littered as the *Discoverie* is with classical allusions and precedents, and advancing its case against the Queen's marriage with eloquent rhetoric, it is unsurprising that such critics as Cyndia Clegg have recognised Stubbs as a likely political insider.[43] This is a view which has been challenged, however, by Natalie Mears' historiographic investigation of the text. Mears notes that whilst Stubbs moved in a 'politically and confessionally aware circle,' his intervention in the matter of the Queen's marriage is likely to have derived from his 'commitment to an active public life' and second-hand information sourced from his inner circle of friends.[44] As such, she contends that the text represents an independent enterprise predicated on a lack of fixedness in the parameters of 'counsel,' with Stubbs nevertheless departing from conventional ideas of parliamentary counsel.[45] At any rate, as an Inns of Court lawyer, his intrusion into the world of realpolitik was an unwelcome, untimely and dangerous misadventure: as evidenced by the Queen's unexpected wrath over his presumption in affecting legitimacy as a counsellor. In attempting to publicly counsel the Queen (and thus call into question, publicly, the abilities of her own counsellors), Stubbs went far beyond the bounds of acceptability. Indeed, his assessment of those

42 Kermode (*Aliens and Englishness in Elizabethan Drama*, p. 64) discusses at length the xenophobic character of early modern England.

43 Clegg, *Press Censorship in Elizabethan England*, p. 132.

44 This view places Mears ('Counsel, public debate and queenship,' p. 644) at odds with Henry Woodhuysen (*Sir Philip Sidney and the Circulation of Manuscripts, 1558–1640*, p. 151) who has argued that Stubbs' *Discoverie* was part of 'an orchestrated campaign to dissuade the Queen from marriage.' Whilst Mears' interpretation is more convincing, for the purposes of this study, interest will be focused not on the motivation behind Stubbs, but the legal reaction in provoked.

45 Mears, 'Counsel, public debate and queenship,' p. 647.

'chief heads … of policy' who pursued the marriage – one of whom was Elizabeth's trusted counsellor, William Cecil – as 'half taught Christians and half-hearted Englishmen,' later condemning them as 'sorcerors,' holding 'enchanting counsels' must have been particularly galling.[46] Here, the dangers of Stubbs' writings become clear in a legal sense – in advancing his case against the marriage, he chose to derogate those legitimate members of the Queen's council who took an opposing view. Inherent, of course, in attacks on such high-ranking individuals via written material is the possibility of prosecution under *Scandalum Magnatum*. Furthermore, that a political amateur should have the temerity to mount an attack on high-ranking members of the government was a thought undoubtedly inimical to Elizabeth, and at least partly explains her wish to prosecute Stubbs in the most severe manner. Accepting Mears' view the Queen's reaction took him by surprise, it is therefore possible to understand her assertion that 'the scene on the scaffold … was a significant moment in Elizabethan history, reflecting how Elizabethans perceived their political roles, especially in regard to counselling.'[47] This might, however, overstate matters a little. It is safer to say that the punishment made clear to politically aware, London-based Elizabethans the lack of safety in publicly demonstrating their political views, and the dangers faced by the subject when airing grievances under the confessional auspices of providing counsel for the good of the commonwealth.

In addition to intruding on the privilege of counsellors (and libelling the Queen's ministers themselves), the treatment which Stubbs afforded the French royal family is worthy of note. Characterising the French as a diseased people under the yoke of the Papacy – the 'scum of all Europe' – Stubbs widened his invective to include the Queen Mother of France, Catherine de Medici.[48] In his words, Elizabeth's putative mother-in-law was a 'trunk, wherein the Pope moveth as her soul to devise and have executed whatsoever for the appetite of that see, even as necromancers are said to carry about a dead body by the motion of some unclean spirit.' In

46 Stubbs, *The Discoverie of a Gaping Gvlf*, p. 5.

47 Mears, 'Counsel, public debate and queenship,' p. 630.

48 Stubbs, *The Discoverie of a Gaping Gvlf*, p. 25.

Catherine, Stubbs therefore scornfully personified what he considered 'the Antichristian Holy League.'[49] Similarly, Alençon himself was labelled a 'prince and good son of Rome, that anti-Christian mother city,' a further crystallisation of the premier argument against the alliance: the fear that reformed England would fall once more into the hands of Rome.[50] Stubbs, a subject, was intruding on foreign policy – which was ultimately the province of the Queen and her government.

Religious calumny was far from the only weapon in Stubbs' slanderous armoury, however, as a tendency to indulge in character assassination is also a common theme of his work. Despite acknowledging Alençon as a 'great prince born and of high lineage,' and alleging a distaste for the 'bruits' concerning the Duke's character, Stubbs nevertheless portrayed the Queen's suitor as an

> Odd fellow, by birth a Frenchman, by profession a Papist, an atheist by conversion, an instrument in France of uncleanness, a fly worker in England for Rome and France in this present affair, a sorcerer by common voice and fame.[51]

Once more setting himself up as a purveyor of truth and an authority on religious matters, Stubbs espoused truth as the prerogative of an honest Englishman – a defence, of course, which could not deflect accusations of slander under *Scandalum Magnatum*. The Duke was further castigated for being 'unmanlike' and 'unprincelike' – particularly vitriolic and dangerous assertions to make against a prospective consort of Elizabeth, casting doubt as they did upon Alençon's performance as a mate (and, as Elizabeth's counsellors would have hoped, as a potential father of the Queen's successor).[52] With such invectives underpinning *The Discoverie*, it is unsurprising that critics have recognised in its suppression and the prosecution of its perpetrators (Stubbs and William Page, his publisher) a need for the Elizabethan regime to protect contemporary foreign policy.[53] As further evidence, Clegg cites the reproduction of the text

49 Stubbs, *The Discoverie of a Gaping Gvlf*, p. 88.
50 Stubbs, *The Discoverie of a Gaping Gvlf*, p. 6.
51 Stubbs, *The Discoverie of a Gaping Gvlf*, pp. 9, 92.
52 Stubbs, *The Discoverie of a Gaping Gvlf*, p. 93.
53 Clegg, *Press Censorship in Elizabethan England*, p. 133.

abroad as at least partially responsible for the legal measures taken against Stubbs; the suggestion is made that due to *The Discoverie* being published in France and transmitted to the Pope in manuscript form, any inaction against the libellers would have provoked accusations that Elizabeth was ineffectual in domestic affairs.[54]

Evidence is certainly available to justify Clegg's argument. For one, it is worth considering that the English courtier, Sir Philip Sidney, voiced similar criticisms regarding the alliance in a letter to the Queen which was widely circulated at court – acting, in Jonathan Gibson's view, as a 'published' manuscript treatise.[55] Like Stubbs, Sidney produced an aggressive attack on the characters of the French royal household, lamenting the public outcry sure to follow the Queen's marriage with a 'husband, Frenchman & a papist, in whome … very common people will know this that he is the sonne of that Jezebel of our age'; further, Sidney writes that Alençon's 'will [is judged] to be as full of light ambition as is possible.'[56] Unlike Stubbs, however, Sidney did not suffer for his forthright criticism of the Queen's proposed marriage. Rather, his contemporary Fulke Greville noted that Sidney enjoyed as great a level of access to Elizabeth as before.[57] Furthermore, Berry lists Edmund Spenser's *Mother Hubberd's Tale* as a directly contemporary literary allegory which presents a 'very well veiled, but … more obvious attack on the Alençon courtship.'[58] That Spenser chose, however, to present his beliefs in a satire rather than adopting the open and conspicuous invective of Stubbs is worthy of consideration; it suggests that not only was the form of *The Discoverie* responsible for its indictment under *Scandalum Magnatum* as 'slanderous news' apt to stir discord, but also relates to Janet Clare's argument that ambiguity and metaphor are the

54 Woodhuysen (*Sir Philip Sidney and the Circulation of Manuscripts, 1558–1640*, p. 147) notes that at least four manuscript copies of the *Discoverie* were preserved by private collectors in England. See also: Clegg, *Press Censorship in Elizabethan England*, p. 134.

55 Gibson, 'Letters,' p. 617.

56 Sidney, 'Sir Philip Sidney to Queen Elizabeth,' pp. 241, 244.

57 Berry, *John Stubbs's Gaping Gulf With Letters and Other Relevant Documents*, p. l.

58 Berry, *John Stubbs's Gaping Gulf With Letters and Other Relevant Documents*, p. liii.

components of Renaissance literary productions.[59] In short, Stubbs' unadorned public denunciation of the Alençon match lacked the protective ambiguity and polysemous equivocation which had grown (as a result of legal censorship) around literature. Consequently, it was almost inevitable that *The Discoverie of a Gaping Gulf* would be viewed by authorities as a purely political and scurrilous work designed to incite rebellion and sedition.

Given the licence afforded courtiers such as Sir Philip Sidney, the distinction must now be made between differing audiences in the law's treatment of slanderous material. Sidney's letter, as Lake recognises, was circulated in manuscript in 'very tight circles,' which suggests that it fits with Harold Love's conception of 'user publication': that is, circulation within a defined social circle.[60] Though he voiced his rather rancorous opinions via manuscript, Sidney certainly did not intend for his writings to be, for example, pinned to the door of a public place for mass consumption, as was to become the fashion for verse libels.[61] Furthermore, in an exhaustive study of the material conditions of the letter (as well as its various, scribally produced versions), Peter Beal has noted that it was carefully framed within the acceptable boundaries of private discourse (however disingenuously). Ostensibly hoping that the carefully argued treatise should 'only come to your merciful eyes,' Sidney may even have 'delivered it as a private letter, even if the alleged privacy of the discourse was a fiction.'[62] Such conventions were not unusual. Daybell has established that 'copies of certain letters … enjoyed wide circulation in manuscript (and print) beyond the named addressee,' and Sidney's letter itself survived and flourished in multiple

59 Clare, *Art Made Tongue-Tied By Authority*, p. 235.

60 Love (*Scribal Publication in Seventeenth-Century England*, p. 47) posits three types of manuscript publication. In addition to 'user publication,' he suggests 'author publication' (publication by the author) and 'entrepreneurial publication,' which sought profit.

61 O'Callaghan, 'Publication: Print and Manuscript,' p. 84.

62 Beal (*In Praise of Scribes*, pp. 131, 111) also notes that the original document presented to the Queen (which does not survive) had to be in Sidney's own hand in order to keep up the rhetorical fiction. See also: Lake, 'The Politics of Popularity,' p. 75; Love, *Scribal Publication in Seventeenth-Century England*, p. 47.

copies made over subsequent decades.[63] Sidney's adoption of the rhetoric of counsel (which had visibly failed when espoused by Stubbs) has been identified by Mears as being central to the difference in the reaction provoked. Pointing out that no action was taken against him, she recognises that 'Sidney's letter operated in a circumscribed forum of policy-making at court. [He] sought to contribute to probouleutic discussion on the marriage and succession at court.'[64] Clearly, the rhetorical use of counsel could be acceptable in proffering political opinions, but it was by no means a safe or reliable mode of expression. Rather, it was contingent on the personal monarchical style of the sovereign, the rank of the would-be counsellor, and, critically, the audience to whom it was expressed.[65] Whilst Stubbs offered the right to determine state affairs to even the meanest person, Sidney did not.[66] The latter's harsh punishment was predicated on the dissent which might be stirred in his wider, lower-ranking audience.

Evidence of Sidney's own recognition of the sensitivity of audiences is further suggested by Beal's assertion that the letter actually sent to the Queen may, indeed, have been for her eyes only – with the various subsequent editions becoming 'a piece of communal property independent of the author.'[67] If one accepts Beal's suggestion that a less salacious version of the text may have been delivered to the Queen (and the fact that various editions of his letter differ in content suggests that we should), significant possibilities arise concerning the ways in which sensitivity to audiences was paramount in attempting to anticipate and avert accusations of slander. Despite Shuger's claim that manuscripts were unregulated, it is clear that even amongst courtiers, there was a degree of self-regulation.[68] There was

63 Daybell, *The Material Letter*, p. 175.

64 Mears, 'Counsel, public debate and queenship,' p. 648.

65 Elizabeth's attitude towards counsel was predicated on her belief that it could be offered only by legitimate counsellors – and even then, she was not compelled to act on it.

66 Bell ('Elizabeth, Stubbs, and the Gaping Gulf,' pp. 99–117) provides an excellent historical background to Stubbs' *Discoverie* but has little to say on the disparity in reaction in engendered in comparison to other writings on the same theme.

67 Beal, *In Praise of Scribes*, pp. 143–6.

68 Shuger, *Censorship and Cultural Regulation*, p. 4.

evidently sufficient ambiguity about what could be safely expressed without inviting the wrath of the Queen that alterations were made to Sidney's text dependent on the eyes before which it would come. Thus, in negotiating and avoiding accusations of slander, it is apparent that words had to be carefully modulated and mediated according to their recipients. Whilst Greg Walker points out that 'direct intervention outside the charmed circle of the court was always a perilous business,' it is clear that even within that circle, a degree of circumspection was required.[69] Although there was no clear way in which 'counsel' and 'slander' could be safely and definitively differentiated, it may be argued that rhetorical strategy, rank, audience, medium and a degree of luck each had a part to play in ensuring the safety of the author.[70]

As a high-ranking courtier, Sir Philip Sidney had a greater degree of liberty in expressing his private reservations to his sovereign and the politically sensitive court; Stubbs, on the other hand, was a commoner. Consequently, the latter's public attacks on privy counsellors and foreign royalty constituted not only a threat to foreign policy, a breach of the Elizabethan parameters of counsel, and an unforgivably public denunciation of Elizabeth's counsellors, but a highly visible crack in the image of social hegemony fostered by the Elizabethan regime. In Loades' terms, it created the intolerable image of the lower members of society turning on the head.[71] It is an argument closely tied to the findings of J. C. Lassiter, who holds that the late sixteenth-century rise in the use of *Scandalum Magnatum* was symptomatic of an upper-class 'crisis of confidence,' stemming from

69 Walker, 'Courtship and Counsel: John Lyly's *Campaspe,*' p. 321. Beal (*In Praise of Scribes*, p. 111) records also an incident in which Leicester himself sent an ostensibly private message on the same theme as Sidney's letter to the Queen via a chaplain. For his pains, the chaplain was clapped in prison.

70 Following the controversy of Stubbs, a government crackdown on public opposition to the match was instituted (Doran, 'Why Did Elizabeth Not Marry?,' p. 49). This resulted in surreptitious objections such as allegorical poetry circulated in manuscript: a clear sign that counsel had been accepted as unwise (and potentially unsafe) whilst handwritten material offered a more covert means of voicing disapproval.

71 Loades, 'The Theory and Practice of Censorship,' p. 141.

a concern on the part of peers that traditional standards of deference and respect were dwindling.[72] Increased use of the statute therefore indicates a legal attempt to compensate for that loss by punishing those guilty of disrespect and, as a result, 'artificially reinforcing weakening social boundaries.' In short, Lassiter convincingly advances the argument that during Elizabeth's reign the statute of *Scandalum Magnatum* came to function as a means by which the conservative elite sought to shore up eroding social and political barriers by legally punishing those who had the audacity to defame them. If one accepts the assertion that Stubbs' attack on politically prominent figures represented a breach of social etiquette, it is undeniable that his injurious derogation – in print – of a blood prince was nothing short of an outrage, exacerbated by the fact that it echoed throughout Europe. Certainly Elizabeth, always vocal in her defence of the divinity of royals, could not countenance a public attack on majesty, nor could she be seen to stand idle whilst a common subject under her jurisdiction sowed discord and defamed potential allies.

Crucially, however, Elizabeth's calls for Stubbs' execution were denied by the Grand Jury – as noted, a move which resulted in the author's punishment under *Scandalum Magnatum* in the King's Bench. Sentenced to lose the hand responsible for writing *The Discoverie*, Stubbs' punishment – derived from a minor statute of *Scandalum Magnatum* issued under Mary and Philip – resulted in a great deal of public sympathy. Coupled with the reluctance of the Grand Jury to execute Stubbs for treason, the public reaction to his dismemberment gives rise to a further complexity which requires attention in any study of slander. Indeed, one cannot ignore the persuasive arguments put forward by Brooks, which suggest that the development of Elizabethan legal thought, far from comprising a unitary belief in an organically structured, hierarchical society, instead included heterodox views of justice as an impartial set of laws hostile to the over-mighty.[73] As evidence, Brooks cites the 1579 Middle Temple work (directly contemporary to the *Discoverie*) of Burghley's associate James Morice's writings which, whilst

72 Lassiter, 'Defamation of Peers: The Rise and Decline of the Action for *Scandalum Magnatum*,' p. 220.

73 Brooks, *Lawyers, Litigation and English Society Since 1450*, p. 193.

advocating obedience to authority, nevertheless openly discourse on the question of the monarch's position in legal proceedings:

> It is a comon sayinge amonge many that the Kinge by his Prerogatyve is above his laws which rightly understode is not amisse spoken … But to say that the Kinge is so a Emperor over his Lawes and Actes of Parliament (bycawse he hath power to make them), as that he is not bound to governe by the same but at his will and pleasure, is an Oppinyon altogether repugnant to the wise and politick State of government established in this realm … [It is] Contrarye to the Rule of Equytie and common reason which sayeth (that laws) beinge made by so grave a Counsell, uppon so great deliberacion and by the Common Consent of all should be followed by the King).[74]

The inference, of course, is that Elizabeth's failure to indict Stubbs for treason, and her subsequent inability to secure his execution, is linked to contemporary legal thought which eschewed absolutist jurisprudence in favour of a system of legality which negotiated potential conflict between 'the power of princes and the liberty of the subject.'[75] Along with the failure of the felony statutes noted by Hamburger, what emerges is a growing sense of distaste for the suppression of public opinion by the monarch: an idea supported by the ambiguous legal terminology of *Scandalum Magnatum* which granted it jurisdiction only over the production of 'news.' Although written material regarded as slanderous was invariably punished when perpetrators were caught, the legal machinery used was variable. So too was the punishment, ranging as it did from the civil penalty of damages to the criminal penalty of the loss of a hand depending, presumably, on the perceived severity of the offence, the audience it reached, the laws invoked at trial, and the disparity in 'quality' between the slanderer and the slandered. Both Stubbs' writings and his subsequent trial, therefore, arose in a period which was both 'obsessed with general fears of social and political chaos' and espoused a theory of legality

74 Brooks, *Lawyers, Litigation and English Society Since 1450*, pp. 212–13. Christopher Brooks adapts the text, sourcing it from a series of lectures given by Morice at the Inner Temple in 1579. The reading survives in two original copies: BL., MS Add. 36081, fos 229 ff and BL., MS Egerton 3376.

75 Brooks, *Lawyers, Litigation and English Society Since 1450*, p. 215.

which emphasised the protection of the weak from the strong.[76] It is therefore fitting that his ultimate punishment was sought through the King's Bench (his comparatively lowly status, it may be considered ironically, protecting him from the ultimate penalty of punishment for treason), yet retained a level of brutality reserved for a sower of sedition who had himself breached the accepted social hierarchy. Further, the fact that Stubbs was tried and found guilty by a jury rather than the Queen's Council (as would have been the case had he been tried in the Star Chamber) was arguably motivated by the need to provide visible proof that his case was not unjustly influenced by the Queen's thirst for vengeance, but rather openly heard by impartial and non-partisan contemporaries.

Interestingly, however, the verdict and punishment announced at the climax of Stubbs' trial did not conclude his participation in the legal proceedings concerning *The Discoverie*. Further legal recourse remained open to him: and, crucially, it was a method of pleading which was reliant on manuscript culture. Following his sentence, Stubbs wrote letters of appeal directly to Queen and council, throwing himself on their mercy, swearing his allegiance to the crown and, in his own words, seeking to 'mitigate' the monarch's 'great indignation.'[77] Central to Stubbs' plea was an open and 'sorrowful' acknowledgement of the sins he had committed, in addition to a recognition of royal wisdom and 'that judgement that is given against me by law': the court having 'recorded [him] a miserable turbulent wretch.' Nevertheless, he stoutly denied that he had ever 'conceived malicious thoughts or wicked purposes' against the state or the crown.' As such, Stubbs presented an argument which was careful to provide a 'supplicatory submission' to the judgement of the legal system whilst continuing to plead against both the severity of its penalty and the justice of its finding a penitent and ingenuous subject guilty. What therefore emerges is the role of the sovereign as the fountain of justice in the realm: a 'natural Queen' who represented the highest tier of the royal courts and whose pardon could

76 Brooks and Lobban, *Communities and Courts in Britain, 1150–1900*, p. 204.

77 Lake ('The Politics of Popularity,' pp. 75–6) discusses Stubbs' letters in the context of his possible connection with (and perhaps sponsorship of) at least one Privy Counsellor.

be sought even after the judgement of her subordinates had been given.[78] It was all part of a great game with very high stakes.

The form of Stubbs' plea is also worthy of consideration. His insistence on his own lack of guile combined with his overt use of the language of submission worked in tandem to create a personal if conventional petition which was clearly aimed at playing on the Queen's supposed inclination to compassion. Although his petition was unsuccessful, one still gains a sense of the importance attached to personal correspondence in the proceedings of the royal courts, with an especial insight into the status of the monarch as a visible representative of the highest level of justice. That visibility was echoed in Elizabeth's public proclamations against the tract, which rather increased the appearance of further 'defamatory libels' sympathetic to Stubbs' anti-French cause than silenced them.[79] The danger of making a public spectacle of intolerable ideas and arguments could and did serve to make them more attractive.

As can be seen, a variety of laws were in place to combat the growing problem of slander – and yet these laws were slow to catch up with the growth in the spread of news and seditious libel. As such, throughout the Elizabethan period, authorities grappled with the remnants of mediaeval legal machinery in a society which was rapidly developing new means of spreading subversive discourse. Consequently, it is not surprising to find slanderers accused of and punished under *Scandalum Magnatum* and the civil tort of libel in the common law courts and Star Chamber, defamation in the ecclesiastical courts, and breaches of statutory law in both the secular courts and Star Chamber. The remarkable case of John Stubbs provides an interesting illustration of the ways in which printed slander was treated, in addition to highlighting how adopting the rhetoric of counsel to avoid slander charges was far from an assured method of engaging in public discourse – particularly when aspirant counsellors lacked the social cachet of their superiors and, importantly, when they had the temerity to open up their advice to a limitless audience via print. However, records from both the common law courts of the King's Bench and the Common Pleas offer

78 Stubbs, *The Discoverie of a Gaping Gvlf*, p. 109.

79 Whitelock, *Elizabeth's Bedfellows*, p. 181.

further invaluable insight into the treatment which the law afforded less celebrated slander suits, as well as providing an important view of the formalities of the courts' operations. Private defamation suits in the King's Bench (a secular court in which the monarch was considered to have some measure of interest and which boasted the added competency of criminal proceedings) increased markedly in the sixteenth century and could be brought by any individual seeking royal justice.[80] Housed at Westminster, the King's Bench utilised bills (as opposed to the cumbersome writs of the court of Common Pleas), making it a popular court for those seeking swift justice. Fortunately, the surviving rolls from the royal courts allow us access to the workings of law courts in slander cases; as a consequence, it is possible to examine contemporary slander suits with a view to uncovering the extent to which factors such as trade loss and the importance of reputation impinged upon the legal treatment of slander. Also worthy of consideration, however, is the physical nature of Elizabethan plea rolls. Invariably produced by court scribes, plea roles illustrate the ongoing dominance of manuscript culture in the period. The central courts produced more than three miles of parchment per year in the sixteenth century – a fact no doubt partly responsible for the difficulties inherent in indexing cases.[81] Consequently, modern access to Elizabethan slander suits is mediated through the existence (and often the ultimate printed publication and translation) of handwritten records.

80 Helmholz provides useful figures illustrating the rise in King's Bench actions for defamation. For Hilary term 1562, the King's Bench roll has nine defamation cases pleaded to issue. For the same term thirty-one years later in 1593, the corresponding figure is sixty, and for Hilary term 1598, it is seventy-one. The Trinity term proportions are not greatly different. These cases, it is further suggested, may not be exact – the editor suggests that he may have missed a few – making the total number possibly larger. It must also be noted that the Common Pleas boasts a lower increase in slander suits, with the conclusion drawn that plaintiffs who could afford royal justice showed a 'natural preference' for justice at the King's Bench. See: Helmholz, 'Introduction,' pp. lxxxvi–ii.

81 Baker, *Legal Records and the Historian*, p. 3.

CHAPTER 2

Slander in the Secular Courts

In the King's Bench case of Netlingham versus Ode (1578), the allegation of slander was brought against one Ralph Ode, whom William Netlingham claimed had uttered the following words: 'If there ever were any witch, thou (speaking to the aforesaid William the plaintiff) art one.'[1] It is further alleged that 'by reason of the utterance and recitation of which words not only is the aforesaid William Netlingham grievously injured and harmed in his good estate and name, in his dealings to which he was accustomed, and in the company which he had with honest persons and subjects of the said lady the present queen, but also the same William has been compelled and coerced to lay out and spend divers sums of money for clearing himself in the matter … and therein he produces suit.'

It is a case in which parallels with Stubbs' accusations of sorcery against the Queen's counsellors and allies can certainly be drawn. According to custom, the previous good character of William Netlingham is established in a prolix defence which renders him 'a good, true, faithful and honest liegeman and subject of the lady the present queen,' in addition to being

> of good name, fame, conversation and condition, and [he] has been held, spoken of, named, reputed and taken of such estate and bearing both among many magnates and all other subjects and liegemen as well of the said lady the present queen … from the time of his birth to the present, and has remained and continued unspotted and untainted by any stains of theft, felony, sorcery, falsity, or whatsoever other magic or noxious art … or ever fallen under any suspicion of such crime.[2]

As Helmholz records, such lengthy defences of character and history are commonly found in the bills of the King's Bench (the court's use of bills

1 Helmholz, *Select Cases*, p. 61.
2 Ibid.

rather than writs presumably allowing for a greater degree of 'extravagant individual creativity').[3] However, the elaboration present in the opening bill of this particular case raises further issues which display the complex potential of a plaintiff's declaration in slander suits.

Firstly, what becomes evident is the opportunity taken by the plaintiff to emphasise his social standing, reputation and 'fame' amongst his peers, whilst simultaneously professing his allegiance and subservience to his betters; again, of course, a legal recognition of the subject's place in society – and his acceptance of it – is tacitly clarified. Of further note is the obvious intention on the part of the plaintiff to equate sorcery – the 'slander' alleged – with what are perhaps more actionable accusations of such criminal acts as theft and falsity: crimes which may be argued to harm a man's trade and professional life. That an accusation of sorcery might be commonly considered a spiritual imputation (and thus entail punishment by the ecclesiastical courts) is therefore mitigated as, despite Netlingham claiming false accusation of an ecclesiastical offence, the focus in the declaration is on the suit being a civil matter. Furthermore, it has been noted that the result of the slander included compelling Netlingham 'to lay out and spend divers sums of money for clearing himself': surely a claim which serves the dual purpose of justifying the case's place in a secular court and making clear the plaintiff's intention is to seek damages for the injurious claims made by Ode.

Here, what is perhaps one of the central themes of slander suits during Elizabeth's reign may be discerned – that is, the interconnection between material or financial loss and the loss of reputation or social standing. Once again, the slanderer is portrayed as occupying the dangerous and unenviable position of a transgressor whose words have the capacity to upset the order of society and economically compromise the position of its members. It is therefore no surprise that, in this case, the malicious intent of Ode is made clear:

> William has led a peaceful, honest and praiseworthy life to his own great comfort; nevertheless, the aforesaid Ralph, not ignorant of the foregoing, inflamed by malice

3 Helmholz, 'Introduction,' p. lxxxiv.

> and envy and stirred up by diabolical inspiration, scheming unjustly and without cause entirely to cut off, impair and denigrate the name, estate and fame of the same William … and to cause the same William to be proclaimed and to fall into the reproach, contempt and vituperation of all liegemen of the said lady the present queen so that all faithful subjects … would entirely withdraw from the company of the selfsame William.[4]

It is further alleged that Ode did 'speak, assert and publish' his 'false, slanderous English words' (words recorded in English as opposed to the Latin which forms the bulk of the original document) in the presence of 'divers faithful subjects of the said lady the present queen.'[5] Such attention devoted to the social consequences of the alleged slander – the host of liegemen and subjects induced to remove themselves from Netlingham's company – is, as will be seen, a customary convention of King's Bench cases. As opposed to suits found in the Common Pleas, which focus their narratives on the personal losses suffered by the plaintiff, it is clear that King's Bench cases show a calculated determination to excuse their place in the court by stressing a wider tear in the social fabric ostensibly caused by the words of the slanderer. It is also quite naturally Netlingham's prerogative as plaintiff to have his counsel portray him in contradistinction to the slanderer, Ode. Still interesting is the sustained claim that, as a result of Ode's malicious, false and even demonic slander, Netlingham himself was forced into the position of a social pariah amongst the Queen's subjects. Once more, the ongoing concern with social disorder is undeniable, with Netlingham's loss of status granted an even greater degree of legal currency than the very tangible loss of £100.

The dangers associated with 'unguarded tongues' in post-Reformation England are well established, with Cressy citing the legion of moral, religious and civic leaders who entrenched the notion that spoken utterances could have 'situation-altering effects,' with a man who lacked 'temperance and moderation in his language' apt to 'provoke violence, discord, unhappiness or sedition … intensifying divisions within communities and eroding the fabric of society.'[6] Particularly dangerous, therefore, were

4 Helmholz, *Select Cases*, p. 61–2.
5 Helmholz, *Select Cases*, p. 62.
6 Cressy, *Dangerous Talk*, pp. 2, 5–6.

defamatory false rumours which, as Painter has suggested, constituted one of the most frequently encountered forms of 'republication,' or 'repetition' of defamation.[7] Thus, the accusation of 'published' slander, which reverberates throughout plaintiff declarations in the period, can be seen to function primarily as a means of underlining the concept of slanderous words as those which, once spoken, leave an indelible stamp on the hearer or hearers as well as the victim.[8] As Baker attests, the basis of an action for words 'was the loss of credit and fame, and not the insult, [and so] it was always necessary to show a publication of the words. A man could not lose credit as a result of words which reached no one's ears or eyes but his own.'[9]

Given that such an overt concern with the power of words forms the basis of Netlingham's slander suit, it is unsurprising that Ode's defence is rooted in the minutiae of language. Indeed, in addition to denying 'force and wrong,' it is Ode's assertion that

> when the utterance and speaking of the aforesaid English words specified in the aforesaid bill is supposed, he spoke and uttered these words following to the said William, namely 'I (meaning the same Ralph) will not say that thou (meaning the aforesaid William) art a witch, but if there is any witch on earth, as some say there are, I think in my conscience that thou art one.' And this he is ready to verify.[10]

Central to Ode's defence is, of course, his contradiction of Netlingham's claim that he made an unequivocally damaging statement; he frames his declaration in order mitigate the action (and subsequent legal actionability) of his words; in effect, he denies having openly called Netlingham a witch. He follows with a use of the conditional, alleging that his accusation was a slander only under the proviso that witches exist – a condition on which he delegates to others the burden of proof. The final line of his defence strategy is an appeal based on conscience.

7 Painter, 'Republication Problems in the Law of Defamation,' p. 1131.
8 Harold Love (*Scribal Publication*, pp. v, 35, 44) offers a useful view of early modern publication. Publication, in the period, could refer to the uttering of words before a third party, the printing of a text in multiple copies or the writing of a manuscript, which would be 'republished' as often as it was copied.
9 Baker, *An Introduction to Legal History, 4th Edition*, p. 444.
10 Helmholz, *Select Cases*, p. 62.

Conscience and truth being so closely associated in the period, Ode's declaration and apparent willingness to prove his truthfulness therefore constitute an assertion that his alleged slander could be defended on the grounds of veracity and good faith.

The desired effect is therefore to internalise his slander (lamented by Netlingham for its very public nature) as a private matter of conscience. In legal parlance, Ode therefore makes use of 'the Special Traverse': that is, the 'express denial that the defendant had spoken the words in the manner and form stated by the plaintiff' – a particularly virulent form of demurral throughout the sixteenth century which aimed at placing emphasis on the defendant's lack of malice.[11] However, it was a defence anticipated by Netlingham's counsel. What therefore becomes apparent is the reciprocal nature of slander suits, as well as a persuasive piece of evidence that words were highly valued and carefully examined by Elizabethan lawyers. One can find in the original plaintiff's declaration clear signs that language was organised and harnessed with a view to ensuring that the defendant's plea would struggle to successfully outmanoeuvre that of the plaintiff. Hence, Netlingham's counsel can be seen to present as fact the idea that 'the aforesaid William says that there were many sorcerers, called witches, within this realm of England, and that the aforesaid art of sorcery, called witchcraft, is a monstrous transgression and offence against the word of God.' As such, Netlingham's lawyers present their plaintiff, too, as a bastion of truth. Further, his personal belief in witches and witchcraft becomes crucial, instantly negating Ode's sceptical attitude by making it clear that, in the eyes of the law, Ode's false accusations undoubtedly imputed a very real wrong in the eyes of his victim and others.

Of further consequence to any consideration of the language employed in legal records is the predominant use of Latin. To Burke, language can be located in the frames of performance and persuasion and has long formed an instrument wielded by the powerful.[12] It was, he argues, a 'device to maintain the power of … professional men such as lawyers.' Indeed, it is Burke's further assertion that 'speaking Latin was a betrayal of the poor,'

11 Helmholz, 'Introduction,' pp. cviii–cix.

12 Burke, *The Social History of Language*, p. 2.

who were rendered unable to understand court proceedings. The caveat is made, however, that it is unwise to 'assume that professional persuaders [and here we must include lawyers] believed all their own propaganda, for ideas, people or commodities, or that they were all cynically detached from it.'[13] We might consequently refrain from adopting an entirely structuralist argument. It is impossible to assume that the use of legal Latin rather than plebeian English in the courtroom mirrored, reflected, or truly upheld the social stratification of Elizabethan culture. Rather, it simply engaged with and reinforced existing society. As evidence, one might cite the growing (though contentious) school of Elizabethan thought which advocated the law's translation and subsequent publication from 'barbarous Latin' to English.[14] Thus, one can conclude that the use of Latin in the courtroom was less an attempt by a monolithic legal system to withhold power from the lower orders of society than it was a traditional method of legal and professional discourse in which lawyers were, perforce, highly trained.

That is not to say that the importance of rank did not play a key role in Elizabethan slander suits across the courts. Although the social caste to which the litigants belong is not recorded, one cannot help but notice, for example, that William Netlingham claims that, in the 'laying out and spending of' money in the process of clearing his name, he is owed damages 'to the value of £100.' It is a considerable sum, despite the eventual damages awarded amounting to a not-insignificant but assuredly less significant £11 5s. Coupled with the amount of financial restitution claimed, it is worth considering that Netlingham's declaration plea neglects to follow the tradition of alternative cases, which habitually stress the occupation of the plaintiff and the resultant financial implications directly affecting the victim's trade as a result of the slanderer's false accusations.[15] It is therefore no great leap to assume that this suit – which took place, it must be remembered, in the court of King's Bench – represented players of a higher rank than that found in the following case, drawn from the records of the

13 Burke, *The Social History of Language*, p. 14.

14 Brooks, *Lawyers, Litigation and English Society Since 1450*, pp. 23–40.

15 Comparable cases in the King's Bench can be found in Helmholz, *Select Cases*, pp. 41–72.

court of Common Pleas (a court which was solely focused on redressing civil matters between subjects, and had no criminal jurisdiction): that of Funnell versus Atmere, which dates also from 1578.

The case of Funnell versus Atmere hinges on the accusation of one William Funnell, who brought a suit against local tailor Francis Atmere and his wife Rose (the identity of whom, despite her being the speaker, is subsumed within that of her husband according to common law practice), alleging that

> the aforesaid Rose, not ignorant of the foregoing, scheming without right to harm the said William and to injure, diminish and impair his name and estate, and in order to bring the selfsame William into vexation, confusion and infamy … in the presence and hearing of many of his neighbours, did speak and proclaim certain slanderous, false and untrue words of the said William, in the English words following, namely, 'William Funnell is a thief, for he has stolen my father's bullocks and my horse, and that I will justify.'[16]

It is further alleged that

> by reason of the speaking and proclamation of which words the same William is not only injured in his good name and fame, but is also grievously harmed in carrying out his affairs with divers honest persons with whom he previously dealt in buying, selling and honestly bargaining.

Unsurprisingly, the conventional polarisation of defendant and plaintiff is evident in the writ; Funnell's 'good name and fame' amongst 'good and substantial men' is placed at odds with Rose's malicious and scheming nature. Unlike the case of Netlingham versus Ode, however, one can distinguish an argument predicated not only upon the dangers slander poses to reputation and standing in wider society, but its more pragmatic effect on a plaintiff's trade and profession. In her defence, Rose's lawyers strive to discredit Funnell's assertion that the words spoken were untrue, by 'denying force and wrong' and suggesting the truth of their slanderous words as judged by 'the common voice and fame.' As has been elsewhere noted, whilst written libel could not be justified as being true, spoken

16 Helmholz, *Select Cases*, pp. 59–60.

slander certainly could.[17] Hence, Rose Atmere's defence centres on the truth of her accusations of thievery, as justified by the court of common opinion. Furthermore, one might consider a further procedural means of defence deployed by the Atmeres: the claim that Rose's words were spoken 'upon certain malicious words spoken and uttered against the same Rose.' Thus, the notion of provocation is introduced, and something of the reciprocal nature of slander begins to take shape.

Key to the Atmeres' defence strategy is, therefore, the undermining of Funnell's claim that the slanderous words were proclaimed 'in the presence and hearing of his many neighbours' by the reduction of the exchange to a reciprocal and prosaic argument of far less import than suggested by the plaintiff's counsel. What emerges, therefore, is a further attempt at a legal 'special traverse,' with which the defendant attempts to show that 'the plaintiff had provoked the words or that the words had been spoken as part of a quarrel for which the plaintiff bore the major responsibility.'[18] In this case, the defence mounted by the Atmeres' lawyers rested both on the special traverse and the legal plea of justification. It was asserted that Funnell was, indeed, guilty of the crime imputed by Rose by virtue of 'various felonies … perpetrated in the area of Carbrooke,' of which the 'common voice' alleged him culpable. We might thus attribute the failure of the Atmeres' defence to the fact that this plea did not justify Rose's imputation because it did not exactly allege the stealing of her father's bullocks or her horse. Rather, it relied on rumour and innuendo.

In sum, it is clear that Francis and Rose Atmere failed to overturn William Funnell's suit because the words Rose freely admitted to speaking were unequivocal in their claim that a specific and unproven criminal act

17 An interesting question arises here of what happened when a plaintiff's slander suit failed based on the defendant's justification of truth. This would, of course, require a plaintiff stupid or brazen enough to take someone to court for slander for defaming them honestly – for accusing them of something they had actually done. Depending on the evidence the defendant used to prove their slanderous words as true, the plaintiff would have to be indicted in an entirely new case, this time as a defendant on trial for whichever crime they had initially tried to claim was a mere slanderous imputation. The lawyers' pockets would be bulging by the end of it all.

18 Helmholz, 'Introduction,' p. cx.

had been laid at Funnell's door. The case may therefore be considered a triumph of the rule of *Mitior Sensus* – a rule which gained currency in the court of Common Pleas in the 1570s and 1580s and sought to stem the flow of actions for slander by maintaining that a specific crime must be imputed (such as the theft of the bullocks) and that 'no action should lie if the words could be construed in a milder sense.'[19] Rose Atmere's unproven accusation that Funnell had stolen specific items of property and her subsequent inability to prove or legally justify that accusation assured William Funnell a successful slander suit. *Mitior Sensus*, though it was designed to stop frivolous suits, was intended also to ensure that serious cases were given justice – and Rose certainly could not avoid justice by claiming she had not meant her words to be taken negatively. Once more the intricacies of language combined to create a world of legal parley in which words were constantly justified and undermined by opposing sides.

19 Habermann, *Staging Slander and Gender*, p. 45.

CHAPTER 3

A Flood Tide of Litigation?

With the cases thus far studied dating from the 1570s, it is useful to examine suits from another decade in Elizabeth's forty-five-year reign. To that end, one might turn to the 1580s: a decade marked by a fresh wave of political instability stemming from newfound succession crises and the perennial concern regarding the machinations of the immured Mary Queen of Scots.[1] Despite its outcome being lost, the 1585 King's Bench case of Coke versus Baxter is particularly noteworthy due to its plaintiff – the esteemed lawyer and later author of *de Libellis Famosis* – Edward Coke, whose suit, according to Boyer may be part of a long-running feud between his friend and patron, Nathaniel Bacon and local landowner Sir William Heydon.[2] Unsurprisingly, given Coke's familiarity with and knowledge of the law, one finds that the case follows familiar protocol, proceeding in what Tim Stretton identifies as the heavily formulaic language of pleading.[3] Coke is characterised as the typically 'good and faithful liegeman of the lady the present queen … [and] has been of good name, fame, condition, conversation, reputation and esteem … among divers venerable, honourable and eminent men.' Reputation, however, is to become the key issue upon which Coke seeks damages and buttresses his case, as it is further established that this

1 The 1580s saw the inevitability of the end of the Tudor dynasty. As Carole Levin (*The Heart and Stomach of a King: Elizabeth I and the Politics of Sex and Power*, p. 60) notes, the dissipation of the Alençon match in 1579 marked the end of the Queen's potential motherhood. In addition, the decade was to see a rise in religious disaffection issuing from such scurrilous quarters as the pseudonymous Martin Marprelate, and Star Chamber decrees which attempted to enforce censorship of slanderous printed material were to face a wave of challenges.

2 Boyer, *Sir Edward Coke and the Elizabethan Age*, p. 70.

3 Stretton, *Women Waging Law in Elizabethan England*, p. 16.

> learned expert in the laws of this realm … has been and still is retained with various honourable, venerable and eminent men … and many other subjects of the said lady the queen for counsel in law, and for his sound and statutory counsel in causes and matters uncertain at law has received, had and won, from divers liegemen of the said lady the queen, his clients, both within the aforesaid county of Norfolk and elsewhere in every part of this realm of England, exceedingly great gains, profits and fees, justly, honestly and lawfully.[4]

Coke's local as well as national reputation for honesty is foregrounded, with his uprightness in his professional life re-inscribed by his rectitude in bringing Baxter to task in this case. The espousal of professional honesty and honesty in pleading is further understandable when one considers the nature of the alleged slander.

Coke's counsel claim that Baxter,

> Not ignorant of but well knowing the foregoing, scheming wholly to deprive the aforesaid Edward Coke of all his credit, good name, fame and reputation … and in order to bring [him] into the hatred of all venerable and other subjects of the said lady the present queen, and to cause the selfsame Edward Coke to be known and proclaimed as an iniquitous, fraudulent and deceitful man and as an ambidexter … did falsely, maliciously and hatefully assert, utter, publish and repeat these false, feigned, slanderous and opprobrious English words … 'Master Coke, at the last assizes in Norfolk, was in counsel with both the plaintiff and defendant, and took fees and was retained by them both, whereby one party's cause was lost; and so [he] did play on both hands.'[5]

Interesting to note is the emphasis placed on the falsity of Baxter's utterance. In maligning Coke's professional activities, his allegations are repeatedly identified as patently false. If one turns to Coke's later *de Libellis Famosis*, it becomes apparent that his assertion there that truth is secondary to intent and potential damage is nascent if discernible at all in this King's Bench case. Here, traditional court conventions are adhered to, as Coke's counsel is careful to decry Baxter's allegation as untrue as a matter of form. By assessing Coke's later views on seditious libel alongside his own pleading strategy as plaintiff, the rupture between the legal view

4 Helmholz, *Select Cases*, p. 66.
5 Helmholz, *Select Cases*, p. 66–7.

of civil defamation and the later crime of seditious libel becomes evident. Indeed, it is a rupture too often glossed over by scholars such as Roger Manning. Manning notes Coke's disregard for the importance of the truth of libels but fails to acknowledge the reasons underlying his 1605 break from the common law precedent that 'a statement has to be factually untrue before it can be deemed libellous.'[6] Truth could (and was) posited as a possible means of defence (which must be mitigated by plaintiffs), but the law was not above selectivity in the period, as the case of John Stubbs will avow.[7] The legal principle here was evidently messy. As will be seen, Coke's later views on the lack of importance of truth in defamatory material will be illuminated by study of the 1605 Star Chamber case which catalysed their publication and entry into the legal canon and sought to tighten up the messy approach taken by the law in prosecuting slanderers.

Of further conventional pleading practice is the later argument put forward by Coke: that is, that the aspersions cast on his legal practice, which he alleges have caused his fall into 'great scandal, infamy and discredit amongst … all other subjects,' causing

> many men, his clients … to hold the selfsame Edward in such distrust and misgiving by reason of the aforesaid slanderous English words … that they have desisted and still do desist from retaining the selfsame Edward as counsel for any of their causes or matters pending at law, or from dealing with him in any other way, so that the selfsame Edward has lost many gains, profits and fees which he … could have had and earned … if the same false crime and slanderous words had not been uttered and put forth.[8]

Though plaintiff's allegations which suggest that attacks on professional life have engendered a loss of business are nothing new, the skill

6 Manning, 'The Origins of the Doctrine of Sedition,' pp. 100–1; Bellany, 'A Poem on the Archbishop's Hearse,' p. 152.

7 Stubbs was indicted under the statute of *Scandalum Magnatum*, which legally allowed for the defence of truth. Yet the alleged truth of his book was unjustifiable given that he had put it in writing – a fact which highlighted a curious quirk in the statute that was not to be shored up until Coke's 1605 common law case.

8 Helmholz, *Select Cases*, p. 67.

with which Coke's lawyers adumbrate both the loss of profit and business opportunities whilst maintaining a cause and effect relationship with Baxter's imputations is notable.

As Boyer notes, to be accused of being a double-dealer 'could wound and damage an Elizabethan attorney as thoroughly as any modern conflict of interest charge,' and so it is perhaps to be expected that Coke's bill centres on the actual loss caused by words which he alleges are false, malicious, and, above all, harmful.[9] The judicial presentation of Coke as an honest and learned expert also deserves further consideration given the broad cultural tendency in the late Elizabethan period to distrust lawyers. Too often was the profession viewed as comprising willing profiteers in the growing multiplicity of lawsuits which plagued society.[10] Inhabiting as Elizabethans did one of the most litigious periods in English history, it was inevitable that many men would subscribe to the Platonic doctrine which held that 'it was a great sign of an intemperate and corrupt common wealth where lawyers and physicians did abound.'[11] The increase in lawyers, furthermore, was seen to be symptomatic of what Brooks calls the 'flood tide of litigation ... which by the 1580s had made the central courts so frequently resorted to.'[12] As a result, the depiction of Coke as an archetypal legal expert adroitly countered contemporary cultural prejudices in addition to providing a means of setting up the conventional dichotomy between honest plaintiff and malicious defendant. In short, Coke's role in this particular judicial narrative was not only that of the upright plaintiff, but a committed and respected member of a generally maligned legal fraternity.

9 Boyer, *Sir Edward Coke and the Elizabethan Age*, p. 70.

10 Brooks (*Pettyfoggers and Vipers of the Commonwealth*, p. 134) notes that 'economic thinking for the most part held that lawyers, instead of adding to the nation's wealth, siphoned their incomes from those farmers, merchants, and trades-men who did.'

11 Burton, *The Anatomy of Melancholy*, p. 427.

12 Brooks (*Pettyfoggers and Vipers of the Commonwealth*, p. 11) goes further in his acknowledgement of the increase in lawsuits in the central courts. He cites the 'increase in wealth of yeomanry; the relative cheapness of the legal process; the decline of local institutions; and the superabundance of legal advisers' as reasons for the expansion in legal business. Demand, of course, must also have played a role.

An increasing cause for concern in slander suits brought during the later Elizabeth period was the problem of what words might or might not be considered actionable: that is, what legitimately constituted grounds for a legal case.[13] Words which could be considered 'mere abuse' had, even by the 1560s, lost all ties with the specific imputation of a crime demanded by *Mitior Sensus*, and had, in fact, entered the domain of pure insult.[14] As a result, there was decreasing tolerance in the crown courts for slander suits over words which could not be considered actionable because they did not imply that a crime had been committed. Nevertheless, cases in which the alleged slander takes the form of one neighbour alleging that another is but a 'false knave' – as in the 1585 Common Pleas action of Ralph Leeson against Henry Coxe for his wife's loose tongue – continued to turn up in the royal courts.

Following the tradition of opening writs, Leeson claims that the words, spoken before 'good and substantial men,' had brought him into 'vexation, confusion and infamy,' harming his dealings with 'divers good and honest persons, with whom he was previously accustomed [to deal] in buying, selling and lawfully bargaining.' As Cressy has noted, allegations of knavery were common, and though it is admitted that lawyers were accustomed to arguing which words in which settings may sustain an action for slander, such allegations were rarely deemed actionable ('knave' itself being an archaic term for a manservant rather than a true word of reproach).[15] It is therefore no surprise to find that the counsel representing defendants Henry and Joan Coxe is careful to point out that 'the writ and declaration aforesaid and the matter contained in them are not sufficient in law for the aforesaid Ralph to maintain his action ... and they are not bound by the law of the land to answer the aforesaid writ and declaration.' It is equally unsurprising to find that Leeson himself, 'solemnly called, does not come;

13 Baker (*An Introduction to Legal History, 4th Edition*, pp. 438–40) provides an adumbration of what was and was not considered actionable in the period. Chief amongst them were words which alleged crime or endangered liberty; words which alleged occupational incompetence and subsequent loss of trade; and words which imputed certain diseases.

14 Helmholz, 'Introduction,' p. xciv.

15 Cressy, *Dangerous Talk*, p. 26.

nor does he prosecute his writ aforesaid,' with the result being that the defendants successfully reverse the focus of the case and recover damages from the supposed victim of the slander.

What emerges from this case is the lack of tolerance in the royal courts for petty, plebeian skirmishes, as even the plaintiff himself shows a disregard for the action he had initiated. Further, the court itself exercises its power of punitive redress against one who has attempted to use it as a weapon in a personal altercation. It is therefore arguable that words which imputed no crime, but rather manifested the problem of prating tongues and personal conflicts, were fast losing the ability to form the basis of slander suits in the courts. However, one must not ignore the fact that this particular case is drawn from the court of Common Pleas and involves lower-ranking members of society (here referred to only as husbandmen). It is therefore possible to argue that, once more, the law's dim view of disputatious and litigious commoners is in evidence. Here the ostensible slanderers were not breakers of hierarchy intent on casting criminal aspersions on their betters, but rather a naturally loquacious couple who had simply and heatedly traduced an equally base neighbour. Certainly, it seems to have been the view of the royal courts that the civil disputes of the lower orders were to be kept in check, with subjects discouraged from indulging in idle lawsuits and refraining from their natural tendency to be contentious. Quite another matter, of course, were words which attacked authority, seditiously stirred up rebellion, or imputed real crimes which affected the accepted social, commercial or religious order of the day; as has been seen, these were apt not to be thrown out of court, but to be treated more seriously as punishable under the civil law of tort or under statutory law.

With case studies thus far drawn from the middling years of the period, it is useful to now turn to the declining years of Elizabeth's rule, the 1590s, in order to compare cases drawn once more from the court of King's Bench and the court of Common Pleas. Retaining an interrogative eye on the importance attached to rank in slander suits, the 1591 King's Bench case of Blunt versus Robertes presents an interesting study. Pleading against one Thomas Robertes, 'citizen and clothworker,' the conventionally self-professed model of moral, legal and economic rectitude, William Blunt contended that Robertes, whilst

> seduced and stirred up by the most wicked malice and diabolical inspiration, scheming and intending not only to strip and deprive the same William of his good name, fame, credit and esteem … but also to bring the selfsame William into public scandal and ignominy … in the presence and hearing of divers faithful subjects of the said lady the present queen … did speak, announce and utter in a loud voice these false, feigned, disgraceful and slanderous English words to a certain Anne Blunt, wife of the selfsame William namely, 'Thy husband (meaning the same William the present plaintiff) was but a bankrupt.'[16]

As a result, it was argued that

> by reason of the speaking and saying of which false and slanderous English words, the same William Blunt has not only been slandered to the highest degree in his credit and esteem, with which he had previously been imbued, but also for the same reason the same William has lost and missed various gains, earnings and profits which he could have had and earned in buying, selling and lawfully bargaining if the aforesaid English words had not been so uttered.[17]

Questions first must be asked about the actionable nature of the words spoken. To assert that an individual is 'bankrupt' is to impute upon them no crime. As has been noted, increasingly strict application of the rule of *Mitior Sensus* was a feature of the court of Common Pleas; the King's Bench, however, took a decidedly more lenient view of cases in which the words allegedly spoken did not impute a specific criminal act.[18] Consequently, plaintiffs who claimed to have been slandered by words which were not criminal accusations were expected to persuade juries that 'the words suggested a corrupt life; that they cut the plaintiff off from society, and that they caused actual loss.'[19]

Certainly, one can discern from the plea allusions to all three as Blunt's counsel attempt to overcome the doubtful actionabilty of the words spoken by Robertes. In so doing, a legal narrative is composed in which he, Blunt, assumes the role of innocent, honest and successful citizen, whose good name is unexpectedly and unfairly traduced by the malicious and devious

16 Helmholz, *Select Cases*, p. 69.
17 Ibid.
18 Helmholz, 'Introduction,' p. xciv.
19 Helmholz, 'Introduction,' p. xcvii.

slanderer before his peers and associates, as an immediate result of which, those 'faithful liegemen of the present queen, and all other foreign merchants … on this account refused to deal further with him, and have withdrawn themselves … from his company, to the selfsame William's great ruin and manifest impoverishment.'[20] Once more, it is clear that emphasis is placed on the slanderer as one who sows discord amongst a previously balanced and ordered society. It is a neat piece of judicial narrative, the goal of which is to stress not only the ultimate loss experienced by Blunt, but to reconstruct the 'real' sequence of events in a way likely to aggrandize William Blunt, blacken the motives of Thomas Robertes, and emphasise the actionability of words which do not fall easily under the category of slander.

The doubtful actionability of the words spoken may also be linked to the insistence placed not only on William Blunt's reputation, fame and name, but his status as one of the 'leading merchants of this realm of England.' Certainly, it is known that the Elizabethan bankruptcy statute required defamation cases to 'set out the status of a merchant to make imputation of bankruptcy actionable.'[21] Further, Helmholz notes that contemporary thought held that 'a person's status helped to determine the extent of compensable harm.'[22] However, Blunt's profession is not only named, his business dealings are described in vivid detail, with his trading activities with 'subjects of England' as well as 'many foreign merchants' cited as being predicated on his trustworthiness and credit. Furthermore, Blunt's counsel present him not only as a successful merchant, but one 'of the greatest repute, credit and esteem among many magnates and nobles of this realm of England, insomuch that Robert, earl of Essex, constituted and appointed the same William receiver and collector of all rents and revenues from all his lands and tenements within the county of Kent.' Such expansive insistence on Blunt's commercial patronage – and sponsorship by none other than the Queen's great favourite and rising star at court – certainly suggest a recognition of the effectual role which a plaintiff's status and noble links could play in court proceedings.

20 Helmholz, *Select Cases*, p. 69.
21 Helmholz, 'Introduction,' p. xcvii.
22 Helmholz, 'Introduction,' p. lxxxi.

What therefore emerges is a sense of the social capital inherent in the late sixteenth century, as the influence of middling and large-scale merchants grew in conjunction with their wealth: a fact which, according to Stone, increased their standing in the eyes of the landed gentry.[23] In a similar vein, stress is laid on Blunt's accustomed business not only with Englishmen, but 'many foreign merchants.' Such overt reference to his international prestige is itself interesting, as Stone further recognises the influence of merchants on foreign as well as domestic policy, given the leverage the merchant community could exercise by the offer or withholding of its facilities for credit.[24] Furthermore, even amongst the 'middling' classes, merchants with foreign connections were afforded a higher status than local wholesalers and large-scale shop merchants.[25] Certainly, Blunt's counsel seem attuned to the nuances of harnessing the attributes of rank and status: the commercial classes were, after all, lawyers' 'bread and butter.'[26] However, it is worth considering that, despite the growth in wealth, numbers and status of merchants and traders, they were still viewed with disdain by many sections of Elizabethan society. Thomas Smith's idealistic *De Republica Anglorum*, for example, is particularly dismissive of 'the fourth sort of men which doe not rule … [who] have no voice nor authoritie in our common wealth,' whilst Stone records contemporary belief that 'merchants do attain to great wealth and riches, which for the most part they employ in purchasing land and little by little they do creep and seek to be gentlemen.'[27] Such a scornful view of this growing commercial elite, may, in part, be related to Helmholz's recognition that 'despite having expansive arguments made in his favour,' the trader was apt to 'leave the royal courts without a remedy.'[28] The presumptuous merchant, it may be argued, can be viewed as becoming as much a threat to social hierarchy as the slanderer himself.

23 Stone, 'Social Mobility in England, 1500–1700,' p. 27.

24 Stone, 'Social Mobility in England, 1500–1700,' p. 28.

25 French, 'The Search for the 'middle sort' of People in England, 1600–1800,' p. 283.

26 Brooks, *Lawyers, Litigation and English Society Since 1450*, p. 240.

27 Smith, *De republica Anglorum*, p. 19; Stone, 'Social Mobility in England, 1500–1700,' p. 19.

28 Helmholz, 'Introduction,' p. xc.

In order to build a fuller picture of the judicial narrative constructed in Blunt's case, we might now turn to the strategy adopted by Robertes' defence counsel. Typically, it is made clear that Robertes 'denies force and wrong.' However, his counsel admitted

> That the speaking of the aforesaid English words in the aforesaid declaration occurred, [but] there was a certain communication held between the aforesaid Anne Blunt, then and there the wife of the aforesaid William Blunt … in this manner, the aforesaid Anne Blunt spoke these English words following to the said Thomas, namely, 'Burchett? What was Burchett's father but a butcher?' Upon which the aforesaid Thomas replied … 'Then what was Blunt but a bankrupt?'[29]

Clearly, the crux of Robertes' defence rests on the contention that the exchange was a private matter rather than the public accusation suggested by Blunt. The context of the alleged slander therefore becomes of primary importance, as the defence counsel reduce the actionability of Robertes' words by removing them from public discourse and placing them in a private, dialogic exchange.

If one accepts Lorna Hutson's view that judicially derived narrative was 'understood to be primarily generated by controversy as to what had happened in a specific time and place,' it becomes apparent that Blunt's lawyers produced a description of a drama played out before an audience of peers.[30] As a response, Robertes' counsel removed the supposed audience to the event and thus rendered the 'drama' a mere description of a private conversation or, in contemporary parlance, altered the 'manner and form' in which the words were spoken. Certainly, it was a successful ploy in this case; not only was Blunt's bill disregarded, but he was ordered to recompense Robertes 'for his charges and costs relating to his defense laid out in this matter.'[31] One can therefore conclude that, despite the dogged promotion of William Blunt's superior status, the words spoken by Robertes were deemed to have affected his business little, if at all. Whilst the plaintiff's attempts to invoke his commercial ties to the country's leading nobility

29 Helmholz, *Select Cases*, p. 70.
30 Hutson, *The Invention of Suspicion*, p. 124.
31 Helmholz, *Select Cases*, p. 71.

indicates an awareness that rank could play a persuasive role in legal argument, it is clear that the both the actionability of the words themselves, as well as the context in which they were uttered, continued to play a dominant role in what was or was not considered legally slanderous.[32]

If the King's Bench displayed a greater toleration for slander suits which did not conform to the rule of *Mitior Sensus* (whether juries ultimately ruled in favour or against such suits notwithstanding), it is no surprise that the following case from the court of Common Pleas centres on the allegation of a slander which ascribes a specific, temporal crime. The 1595 case of Holman versus Penfounde is noteworthy not for the allegation of slander for which it is brought, but rather for the method of defence successfully employed by the defendant. The crime imputed is conventional enough, as one Arthur Holman alleges that Diggory Penfounde of Cornwall

> Did openly and publicly speak and utter certain false, slanderous and untrue words of the aforesaid Arthur, in these English words following, namely, 'Thou art a thief. Thou hast stolen sheep'; by reason of the utterance of which false and slanderous words the same Arthur is not only injured in good name and fame, by which he was previously reputed, but he is also most grievously oppressed and weighed down by divers labours and expenses for clearing himself in this suit.[33]

As in the case of Blunt and Robertes, one can again trace the rising currency of the word 'slanderous' as a means of emphasising both the supposed falsity of the words and the temporal damage they have incurred. Further, the well-established pattern of previous cases is adhered to; Holman's counsel constructs a narrative in which the players are polarised

32 It must be here noted that reconstituting the context in which words were spoken was not a certain way of ensuring the courts' favour. Sir Edward Coke defended Edward Denny, a Norfolk clergyman, in around 1579. Denny had been charged with slandering Henry, Lord Cromwell, and Coke asserted that 'the words spoken were a private act.' Nevertheless, the Lord Chief Justice 'delivered the opinion that anything which touches prelates, great nobles or certain officers of the crown is a public act and that the slandering of any of these magnates concerns the king.' The outcomes of the cases are therefore quite different, but both demonstrate the preoccupation with rank in relation to the effects of slanderous discourse.

33 Helmholz, *Select Cases*, p. 73.

into the upright plaintiff and the devious defendant whose motives are malicious and self-interested. To underscore this point, clear reference is also made to Penfounde's 'pure and considered malice,' as a counterpoint to the 'good name, fame, conversation and condition' which reputedly characterises Holman. Rather than respond to the allegation of slander by reconstructing the narrative of events, however, Penfounde's lawyer 'denies force and wrong' by strenuously claiming the truth of his words, arguing that

> The aforesaid Arthur, before the time and speaking and utterance of the aforesaid English words specified in the aforesaid declaration is supposed to have occurred ... did with force and arms, etc. feloniously take and carry away a wether belonging to a certain Edward Holman ... against the peace of the said lady the queen, by reason of which the same Diggory, afterwards ... did speak and utter of the aforesaid Arthur the aforesaid English words ... as he was well entitled to. And this he is ready to verify.[34]

The defendant's plea, therefore, constitutes a further example of the plea in justification: that is, that the crime imputed in the alleged slander was justifiable by its veracity. In creating a response to Holman's accusation of slander, it is the strategy of Penfounde's legal counsel to, as Gowing would suggest, build a recognisable, oral narrative with 'space for flashbacks, parenthetical explanations, and chronological and spatial shifts to blend different moments towards one theme': that being, in this case, the justification of Penfounde's words.[35]

Unlike the case of Funnel versus Atmere, however, Penfounde does not allege Holman guilty according to any dubious court of common voice. Rather, the case proceeds according to a refinement adopted by the Common Pleas in the 1590s, which encouraged a reciprocal series of demurs, replications and rejoinders in order to 'take issue more specifically on the commission of the crime.'[36] Thus, the fact that the case proceeds with a further denial of thievery by Holman, followed by repetition of Penfounde's claim that Holman was, in fact, responsible for the theft, is

34 Helmholz, *Select Cases*, p. 73.
35 Gowing, *Domestic Dangers*, p. 235.
36 Helmholz, 'Introduction,' p. cviii.

understandable. As a result of this heightened level of disputation, however, it was made clear that 'the rule in these cases was that the answer must fully justify the words spoken.'[37] Hence, the case was referred to the Michaelmas Assize, which inquired not into whether or not the slanderous words were spoken, but rather whether or not the plaintiff had stolen the sheep. With the imputed crime thus at the forefront of the legal case, and the Assize jury judging Holman guilty of the theft (which was related, via report, back to the King's Bench) it is no surprise to find Holman not only failing to benefit from his writ, but ordered to pay Penfounde damages for the costs incurred.

Justification of truth, therefore, can be seen to take a role in slander suits in the Common Pleas courts of the 1590s, with rank, in this particular case, playing a far less visible role than in the King's Bench. Indeed, Holman's status is referred to only insofar as conventional pleading dictates. He is 'reputed well amongst his neighbours' and a 'true and faithful liegeman of the said lady the present queen,' and yet neither his trade nor any fiscal threats to his livelihood are mentioned in the writ.[38] Arguably, such a lack suggests a gap in Holman's original writ; he lacks the security of status and demonstrable loss in trade that attacks on reputation are often claimed to have caused. Indeed, it may be argued that it is this very lack that allows the defendant to produce such a successful counter-argument: the statusless man seeking to profit by allegations of slander against his neighbour is not only a figure of suspicion, but one well-recognised in a legal culture populated by 'uneducated peasants and townsmen [who] used and manipulated courts for their own purposes.'[39] The potential of lawsuits to result from 'the ill will of men' and 'encourage contention between neighbours' is therefore particularly interesting.[40] If one accepts that contemporary thought included scepticism of the burgeoning practice of law as a 'social evil' – as recorded in the writings of Sir John Davies, Sir Anthony Benn and Robert Parsons – then it may be argued that a case which exhibits false

37 Ibid.
38 Helmholz, *Select Cases*, p. 73.
39 Brooks and Lobban, *Communities and Courts in Britain, 1150–1900*, p. 45.
40 Brooks, *Lawyers, Litigation and English Society Since 1450*, pp. 23–4.

accusation and misuse of the courts for attempted personal gain was bound to fail. The court, it seems, sought to regulate its disputed and criticised powers by exercising a sharp and legally upright stance against members of the lower orders who attempted to manipulate the law for their own gain.

CHAPTER 4

Slander in the Court of Star Chamber

Of course, as the opportunity for subjects to air private grievances and seek financial redress for civil disputes was reserved for the secular courts, it is unsurprising that civil cases fought between subjects of the lower and middle classes dominate the plea rolls of the Common Pleas and King's Bench. Conversely, the powerful court of Star Chamber had, by the reign of Elizabeth, become an exclusively criminal court and, provided the Grand Jury were willing to indict defendants, focused its attentions on punishing or protecting the interests of high-ranking individuals involved in (often politically sensitive) criminal cases. In terms of slander, this proved problematic, as prior to the birth of the crime of seditious libel, jurists in the criminal court of Star Chamber were placed in the invidious position of having to cobble together existing civil libel law (which, as we have seen, proscribed slanderous speech and did not tolerate slanderous writing, but was focused on financial recompense) and statutory laws (such as felony statutes, *Scandalum Magnatum*, and treason laws) to punish offenders as criminals – a task that was probably made easier by the fact that felony trials admitted no counsel for the defence.

So named for the gilded stars which decorated the ceiling of the chamber in which the court sat, its jurisdiction was, strictly speaking, available to anyone who wished to bring criminal activity to the attention of the Crown (although the costs of attempting to sue in the Star Chamber were both prohibitive for those of lower rank and reliant on demonstrable allegations of criminal behaviour).[1] It is thus understandable that Sir Thomas Smith, in his *De Republica Anglorum*, viewed the court as a means of 'bridling stoute noble men, or Gentlemen which would offer wrong by force to any manner of man, and cannot be content to demaund or defend their

1 Guy, *The Court of Star Chamber and its Records to the Reign of Elizabeth I*, p. 62.

right by order of law.'[2] Nevertheless, the court did follow the protocol of the common law courts, with Barnes identifying the 'scrupulous formality' with which the court of Star Chamber adhered to the principles and protocols utilised in the common law courts.[3] Thus, Star Chamber pleadings comprise the familiar format of pleas, demurrer or answer, replication and rejoinder. Whilst private suits therefore constitute a significant part of the activity of the court, official or government prosecutions in the Star Chamber (which increased during the reign of Elizabeth) were initiated by the Attorney General, and could proceed either by the filing of written charges, or *ore tenus*, with the defendant commanded either to make vocal answer to the charges directly or sign a pre-prepared confession.[4] Witnesses were not produced in either type of suit, but rather privately interrogated, with any relevant evidence produced in writing and, with justice then administered directly by the Privy Council, the modern understanding of the court's activity as summary and arbitrary is understandable.

The jurisdiction of the Star Chamber was, of course, wide-ranging and varied. Writing of the court's history in 1641, Richard Crompton lists amongst the criminal activities which fell under the Star Chamber's cognizance such varied crimes as routs (unlawful assemblies), riots, forgery (with intent to defraud), perjury and, of course libel.[5] To Crompton, libellers 'bee oftentime dealt with in Star-Chamber, as offenders not sufficiently provided for by lawes otherwise.'[6] Particularly dangerous were those libels which Crompton recognises as 'famosus libellus': writings or utterances which touched public figures and constituted more than just a 'written injurie.' In a period which Andrew McRae recognises as characterised by an 'intermeshing' between the spheres of the personal and the political, it seems obvious that slander and libel posed particular problems to those in authority: effectively, attacks on the reputations of high-ranking figures struck not only at the figures themselves, but could be employed as

2 Smith, *De Republica Anglorum*, p. 51.
3 Barnes, 'Star Chamber Mythology,' p. 5.
4 Guy, *The Court of Star Chamber and its Records to the Reign of Elizabeth I*, p. 37.
5 Crompton, *Star-Chamber cases*, p. 1.
6 Crompton, *Star-Chamber cases*, pp. 10–11.

weapons against state structures.[7] The necessity of halting slanderous activity between and against public figures was well recognised and found its voice in contemporary political and legal writing. In his 1630 treatise on the 'Arraignment of slander, perjury and blasphemy, and other malicious sinnes shewing sundry examples of Gods judgement against the offenders,' commentator William Vaughan recognised that

> Every libel which is called a famosus libellus or Infamoria Scriptura, is made eyther against a private man or against a Magistrate, or publique person. If it be made against a private person, that deserves a severe punishment. For though the Libel be made but against one, yet notwithstanding it incites all of them of the same family, kindred, or society to revenge, and so tends consequently to quarrels, & to the breach of the peace, and may be cause of the effusion of bloud, and of great inconveniences. If it be made against a Magistrate, or any other publique person, that is a greater offence; for that concernes not onely the breach of the peace, but the scandal of the government.[8]

Once again, the overt and pervasive concern with the regulation of public order becomes evident; the slanderer, as in the common law courts, occupies a position of social outsider and malfeasant whose intent is to disturb the harmony and ordering of the realm by means of inciting disorder and compromising the position of his betters. The court of Star Chamber had developed in concert with increasingly punitive laws aimed at severely discouraging seditious utterances in the form of political prophecy or rumour, and the advent of the legal offence of criminal libel (instituted in 1605 after a lengthy period of uncertainty and malleability in the deployment of various legal tactics in the punishment of felons) was characterised by its initial definition and punishment by the Star Chamber.

Naturally, this had repercussions for the ways in which slanderous speech and writings were treated. As Manning further recognises

> it was axiomatic that slander or libel could lead to factionalism and that factionalism in turn could lead to a breach of the peace, which was the justification for the court of Star Chamber assuming jurisdiction over the several species of crime that were included under the general heading of sedition … which comprised slanders or libels

7 McRae, *Literature, Satire and the Early Stuart State*, p. 52.
8 Vaughan, *The arraignment of slander*, p. 97.

> upon the reputations and/or actions, public or private, of public officials, magistrates and prelates, which sought to divide and alienate 'the presente governors' from 'the sounde and well affected parte of the subiectes.' It was not necessary for seditious utterances or writings to be published, and if the facts alleged were true, that only made the offence worse, since a true slander was more likely to cause a breach of the peace than a public one.[9]

Given such autocratic attempts to regulate social order and punish malfeasants, it is tempting to consider the court of Star Chamber, by virtue of its status as the judicial arm of the Queen's Council, as synonymous with despotic, prerogative justice; indeed, it is a view which has long been endorsed by modern scholars critical of the court's alleged use of torture, inquisitorial procedure and trial without jury. However, Thomas G. Barnes has gone some way to demythologising much of the common and often erroneous perceptions of the court which, as he recognises, had steadily grown in currency since the first generation of post-Cromwellian judges, abetted by successive generations of Whig historians, began to vociferously condemn the abolished judicial system.[10]

Attempting to contextualise the operations of the court, Barnes recognised that, whilst punishments ran from the relatively innocuous (a gentleman of Kent who 'falsly and malitiously' slandered his cousin by 'going about to prove [him] to be a traytor' was ordered to ride about Westminster Hall with his face to the horse's tail) to the barbaric (nostrils could be slit and ears cut off), such corporal punishments were handed down just as frequently in the King's Bench: a court which was also, in its time, even more noted for its summary use of torture. Both courts could maim slanderers, but the legislation with which they did so was problematic enough to require clarification under James I. Sentence of execution, it will be noted, also fell outwith the jurisdiction of the Star Chamber, the court having no cognizance over cases of treason. Although the records of the Star Chamber are disorganised (and many damaged or lost), surviving records and material relating to the court's practices allow us to uncover the most

9 Manning, 'The Origins of the Doctrine of Sedition,' pp. 100–1.
10 Barnes, 'Star Chamber Mythology,' pp. 1–11.

common form of punitive redress handed down by the Privy Council.[11] Far outweighing mutilation and corporal punishments were imprisonment, fines (of varying size) and orders of public penance. It therefore becomes clear that the primary goals of the Star Chamber were not merely to secure public order and punish the criminal activity of high-ranking noblemen, but to provide a forum in which convicted criminals were forced to atone for their crimes via public mortification.[12]

Crucially, however, Barnes accepts that cases involving political offences were (in both the Star Chamber and King's Bench courts) unencumbered by burden of proof, with the Tudor monarchy not scrupling to 'use [the Royal Prerogative] shamelessly in any court to crush an enemy of the state.'[13] Whilst Barnes' attempt to re-historicise the Star Chamber without the impediment of centuries of historical bias is admirable, it is perhaps worth noting that he failed to address what was likely one of the greatest reasons for the court's contemporary popularity. Although the lack of jury seems incompatible with modern ideals of justice, it remains a fact (indeed, even the briefest look through the court's records will confirm) that the Star Chamber nevertheless offset the omission by comprising counsellors who readily and enthusiastically engaged in an open, deliberative process. It was, one might reasonably assume, therefore an asset of the court that

11 Useful material which explains the Star Chamber's punitive exactions include John Southerden Burn's *The Star Chamber: Notices of the Court and Its Proceedings* (1870), which draws on the records themselves) and Richard Crompton's *Star-Chamber cases Shewing what causes properly belong to the cognizance of that court. Collected for the most part out of Mr. Crompton, his booke, entitled The iuristiction of divers courts* (1641).

12 The fines imposed by the Star Chamber could also provide a source of revenue for the Crown, although Southerden Burn (*The Star Chamber: Notices of the Court and its Proceedings*, p. iv) notes that the court was mainly used for this purpose by Henry VII, James I and Charles I, who 'were especially active in appropriating fines for their own benefit, or assigning them to their relations or dependents.' G. R. Batho ('The Payment and Mitigation of a Star Chamber Fine,' pp. 4–51), however, has provided a more nuanced account of the ways in which fines – particularly exorbitant ones – could be mitigated. Further, such mitigation was not only common; it was even usual.

13 Barnes, 'Star Chamber Mythology,' p. 11.

it constituted a gallery of educated and experienced peers; and further, an even greater asset that those peers conducted proceedings not in secrecy, but in a legally accessible courtroom, wherein the invited public could witness their deliberations.[14] The latter fact, naturally, meant that the judges could in turn observe the public mood and tailor those deliberations accordingly. With this understanding, it is possible to examine records from the court through a socio-historical lens, recognising that the Star Chamber had not acquired an indelibly black reputation, but followed the example of the common law courts in seeking to maintain social hierarchy and order by punishing slanderers according to the perceived severity of their crimes.

Predictably, tension arose between spoken and written slanders. Indeed, by the reign of Elizabeth, the Star Chamber was already familiar with the meting out of punishment to those who had taken to libelling others with their hands. In the year prior to the Queen's accession, the court (under Mary Tudor) had presided over a case in which one Veer was convicted in the Star Chamber for 'malicious counterfeiting of traitorous letters against one And[re]w Ryvett and Bygott, whereupon they were sent to the Tower.'[15] For his crime, Veer was committed to the Fleet and pilloried in Cheapside. As in the common law courts, it is apparent that conviction for slander rested predominantly on the assertion that the alleged slander had imputed a crime punishable by law onto the victim.

What is of particular interest, however, is the role played by the libellous letters produced by Veer. Whilst the common law courts relied predominantly on slanderous speeches uttered in the presence of neighbours

14 Cheyney ('The Court of Star Chamber,' p. 731) recognises that the when the Star Chamber operated judicially, it was 'as public as any other court.' Though the rank of spectators cannot be definitely identified, Cheyney further notes that 'the situation of the Star Chamber itself on the extreme edge of the group of Westminster buildings gave ready access to it to all, except for the control exercised by the usher of the chamber. We hear of that official receiving profitable fees for providing convenient seats or standing-room for young noblemen and gentlemen which flock thither in great abundance when causes of weight are there heard and determined.' Evidently, the Star Chamber's judicial proceedings made it a useful tool of the state in making a public example of criminals.

15 STAC 4/3/2.

to the civil derogation of the victim, the Star Chamber was not unfamiliar with the dangers which the dissemination of handwritten libel could pose for victims. As a consequence, one can identify a solid, pre-Elizabethan foundation of the recognised potential of manuscript material to be misused by slanderers with malicious and damaging intent.

Manuscript circulation was not, of course, the only means by which defamatory material could be spread, as evidenced by the telling case of the Attorney General versus Sir Rich[a]rd Knightley for 'contempt against certain proceedings and decrees against printing, and maintaining those who printed seditious and libellous books and pamphlets.'[16] Knightley and his cohorts were summarily tried in the Star Chamber, with imprisonment and a £2,000 fine imposed as punishment. Similarly, one Vallinger was convicted, *ore tenus*, in 1582, 'for libels against the Government and religion, the manuscript originals being found in his lodgings.' Fined £100, Vallinger was also pilloried both in Cheapside and Westminster, losing an ear at each site and being fined £100.[17] Nor were such cases rare during the Elizabethan period, and it consequently becomes clear that, to the Star Chamber, the potential of both handwritten and printed defamation to promote disorder and threaten both the security of the kingdom and social harmony were well recognised, with the judicial system gaining momentum in punishing and curtailing the activities of those offenders it could catch. Thus, at this stage, it can be seen that written defamation (produced by pen or press) had already entered into the realm of seditious libel – an early sign of the legal developments that were to be aimed at handwritten material in ensuing decades.[18] Written material, it might here be suggested, was beginning to be used as a vehicle for slander that was only to become ever more divided from its spoken counterpart as the century wore on.

The Marian case of Veer versus Ryvett and Bygott, whilst interesting as an example of the way in which handwritten material was recognised

16 Southerden Burn, *The Star Chamber*, p. 71.

17 Southerden Burn, *The Star Chamber*, p. 71.

18 The common law crime of seditious libel, established in 1605 was, it will once again be noted, to be used primarily against handwritten material for the majority of the seventeenth century.

as a means of disseminating slander (and consequently punishable in the Star Chamber), provides also an example of what may be termed a 'private' suit: that is, a case in which private citizens filed a complaint against a slanderer, citing his criminal activity and beseeching the Council to administer justice. As has been noted, such cases were common in the Star Chamber – however, it is not without complication that a court sensitive to the importance attached to rank accepted suits from individuals who had the means to pay for justice for alleged criminal wrongs. Further, it was a sensitivity to which the players in Star Chamber cases were well attuned, as can be seen in the case of Tyringham versus Ardis, which dates from the 1570s.[19] Primarily a suit concerning forgery, it was Thomas Tyringham's assertion that Edward Ardis, along with his wife and brother, were responsible for the forgery of title deeds to the manor of Linford, in addition to slandering 'the sayd Thomas before dyvers witnesses in the sayd countie of Wiltshire.' As the court had become the site of exclusively criminal matters, it is perhaps to be expected that slander, which often constituted a tort touching only a man's reputation and business, could and was attached to actual crimes. In this case, therefore, slander represented a means of bolstering the suit and adding a further charge as an adjunct to the crime of forgery, the slander being the less than actionable claim that Tyringham was not the lawful owner of the manor.

What is interesting, however, is not the appearance of an accusation of slander in a shady property dispute, but the way in which Ardis responded to the accusation in the answer which he brought before the Star Chamber:

> The said Edward Ardis one of the defendants for himself sayth that the said Bill of complainte againste him exhibited in this honourable courte is for the most parte insufficient in the lawe to be answered unto And the matters therein conteyned merely devised and prosecuted against him of purpose only to impoverishe and hinder the saide defendant he being but of meane wealth and abilitie and now heretofore unacquainted with matters of suche charge especially in things that do not greatly concerne himselfe for plaine declaration of the trewthe and direct answere to the said Bill … [and] further the that [*sic*] said defendant as to any forgery, contriving of

19 STAC 7/6/9.

> any false deed, slander or any other misdemeanour contrary to the lawes and Statute in the sayd Bill mentioned is not guiltie.[20]

The claim that the complaint made by the plaintiff is insufficient in the law to be answered is familiar enough; however, Ardis's protestation that he was but of 'meane wealth and abilitie' were peculiar to the court in which he found himself arraigned. As has been demonstrated, the primary function of the Star Chamber (particularly during Elizabeth's reign) was the curbing of criminal activity amongst the upper echelons of society, and the protection and punishment of those unlikely to submit or be arraigned by the common law. Certainly, it is obvious that this is a perception of the court shared by Ardis' defence. In addition to the expected attempt to transfer guilt from defendant to plaintiff (Ardis asserting that the suit was merely a fraudulent fabrication aimed at blackening his name), it will be noted that Ardis is also pointedly described as of 'meane' birth and lacking in understanding of the weighty matters alleged by the plaintiff. The presentation of a defendant in such ignoble terms may seem, at first, somewhat counter-constructive, and yet given the status of the Star Chamber as a powerful court which concerned itself with 'stoute noblemen' and the direct administration of justice in the name of the Crown, it is clear that Ardis' defence centred on his convincing the Council that the plea against him was neither legally valid nor a fit matter for the country's premier arbiters of justice. Unfortunately, as with the manuscripts of many records from the court of Star Chamber, the final verdict in Tyringham's suit is lost. Nevertheless, what remains provides compelling evidence that the court and those brought before it were acutely aware of the importance of rank and its effective role in negotiating the legal system. If rank played a significant role in the common law courts, it may be argued that it formed one of the major factors which influenced the way in which suits were brought, fought and judged in the Star Chamber.

With the court's preoccupation with rank thus illustrated, it is possible to turn to some of the cases for which the Star Chamber is perhaps most

20 Ibid.

infamous: those in which both plaintiff and defendant were drawn from the upper reaches of Elizabethan society. As has been noted, those who occupied public positions were, in the eyes of the law, more susceptible to the slanderous speeches, writings and actions of those attempting to destroy reputations or sow sedition. In addition to the magistrates and 'publique persons' whom William Vaughan categorised as at risk of the tongue, pen and press of slanderers, he was to add churchmen and religious officials. In his treatise, Vaughan recognised that

> if one speaks scandalous words of an archbishop or a bishop, he may sue him in this court to have him punished; or else he may have an action upon the Statute *de Scandalis Magnatum*, as happened in Sandes and his case, Arch-bishop of Yorke, betwixt him and one Sir Robert Stapleton Knight, in the Star-Chamber.[21]

Although the records from the court case do not survive, the extraordinary arraignment of Robert Stapleton for the 'contriving of a slander against the Archbishop of York by conveying a harlot into his chamber and bed' can be readily traced in the dispatches and letters which form the domestic Calendar of State Papers for 1582. Devised as a means of extorting money from Archbishop Sandys, the alleged slander takes the form of

> [a] plot to entrap the Archbishop with Mrs Sysson. Her resort at an appointed time to his chamber. Forcible entry of Stapleton, Sysson and others into the chamber, and detection of Mrs Sysson in naked bed [*sic*] with the Archbishop. His attempts to secure secrecy by bribing Sysson with 500*l* and Stapleton with 200*l* and a valuable lease worth 1500*l* and with the loan of much money. Stapleton denies being a party to the plot, but merely a looker on in answer to what the Archbishop charges him with.[22]

Clearly, the category of 'slander' into which Stapleton's alleged crime falls is markedly different from the written or spoken utterances which have been previously examined. Rather, it becomes evident that 'slander' had a fluidity of meaning which could be broadened to encompass any act or action intended to bring an individual into public disrepute, or

21 Vaughan, *The arraignment of slander*, p. 91.
22 *CSP, Domestic, Elizabeth – Vol. CLVIII.*

to misrepresent that individual as the perpetrator of an actionable crime (in this case, an ecclesiastical crime). Consequently, the role of the slanderer is similarly widened. Rather than a dangerous troublemaker whose deeds are marked by malicious loquaciousness or a private grudge, he can be an active player in intrigues designed to destabilise existing structures of power. This, to Ina Habermann, is a key facet of criminal slander. She argues that 'on the criminal side, where a much clearer hierarchy of power is involved, actionable slander is defined by the authorities; it is not open to interpretation, and its meaning and outcome are pronounced to be unambiguous, which makes this type of slander illocutionary and equates it with a physical action, that is, turns it into a performative.'[23] The notion that 'slander' is what the state decrees is, as will later be seen, particularly important – especially in criminal cases in which a considerable degree of elasticity was involved.

Stapleton's claim to be no more than a 'looker on' is therefore of particular importance. In his representation of the narrative, his attempts to stress his own lack of agency are contingent on his self-portrayal as distinct and apart from the plot: not an active player, but a disinterested witness. Such a defence, however, failed to convince the Archbishop, who wrote to the Queen's chief minister, Lord Burghley, to express his desire that 'a fuller commission may be set for the examination of witnesses … [and that his cause] be heard in the Star Chamber [because of the private commission's] unjust and partial dealings.'[24] Stapleton and his fellow conspirators were subsequently tried in the Star Chamber for their attempts to 'bring upon the Archbishop a horrible slander.'[25] Whilst his companions were variously mutilated, fined and pilloried, Stapleton was 'degraded from his Knighthood,' sentenced to eight years' imprisonment and given a considerable fine of £3,000. All parties, it is further recorded, were forced to restore to the Archbishop the monies which had been extorted. Here, one of the key differences between the treatment of slander as a crime and as a tort becomes obvious – whilst civil suits were aimed primarily at extracting

23 Habermann, *Staging Slander and Gender*, p. 48.
24 *CSP, Domestic, Elizabeth – Vol. CLVIII.*
25 Southerden Burn, *The Star Chamber*, p. 75.

damages from defendants, the former, according to criminal law, viewed slander suits as a means of publicly (and sometimes brutally) condemning those who sought to upset the established hierarchy. At the criminal level, even before 'criminal libel' was codified, slander was sedition. Measured by effect, it was the malicious upsetting of order by words or deeds.

Like the late Marian case between Veer and Ryvett and Bygott, that of Sandys versus Stapleton and his cohorts is notable not least because it portrays the slanderer not merely as loose of lips and poisonous of pen, but of actively malicious intent and apt to criminal machinations in the pursuit of slandering an enemy (the portrayal of Sandys as a bawd being of particularly actionable force given his profession). However, it will be remembered that churchmen were not the only public figures at the mercy of slanderers. So too were magistrates and officers of the law: a not surprising fact given the ability of defamation to attack the characters of those whose 'very essence of ability to govern' hinged upon their reputations.[26] Thus, one might turn to the 1599 case of the Attorney General versus Smith and Fisher: a case which resulted in the corporal punishment of two prisoners for their part in the dissemination of a slanderous petition against the warden of the Fleet prison, the destination of many who faced justice in the Star Chamber.[27]

Of key interest to any consideration of the case are the aptly named Interrogatories, which survive in manuscript form and illustrate at some length both the pressing concerns which motivated the Attorney General's arraignment of the defendants and the means by which Smith and Fisher were questioned. Amongst the queries put to the pair are

> whether were these articles nowe shewed unto you at the tyme of your examynacon entitled with these wordes (viz) Articles of p[ar]ticular matters wherein prisoners of the ffleete are grieved and have and doe receive … oppression and abuse at the handes of George Reyvell nowe warden … [were] sett down written or published or caused to be sett down written or published by you, yea or noe! Whether be the said Articles conteyned in the said paper trewe or not, whether be any of them true

26 Shuger, *Censorship and Cultural Regulation*, p. 68.
27 STAC 5/A10/13.

> or not, and declare which of them in certain either the first, seconde, thirde or any of them, yea or noe![28]

The harangue continues, as the interrogation further demanded answer to

> whether was this petition directed to the righte honourable S[i]r Thomas Egerton, Knight, Lorde Keeper of the Greate Seale of England … by you or by your meanes. What person delivered the same, who did write the said petition, declare his name and dwellinge place, and the truthe thereof uppon you othe. Whether you did at any tyme say that the nowe warden of the ffleete doth extract under colours of false orders [and] taxes … to the charge and spoil of her Ma[jes]ties prisoners … [using] craftie means and under cloke and color [for your] false suggestions to be exemplified under the Greate Seale of England.[29]

Particularly worthy of consideration is the persistent polarisation of truth and falsehood: a line of demarcation which places the slanderer on one side and the weight of justice and the law firmly on the other. Although the line of questioning demands answer to whether any of the slanderous accusations contained in the position contain any elements of truth, the dogged insistence that the claims are 'falshood' is particularly telling, as is the allegation that the slanderers caused their writings to be fraudulently 'exemplified' under the Great Seal of England by virtue of their being directed, 'by craftie means and under cloke and color,' to the Lord Keeper. Once more, the accused are avowed guilty of deception, chicanery and guile before judgement has been passed. The insistence on the perceived falsity of the accusations contained in the petition is itself interesting. The Privy Council was, as will be seen, increasingly unconcerned with the truth or falsity of written material, and 'in prosecutions for written defamations … the defendant could never justify his words as true.'[30] Why, then, the concern with establishing the petition as false? The answer can only lie in the nebulous development of the law. With written and spoken slanders as yet legally undistinguished, and the law apt to take what we

28 Ibid.

29 STAC 5/A10/13.

30 Hamburger, 'The Development of the Law of Seditious Libel and the Control of the Press,' p. 670.

may term a selective approach to prosecution based on the perceived severity of the effects of the words, it is possible that here the Attorney General sought to ensure conviction by establishing the criminality of the text not just as illicit (and therefore illegal regardless of truth) but as untruthful and, regardless of the delivery method, unjustifiable.

Although the Attorney General is keen to affirm the falsity (and therefore criminality) of the handwritten petition, anxiety is betrayed by the zealous and protracted demands made to the defendants to reveal the means by which the inflammatory material was circulated. Such overt exhortations to divulge information concerning delivery, authorship and the identity of everyone involved in the creation of the petition betray a general uneasiness about the dangers of slanderous manuscripts. Equally interesting, however, are the further issues raised the by Attorney General's forceful pressing on matters of authorship and distribution. For one, it becomes apparent that written slander could make a felon not only of one, but of many. It will be noted that early modern authorities were increasingly concerned not simply with the words of slander, but in the act of publication itself. This is a point neatly underscored by Harold Love, who recognises one of the dangers of slanderous and seditious manuscripts as lying in their 'republication,' which took place as often as they were copied.[31] Complications arose when, unlike in many civil cases, the slander was not simply spoken by an identifiable individual before a third party, but rather anonymously produced and covertly imparted. It was a concern which grew in magnitude as the Elizabethan period wore one.

As Manning suggests, 'each new crisis in Elizabeth's reign' culminated in renewed proclamations ordering martial law.[32] One of them, in the 1590s, resulted in rewards of £100 being offered in the capital for those who provided information which would lead to the apprehension of any authors of seditious libel, that they might be punished under felony statutes or, depending on the content of the libel, treason or sedition. Another, issued during the increased fears of Spanish invasion, proclaimed death for anyone who imported or owned books containing 'seditious or slanderous libels'

31 Love, *Scribal Publication*, p. 44.

32 Manning, 'The Origins of the Doctrine of Sedition,' p. 108.

against Elizabeth.[33] The rarity of catching the authors of libellous material (manuscripts providing a readily anonymous mode, with the 'distance' of anonymity offering slanderers greater power of expression) greatly complicates traditional notions of authoritarian state suppression and censorship.[34] Given that those in authority demonstrably sought to curtail the defamatory activities of the lower orders, it is obvious that handwritten material presented a much greater challenge than that spoken or printed. Not only was it frequently aimed at public figures and officials (and therefore synonymous with what was to become the crime of seditious libel), but perpetrators were likely to be far more difficult to identify and bring to justice. In addition, they retained the ability to covertly and informally distribute material which was increasingly apt to lampoon public figures and evade systems of censorship. Consequently, it is arguable that the crime of producing a handwritten slander in order to discredit a social better combines two Elizabethan perceptions of slanderous activity that have already been witnessed: the social malcontent whose words represent a danger, and the invidious and cunning actor whose insurgent actions are calculated to arouse societal discord. That these perceptions of the slanderer were to become increasingly intertwined is of some consequence. As Pauline Croft notes, scurrilous items were particularly suited to manuscript circulation, and despite their propensity to be repeated orally, their writers (rather than being silenced) began to flourish artistically, and even to attach value to their handwritten slanders.[35] Whilst Fisher and Smith may have been far removed from the railing verse libellers who were to grow in number in subsequent decades, one can confidently conclude that it was in the Star Chamber that the (as yet unwritten and unofficial) distinction between written and spoken slander was, in practice, most acutely understood.

In 1594, that same Edward Coke who was later to condemn written slander whether it was true, false, public, or private, succeeded to the position of Attorney General. It was in this role that he was to preside over

33 Capua, 'Early History of Martial Law,' p. 169.

34 McRae, *Literature, Satire and the Early Stuart State*, pp. 32–3.

35 Croft, 'Libels, popular literacy and public opinion,' p. 266; Fox, 'Ballads, Libels and Popular Ridicule,' p. 64.

a 1596 slander case concerning words spoken against two of the realm's leading courtiers:

> Kuke [*sic*], the Queen's Attorney moved against three for slanderous words against the Lord Admiral and the Earl of Essexe, but he proceeded only against one Smithe on his confession for spreading sclaunderous newes. He laid his information under the statutes of Edward I and Philip and Mary … Smithe had confessed that he being a pressed soldier at Dover and the news being there that the Spaniards were on the sea (which was false, for they were Hollanders and friends of the Queen), they were shipte, bu [*sic*] as it turned out to be 'Grave Morris' [Maurice of Nassau, Governor of the United Provinces] they were dismissed; and he came to London and reported that the news was throughout the soldiers that the Lord Admiral's shippe beinge searchte by th'erle of Essexe & openinge divers barrelles wherein he supposed to haue been gunpowder … & thereupon he Called him Traitor, and so theye Came bothe to the Cowrte & there the'erle of Essexe … before the Queene tooke the Lord Admiralle by the Berde & sayde 'ah thou Traytor'; and this Smythe, trauellinge by Windsor, called at the howse of a Justice of peace thereby for drinks and reportinge the like there, was … himselfe apprehended.[36]

As has been noted, the statute of *Scandalum Magnatum* (which foregrounded libel – either written or spoken – as a statutory crime) provided a legal basis for specific condemnation of those spreading 'false news' about public figures and officials with the intent of sowing discord between the sovereign and her magnates. Pre-1605, it was one of the most popular means of criminalising and prosecuting those who defamed public figures. A political crime – and an early form of criminal libel – *Scandalum Magnatum* was unique in that it 'punished the fact of publication as a crime.'[37]

Thus, the statute neatly assumed jurisdiction over speakers, repeaters, writers and publishers of slanderous material, with a broad remit covering a variety of forms of libel against peers and officials. Nevertheless, the

36 Hawarde, *Reportes*, p. 39.

37 Manning, 'The Origins of the Doctrine of Sedition,' p. 111. Bellany ('The embarrassment of libels,' p. 146) recognises that the Star Chamber increasingly placed emphasis on the effect rather than the content of libels. This had the (presumably intended) effect of making the truth of a libel's allegations irrelevant to the legal determination of an offender's guilt or innocence.

successful prosecution of malefactors under *Scandalum Magnatum* was not without obstacles. For one, truth could legally be posited as a successful defence under the statute (provided the news alleged was proven true, unwritten and not designed to cause a breach of the peace). This presented difficulty for the politically sensitive Tudor monarchy which began, under Elizabeth, to use the Star Chamber to punish both seditious and ordinary libels and slander – whether true or false.[38] It is therefore unsurprising to recognise in the case of Coke (as Attorney General) versus Smith a clear example of the way in which the statute was invoked in order to punish an individual who had repeated patently untrue allegations about the activities of his social superiors.

The politically subversive nature of Smith's claims is of especial significance. With contemporary beliefs regarding the divinity of social hierarchy (as considered at length in E. W. M. Tillyard's *The Elizabethan World Picture*) still very much propounded by authorities, it is understandable that those who spread false claims about the activities of their betters were considered worthy of punishment for sedition. Of course, the very existence of slanderous and seditious discourses attests to the fact that Tillyard's perception of a dominant 'world view' is problematic. As Kevin Sharpe has noted, alternative political ideologies to that advanced by the adherents of the *status quo* were far from unthinkable; they were thought.[39] It may be further argued that Smith's claims of a rift between two powerful figures not only constituted a dangerous and subversive lie, but recognised and bolstered factionalism and divisions between members of the Queen's court. That the Lord Admiral is also claimed to have been called a traitor is also relevant. A capital crime punishable by death, the accusation that the Admiral has committed treason, although ostensibly only repeated rather than created by Smith, falls easily into the category of slander, comprising as it does the false allegation of an actual crime.

38 Manning, 'The Origins of the Doctrine of Sedition,' pp. 112–13.

39 Sharpe, *Remapping Early Modern England*, p. 223. David Norbrook (*Poetry and Politics in the English Renaissance*, pp. 282–3) has further criticised Tillyard's perception of the success of hierarchical ideals as representing a 'static and frozen' model. Bearing in mind, however, Elizabeth's use of the motto *semper eadem*, it is clear that just such a model was paradigmatic if not realistic.

Subsequently, though Smith himself seems a remote figure who, rather than acting out of malicious intent, was satisfied to simply repeat 'the news throughout the soldiers' (his lack of guile suggested, if nothing else, by his naivety in sharing his 'news' with a Justice of the Peace), it is to be expected that under the jurisdiction of the Star Chamber, his lax attitude to social order and the alacrity with which he spread news about members of the aristocracy merited severe punishment. Once more without the benefit of a written defence or the chance to present himself before a jury and make answer or rejoinder, Smith was

> sentenced *per totam curiam* to loose one of his ears vpon the pillorie at Westminster, the other one at Windsor, to be whipped, & to haue a paper one his head Contayninge the wordes, & imprisoned during pleasure, & fined *20l*, w[hi]ch should haue bene farre greater but for his baseness beinge a peasant & a boye.[40]

The multitude of punishments (covering almost the full array of those usually inflicted by the Star Chamber in such cases) reveals just how seriously the government took the spreading of slanderous news, especially when it touched the kingdom's premier nobles and held the potential of breeding factional dispute. Whilst Elizabeth's chief minister, Burghley, was to caution that the 'the vulgar sort had no business in affairs of the state,' an atmosphere of gossip, rumour and false information-circulation prevailed.[41] It is therefore possible to discern an indication that the increasingly severe measures meted out towards offenders were at least partly symptomatic of the state's inability to eradicate or effectively control a problem which was to invite accusations of libel via a plethora of means, including the publication and circulation of slanderous discourses in ways which actively resisted containment.

The fact that the defendant was also 'base,' 'beinge a peasant & a boye' is also worth noting. Whilst the Star Chamber is perhaps most famed for its treatment of high-ranking individuals (one must not forget those 'stoute noblemen' recognised by Sir Thomas Smith), it could nevertheless proceed against all or any who could be indicted or proven to have committed acts

40 Hawarde, *Reportes*, p. 40.
41 Cressy, *Dangerous Talk*, p. 11; Fox, 'Ballads, Libels and Popular Ridicule,' p. 243.

which warranted immediate prosecution for political crimes. It therefore seems obvious that throughout the Elizabethan period the law proceeded to loom ever larger in the lives of people 'all the way down the social order' (what is difficult to gauge is only how heavily its shadow fell every time someone opened their mouth in company).[42] It is a persuasive notion, and the punishment of Smith in the Star Chamber also provides compelling evidence that authorities considered 'word of mouth' transmission of false news amongst the increasingly politicised lower orders intolerable. Despite his lowly status, Smith's public, verbal 'republication' of contentious state matters ensured that his activities became a matter for the judicial arm of the Queen's council, whose business was increasingly concerned with stemming the spread of seditious slander. The case study of Smith, it may therefore be seen, suggests clearly that news (especially false news) could provide a bridge between the civil offence of intemperate speech and the more serious, statutory crime of sedition. In this case, at least, rank was recognised – as affirmed by Smith's comparatively small fine, and yet his crime and the perceived potential of his slanderous activity in fostering dissent and division were enough to warrant his arraignment and summary punishment in the Star Chamber.

It is one of the ironies of the law that although it sought to punish and control the spreading of slanderous words and speeches, the courtroom provided a forum in which those words must, perforce, be amplified and repeated. Concerns over the notion of the court as a site of slanderous re-publication are therefore to be expected, and, indeed, are openly voiced in the 1596 case of Wheeler versus the Dean of Worcester. The case involves a bill, devised and entered into the court by Wheeler as plaintiff against the Dean of Worcester. However, the bill itself was judged slanderous, containing as it did '74 offences in the Dean, and others in High Commission and others in authority.'[43] As a result, the Dean seized the opportunity to counter-sue Wheeler, which led to a further examination in the Star Chamber, culminating in

42 Fox, 'Ballads, Libels and Popular Ridicule,' p. 333.

43 Hawarde, *Reportes*, p. 52.

> the interrogatories on the one side being 155, and on the other 125, and 77 witnesses were examined, interrogating things of doctrine and religion, over which this Court has no jurisdiction.[44]

The apparent distaste with which the officials of the Star Chamber viewed such treatment of the court is evident, as the report states that 'the hearing was tedious, and a slanderous libel ... And of which the Counsellor ought to be well advised, and of such tedious depositions.'[45] Nevertheless, the case proceeded apace with obvious intent: the punishment of the original plaintiff, Wheeler, who had attempted not only to slander a religious official, but to misuse the courtroom and the law as a weapon in order to do so. Particularly galling to the Lord Keeper, who presided, were

> the hugeness of the depositions of the slanderous bill, and [he] condemned the plaintiff [Wheeler] for a notorious villain; and his offence is the greater in this, that he made this Court (of such authority and state that [the Lord Keeper had] not heard nor read of the like in the world) an instrument to publish [and] record his blasphemies, and to have the nobles of the land from her Ma[jes]ties side, vpon whose sacred person they showlde attend, to hear his slanders and libels, and thus a great shame to her Ma[jes]tie and this Courte.[46]

A lack of tolerance towards those who attempted to misuse the court is clear, and it will be noted that the Star Chamber was active in regulating court procedure and punishing those whose attitude to the law was considered subversive.[47] Certainly, it was not unusual to find records of the punishment of those who, like Wheeler, attempted to bring false suits to court as a weapon, nor is it rare to find cases of the Star Chamber punishing juries who had returned unfavourable verdicts in the common law courts.[48]

44 Hawarde, *Reportes*, p. 54.
45 Ibid.
46 Hawarde, *Reportes*, p. 55.
47 Those who sought to use the law as a weapon in civil disputes were increasingly likely to eschew the secular courts in favour of the ecclesiastical courts (Gowing, *Domestic Dangers*, p. 37).
48 Southerden Burn, *The Star Chamber*, p. 53.

However, the worries of the Lord Keeper betray a more general tension in the legal treatment of slander. Arguably, it was a source of anxiety to lawmen that the punishment of slander required the words to be repeated (the very act of repetition being one which it is the court's business to curb). Furthermore, the noticeable distress with which the repetition of the slanderous articles before the council was viewed is obvious. What it suggests, however, is not only the professed tedium engendered by the copious depositions and interrogatories, but also a tacit belief in the potential effects which slanderous discourse might have on the hearers, even in the inquisitorial confines of the courtroom. It was a belief well-founded, as Lord Keeper Bacon had, in 1567, expounded the dangers of 'contemptuous talk' and 'unbridled speeches' which 'led to factions and seditions ... [and] maketh men's minds to be at variance with one another, and diversity of minds maketh seditions, and seditions bring in tumults, tumults make insurrections and rebellions.'[49] Similarly, slander of the clergy had also long since been a source of disturbance, 'because it undercut the spiritual authority of God's ministers on earth.' Coupled with what Cressy further recognises as an unfortunate tendency on the part of both readers and listeners to believe libellous words, it is not surprising that the Lord Keeper who condemned Wheeler to 'imprisonmente during pleasure' and 'naillinge at the pillory' also ordered the depositions 'to be withdrawn from the Courte.'[50] The corrupting influence and subversive potential of words in breeding dangerous thoughts and actions in listeners is, therefore, illustrated with some clarity.

The case between Wheeler and Worcester is noteworthy not only for the insight it provides into the level of trepidation with which slanderous words were repeated in the courtroom, however, but also because it provided a catalyst for a further royal proclamation concerning slander, which was issued in tandem with sentencing. Crucially, part of the Queen's commandment ordered that 'vagrante & idle persons, especially those w[hi]ch flocke together, [are] to be punished seuerely.' It was further commanded that the law was to 'haue circumspecte note of sclaunderers, haue loose

49 Cressy, *Dangerous Talk*, p. 42.

50 Hawarde, *Reportes*, p. 55.

tongues, & to punishe them *non oscitander*.'[51] The governmental concern regarding the dangers of collusive and subversive social groups is obvious; so too is the pervasive belief in the malevolent, seditious and incendiary potential of loose tongues and intemperate speech. Worthy also of discussion is the role which the royal proclamation had to play in providing a 'legitimate' counterbalance to the 'illegitimate' writings of the slanderer.

As Kevin Sharpe has illustrated, early modern England recognised a close relationship between the word and the exercise of power, with the development of print extending authority.[52] He further notes that 'through the printed proclamation, the king [or queen] could reach to all corners of the realm … The proclamation spoke to and commanded even the illiterate. Pinned to the market cross, its typography and form announcing it to be the royal word, it was the medium through which subjects most frequently experienced royal authority.' Thus an objectification of authority, one might question the operation of Elizabeth's proclamation in light of the case which engendered its publication. Arguably, it was the purpose of the proclamation not merely to provide instructive information about legal commandments, but to serve as a written antithesis to Wheeler's written slanders: the idea was to fight dangerous fire with state-authorised, controlled fire. In short, Elizabeth's proclamation symbolised the true and legitimate word of authority, publicly displayed as a remedy to the illegitimate, abusive, written words of a slanderer. Further, the proclamation was undoubtedly intended to implicitly carry a whole range of dichotomies: legitimate and illegitimate, true and false, legal and illegal: all distinctions which further underlined the vast gulf between authority and slanderer.

However, the issue of the proclamation, made as it was alongside a pronouncement of sentencing against a slanderer, provides further evidence that, rather than the Elizabethan regime conducting a consistent and organised attack on slanderous activity, its legal attempts at suppression and control comprised pragmatic and politically expedient responses to discrete crises. That public opinion and social realities interacted with the actions of the courts is no revelation; one might reconsider, for example,

51 Hawarde, *Reportes*, p. 57.
52 Sharpe, *Reading Revolutions*, p. 27.

the case of publisher John Stubbs, who was spared treason charges due, at least partly, to his airing of views which were universally greeted with sympathy. Nevertheless, whilst Stubbs was tried in the King's Bench for his actions, it is arguable that the Star Chamber acted with similar regard for expediency. In 1599, one Mison was brought before the court for

> seditious words in contempt of Justices of the Peace and their authority on the orders as to Corn and the poorer people in the time of the great dearth, and for seditious words against the Council and the Queen (viz: 'they are knaues, I will keepe none of there bastardes, my goodes are my nowne, they, nor the queene, nor the Councelle haue to do wi[th] my goodes, I will doe what I list wi[th] them,' etc.).[53]

For his midemeanour, Mison was sentenced to a fine of '£100, imprisonment, to wear papers, to confess his fault, and to be bound for his good abearing.' A comparatively lenient punishment in that Mison did not suffer mutilation, it may surely be argued that both Mison's speech, which signifies more a malcontent view of the government rather than the spreading of false news held in such suspicion by the statute of *Scandalum Magnatum*, was judged to be a response to the agricultural problems which blighted the 1590s rather than a dangerous attempt to sow sedition. Accordingly, the Council dispensed with the severer punishments commonly meted out against those who spoke ill of those in power, trying him for a misdemeanour rather than a felony.

What therefore becomes apparent is that the government took careful account of public feeling as well as exercising an acute sense of social realpolitik when sentencing slanderers. It is a view, furthermore, supported by Manning, who sees the 1590s as a period in which martial law began to fail as an effective means of curbing seditious material, leading the Privy Council to develop 'the practice of distinguishing between seditious words and writings which were serious enough to be considered treason, and lesser offences of seditious slander and libel, which were tried as misdemeanours in the Star Chamber.'[54] It may therefore be argued that, as Mison's words

53 Hawarde, *Reportes*, p. 104.

54 Manning, 'The Origins of the Doctrine of Sedition,' p. 110. The difference in treatments – whether felony or misdemeanour – depended on the case. It is notable that

were uttered during a period of widespread social unrest and a popular mood of disaffection ('the time of the great dearth'), his slanderous speech was measured carefully against public opinion rather than condemned with indifferent barbarity. The actions of the court of Star Chamber therefore take on a slightly different complexion. In moments of political turmoil, it was the prerogative of the court to gauge the 'common voice' of the nation and, when necessary, mitigate the punishment of slanderers rather than sentence arbitrarily. Key, it may be seen, was the importance of maintaining an *ad hoc* attitude towards justice which balanced the need to maintain and regulate social order during periods of national agitation with the tradition of ruthlessly silencing incontinent and dissenting voices. This was not, however, to suggest a benevolent institution (the unfortunate young Smith would no doubt be appalled by any such suggestion, were it possible for it to reach his remaining ear), but rather one that could vary its sentences when it was considered politic to do so.

In short, such cases indicate the need for caution when considering legal records as evidence of shifting legal trends; the treatment of slanderers, it can be seen, depended equally on local and periodical fluctuations in circumstance as on an encroaching and increasingly paranoid, autocratic government.

---

misdemeanours allowed for defence lawyers whereas felonies did not. See: Beattie, 'Scales of Justice,' p. 221.

CHAPTER 5

After Elizabeth: Slander in the Early Jacobean Star Chamber

Despite the various attempts of the government to quell the tide of slanderous and seditious speech, the Queen's Attorney was to note in the penultimate year of Elizabeth's reign that '[libel] is a growing vice, and there are more infamous libels within a few days than ever there were in the ages last past.'[1] Certainly, the Star Chamber of the Jacobean period was to continue to be inundated with suits against slanderers and writers of seditious material. Addressing the jurisdiction of the court, Adam Fox has recognised the varied types of slanderous activity there punished – from 'derogatory songs or verses to derisive letters, pictures or objects with some scandalous imputation or false allegations made before another authority against an individual or group.'[2] Despite increasingly stringent measures and a pragmatic and expedient attitude towards punishing malfeasants, slander continued to flourish throughout the early modern period. However, the Elizabethan age represents an enormously important era in the development of the legal status of, and legal attempts to discourage and punish, slander. In particular, the decisions and precedents set down in the Star Chamber when dealing with spoken, scribally produced, and printed material were to have repercussions on the legal treatment of defamation as exercised throughout the early modern period. The legacy of the Elizabethan Star Chamber has particular resonance in the period immediately following the Queen's death, and of especial interest to any study of the reputation which slanderous manuscripts had acquired by the close of the Elizabethan age is the 1605 case of Attorney General Coke versus Lewis Pickering.

1 Hawarde, *Reportes*, p. 143.
2 Fox, 'Ballads, Libels and Popular Ridicule,' pp. 47–83, 55.

The facts of the case are as follows:

> One Lewis Pickering was charged with writing a libel against Queen Elizabeth and the late Archbishop Whitgift. He subsequently showed the writing to a Minister named Bywater, who made a copy. Pickering claimed that this was done privately and did not constitute publication. Bywater later procured several colliers who sang the libel at Whitgift's funeral. Although Bywater had technically published the libel twice, only Pickering was punished in order to emphasise that even the private delivery of a libel was to be construed as a publication.[3]

The case, clearly, raises a host of questions regarding the legal status of written defamation, which, at the close of the Elizabethan period, was taken seriously as a criminal act rather than a tort (the 'plaintiffs' both being deceased making no difference to the court's views on the relevance of *Scandalum Magnatum*). Furthermore, it is evident that the 'manner' (or publication of the slanderous material) was more worthy of punishment than the 'matter' (or content). That is, the act of showing slanderous material to another (who may or may not redistribute it) was, to the legal mind, representative of criminal activity, the exact nature of the slander notwithstanding. Significant also is the importance attached to Pickering as inventor of this particular libel. This case is particularly indicative of the government's perception of slanderers as those who seek to corrupt others by creating and spreading libels.[4] The fault, and therefore the judgement of the court, falls upon the originator of the material, and suggests that the courtroom continued apace in seeking to control and punish even those slanderers whose creative activities were conducted privately. Written material, it seems clear, had become stigmatised by its ability to be read and carried forward even by those who had viewed it privately – an

3 Manning, 'The Origins of the Doctrine of Sedition,' pp. 47–83.

4 Bellany ('Railing Rhymes Revisited,' p. 1150) recognises that 'whoever posted Pickering's libellous epitaph on Whitgift upon the late archbishop's hearse daringly usurped a space and a practice supposed to honour the deceased, and thereby intensified the force of the libel text's mock reimagining of the funeral.' However, it may be argued further – the text, though produced by Pickering, was appropriated by Bywater and then further vocally published by his hired colliers in a crass parody of a funereal choir.

understandably vexatious problem in a society which was characterised by increasing literacy, especially in the capital and urban areas.[5] Nevertheless, it was not completely without regulation. Complicating Shuger's claim that handwritten material was unregulated is the very fact that Pickering was identified, caught and prosecuted.[6] There is a strong distinction to be made between a lack of regulation and poor, informal, reactionary regulation. Although the discovery of the text in Bywater's chambers a year after its production was, as Bellany recognises, largely fortuitous, the fact remains that a level of regulation existed; royal officers could (and did) perform searches in suspects' domestic spaces and illicit material constituted evidence of malfeasance.[7]

Whilst Manning's view of the increased importance placed on the 'manner' of publication at the expense of the 'matter' reveals persuasive and pertinent information concerning the status of manuscripts and their potential for unlicensed verbal or written republication, it is arguable that 'matter' and 'manner' cannot be so readily nor so completely divorced. Indeed, the offence with which Pickering was charged and punished was the creation of a 'verse libel': a particularly slippery and vexatious mode of expression. Often containing licentious accounts of individuals or political events, the developing vehicle of the verse libel was rapidly becoming a recognised feature of political and literary culture.[8] These pithy little poems were naturally anathema to the law, not least because they were characterised by their invariably anonymous manuscript circulation. Anonymity itself proved to be an extremely useful means of circumventing legal reprisal, and explosive libels 'were at one and the same time both written and spoken, simultaneously oral and textual.'[9]

In his exhaustive study of the Pickering case, Alastair Bellany has convincingly isolated what he determines to be the driving factor in the production of the libel – namely, the outpouring of Puritan dissatisfaction

5 Fox, 'Ballads, Libels and Popular Ridicule,' p. 18.
6 Shuger, *Censorship and Cultural Regulation*, p. 4.
7 Bellany, 'A Poem on the Archbishop's Hearse,' pp. 140–1.
8 McRae, *Literature, Satire and the Early Stuart State*, p. 1.
9 Fox, 'Ballads, Libels and Popular Ridicule,' p. 65.

fomented by the Elizabethan Puritan movements (if they can be called that) of 1603–4.[10] Bellany is likely correct in his conclusions about the religious underpinnings of Pickering's motives. However, decidedly less attention is given to the potential which the case offers in illuminating the development in the Star Chamber's attitude toward slanderous activity. It was, it is worth noting, in response to this particular case that Attorney General Coke crystallised his thoughts on libel in his *de famosus libellous*, that canonical work which introduced a hitherto unknown emphasis on previously blurry lack of importance of truth in cases of written defamation: truthful allegations about officials being, indeed, a greater incitement to public disorder given that they were held likelier to disturb the peace. The influence of the statutory power of *Scandalum Magnatum* is evident in Coke's creation of the common law crime of seditious libel:

> A libel is made either against a private person, or a magistrate, or public person; and in either case is punishable, although the party libelled is dead at the time of making the libel. A libeller shall be punished either by indictment by common law, or by bill, or *ore tenus* on his confession in the Star Chamber, and may be punished by fine, imprisonment, and by pillory of loss of ears. It is not material whether the libel be true or false. A libel is either in *scriptis* or *sine scriptis*. A libel in *scriptis* is when an epigram, rhyme, or other writing is composed or published, to the scandal or comtumely of another. The publication may be 1. *Verbis aut cantilenis*. 2. *Traditione*. A libel *sine scriptis* may be 1. *Picturis*. 2. *Signis*. If one find a libel against a private person, he may either burn it or deliver it to a magistrate: but if it be against a public person, he ought to deliver it to a magistrate.[11]

10 Bellany, 'A Poem on the Archbishop's Hearse,' p. 142. The idea of a Puritan movement or movements is loaded. The name 'Puritan' was applied, with increasing disparagement, to a variety of sects and loosely connected (or totally unconnected) factions whose members desired further reform than the official Church of England espoused. Some were inclined to promote Presbyterianism after Calvin, some were in favour of sharing ideas at intimate meetings called prophesyings, and so on. The 'Puritan' as a figure was defined largely by the attitude of the current face of the English Church, the Archbishop of Canterbury, and thus became somewhat Protean over the reign of Elizabeth.

11 Coke, 'De Libellis Famosis,' p. 255.

Clearly, the establishment of the common law crime of seditious libel was not simply a knee-jerk response to the Pickering case, but the product of decades' worth of growth in slander and sedition, previously governed messily by statutory law, treason charges, civil redress and legal calisthenics performed over definitions of 'news,' 'truth' and 'falsity.' It is arguable that the proliferation of verse libels had caused the existing approaches of the law to be unfit for purpose, and the abolition of the justification of truth in the prosecution of libellers (libels being, as Fox notes, either in 'word or writing') sought to ensure that those who realised that anonymity was a means of avoiding legal censure would still be aware that, if caught, they would be subject to criminal penalties without the possibility of justifying their actions.[12] Nevertheless, by the middle of the 1630s some judges were beginning to allow defendants to plead truth as a defence for defamatory words, but still not when the libel had appeared in writing.[13] Alan Harding has suggested that this is the source of the modern distinction between libel and slander.[14] However, it must be pointed out that the law did not arbitrarily decide to differentiate between acceptance of truth in spoken and written libels in the 1630s. Instead, this was the result of cultural shifts which had, for decades, seen the growth of written libel as a mode of unlicensed expression which confounded state attempts at censorship, repression and punishment. In essence, if we want to understand the distinction, we must not simply look at the authorities' role in differentiating the two, but at what those authorities were reacting to. That was, evidently, a culture of active libelling which saw libellers adopt strategies such as satire and written anonymity (often in manuscript) in order to thumb their noses at existing laws and take advantage of the legal blurring of the two accusations in order to claim one as a useful mode of voicing dissent.[15]

12 Hawarde, *Reportes*, p. 143; Fox, 'Ballads, Libels and Popular Ridicule,' p. 65.

13 Manning, 'The Origins of the Doctrine of Sedition,' p. 120.

14 Harding, *A Social History of English Law*, pp. 80–1.

15 Why 'libel' was the mode of expression reclaimed by those who recognised the blurring of 'slander' and 'libel' is an interesting question in itself. In addition to its written connotations, which allowed for the adoption of anonymity, David Colclough (*Freedom of Speech in Early Stuart England*, pp. 206–7, 249) suggests

Given the means by which litigators and judges grappled with a variety of laws and statutes in punishing slander, it is certainly unsurprising that, following the Pickering case and the visible difficulties it presented in securing a conviction under existing legislation, Coke was to provide a definitive common law remedy which took the opportunity to clarify ideas and autocratic beliefs about slander, sedition and libel which had been of vexing import throughout the Elizabethan age. As a consequence, the breadth of defamatory activities was codified more neatly than it had been. So too were the delineation of punishment; the clear end of the justification of truth in the cases of famous personages (dispensing with the often-ignored 'false news' requirement of statute); the lack of importance of the decease of the individuals slandered (borrowed, of course, from statute law); and the proper means of disposal. 1605 thus marked the tightening up of slippery Elizabethan legal policy on slanderous writing, speech, and display, and the beginning of a more visibly draconian judicial system – although it should be noted that this system rather lent legality to what had been going on in practice for years. The advent of such a draconian system, however, would not contain slanderous and seditious language, but rather produce more clandestine methods of negotiation and resistance. *de Libellis Famosis* at a stroke made it a common law crime to ridicule or defame private individuals of high rank in speech and writing. It thus outlawed (even accurate) satirical jabs (the privilege of which, as we will see, were increasingly debated, and claimed by the literary figures of the age) and truthfully felt religious attacks (which had come to be framed more and more in personal terms). The law sought to curb a troubling tide, but such laws seldom stop behaviour; they drive it deeper underground, encouraging invention, innovation, and the learning of lessons from what worked and did not work in the past. As always, high-handed laws tell us two things: what was of major concern to the instigators (as Shakespeare knew when penning the sexually repressed Angelo in *Measure for Measure*) and what people were eager to do in spite of them (and, again, it is notable

---

the importance of the classical antecedents of the libel, with libellers increasingly attempting to situate their work in the tradition of vituperative epideictic rhetoric.

that Angelo plots to flout the anti-fornication laws almost as soon as he reissues them).

Arguably, the case therefore provides a pivotal moment in the division between traditional, common law perceptions of libel as a maliciously false aspersion on reputation and an emerging belief (which gained wide currency) that truth (despite falsity being a prerequisite in both common law definitions of slander and under *Scandalum Magnatum*) no longer constituted a sound or acceptable defence. Instead, the courts were able to display a keen facility for adapting the rule of law according to the political situation. Coke and the Star Chamber judges took the opportunity of extracting traditional notions of libel from statute, common law and elsewhere and 'fused them into a whole that served their immediate purpose of demonstrating the libellous and seditious nature of the verses against Whitgift.'[16] One must go further, however, in realising that in addition to following the legal tradition of adapting the law to political (and religious) circumstance, the case is also something of a watershed in the uneasy relationship between truth and falsity which had long complicated the law's attitudes towards slander. Ironically, it may be added, it was the prerogative of the verse libel to itself artfully blur fact and fiction in providing a growing cultural mode which demanded obscenity and insult as a feature of expression.[17] This demand, it may be argued, constituted not just an engagement with libel, but a reclamation of it from a state which blurred the lines between 'slander' and 'libel' in denouncing language which it could not contain. One retained the imputations of false and unruly speech; the other took on connotations of criticism, writing, poetic form, political engagement and even the possibility of truth (for which the law showed no regard). With this understanding, the legal system's growing intolerance and attempts to quash both truth and lies deemed libellous becomes more understandable – as does the growth in often anonymous, written verse libels which resisted them. Ironically, in definitively making clear that truth did not matter in prosecuting libels, the law made audiences

16 Bellany, 'A Poem on the Archbishop's Hearse,' p. 155.

17 McRae, *Literature, Satire and the Early Stuart State*, p. 34.

more likely to accept defamatory texts as probably truthful – and thus all the more damaging.

Consideration must also be given to the fact that the libel for which Pickering was indicted centred on two recently deceased public figures. Moreover, the case revolves partly around a slander levelled against the late Queen, whose enduring memory had already begun to pass into the realm of fetishised mythology (it will be remembered that Thomas Heywood's *If You Know Not Me, You Know No Bodie* – a laudatory biographical play about Elizabeth – was first published in 1605). As a result, one must question the effects which slander was considered to have upon the reputations of former notables, and the extent to which slanderous attacks on Elizabeth were as threatening to the institution of monarchy as those on Whitgift were of concern to the church. Many of the contemporary concerns are to be found in the surviving records of the case, which display with considerable gravity the tensions arising from Pickering's libel. Whilst Pickering affirms that 'he tooke it to be no lybelle … beinge of a deade man he took it no offence,' the court maintains that 'it is a poison. And … these three things be in theise libellers, 1. Masked impietie, 2. Cunninge hipocrasie, 3. Colored Conformitie.'[18] Once more, the slanderer is defined in delineative terms as villainous, duplicitous, hypocritical, and archetypically subversive. He was, in all ways, a threat to the security of the state and deserving of punishment.

The members of the Council then joined in the litany of criticism in their haste to condemn the slanderer and defend the slandered. The Lord Chief Justice reinforced the well-grounded belief that 'For a libelle and sclaunder againste a priuate man, he shall haue an accion of the case; againste a noble man, Scandalum magnatum. A libelle is a breache of the peace, & is not to be suffered, but punished,' before reiterating the view of the Attorney General that, '[a libel] is a poison in the Common wealthe, & no difference of the deade or liuinge: & th'offence to the state dyes not.'[19] Once more, the perception of the slanderer as one whose actions 'poison' and seek to destroy an organically conceptualised society are paramount,

18 Hawarde, *Reportes*, p. 224.
19 Hawarde, *Reportes*, p. 226.

and in order to promote the gulf between corruptive defamer and virtuous defamed, Robert Cecil, by then Lord Salisbury, noted

> A libelle in general & particular, called a wrytinge defamatory, published wi[th] hande, worde or wrytinge, & he doe not produce an author, he is the publisher … [His] ende is faction, [his] zealle blinde Furie: & there is no presydente [precedent] to equalle the Archbishop that ys deade: & it is no vice to be an olde virgin and haue spectacles: & benefits binde mee: she was a woman by Creation, but by byrthe a Queene, by her gouermente memorable, by her deathe happie, & the wonder of her sex … she did an acte of essence 24 howres before her deathe, ingeniouslye & loueingly declare that shee woulde hate her selfe yf any but K[ing] James showlde succeede her.[20]

Once again, slanderous material in handwritten, spoken and printed forms was conflated in the eyes of the law, which recognised the potential of material to circulate in all three forms. However, the circumstances of Pickering's role are particularly relevant, as both 'author' and 'publisher' – his initial, private transmission of the material led to its ultimate circulation and republication. Equally interesting is the creative historiography employed in order to legitimise James I's place on the throne (his right to which was as questionable as Elizabeth's had been given both his Tudor descent and Henry VIII's will, which barred foreign-born princes from the succession). The reasons for the inclusion of Elizabeth's ostensibly earnest desire to see James succeed her are obvious: in the promotion of a harmonious and legitimate succession, Salisbury turns Pickering's slander not only into an acerbic calumniation of the late Queen, but an attack on an undying body politic which, according the commonly held belief in divine succession, enshrined the sovereign's body politic in eternal life. This argument greatly expands the potential of defamation and slander in damaging reputation.

As has been repeatedly shown, the protection and defence of reputation was a predominant concern even to those litigants who sued at the common law. However, the libelling of the state through its former officials provides a concrete example of the extremes to which slander

20 Hawarde, *Reportes*, p. 227.

could be taken: libels were at once carnivalesque and deadly serious, for they 'provided vehicles through which contemporaries could reassess the mechanics of power and the structures of ideology.'[21] It is a belief further alluded to by the Lord Chancellor who, in his contribution to the case, confirms that 'albeit there be a Cession, yet the Crowne dyes not.' He adds, 'the Cause of lybellinge proceedes from an inquiete & intemperate spirite, not obeyinge gouerm[ente]; the ende is … the ouerthrowe [of] peace of churche & Common wealthe bothe: not vniformitie, but multiformitie … Pickeringe's faulte is the Contriuinge & publishinge.'[22] Thus roundly vilified for his alleged attempts to subvert church and state by showing a privately produced manuscript to another, it is no surprise to find that Pickering's punishments included a fine, imprisonment and pillorying at various locations (although, due to his spoken confession, he was spared his ears).

It can thus be concluded that, by the beginning of the Jacobean period, the Star Chamber was well versed in the necessity of suppressing slanderous material – especially when it was of a politically sensitive nature – as well as the means by which slanderers ought to be punished. Furthermore, it can be seen that handwritten slander, even when privately produced and displayed discreetly, was viewed with as much or more tolerance than printed or spoken material – so much so, in fact, that the creation of a new criminal law, seditious libel, was necessary to punish it. Such attitudes were, of course, not born in a vacuum, but rather as a result of such interconnecting factors as the growth of the legal profession and an increasingly watchful government which responded to each political and social crisis with expedient legal developments. In this way, the development of the law and the activities of the legal profession shared a recognisable bond with authoritarian attitudes towards censorship which, as will be seen in the following chapter, maintained a rather more politically reactive than actively aggressive policy when it came to slanderous material.

At any rate, the Star Chamber, like the lower courts, displayed a tacit adherence to the advocacy of staunch hierarchical order, with its primary interests focusing on the punishment of criminal libellers and publishers

21 McRae, *Literature, Satire and the Early Stuart State*, p. 52.

22 Hawarde, *Reportes*, p. 228.

(be they speakers, writers or printers) of seditious material, whilst displaying a familiar antipathy towards those who sought to misuse the court for personal reasons. Furthermore, the Star Chamber itself was to have the dubious honour of playing host to the birth of a lasting, controversial turning point in English legal history – the birth of the common law crime of seditious libel: a culmination of intolerance towards (and technical, if not actual, impotence in outlawing) slanderous and seditious dissent aimed at the government – whether true or not. It is entirely possible that it was cases and laws such as that resulting from 1605's *de famosus libellus* – representing as it did a fresh attack on civil liberty and speech – which contributed to the Star Chamber's reputation as a symbolic site of royal tyranny. In attempting to outlaw defamatory speech and writing just as it was blooming, the Star Chamber made itself an opponent of public discourse rather than a fair and impartial regulator. And opponents breed proponents.

CHAPTER 6

Conclusions on the Courts: Clarity or Confusion?

To the law courts, slander could take the form of spoken defamation against a neighbour, the spread of false or subversive news, misuse of the legal system and aspersions cast upon the reputations of those in authority in writing, print or speech. Accordingly, the various law courts dealt with different categories of slander by variant means: a fact with which the increasingly litigious Elizabethans were well cognizant even if they required more lawyers than ever to guide them. Certainly, the fact that plaintiffs seeking financial redress flocked to the common law courts in order to sue slanderers for damages in civil cases, whilst the Star Chamber busied itself punishing defendants as criminals, indicates a level of recognition of contemporary jurisprudence and the means by which it was best negotiated. Similarly, the courts regulated power by both vilifying slanderers and maintaining a pragmatic and expedient attitude towards administering justice: a necessity in a culture which was required to balance an autocratic justice system geared towards eliminating dissent and upholding social order with a common perception that lawmen were 'ever malicious, litigious and full of mischiefe.'[1]

In the course of this balancing act, however, one constant remains – the figure of the slanderer was frequently portrayed as a subversive social deviant, a poisoner, a corrupting influence on social order, a vengeful malcontent and a thorn in the side of the body politic. The slanderer thus represented a figure who presented a threat across the social spectrum, as evidenced by suits both at the common law and in the Star Chamber. As can be seen, therefore, the Elizabethan law courts, though stratified in their treatment of slander as either a criminal or civil matter, were united in their attempts to stifle a common enemy: an enemy who showed no respect

1 Vaughan, *The arraignment of slander*, p. 75.

for the ideological ideal of hierarchical unity, whose threatening presence signified social disorder, and, crucially, one who was equally apt to wield tongue, pen or press with dangerous and destructive intent.

Nevertheless, it will be noted that, by the early Jacobean period, demonisation of the slanderer had not contained him. Instead, slander suits were to remain a mainstay of the courtrooms throughout the seventeenth century. Not only that, but a new figure had risen: the popular verse libeller, who revelled in anonymity and thus frequently flouted the law, encouraging others to follow his example by providing them with defamatory songs, ballads, short poems and rhymes.[2] In relation to the law, a variety of reasons may be posited for the rise of the popular libeller. Primarily, the difficulty of catching the writers of anonymous works is obvious – indeed, it was something of a sticking point for authorities, who were forced by their lack of effective policing to develop increasingly punitive laws designed to stall the spread of libel and punish whoever they could find, originator or not. The lack of distinction between 'libel' and 'slander' is also of consequence. Whilst the law routinely collapsed the two terms, the rise of anonymous, defamatory writings allowed those who sought to indulge in slanderous activity to claim non-verbal expression as their own, before opening up their work to those who wished to republish it verbally. Finally, the lack of safety inherent in direct and open attempts to engage in what Lake and Pincus (2007) have recognised as a developing public sphere certainly fostered a need for politically motivated subjects to find another avenue of expression (not wishing, presumably, to suffer the fate of would-be counsellor John Stubbs) whilst those disaffected with superiors and neighbours might avoid lengthy, costly and potentially dangerous slander (or criminal libel) suits by penning – if they were literate – covert verse libels. Such libels, moreover, allowed for the expression of classical, literary satire which, as will be seen, were highly prized by poets who otherwise lacked safe methods of delivery.

2 Knowles, 'To Scourge the Arse,' p. 80.

PART II

Slander and Sedition in Elizabethan Drama

CHAPTER 7

Slander and Sedition in Elizabethan Dramatic Performance

Slander and sedition intersected with drama in a number of interesting ways. As in our introduction to the law courts, it is worth considering a number of them.

1. John writes a play, bound for the public stage, which depicts slanderous or seditious behaviour within the drama. Depending on the action of the drama – is the slanderer justly punished? – this might well meet with the approval of the state censor.
2. John writes a play which depicts slanderous or seditious behaviour and is bound for the private stage, whether meant as instruction in the Inns of Court or for private amusement amongst a coterie.
3. John writes a play which itself might contain slanderous or seditious words against the state, other states, or individuals. In theory, such passages should be excised by the censor. Yet this was a highly subjective and rather haphazard process. If the words attack a private (or public) subject, the whole thing might end up in the law courts.
4. John writes a play which itself contains slanderous or seditious words, bypasses or is accepted by the censor, and then later provokes an outcry when it reaches print. Those who licensed the text might find themselves with much to answer for, as might John. It will be remembered that committing words to paper put them past justification of truth; but where sat truth in the world of fiction?
5. John writes a play which contains material that might inadvertently be construed as slanderous or seditious but intends it only for private performance. What if those who do read it find

it dangerous? How might he defend himself from what others interpret?

6. John writes, has performed, or publishes a play which is, on its initial releases, completely innocuous, but which contains material which becomes liable to give offence or provoke a breach of the peace at a later time. Can he remain safe in the knowledge that he had followed the correct channels of publication initially?
7. John writes a play which is either performed publicly or licensed for sale, only for others to use the material contained with slanderous or seditious intent. If those hijacking the material cannot be found, might John expect trouble – and, given the vagaries of the law, what form might that trouble take?

Each of the above find expression in the records, which suggests that any understanding of how drama and slander operated must perforce be multifaceted. It is unlikely that any single model of how the two operated can account for every scenario.

Given the high number of slander and defamation suits in the early modern law courts, and the strategies commonly employed amongst both litigants and lawmen in condemning and defending libellous language, it is no surprise that the politically charged arena of the stage – bolstered as it was by the dramatic output of the Inns of Court – was intertwined with legal developments. Both the felonies and tort of slander, in handwritten, spoken, and printed forms were public dramas played out with remarkable frequency in the law courts. It is therefore understandable that the dramatic possibilities of slanderers' actions provided material suitable irresistible to writers.

Perhaps the most commonly analysed intersection of early modern drama and slanderous discourse is that recognised by M. Lindsay Kaplan in her *Culture of Slander in Early Modern England*: that is, the role of the state censor in suppressing and editing plays. Certainly, this seems to be a well-trodden path in the academic study of theatrical defamation. In his overview of recent study in the area, Andrew Hadfield recognises the 'productive and lively debate' which surrounds historical and scholarly examination of censorship. As a result, a multitude of models of early modern censorship have been proposed, from Janet Clare's autocratic, dynamic and unpredictable mechanism under which all plays were written to Cyndia Clegg's proposed model which posits the notion of an *ad hoc*, unplanned style of censorship which responded to inflammatory literary texts both dramatic and otherwise.[1] Similarly, Richard Dutton argues that the role of the censor (in the Elizabethan period, the Master of the Revels) was one of intermediary, whose job was 'to arbitrate between the court and playwrights and performers,' with controversy arising only when the 'normal checks and balances had broken down.'[2] This would certainly explain the later ambitions of Ben Jonson, who, having achieved a degree of notoriety and literary fame, was considered a potential Master of the Revels himself (albeit he never got the post). Hadfield further suggests the benefits of considering the models of censorship proposed by Clegg and Dutton in tandem, implying as both do a general liberality of speech and writing at those times in which there was no political or socially expedient need for suppression. The problem was that times would change whilst the texts remained, once available to the public, static and ripe for appropriation. No writer could predict what others might do with their work in a future political climate. One might consider, for example, the notorious 'Dutch libel' of 1593, which saw a response to parliament's extension of privileges to Dutch immigrants in the form of a placard promising civil disobedience and telling the Dutch to go home. It was signed 'Tamburlaine' and borrowed the style of Christopher Marlowe, dramatist of the popular 1587 play of the same name. The text had taken on a life of its own, but the author of the placard remained elusive. Nevertheless, Marlowe and his roommate, the playwright Thomas Kyd, were implicated, the latter tortured into blaming Marlowe, who was bound over to be watched before being killed in an affray the same month.[3] The times, marked by unrest and a ban on playing, had changed indeed. *Tamburlaine*, judged acceptable in 1587, had become apt to help cause trouble in 1593. In the absence

1 Clegg, *Press Censorship in Elizabethan England*, p. 22.

2 Hadfield, *Literature and Censorship in Renaissance England*, p. 3; Dutton, *Mastering the Revels*, pp. 46–7.

3 Freeman, 'Marlowe, Kyd, and the Dutch Church Libel,' pp. 44–52.

of a proverbial smoking gun – or dripping quill – proving the authorship of the libel, authorities desperate for scapegoat turned angry eyes towards the dramatist. If this can be accounted censorship, it was of the most reactionary, messy, and scattergun kind.

One might, however, argue further. It is certainly true that such a notion of censorship bears a remarkable similarity to the workings of the law courts and legal proclamations, both of which have been demonstrated as showing a propensity for reacting to rather than autocratically anticipating the actions of slanderers. If Dutton and Clegg complement one other, one must question another crucial facet of the study of censorship: genre.

Whilst Clegg's focus centres on the workings of press censorship, Dutton's emphasis is on theatrical suppression. Reacting to Annabel Patterson's overarching view that all material was liable for censorship, Clare has pointed out that genre itself 'must to some extent determine modes of communication and evasion … with drama being the most dangerous and topical form of literary production.'[4] The problem here is that playwrights seldom appear to have been hanged, mutilated, or fined in the way that writers of others kinds of seditious topical texts – and loose speakers – suffered. Central to Clare's approach are the ways in which censorship can be shown to affect the working practices of the early modern dramatist. As a result, much of her interest lies in 'the cumulative evidence in manuscripts and various editions of plays,' with a view to exposing those manuscripts which bear 'traces of the censor's hand.'[5] Her approach certainly bears fruit, and her deployment of 'traditional bibliographical and philological skills' in tracing the mechanisms of censorship are particularly useful in identifying just what early modern censors found objectionable.[6] Further,

4 Clare, *Art Made Tongue-Tied by Authority*, p. 16.

5 Clare, *Art Made Tongue-Tied by Authority*, pp. 9, x.

6 In particular, Clare provides useful recognition of censorship in John Marston's 1603 play, *The Malcontent* (pp. 136–9) and Ben Jonson's 1605 play, *Eastward Ho* ('Review of *Art Made Tongue-Tied By Authority*,' p. 139). However, in reviewing her book, N. W. Bawcutt ('Review of *Art Made Tongue-Tied by Authority*,' p. 546) questions whether Clare's view of censorship as a mechanism both 'unpredictable' and 'arbitrary' would not be better glossed as 'inefficient' and 'incompetent.' A compelling suggestion, varying levels of competence and operational efficiency will later be considered.

her claim that scholars must 'consider the specificity of individual works which encountered censorship and register the character of the cultural practices which sought to determine them' is well taken.[7] Here, however, we are met with an obvious difficulty. Whilst censored manuscripts might suggest much, the modern critic is nevertheless hampered by omission, lack of information and historical revisionism. In short, one faces the impossibility of recovering a 'true' text – a notion made doubly complicated by the persuasive argument of Richard Burt that

> there can be no original moment of the text as the author designed it which has been repressed or hidden, because all texts exist as forms of negotiation and are never pure: any search for the origin of censorship will be frustrated by an infinite regression: court censorship (defined in its repressive and productive senses) generates self-censorship in the actors and the author that may be regarded with equal validity either as being an anticipation of court censorship or as following after the suggestions and demands of the censor.[8]

Thus converging with Clare's view of the playwright inherently repressed by the foreknowledge of the possibility of censorship, one must surely question the purity (or recoverability) of manuscripts. It will be noted, after all, that plays reached the Master of the Revels in manuscript form, occasionally with offensive or satirical references already marked.[9] Nevertheless, the editing and censorship of plays in their nascent, manuscript form is of enormous consequence, for it informs not only Clare's view of literary suppression, but Clegg's. Citing the notorious incident of John Stubbs' *The Discoverie* and the disparity between Stubbs' public slander and the concerns of Philip Sidney expressed amongst a 'very tight circle,' in addition to recognising the dispersal of manuscript translations of the book across Europe, it becomes clear that state censorship of defamatory and seditious material had as close a relationship with medium as it did with genre.[10]

7 Clare, *Art Made Tongue-Tied by Authority*, p. 18.
8 Burt, '(Un)Censoring in Detail,' p. 28.
9 Hadfield, *Literature and Censorship in Renaissance England*, p. 5.
10 Lake, 'The Politics of Popularity,' p. 75.

With Janet Clare and Richard Dutton each presenting cases for their models of censorship as, respectively, a monolithic system which impinged implicitly on the writings of playwrights and a reciprocal process less concerned with autocratic repression than with mediation, it has been up to M. Lindsay Kaplan to explore theatrical censorship 'in terms of the wider [legal] question of slander and defamation.' Recognising slander as a 'central social, legal and literary concern of early modern England,' it is thus Kaplan's intention to provide a 'more historically grounded and fluid account of power relations between poets and the state than that offered by the commonly accepted models of official censorship.'[11] In so doing, Kaplan recognises the growth of defamation cases in the Elizabethan law courts (although the scope of her study does not allow her to examine the development of that growth) as being testament to the state's impotence in successfully repressing criticism whilst simultaneously highlighting the 'slipperiness' of slander and its consequent benefits in reversing the commonly understood power relations between censor and playwright. What therefore emerges is a model of censorship which displaces the traditionally held (and, as Kaplan would have it, anachronistic) view of censorship as a form of repression which is operated solely by the state, and instead assimilates the 'self-censorship' notions espoused by Dutton, Clare and Burt, whilst foregrounding the legal machinations of slander and counter-slander suits in order to illustrate the contestatory powers of the poet-playwright in challenging his oppressor. Stressing the instability of slander's power, Kaplan thus concludes that, 'models of censorship focus on the exercise of state power; in so doing, they ignore what a defamatory model reveals: the elusive power of discourse.' In order to bolster her case – and a convincing case it is – Kaplan cites as evidence Edmund Spenser's defence in *The Faerie Queene* against defamatory attacks levelled at poets, Ben Jonson's similar concerns over satire as a result of the 1599 Bishops' Ban, and Shakespeare's 'reconfiguring of the terms of the debate' through the presentation of slanderous discourse employed by Lucio and the Duke in Measure *for Measure*: a play whose various plot threads rely on the politics of reputation. Yet none of these texts uphold the right to slander others – indeed, *The Faerie Queene*

11 Hadfield, *Literature and Censorship in Renaissance England*, p. 7.

all but condemns slanderers as worthy of having their tongues nailed to posts – and this is crucial. Poets sought the right to write, and to write in decorous ways, rather than a proverbial free-for-all of defamation.

Though Kaplan's study cannot explore in great depth the nature of slander in the law courts, it is impossible not to draw parallels between the law's now familiar accusations, counter-accusations, replications, rejoinders and surrejoinders and her notion of slander as a slippery category which provides for more fluid power relations between dramatist and censor. Furthermore, her focus on literary material provides a particularly interesting consideration of the power relations exposed by slander in *Measure for Measure* (1603). Any comprehensive consideration of Elizabethan slander, it may be argued, can benefit immensely not only from study of those moments, recognised by Dutton, in which relations 'broke down' – or, as Clare would have it, when state apparatus was successful in its campaign of suppression – but also from a close examination of the figure of the slanderer and the legal ramifications of libel as presented and culturally ratified on-stage. In short, as much as the defendant and plaintiff adopted the role and customary language of the law at court, so too did the playwright actively engage with the language of slander and the contentious relationship it illuminated between authority and transgressor. As Kaplan demonstrates, this approach can yield extremely useful results, and yet it remains, largely, of little consequence to those whose models of censorship are based predominantly on the censorious actions of the state on the playwright's work. Thus, consideration of state suppression of plays deemed slanderous alongside plays which actively sought to explore the actions of the slanderer and the slandered on-stage, in light of the growth of litigation and development of more stringent laws, is necessary. Furthermore, with current models of censorship and dramatic suppression focusing their attention on relationships between poet and state-appointed censor, one must also examine the dramatic production of those sites in which the censor is either displaced or lacks jurisdiction.

CHAPTER 8

Staging Slander in the Inns of Court

Whilst the historical origins of the Inns of Court remain notoriously elusive, the close bond between the Inns' activities and the foundations of early modern English drama are well documented. Often collectively referred to as 'the third University of England,' the collective London Inns (Gray's Inn, Lincoln's Inn, the Inner Temple and the Middle Temple) had, by the Elizabethan period, grown in both stature and members.[1]

As sites of organised legal training, these institutions provided students of the law with an educational community and places of residence and, whilst the quality of that legal education has been reflected on with some cynicism, the Inns were the 'literary centre of England' for the bulk of Elizabethan period.[2] Indeed, to Adam Wigfall Green, it was the very lassitude of the common law curriculum of the Inns of Court which stimulated writing, as the sites became a focal point for 'poets, dramatists, and many of the juvenilia.'[3] He further recognises that the Inns 'provided a better background for literature than did the great universities, which were for a long time confined to Latin and Greek mathematics.'[4] In order to underscore his

1 Reviewing the recent publication of Jayne Elisabeth Archer, Sarah Knight and Elizabeth Goldring's, *The Intellectual and Cultural World of the Early Modern Inns of Court* (2013), Sukanta Chaudhuri recognises that the term 'derives from George Buc's 1615 treatise 'The third universitie of England,' where Buc applies it to London as a whole, including, *inter alia*, not only the Inns but St Paul's, Westminster Abbey, and all the city churches; the College of Heralds, College of Physicians, Gresham College, and even two schools for poor children.' What therefore emerges is a sense of the Inns at the heart of a cultural and educational movement based in London. See: Mukherji, *Law and Representation in Early Modern Drama*, p. xvi.

2 Prest *The Inns of Court under Elizabeth I and the Early Stuarts*, p. 153.

3 Wigfall Green, *The Inns of Court and Early English Drama*, p. 2.

4 Wigfall Green, *The Inns of Court and Early English Drama*, p. 3.

point, Wigfall Green goes on to note the cluster of notable minds which passed through the Inns' various halls during their educative years: from Sir Thomas More and Sir Philip Sidney to Ben Jonson and Francis Bacon. So too does Shakespeare retain a connection, with his *Comedy of Errors* reported as first being presented to the assemblage of Gray's Inn in 1594. In such an overwhelmingly literary and artistic atmosphere, it is unsurprising that these legal guilds are synonymous with the origins of early English drama as sanctioned by each Inn's own internally elected Master of Revels.

Chiefly, Norton and Sackville's *Gorboduc* (1561; later praised in Sidney's 1595 *Defence of Poesy*), a play which holds the triple distinction of being the first English tragedy, the first play composed in blank verse, and the first to employ native legendary material, was a product of the Inns. Similarly, the Inns' liberal study of the classics resulted also in Gascoigne's *Jocasta* (1566) and *The Supposes* (1566) in addition to the collaborative effort, *Tancred and Gismund* (1566) and Hughes' *The Misfortunes of Arthur*. Respectively, these dramatic efforts represent the first English adaptation of a Greek play, the first English prose comedy, the oldest adaptation of an Italian novella and the first English play to engage with Arthurian legend.[5] Given such illustrious contributions to the history of English drama, it is tempting to accept Wigfall Green's assertion that the Inns sacrificed exhaustive study of the common law in favour of artistic expression. It is by no means a new opinion – contemporary commentary mocked the supposed licentiousness of the Inns, with a printed satire of 1601 reading, 'You kept such reuell with your careless pen,/ As made me thinke you of the Innes of Court:/ For they vse Reuels more then any men.'[6]

It is, however, a notion complicated by Wilfrid Prest's recognition of the considerable lapse in time between the highly creative plays produced by the Inns in the 1560s and 1587's *The Misfortunes of Arthur*, after which the societies relied entirely upon professionals. As such, the image of the Inns as exercising a wholly lackadaisical approach to the study of the law in deference to a systematic commitment to developing drama is untenable, and made doubly so by the proliferation of practising lawyers who,

5 Wigfall Green, *The Inns of Court and Early English Drama*, p. 17–18.
6 Davenport, *The Whipper Pamphlets*, p. 36.

it has been seen, were of considerable concern to those Elizabethan commentators who viewed the growth of a litigious society with increasingly jaundiced eyes. Although the curriculum of the Inns of Court may have been lacking in the academic rigour favoured by early modern universities, the Inns nevertheless found the means to instruct their members in legal discourse, including, of course, identification of the frameworks of slander and sedition. Graduates of the Inns of Court 'were condemned for lacking morals, not learning.'[7]

The earliest recorded Inns of Court play, 1561's *Gorboduc* – something of a *cause célèbre* given its triumvirate of advances in English literary history – also raises interesting issues regarding the nature of early Elizabethan dramatic expression and theatrical engagement with state matters. Jessica Winston explores in considerable depth the historical circumstances of the play.[8] Sponsored by Robert Dudley (somewhat unsurprisingly, given his vested and enduring interest in the Queen's marriage), the play was originally performed at the Inner Temple before being played before Queen Elizabeth at Whitehall two weeks later. To Sara Watson, *Gorboduc* simultaneously analyses the political-philosophical ideas variously (and contradictorily) expressed by the two writers.[9] Central to Watson's argument is the belief that the play is the sum of two parts: those acts penned by the evangelical Thomas Norton and those attributed to the well-connected and politically conservative Sackville. To Watson, the product of this collaboration (or rather clash) of beliefs (that is, the radical and potentially subversive reformist notion that tyrannicide was just if a ruler's crime was a great one, and the belief that no subject could consider himself the judge of a divinely appointed ruler's actions) is a play which 'was amongst the first to promulgate the idea of tyrannicide in the consciousness of the English people.'[10] Certainly, this reading of the play is somewhat borne out by textual evidence. At an early stage of the play, as Gorboduc expresses

7 Prest *The Inns of Court under Elizabeth I and the Early Stuarts*, p. 150.
8 Winston, 'Expanding the Political Nation,' pp. 11–34.
9 Watson, 'Gorboduc and the Theory of Tyrannicide,' pp. 355–66.
10 Watson, 'Gorboduc and the Theory of Tyrannicide,' p. 366.

his desire to install his sons in their kingdoms and inculcate in them the course of wise and able governance, he hopes that they

> Not be thought, for their unworthy life
> And for their lawless swarvinge out of kind,
> Worthy to lose what law and kind them gave;
> But that they may preserve the common peace-
> The cause that first began and still maintaines
> The lyneall course of kinges inheritance.[11]

The words are likely by Norton: the sentiments expressed are unmistakeably reformist in their belief that a sovereign's duty is to the continuance of peace, and that the crown rests on a foundation of good governance and legality. However, the perception of 'the lyneall course of kinges inheritance' betrays an over-arching acceptance of royal continuity. According to Watson, however, the alternative, conservative view is not expressed until Sackville's pen reaches paper. Noting in particular the following lines, she recognises a direct refutation of radical ethos:

> I holde it more than neede with sharpest law
> To punish this tumultuous bloudy rage;
> For nothing more may shake the common state
> Than sufferance of uproares without redresse
> *That no cause serves whereby the subject maye*
> *Call to accompt the doynges of his prince,*
> *Much lesse in bloode by sworde to worke revenge,*
> *No more than maye the hand cut off the heade.*
> *In acte nor speache, no, not in secrete thoughte,*
> *The subiect maye rebel agaynst his lorde,*
> *Or iudge of him that sittes in Caesars seate,*
> *With grudging minde to damne those he mislikes.*
> Though kinges forget to governe as they ought,
> Yet subiectes must obey as they are bound.[12]

11 Norton and Sackville, *Gorboduc*, I.II.88–93.
12 Norton and Sackville, *Gorboduc*, V.I.32–43.

This section, to Watson, forms Sackville's conservative defence of sovereignty – full as it is of the imagery of rebellious subjects turning on their king armed with violence and disloyal speech, thought, and judgement. Crucially, however, the lines which deal with these actual acts of treason (that is, those italicised above) were omitted in the 1570 edition of the text. While Watson conjectures that this may be a concession to the proto-Puritan values of Sackville's co-author, or reformist printer John Day, the actual reasons for this excision remain debatable.

It is possible that the removal of these lines may not be due to evangelicalism, but rather the opposite. One might therefore make the argument (given what is known about authoritarian sensitivity to the representation of rebellion and sedition) that the lines, although conservative and condemnatory in their meaning, would nevertheless present to audiences the variant means by which malcontents could show disaffection with authority. In essence, just as the court of Star Chamber recognised lamentably that punishing slanderers involved public repetition of dangerous words, so here does it seem that condemning the strategies by which malfeasants challenge authority ought not to involve presenting those strategies in a public forum. Thus, whoever sanctioned the excision of the lines which illustrate the actions and agency of rebels, the idea seems clear – the message that subjects must obey their ruler ought to be expressed publicly, but without an accompanying catalogue of stratagems which constitute the rebel's arsenal. As a consequence, what was acceptable to present before the Queen within the relatively private confines of a performance at Whitehall was evidently deemed unsuitable for public consumption.

That the play was performed before the Queen by the gentlemen of the Inner Temple under the patronage of Robert Dudley has, according to the detective work of Greg Walker and Henry James, shown that *Gorboduc* is open to alternative readings.[13] Key to Walker and James' revolutionary reading of the play is the relatively recently uncovered Beale manuscript which comprises an eyewitness account of the first, semi-private, courtly performance of the play. Noting the courtiers, administrators and lawyers which comprised *Gorboduc*'s first audience, Walker and James foreground

13 Walker and James, 'The Politics of Gorboduc,' pp. 109–21.

contemporary political circumstances in their assessment. Of key importance, it is argued, was the question of the Queen's marriage – thrown into stark relief both by her close association with Dudley, her Master of Horse, and Eric XIV of Sweden, at that time a prospective bridegroom. Certainly, the subject matter of the play – a kingdom fallen into disrepair due to the rebellions and civil wars engendered by an uncertain succession – seem to bear out the notion that the play contains allegorical associations with the young, unmarried Queen, herself an illegitimate heir to a contested throne. Citing the reordering of the play's dumb shows as evidence (they are missing from the printed editions of 1565 and 1570) Walker and James make a persuasive argument that the 1561 performance of *Gorboduc* constituted a discussion of marriage designed to press Dudley's suit to the Queen at the expense of the mooted Swiss alliance.[14]

Convincing as Walker and James' assessment of *Gorboduc*'s political and rhetorical function is, Jessica Winston raises the important question: should we trust the interpretation of the eyewitness entirely?[15] Recognising that the opinion of the play found in the Beale manuscript is 'more personal than objective' in its belief that *Gorboduc* represented a pressing of Dudley's suit, Winston provides an arresting (and relevant) interpretation of the play as a study in the theory and practice of counsel.[16] Recognising that the performers were 'men of authority, learning, and wisdom, playing before grave and discreet persons' Winston presents an argument which foregrounds not the play's didactic lessons on the necessity of the marriage game, but its consideration of a unified political nation and subsequent urging of 'a form of collaborative counsel.'[17] Subsequently, whilst the play might be – and certainly was – interpreted as a commentary on Elizabeth's marriage negotiations, it also functioned as a means of turning lawmen into counsellors; of testing the boundaries of collaborative counsel; and of 'arguing

14 A compelling discussion of the play's place in Elizabeth's marriage negotiations can be found in Marie Axton's *The Queen's Two Bodies: Drama and the Elizabethan Succession* (1977). The work of Walker and James, as well as Winston, offers a fresher perspective.

15 Winston, 'Expanding the Political Nation,' p. 26.

16 Ibid.

17 Winston, 'Expanding the Political Nation,' pp. 23, 22.

for a form of government in which different institutions of the political nation [could] play equally authoritative and mutually reinforcing roles.'[18] Nevertheless, the playing space and performers remain important. The play certainly depicted a multitude of governmental models (from a coalition of nobility to rule by council and rule by parliament), but it did so within a private space and via men who were likely to ultimately seek a position within the political regime. Thus, it seems clear that whilst *Gorboduc*, might have 'contributed … to the contested expansion of the political nation in the sixteenth century,' it did so within accepted boundaries of decorum and rank.[19]

It is impossible not to recognise parallels between such an acceptable discussion of the succession (within the framework of counsel and its participants) and John Stubbs' later, very public *The Discoverie*. Myriad reasons, of course, might account for the difference in treatment of Norton and Sackville's possible attempts to warn the Queen of the dangers of an unstable succession and that of Stubbs. One could argue with equal legitimacy, for example, that the Queen, in her more tender years, was less inclined to the bellicose passions of her middle and old age, or that her fondness for Dudley – and, as Watson notes, her kinship with Sackville – safe-guarded them from rebuke (as Sir Philip Sidney's status may have helped ensure his safety when circulating his letter against 1579's proposed French alliance).[20] It may also be argued that, just as the laws and proclamations against slander and sedition tended to be expeditious and reactive to discrete crises and uprisings of disorder, castigations about the succession and allegedly unwise alliances were permissible when they did not intrude upon foreign policy. However, it is worth considering Stubbs' audience. Though an Inns of Court lawyer himself, his intervention on the subject of the Queen's marriage (also, it will be recalled, couched in the ostensible need to counsel his monarch) was neither private nor even semi-private: it was public, unlicensed, and evidently went beyond the boundaries of decorum which

18 Winston, 'Expanding the Political Nation,' p. 20.
19 Watson, 'Gorboduc and the Theory of Tyrannicide,' p. 357.
20 Ibid.

Gorboduc did not cross.[21] Reading the rhetoric of counsel as portrayed and interrogated in the play, Dermot Cavanagh argues that its chief concern was not in counselling the Queen, but in 'meditating upon the limits of counsel.'[22] Suggesting that Norton and Sackville sought to explore the ways in which history could be used to highlight the difficulties attendant on public dialogue and debate, his interpretation of the play offers a partial solution to the difference in treatment afforded the unfortunate Stubbs.[23] Claiming the right (or need) to counsel the sovereign did not grant a licence to write with impunity. Instead, men of any rank who sought to offer counsel (however disingenuously) had to bear in mind their audience (as did Sir Philip Sidney). Audience, it may be argued, was a principle issue in the practice and rhetoric of counsel. Norton and Sackville portrayed the necessity of a well-counselled monarch before discreet audiences and depicted the practice as potentially dangerous mode of expression. Further, their play underwent a degree of censorship prior to publication.[24] Stubbs, on the other hand, fell into a trap that the playwrights would undoubtedly have recognised, as what was intended to be read as counsel became slander when it reached indiscriminate (and meaner) eyes and ears.

Whilst such a view provides useful insight into the ways in which texts on similar themes could be treated very differently by authorities sensitive to potential slanders, there is more to be said on the pre-publication excisions from *Gorboduc*. Astutely recognising the overlapping spheres which drama and politics inhabited in the period, and the consequent invitation

21 Quite clearly, adopting the rhetoric of counsel as a model for resisting accusations of slander was no safer or surer a defence than slander or censorship were fixed or stable categories deployed by authorities. Lacking the licence to address advice to the monarch, Stubbs played a dangerous game and lost. Norton and Sackville, however, met with more success, not only in providing a text which was considered by at least one witness (without, apparently, much concern) as a warning to the Queen, but in calling into question just who could participate in state politics.

22 Cavanagh, *Language and Politics in the Sixteenth-Century History Play*, p. 54.

23 Cavanagh, *Language and Politics in the Sixteenth-Century History Play*, p. 56.

24 As Gurr (*The Shakespearean Stage*, pp. 72–6) has noted, the Master of the Revels was not involved in the licensing of plays for printing until early in James' reign. The likelihood is therefore that censorship was carried out either by the authors or the publisher.

made to Elizabethan audiences to view drama as a direct commentary on contemporary debates, Walker and James use the differences in performance outlined in the Beale manuscript as evidence that the published *Gorboduc* of 1565 and 1570 was adapted precisely because a specific political moment was no longer relevant. That is to say, the need to denigrate the Swedish marriage suit in favour of Dudley's proposal had, by 1565, been lost to the ever-changing rules of the Elizabethan marriage game. It is a point well made. However, whilst Walker and James' examination of the history of Elizabethan politics makes a good point, it is their subsequent recognition of the differences between the play as performed in the controlled space of a semi-public Inner Temple (and later, private Whitehall) stage and that later printed (complete with excision of more specific political allusion) that is of especial interest to the student of dramatic censorship and its relationship with potentially seditious material.

What is abundantly clear is the licence afforded the play as staged in the forum of a courtly performance overseen by a festive Master of the Revels, and the more rigorous attention devoted to the censorship of volatile material when it was to be printed and available for public consumption. Thus, the fissure between Norton and Sackville's original production (as suggested by the Beale manuscript) and Stubbs' later incendiary public admonishment regarding the Queen's marriage crises are neatly explained by the politics of performance. The controlled playing spaces of courtly performances were allowed a degree of freedom of expression which, under the Elizabethan regime, was admissible as long as, in the transfer to the public sphere, the text passed through the mediatory hands of the censor. Here we may recall legal definitions of slander, which posited that even private material could be deemed defamatory.[25] What seems apparent is the slipperiness of censorship, a mechanism which lacked any fixed or stable categories of permissibility. Norton and Sackville's text was evidently acceptable as a depiction of the necessity of wise counsel, but a sensible censor was apt to remove passages which might incite rebellion when played before a public audience.[26] The law might have provided a broad and, in

25 Manning, 'The Origins of the Doctrine of Sedition,' p. 121.

26 Here, it must be restated that 'a censor' does not necessarily mean the state's official censor. As has been noted, the Master of the Revels had not yet acquired power

principal, autocratic purview over textual material; in practice, a degree of discretion was required when material was published.

Of course, what this confusion of expected power relations – the play text enjoying freedom of performance on a private stage, followed by alteration prior to publication – eludes is any one of the accepted models of censorship, which tend to focus on either the initial self-censorship of the playwright, the aggressiveness of the Queen's Master of the Revels, or a symbiotic and mutually beneficial relationship between writer and censor. In short, the Beale manuscript informs us, crucially, that the print editions of *Gorboduc* in 1565 and 1570 were altered from 1560s courtly performance. Although it is unknown whether these alterations were made by censor, playwrights or publisher, it may be argued that this is irrelevant. Whilst knowledge of the agent behind the excisions might allow us to fit the public version of the play into an existing model of censorship, one cannot help but notice that such models only become relevant when considering the printed text. All mechanisms of existing models, it can be seen, explain excision or alteration, by whichever party, only when the play came to publication. The initial performance, in its full form and without the consideration of public staging, has remained elusive, for the simple fact that we can never see exactly what contemporary audiences saw and heard. Without proof of either the censor's hand or the playwright's need to abridge his work for a general audience, we are left with the puzzling question: to what extent was privately staged material free from state suppression?

It must be noted that whilst the Inns of Court provided fertile ground for writers to develop skills in playwriting through the production of stage plays, their output was certainly not confined to the five act model espoused by their classical antecedents. On the contrary, students of the Inns found dramatic expression through a variety of forms, perhaps most notorious of which were the elaborate revelries staged throughout holiday periods. Such events encompassed the courtly trivium of fencing, dancing and music, and as Alan H. Nelson and John R. Elliott, Jr further note,

over the licensing and censorship of printed materials, and instead censors were to be found in printers, authors, stationers and other figures of authority.

> a conventional Christmas at the Inns of Court was presided over by a Master of the Revels (one of many Christmas officers) who was typically appointed in November. The revels which he supervised consisted primarily of feasting, music, dancing, and gaming, especially on the three or four Saturdays leading up to Christmas, and on major post-Christmas holidays such as Holy Innocents' Day (28th December), New Year's Day, Twelfth Night and Candlemas. Less frequently, a Lord of Misrule or Christmas prince presided over a more elaborate and scripted Christmas season, often at enormous cost to himself and others.[27]

Nelson and Elliott have compiled much of the 'elaborate and scripted' material from these revels, drawing on manuscripts and printed books from the archives and libraries of all four Inns. By drawing on material derived from original, contemporary masque texts, it is possible to discern the diverse means by which the inhabitants of the Inns of Court entertained their fellows (and occasionally their sovereign) through dramatic display. Additionally, it is possible to trace the interaction of that drama with the legal knowledge which accompanied classical education within the Inns.

One such collection of scripts, titled the *Gesta Grayorum* [the deeds of Gray] and attributed in part to Francis Bacon, lays out in considerable detail the words and actions of the company of Gray's Inn over the festive period of 1594–5. An ostentatious display, the Gray's Inn frolics were presided over by one Henry Helmes, elected to the position of Prince of Purpoole (the position of mock prince being traditionally titled so at Gray's Inn – with the Prince d'Amour overseeing the Middle Temple revels, the Prince of Sophie holding court at the Inner Temple and the Prince de la Grange ministering his erstwhile fellows at Lincoln's Inn). Furthermore, complementing the newly crowned Prince's retinue were a full Privy Council and administrative staff. In celebration of his elevation, the *Gesta Grayorum* acquaints the reader with Purpoole's issue of a general pardon throughout his newly acquired dominions:

> General pardon by the Prince of Purpoole for 'all manner of Treasons, Contempts, Offences, all manner of Mis-feasance, Non-feasance, or too much Feasance.' Except, and always fore-prized out of this general and free Pardon, All and every such Person

27 Nelson and Elliott, *Inns of Court: Records of Early English Drama, 3 Vols*, p. xviii.

> and Persons as shall imagine, think, suppose, or speak and utter any false, seditious, ignominious, or slan-|derous Words, Reports, Rumours, or Opinions, against the Dignity, or His Excellency's honourable Actions, Counsels, Consultations, or State of the Prince, his Court, Counsellors, Nobles, Knights and Officers.[28]

The satirical mockery is obvious as the language of authority is rendered absurd. Of particular interest, however, is the attention drawn by the shift from the playful 'non-feasance, or too much Feasance' to the rather more businesslike and authoritarian tone concerning those exempted from the Prince's general pardon.

A variety of forces are at work. Firstly, there is an inherent ridicule (as must be expected) of authority in the apparently ironical willingness to exempt treasonous rebels yet refuse to countenance those who might slander or injure the ruler's dignity. This was a notion to be taken up with alacrity by Stuart libellers, who worked underground and were keen to associate their lampoons of high-ranking individuals with a sense of festivity and the carnivalesque, despite this not excusing their texts in anything like a legal sense; one can discern a knowing wink on the part of the students in foreseeing it. It is also arguable that the ability to make use of (indeed, to subvert) the language of government betrays a sound knowledge of legal parlance both on the part of the writer and of the (presumably appreciative) audience of fellows to whom the address was read. To libel was ostensibly to be a grubby and intolerable malcontent pinning lazy insults to doors; but in the satire this idea itself is sent up. As Shakespeare was to exhibit in *Measure for Measure*, there is a definite awareness that authorities had a proverbial bee in their bonnets about defamatory speech levelled against them.

It is arguable, therefore, that the satire exposes what is a more general understanding amongst the performing law students of the dangers of slander perceived by the authorities they seek to parody. Certainly, on reading the Prince's pardon (and consequent exemptions), the obvious question arises: why were slander, sedition, rumour and the injury of dignity chosen as matters fit for continuing punishment in the mock fiefdom awarded to the Prince? Given what has been seen regarding the very real

28 Nelson and Elliott, *Gesta Grayorum*, p. 391.

Elizabethan intolerance of such crimes, their place on the list of exemptions stems directly from the writer's tacit mockery of what is considered the real court's hysterical attitude towards dangerous speech. In short, as it is the prerogative of the satirist to parody what is perceived to be the beliefs of the object of the satire (and during the Christmas revels, this was invariably the court and justice system), the satirical thrust of the Prince of Purpoole's general pardon exposes and makes ridiculous what were common attitudes espoused by the authoritarian regime with which the Inns were familiar.

Further evidence of the newly formed court of misrule's general mockery of the fundamental beliefs and rules of the Elizabethan court are to be found also in the list of ordinances produced and read to the assemblage governing behaviour in the Prince's reign. One such rule holds that

> Every Knight of this Order shall Endeavour to add Conference and Experience to Reading; therefore shall not only read and peruse Guizo, the French Academy, Galiatto the Courtier, Plu-|tarch, the Arcadia, and the Neoterical writers, from time to time; but also frequent the Theatre and such-like places of Experience; and resort to the better sort of Ord'naries for Conference, whereby they may not only become accomplished with Civil Conversation and able to govern a Table with Discourse; but also sufficient, if need be, to make Epigrams, Emblems, and other Devices appertaining to His Honour's learned Revels.[29]

Again, the speech must be viewed through the lens of satire which characterised each of the scripts produced and read as part of the Inns' Christmas revels. Particularly interesting is the reference to the theatre – which Knights of the mock court are advised strongly to attend. One might recall Prest's observation that plays themselves had, by the 1590s, begun to disappear from the records of the dramatic output of the Inns; instead, plays staged within were increasingly produced and written without, and acted by professional players rather than the law students. Such, indeed, was the case during these very revels, at which Shakespeare's *Comedy of Errors* was performed by an outside troupe. Indeed, elsewhere in the *Gesta Grayorum* (crucially, during a further parody of judicial inquiry into the causes of disorder) these players are denigrated as a 'company of base and

29 Nelson and Elliott, *Gesta Grayorum*, p. 403.

common Fellows' who had been 'foisted' on the distinguished gentlemen of Gray's Inn. The variations in intent can be explained by the circumstances of each satirical jab – the 'rules' governing the court sanction theatricality whereas the 'judicial inquiry' into the resultant disorder mocks a more general distrust of actors by artfully and ironically contrasting the 'distinguished' members of the Inn with the 'base and common' players. As Michael Bristol has noted:

> Unlike the consecrated minister of God's word or the political orator, an actor is a man whose public utterance does not represent what he feels or thinks, although it is said with full conviction and the sound of authority. An actor is not just someone whose speech is 'dissembling': the deeper problem is that he is valued for his ability to dissemble convincingly.[30]

Certainly, there is ample evidence to suggest that the negative attitude towards actors that the revels present was not an uncommon Elizabethan view. Anti-theatrical polemicists such as the staunch moralist Stephen Gosson flourished in the 1580s and 1590s, vociferously attacking the perceived licentiousness and lack of godliness inherent in theatricality. In his objurgatory *Schoole of Abuse, Conteining a pleasant invective against Poets, Pipers, Players, Jesters, and such like Caterpillers of a Commonwelth* (1579), Gosson denounces at length the dangers of public mimesis and calls for the suppression of theatrical activity. Central to Gosson's view is a belief in acting's place in a sequence of unruly and dangerous behaviours – 'from pyping to playing, from playing to pleasure, from pleasure to slouth, from slouth to sleepe, from sleepe to sinne, from sinne to death, from death to the devil.'[31] The work was followed by the equally censorious (and thematically repetitive) *Playes Confuted in Five Actions* (1582) as a war of words erupted between the theatre's opponents and its defenders. In the midst of this conflict of opinion appeared Philip Stubbes' oft-quoted *Anatomy of Abuse* (1583). Similar in tone to the work of Gosson, Stubbes' writing deals only perfunctorily with the theatre, but those few pages devoted to 'Stage-playes, and Enterludes, with their wickednes' are particularly

30 Bristol, *Carnival and Theatre*, p. 113.
31 Gosson, *Playes confuted*, p. 7.

telling. Not only is the Elizabethan theatre attacked for its alleged immorality and penchant for representing vice, but Stubbes recognises also the abuses and excesses of revelry, and in particular, those who indulge in the fripperies of 'courts of mis-rule.' They are, to Stubbes, 'hel-hounds (the Lord of mis-rule and his complices) … but if they knew that as often as they bring any thing to the maintenance of these execrable pastimes, they offer sacrifice to the devil.'[32] Thus, censure of the revellers of the Inns of Court is collapsed with that denouncing professional players. One can imagine what the high-spirited students made of Stubbes and his fellows.

As a consequence of the animadversions of increasingly voluble anti-theatricalists, the satirical bent of the *Gesta Grayorum*'s view of players is therefore wholly explicable. It is such views as those of Stubbes and his anti-theatrical cohorts that are held to ridicule, as the students of law utilised the period of misrule to claim kinship with actors as confederates in an activity laid open to obloquy by a small but well organised and militant sect authorised by the city fathers. Such a kinship is understandable, it may be further argued, not merely due to the theatrical activities of the law students, but to their position as marginalised and popularly denigrated members of Elizabethan society. If attacks on theatres and players were rife, so, it will be remembered, were attacks on the growing multitude of lawyers who, it was alleged, encouraged civil discord in order to profit from an increasingly litigious society. Whilst not all students of the Inns of Court would go on to become lawyers (some used the Inns as a means to 'experience the metropolis'), the Inns themselves remained sites of legal

32 Stubbes, *The anatomie of abuses*, p. 93. Festive 'Lords of Misrule' were not, of course, peculiar to the Inns of Court. Indeed, as Ronald Hutton (*The Stations of the Sun*, pp. 105–10) recognises, the tradition of carnivalesque mock Kings and figures of Misrule endured (with varying degrees of popularity) in the civic spaces of England, in aristocratic households and in the Inns of Court until the Civil War. Nevertheless, the festivities laid on by the Inns were arguably the most notorious, managing as they did to secure the participation of luminaries such as the Queen's favourite, Robert Dudley, in 1561/2 (the season which included *Gorboduc*'s first performance). Stubbes' distaste likely extended to festive misrule across all domestic, civic and professional sites – but it is impossible to ignore the celebrated role of the Inns of the Court in the tradition for which he showed particular intolerance.

training.[33] Attacks on lawyers (and particularly on their proliferation) can only have reflected on the source of that proliferation: the Inns themselves. Whilst it is tempting to believe that the mockery of actors is as conventional as that afforded other sections of society during the festive period, the fact that the Inns of Court students were 'regular playgoers from the start' and equally liable to be victims of conservative censure suggests a playful kinship.[34]

Accepting that the revelry recounted in the *Gesta Grayorum* recognises (via its satire of the view of actors and theatrics) the link between lawmen and actors as one of popular censure, the advisory speeches (attributed to Bacon's pen) which were addressed to the Prince of Purpoole become clearer. The advice of the Fifth Counsellor charges that the Prince

> look into the state of your laws and justice of your land; purge out multiplicity of laws, clear the incertainty of them, repeal those that are snaring, and press the execution of those that are wholesome and necessary; define the jurisdiction of your courts, repress all suits and vexations, all causeless delays and fraudulent shifts and devices, and reform all such abuses of right and justice; assist the ministers thereof, punish severely all extortions and exactions of officers, all corruptions in trials and sentences of judgement. Yet when you have done all this, think not that the bridle and spur will make the horse to go alone without time and custom. Trust not to your laws for correcting the times, but give all strength to good education; see to the government of your universities and all seminaries of youth, and to the private order of families, maintaining due obedience of children towards their parents, and reverence of the younger sort towards the ancient. Then when you have confirmed the noble and vital parts of your realm of state, proceed to take care of the blood and flesh and good habit of the body. Remedy all decays of population, make provision for the poor, remove all stops in traffic, and all cankers and causes of consumption in trades and mysteries.[35]

As may be expected of Bacon – himself an alumnus of Gray's Inn – the speech is overtly concerned with the right practice and maintenance of law (and the reference to multiplicity and uncertainty might have been directed at slander laws, were it not a problem common throughout

33 Love, *Scribal Publication*, pp. 224–5.

34 Gurr, *Playgoing in Shakespeare's London*, p. 67.

35 Nelson and Elliott, *Gesta Grayorum*, p. 410–11.

the legal system). It will also be noted that the irony is structural rather than verbal; Bacon does not mock any particular view or attitude in his speech, but rather expresses satire by drawing on his growing experience in state matters (and penchant for dispensing advice) in order to produce a convincing and delusory speech which is, perforce, to be wasted on a mock king.

As such, the matter contained within that advice quite deliberately illustrates matters which were of concern to the legal minds of the age. Particularly relevant are those calls to 'define the jurisdiction of courts' (it will be recalled that slander, in particular, was a matter over which various courts claimed jurisdiction); to 'repress all suits and vexations' (a direct reference to the perceived litigiousness which plagued England); to 'repress fraudulent shifts and devices' (again, one might recall the concerns of the Star Chamber over those who sought to manipulate the court); and 'to give all strength to good education' (the charges against the ostensible lack of learning within the Inns of Court already having taken root). Thus, the revels were not purely times of unchecked revelry and frolics, but rather a period in which matters of real concern both to students of law and Elizabethan society at large could be addressed. Within the framework of performance, revelry, gaiety and mockery, satirical speeches were deployed in order to expose problematic attitudes towards and issues within the law and legal profession.

This notion of the educational power of performance played a central role not only in the revelries staged during the 1594/5 Gray's Inn festive period, but across the four Inns throughout the early modern period. Especially noteworthy to any scholar interested in the legal and dramatic development of slander are the activities of the Middle Temple's mock ruler, the Prince D'Amour's court during the revels of 1597–8. Amidst the revelries (over which presided a Master of the Revels whose main charge was ensuring that the court 'danced in measure and loved beyond measure') was a highly dramatic mock trial, in which the defendant was charged with a number of offences and the Prince's Attorney demonstrated his oratorical skill in expounding at paraleptic length on the prisoner's faults:

> I will not amplifie his crimes by the common induction of vita anteacta, nor rip up his faults from his Infancy; onely I say that his familiars have great suspicion of his nature, knowing him from a Whelp; as the Servingman hath great confidence in his Sword which he hath bred up from a Dagger. I let pass most part of his education, spent in the practice of enchantments, and penning of dangerous Speeches, able to corrupt the minds of them that had beauty without discretion …
>
> I will onely insist upon the matter of this Indictment. First for the words which he spake; wherein I make out,
>
> First (for our better note) who spake it.
> Then what.
>
> Then where.[36]

Addressing the 'courtroom,' the Attorney, it will be noted, follows carefully the processes of a real court of law. The defendant is portrayed in ignominious terms, as the Attorney constructs a judicial narrative in much the same manner as barristers at the common law routinely did; indeed, the attention devoted to orderliness (the recitation of the words allegedly spoken, followed by where) are lifted directly from the schema of narratives which formed the lawyerly presentations of plaintiffs' bills and writs across the judicial system.

The effect, therefore, is the construction of an imaginary reality. As Holger Schott Syme has argued in his *Theatre and Testimony in Shakespeare's England* (2011), Elizabethan law courts themselves relied on a similarly imaginary reality, as the fictitious presence of the Queen as officiating figure was invoked through the reading of her laws.[37] In addition, it can occasion no surprise that the 'supposedly spontaneous' exchanges of real Elizabethan law courts were also highly scripted, produced as they were during pre-trial examinations before being produced orally, in the courtroom, as performances. As such, it is possible to argue that the humorous little dramatic reconstruction occasioned by the Inns of Court revelry goes further than simply providing students with an opportunity to experience a mock courtroom and indulge in the chance to learn whilst enjoying a witty performance; rather, it reflects on the very theatricality of the law

36 Nelson and Elliott, *Le Prince D'Amour*, p. 472.
37 Syme, *Theatre and Testimony in Shakespeare's England*, p. 22.

in practice, from its deferral to its representation and reconstruction of an event through narrative. In short, to borrow Schott Syme's wording, the Attorney's scripted, highly performative oral recitation of traditional lawyerly rhetoric takes advantage of drama's 'propensity to reflect on the mechanics of its own illusion-making.' It may be argued further, however, that the Middle Temple's *dramatis personae* reflect not only on drama's self-reflexivity, but on its place and usage within the mechanisms of law.

Nor does the dramatic action end with the Attorney's opening allegations. After castigating the defendant for his alleged 'speeches against love' (apparently an indictable offence under the rule of the Prince d'Amour), the charges continue apace:

> But to the next of his speeches against his Mistris, whose constancy and kindness he requites with disdain and ingratitude, wishing that he might shift her as often as he shifts his clothes; the ex-example whereof would draw many changes and innovations in this Kingdom. For so, by all likelihood, he would change his Mistris once in two years at least. How contrary this were to his often protestations, might appear by divers his Letters to her, found in his Study upon a late search for conjurors, suspected to cause this alteration of a Weather, by vertue of a Warrant from the Lord chief Justice; yet in one of them appears this his odious mutability and slanderous presumption against our honorable Judges of this Court; in confidence whereof he presented himself here, hoping to be delivered by corruption.[38]

Looking through the obvious levity of the charges, one is once more acutely aware of the opportunity taken by the Attorney to exhibit his oratorical skill. Interesting also, however, is the role which 'slander' plays in the allegations. Firstly, it might be remembered that the real crime of seditious libel (as yet in its infancy and in practice prosecuted via statutory law) strictly forbade specific kinds of speech and writing, which held similar perlocutionary force, on the grounds that it sought to effect change in the kingdom by illegal means. Certainly, such a notion appears to be at work here. Within the purview of the Prince d'Amour's jurisdiction, speech and actions against love and constancy are strictly forbidden; indeed, amongst the rules of the mock court is the warning that

38 Nelson and Elliott, *Le Prince D'Amour*, p. 472.

> If any man do speak words of defamation of any Lady or Gentlewoman, or do directly or | indirectly use terms of Scurrility, or Ribawdry in any discourse, verse, or Oration; he shall stand in the Pillory and lose his best ear, unless within two days he publickly signifie his unfeined repentance, and make such satisfaction as shall be enjoyned at his confession by his Excellencies Archflamen.[39]

Yet here the accused is charged with railing against both, the example of which is held to have occasioned the possibility of 'changes and innovations in this Kingdom.' Further – as allegation falls upon allegation – the claim is made that the defendant (already characterised as seditious of intent and imprudent of speech) is a slanderer by virtue of his writings against the court, thus collapsing his insurgent nature with a general contempt for the law, in addition to conflating the dangers of speech and writing. What is therefore exposed is the contemporary legal weight attached both to the slanderer's place within a larger framework of sedition and corruption, and the potential which – highlighted through the parody – was increasingly becoming attached to seditious libel.

Slander against the court having been roundly vilified, the dramatic reconstruction continues in its humorous vein, as the jury – thus far bystanders before the Attorney's rhetorical demonstrations – are let in on the dramatic action. The narrative of the mock trial accordingly progresses from the reading of the defendant's bawdy letters to his mistress, to the extraordinary claim that he slandered her dog:

> he in scorn spurned [the dog] and called him Jew, when his name indeed was Iewel; a barbarous wrong, and a Turkish contradiction, such as I hope you my Lords, and you the Iury will justly think of. (Whereat they gave a severe Nod).[40]

Once more, we must place to one side the obvious wit of the pun, as well as the deliberate absurdity of the situation, in order to discern the nature of the slanderer being here depicted by the Attorney. In allegedly engaging in a dispute with a dog, the defendant, it may be argued, is accused not only of reducing the speech act to a level of animality, but through the art of punning (the obvious Jew/Jewel distinction), of misusing the artistic

39 Nelson and Elliott, *Le Prince D'Amour*, p. 467.
40 Nelson and Elliott, *Le Prince D'Amour*, p. 476.

expression and possibilities of language in a thoroughly base and unnatural exchange. In so doing, the jury are invited also to consider the accused slanderer as an agent who makes a mockery both of speech and the law through the ridiculousness of his usage of the former and treatment within the latter. Such propositions, to be sure, would have been met with general acquiescence from the select audience of lawmen; it may be remembered that any view (however exaggerated) of slander as a mode of expression simultaneously transgressive, disorderly and unnatural accords well with the Elizabethan regime's view of those who were avowed guilty of using speech to defamatory effect.

The idea that speech could be used with malicious, dangerous, or otherwise unnatural intent finds further ratification in the latter stages of the mock trial:

> The next matter of this Indictment is the perverting of honest speeches into unhonest meanings; which though he hath excused (for his guiltiness hath been often taxed) with this answer, that for the words they were his, but the sence was in the Audience, and every one of them brought hither a minde of his own; and so returned all the dishoneesty upon the hearers construction: Yet can he not save himself with this evasion; for the imputations of such, to the discredit of this Court, have been very common, and the offence very publike. The fault onely his, by his own confession; For, he hath so crept into the service of penning some speeches, in this Princes raign, with a pernicious in-|tent of disgracing the Government, and hath thereby so impeached the estimations of our Profession, that some are of opinion that our common Law is scarce written in an honest language.[41]

Of chief import in the Attorney's closing allegations is, it may be seen, the exploration of the relationship between subversive speaker and credulous listener. The defendant's claim that his words were misconstrued by his listeners is certainly nothing new – it is little more than the special traverse commonly found in the defence strategies of accused slanderers – and it is similarly nothing new to the mock court, which recognises the 'evasion' as a common defence, easily negotiable by the extent of the 'very publike' audience. Equally interesting, however, is the way in which the narrative parodies authoritarian concerns over seditious speeches, which

41 Ibid.

are histrionically claimed to disgrace both the government and the legal profession. It will further be noted, however, that the guilt subsequently attributed to the defendant here hinges on the equality of culpability between the perversion of 'honest speeches into dishonest meanings' and the 'penning of speeches' seditious in content. It is therefore possible to read within the allegations a further lack of demarcation between spoken and written slander – a distinction which, it must be remembered, had yet to be made. In short, the amusing drama of the mock trial concludes with implicit evidence that guilt of written slander provided ample evidence of guilt of spoken slander – the two were, in the eyes of the law, either side of the same coin.

As can be seen, the Inns of Court – those institutions which housed both dramatic revelry and legal training – produced important artistic output which allows the scholar to excavate contemporary attitudes, mechanisms and legal approaches to slander. As schools of law, as well as the cradles of early modern English drama, it is no surprise that the Inns provided a site in which legal practice and dramatic material overlapped, as evidenced not only by the variant ways in which practices of the law informed or were engaged with by the Inns' dramatic output, but by intersection of lawmen and players, increasingly linked in terms of marginalisation by Puritan sects in addition to the relatively close proximity of the Inns and playhouses. What cannot be overlooked, however, is the crucial aspect of the audience in terms of both potentially slanderous dramatic material and representations of slander and slanderer in the dramas enacted during the Inns of Court revels.

As noted, 1561's *Gorboduc* – a play potentially inflammatory in its perceived (by at least one witness) attempt to chide the Queen about the dangers of an insecure succession – escaped the censure afforded similarly themed works for a variety of reasons, not least of which was the semi-private staging of its initial performances. Similarly, those scripted, dramatic revelries staged during such periods of misrule as that recounted in the *Gesta Grayorum* or the Prince d'Amour's court, whilst they satirised authority in their representations of the slanderer, were both private affairs amongst the revellers and enjoyed the traditional licence of festive carousals. A figure who remains conspicuous by his absence in the semi-private dramas of the Inns of Court is the real Master of the Revels. Nominally invested with powers over all dramatic production in the kingdom and one of the central figures in many proposed models of censorship, it is notable that the Master of the Revels had no official involvement in the dramatic material performed by the law students during their Christmas festivities.[42] Although, the Inns of Court traditionally elected their own, internal Master, it has been seen – most notably in the Prince d'Amour's court – that this figure served the predominant purpose of lampooning rather than upholding authority.

We are therefore left with the question, where do semi-private dramas fit into the models of censorship (designed to account for the regulation of slanderous and seditious dramatic material) variously proposed by such critics as Kaplan, Clare, Dutton and Clegg? The answer, it may be confidently proposed, is that existing models of censorship are largely predicated upon the publishing and playing of commercial drama on the public stage. Conversely, the semi-private material produced and performed by the Inns of Court was, it has been demonstrated, regulated by internal mechanisms: from the nominal Christmas Master of the Revels; to the knowledge that staged plays may be called for performance before the sovereign; to questions of patronage; a de facto knowledge of the law and the relative freedom of traditional misrule. The politics of performance were, for the semi-private stage, redrawn. In a similar vein, it is impossible to ignore the links between audience and content, especially in the Inns' satirical performances. Inarguably tailored to an audience of lawmen – the satire, indeed, relying on a shared knowledge of the law and legal authority only likely to be found in such a cultural sphere as the Inns of Court – attention is once more drawn to the intimate, esoteric nature of scholarly dramatic output which did not conform to the traditional play form. As such, one must then ask what mechanisms (if any) were in place to monitor dramas which were not intended for public performance. Here, we arrive at the 'closet drama' – a medium which has only relatively recently begun to garner deserved critical attention.

42 By the time of the *Gesta Grayorum*, the authority of the Master of the Revels had been officially extended to include control over all dramatic material in the kingdom.

CHAPTER 9

The Politics of Publication and Performance in Closet Drama

Existing models of censorship, including M. Lindsay Kaplan's slander model, which foregrounds the power relations between poet and state as exemplified by the 'elusive' power of slanderous discourse in theatrical production, are alike in their preoccupation with the role of the censor. As divergent as these models may be on the actual influence of the Master of the Revels, his relationship with playwrights and the extent of their awareness of the bounds of decorum, each, in its own way, hinges on a tacit acceptance of the state's authority and jurisdiction (to varying degrees) over play texts. However, as we have seen, there were sites in which drama could be performed with degrees of licence different from that of the public stage. Naturally, this encourages us to ask the question, what happens when the censor and all questions of public performance and authoritarian censure – whether that be in the form of the foreknowledge of a sovereign audience or otherwise – are entirely removed from dramatic production? In attempting to address such a question, it is useful to turn to the actual power of censorship and licensing which lay in the Revels Office.

Virginia Crocheron Gildersleeve, in her comprehensive history of the government regulation of Elizabethan drama (1908), recognises the growth throughout the period of the censor's jurisdiction. His initial responsibilities were limited to ensuring that no offensive word met the Queen's ear during performances enacted as part of her court's revels, but Gildersleeve points out that jurisdiction over performances outside the court was formally given in the patent granted by Elizabeth to the Earl of Leicester's players in 1574.[1] The restructuring of the Revels Office, as overseen by

1 The patent for the Earl of Leicester's Servants can be found in Wickham, Berry and Ingram's *English Professional Theatre, 1530–1660*, p. 206. It will be noted that the

Edmund Tilney – appointed to the post in 1579 – further ensured a tighter and more organised approach to the regulation of performance which had nominally existed since the Queen's first year on the throne, during which she had issued the proclamation:

> The Queen's majesty [doth] straightly forbid all manner interludes to be played either openly or privately, except the same be notified beforehand and licensed [by mayors, queen's lieutenants or justices of the peace] ...
>
> And for instruction to every of the said officers, her majesty doth likewise charge every of them as they will answer: that they permit none to be played wherein either matters of religion or of the governance of the estate of the commonweal shall be handled or treated, being no meet matters to be written or treated upon but by men of learning, and wisdom, nor to be handled before any audience but of grave and discreet persons.[2]

A number of issues may be drawn from Elizabeth's early attempts to assert authority over performance, not least of which is her evident wariness over the potential political hazards of unchecked dramatic performance. One also cannot help but notice the emphasis placed on the rank of both audience and players. Initial concern, it seems, was not on the wholesale curbing of theatrical output, but focused on the licensing (by the Queen's officers rather than an authoritarian Master of the Revels, whose right to censor all plays was not granted until 1581) of plays of fit purpose, and that purpose fit for 'learned' and 'discreet' persons.[3] This, it will be seen, is of key consequence to any study of the history of the dramatic censorship of slanderous or seditious material; indeed, this early proclamation makes explicit the state concern over both audiences and playwrights. Just as the law made plain its tension regarding the perceived quality of the subjects

---

patent stipulates that 'the said comedies, tragedies, interludes, and stage plays be by the Master of the Revels for the time being before seen and allowed.'

2 *Proclamation 509*, Elizabeth I, 1559.

3 As noted, the Master of the Revels was required to see and grant permission for plays to be performed by Leicester's Servants in 1574. His right to 'censor' *all* plays was, however, formally granted in the 1581 patent which appointed him Master of the Revels. The patent is recorded in Wickham, Berry and Ingram's *English Professional Theatre, 1530–1660*, pp. 70–1.

and speakers of defamation, so too did authority display a predominant anxiety over the rank of subjects exposed to hazardous or inflammatory dramatic material. A firm link can therefore be drawn between the flexible and ever-developing legal system as it operated in maintaining hierarchical order via laws against defamation and matters of censorship which sought also to protect the state from critical, potentially insurgent plays.

Emerging also from this early Elizabethan proclamation is the ostensible legal jurisdiction granted to local authorities over private as well as public performance. It was, perforce, a jurisdiction which, whilst austere and authoritarian in intent, was virtually impossible to enforce in practice. Indeed, the official stance on the licensing and playing of drama was, as Gildersleeve further recognises, an ideal rather than a practicable diktat, at least for the majority of the Elizabethan period. As has been seen, the political content of plays like *Gorboduc* was certainly not censored or altered until such a time as a publication licence was to be granted – and to Gildersleeve the authorities were in no way averse to such performances as that of 1561's original production of *Gorboduc*. Indeed, 'there were plays given by pupils in schools, by student in universities, by the young lawyers of the Inns of Court. All of these were more or less amateur performances, approved by public opinion; the actors were persons of definite standing in the community; there was, of course, no suspicion of their being "rogues and vagabonds."'[4] Evidently, for much of Elizabeth's reign, the mechanisms of censorship were, when men of rank were concerned, used with great laxity. The idea of an authoritarian state which could exercise unlimited powers over dramatic expression is therefore hugely problematic. Such powers existed nominally, but practical difficulties made them unenforceable. Censorship was less a repressive tool than an ideal. Provided that dramatic material was performed by writers and players who conformed to the public's good opinion and were members of a respectable societal rank, it is evident that the state was unlikely to be mobilised into repressive censorship.

Tilney's accession to the role of Master of the Revels heralded a general shift towards the more autonomous, structured approach to censorship

4 Gildersleeve, *Government Regulation of Elizabethan Drama*, p. 22.

with which we are likely to be familiar. Whether due to his own proactive methods of governance, his fondness for the munificent remunerations of licence-granting, or simply a growth in demand for public performance and a blossoming of exceptional writers, Tilney's tenure certainly coincided with an increasingly active Revels Office. A scant two years after taking office the Crown granted him a patent to 'order, reform, authorise and put down all plays, players and playmakers, together with their playing places, throughout the kingdom,' vesting within the Master of the Revels the right to censor and license not just London-based courtly performances, but all plays and, crucially, the increasingly contested sites of playhouses, throughout the kingdom.[5] His jurisdiction growing apace, it can occasion no surprise that 'by the end of Elizabeth's reign, the authority of the Revels Office over performances outside the court was fairly well established.'[6] An obvious issue, however, is that with such empowerment came a degree of authority conferred upon texts which, once authorised by the Revels Master and thus by the state, were later put to potentially subversive uses.[7]

Combining the growing geographical remit of the Master of the Revels with the authority over all dramatic material to be performed – either privately or publicly – granted by patent, there remains a category of drama which, nevertheless, fell outside the purview of the censor. This is, of course, the closet drama. It is perhaps curious that it has historically been met with relatively little critical attention – with some notable exceptions, as outlined by Cerasano and Wynne-Davies – until its reclamation by proponents of women's drama in the 1990s; after all, as Brander Matthews recognised in 1908, the closet drama has been something of a constant throughout English literary history – finding expression in the works of Byron, Eliot and Swinburne.[8] Even Matthews, however, neglects the early modern period as one in which the closet drama was a popular if difficult

5 Gildersleeve, *Government Regulation of Elizabethan Drama*, p. 35.

6 Gildersleeve, *Government Regulation of Elizabethan Drama*, p. 22.

7 Veerapen, 'Slanderisation and Censure-ship.'

8 Cerasano and Wynne-Davies, *Readings in Renaissance Women's Drama*, p. 9; Matthews, 'The Legitimacy of the Closet Drama,' p. 214.

to categorise genre. Nevertheless, his adumbration of what constitutes a 'closet drama' is noteworthy:

> It is a play not intended to be played. It is a poem in dialogue, conceived with no thought of the actual theatre. It is ... a piece of literature, pure and simple, not contaminated by any subservience to the playhouse, the players or the playgoers. It is wrought solely for the reader in the library, without any regard for the demands of possible spectators in the auditorium. Its essence is to be sought in the obvious fact that the poet who essays it is firm in the conviction that the playhouse has no monopoly of the dramatic form.[9]

Euphuistic as Matthews' expression is, his sentiments are sound: the closet drama is one which is not intended for performance. Hence, it lies outside the very paradigms of censorship as, in practice, governed by the Master of the Revels. The closet drama was not meant to be performed in the traditional sense and, much as the dramatic material performed by the respected amateurs of the Inns of Court was not subject to official scrutiny for much of the period, neither were closet dramas. In short, the right of the Revels Office to 'put down all plays' neglected the manuscripts of private, handwritten material – a curious omission given the propensity of scribally published material to be, as Marotti notes 'obscene ... satiric or libellous or both.'[10] Whilst the law, of course, forbade scribal publication of slanderous or seditious material (the truth of its matter being immaterial), Harold Love has suggested that 'scribal communities' were bonded by the exchange of manuscripts and could evade censorship entirely.[11] Naturally, one would expect those bonded by manuscript circulation to be bonded by ideas and ideologies – and so the lack of prosecutions for slanderous or seditious closet dramas is perhaps to be expected. Of course, whether this is due to the largely circumspect nature of much closet drama or to the quixotic efforts required to monitor and regulate the activities of the library, closet and private chamber is highly debatable.

9 Matthews, 'The Legitimacy of the Closet Drama,' p. 214.
10 Marotti, *Manuscript, Print and the English Renaissance Lyric*, pp. 75–6.
11 Love, *Scribal Publication*, pp. 180–5.

It is thus tempting to envision the closet drama as a means of free expression: a mode of dramatic production which defied the censor, was free from the scrutiny of public performance, and allowed the playwright free reign to produce material unencumbered by fear of reprisal or authoritarian interference. Curiously, however, any such potential has been largely side-lined by scholars who – for the quite understandable reason that early modern closet drama was predominantly the domain of female writers – have focused research on the closet as a domestic site which allowed women a mode of expression, drama, usually limited to the male-dominated public sphere. Certainly, this approach is not without textual evidence, both in terms of authorship and the sentiments expressed in, for example, Mary Wroth's *Love's Victory* (*c.* 1620) which allude to a belief in the lack of patriarchal censure inherent in female coterie reading:

> Now we're alone let everyone confess
> Truly to other what our lucks have been,
> How often liked and loved and so express
> Our passions past; shall we this sport begin?
> None can accuse us, none can betray,
> Unless ourselves, our own selves will bewray.[12]

As such, it is not without reason that feminist readings of the closet drama have dominated. Indeed, female writers themselves took advantage of the closed and private nature of domestic dramatic production in order to explore women's concerns within female assemblies in addition to their freedom of expression outwith patriarchal order: in short, it was the prerogative of the female closet dramatist to address, in her writings, matters closest to the hearts of her small audience of readers. Nevertheless, Marta Straznicky has outlined at length the dangers of any facile de-politicising of, or, indeed, distinguishing between private play-reading and public performance.[13] To Straznicky, the closet drama is to be situated in a cultural field in which 'private and public are shifting rather than fixed points of reference.' Indeed, she further contends that early modern women's plays

12 Wroth, *Love's Victory*, III. ii. 21–6.
13 Straznicky, *Privacy, Play Reading and Women's Closet Drama*, pp. 1–6.

are far from unperformable (whatever their intent), and thus cannot be held in fixed opposition to the public stage. The act of reading in a group was and is itself a performative act.

This distinction thus collapsed – whilst the remaining lack of authoritarian censure remains – scholars of the closet drama are invited to recognise the possibility of association between play-reading and political dissent in the early modern period. Furthermore, one must understand the 'closet' not merely as a closed, private chamber, but, like the public or courtly stage, a site of collaborative dramatic production. Whilst Cerasano and Wynne-Davies have recognised the physicality of the 'seeled chambers and dark parlour rooms' as a protected location in which both male and female creativity could flourish, they allow that these havens were nevertheless controlled by elite men.[14] As such, the idea of politicised plays is further underscored by what Natalie Mears has identified as the link between elite social networks and Tudor policy.[15] In short, the participants in closet drama (whether readers or performers within the confines of a secure household) were nevertheless apt to be connected either socially or politically with the court, and yet the very security of these households (filled with retainers, social networks and, likely, acquaintances of similar political persuasions – in effect, a 'safe' audience) created a site of dramatic production and performance (in either the oral or mini-theatrical sense) free from the encumbrance of gaining licence, the dangers of hostile response or the threat of state censorship.

Evidence certainly exists to show that closet dramas of both male and female authorship engaged with contemporary political debate without alerting the Master of the Revels and inviting censorship. Indeed, Straznicky is quick to recognise that, whilst plays not intended for commercial performance could (and did) cross between private play-reading and the public sphere through the medium of print, public censure could still be avoided by insistence that the play not be staged before an indiscriminate public.[16] As a consequence, the role of censorship and the Revels Office in curbing

14 Cerasano and Wynne-Davies, *Readings in Renaissance Women's Drama*, pp. 60–8.
15 Mears, 'Courts, Courtiers and Culture in Tudor England,' pp. 703–22.
16 Straznicky, *Privacy, Play Reading and Women's Closet Drama*, p. 1.

potentially seditious or slanderous material is again problematised, as once more the overlapping spheres of public and private (and semi-private) conspire to confound many existing models of censorship predicated on the relationship between commercial playwright and state authority. Nor were women alone engaged in the production of politically sensitive manuscript dramas. One can turn to the notorious example of Fulke Greville's manuscript *Antony and Cleopatra* (*c.* 1600–1). Written, as Raber notes, for a carefully limited, elite coterie, the play was nevertheless committed to the flames by Greville himself due to concerns raised

> by the opinion of those few eyes which saw it, having some childish wantonness in them apt enough to be construed or strained to a personating of vices in the present governors and government.[17]

Understandably, given the scope of her study, Raber is quick to contrast Greville with Mary Sidney, who penned her own, similarly themed *Antonie*. In so doing, she constructs a convincing argument which posits Sidney's success as due to her gendered approach to dramatic production. Whilst Sidney and Greville shared 'class, a commitment to a style of drama and to a patronage which supports the genre,' the former was singularly more adroit in 'situating her work within a network of gender-sensitive strategies and arguments,' thus manipulating the structures (or buffers) that linked domestic and public life.[18]

It is futile to argue with Raber's point; the evidence for female licence in filtering potentially politically sensitive material through such traditionally feminine channels as translation and domestication is overwhelming. However, what her study sidesteps lies in the causes of Greville's burning of his play – the mechanisms by which the censure of 'those few eyes' which were privy to his work necessitated its destruction. Certainly, the figure of the censor as embodied by the Master of the Revels is here conspicuous by his absence – instead, it was potential misinterpretation by Greville's own small coterie which led to *Antony and Cleopatra*'s immolation. Concurring with Raber, Susan Hrach Georgecink succinctly points

17 Raber, *Dramatic Difference*, p. 112; Greville, *A Dedication to Sir Philip Sidney*, p. 93.
18 Raber, *Dramatic Difference*, p. 112.

out that 'the infelicitous reception of a stage play could always be blamed on the performance rather than solely on the playwright,' mitigating the authorial culpability associated with closet drama.[19] But what dangerous state retribution did playwrights perceive against dramas which were not intended for performance? This seeming paradox – the private closet dramatist's need to destroy his work based on fear of reprisals by an authoritarian regime whose interest is ostensibly centred on public performance – can, in part, by explained by the politics of elite play-reading.

Addressing the political aspects of reading in early modern period, Kevin Sharpe cites the most important move in hermeneutical and critical theory as 'a concern with the reading and consumption of texts.'[20] In pursuing early modern readerships, it is a task made doubly difficult not only due to shifting cultural sands, but the tangle of gendered networks, and – as we have seen – issues of censure, even amongst reading coteries. Authors in particular, Sharpe argues, were required to tread a fine line when the state functioned as reader – the penalties for libel or sedition being mutilation or death.[21] Of course, this applies, in the main, to those authors who actively sought to open their texts up to unknown readers – and the strategies for doing so safely included functional ambiguity, a method of literary production tacitly accepted by the state.[22] Attempts at ambiguity, however, courted the possibility of misinterpretation. It was, further, a problem well recognised, as Sharpe acknowledges in his list of contemporary commentators who decried the blatant misreadings which were of concern to writers:

> Hayward ... while admitting that readers would be interpreters, pejoratively spoke of them as potential 'wrestlers,' and 'corrupters,' and 'depravers' of what they read. Bacon too felt that some readings of a text claimed to discover 'meaning which it was never meant to have' and accused Machiavelli of expounding the fable of Achilles 'corruptly.'[23]

19 Georgecink, 'Review of *Dramatic Difference*,' pp. 597–8.
20 Sharpe, *Reading Revolutions*, p. 34.
21 Sharpe, *Reading Revolutions*, p. 43.
22 Sharpe, *Reading Revolutions*, p. 40.
23 Sharpe, *Reading Revolutions*, pp. 43–4.

Interestingly, Sharpe cites Ben Jonson as an example of an author who actively resisted literary equivocality – a fact which must be borne in mind when we turn to the commercial stage.[24] Nonetheless, within the tradition of early modern reading, ambiguity and the dangers of misinterpretation evidently constituted a matter of considerable weight in literary production. Consequently, the period coincided with 'the development of strategies to contain the hermeneutic liberties of readers … As readers in turn became more sophisticated in "reading" and seeing beyond those gestures, so authors adopted different and more sophisticated techniques … [ultimately] claiming cultural authority as authors.'[25]

This preoccupation with interpretative possibilities and the dangers of misreading – along with the developmental game of one-upmanship designed to combat the perversion of meaning – has obvious consequences for our understanding of Greville's destruction of *Antony and Cleopatra*. By his own admission, Greville found himself writing for just such a network of 'misinterpreters' and, in a culture which was familiar with the dangers which misreading attracted, opted to destroy the text – whether due to his acceptance that it invited misinterpretation or because he feared what misreadings might engender we cannot know. Where we can safely place Greville's actions, however, are within a microcosmic interpretative community – a coterie readership – which echoed early modern English concerns about misinterpretation, the fear of autocratic retribution and the dangers of seditious writing. In short, what becomes clear is that, even in matters in which the censor played no active role – the legal right to

24 Arthur Marotti (*Manuscript, Print and the English Renaissance Lyric*, p. 242) provides a useful contextualisation of Jonson's difficulties in controlling the reception and interpretation of his writings, as necessitated by 'the new conditions of literature in a print culture that made possible was virtually impossible in a system of manuscript transmission, where the uses and interpretation of texts were more obviously under reader control.' To Marotti, print offered authors not only 'property rights over corrected texts but also … issues of meaning and interpretation.' Arguably, there were repercussions here for texts deemed slanderous or seditious. In print, such property rights could also apportion blame and guilt should texts be received with official hostility.

25 Sharpe, *Reading Revolutions*, p. 44.

license private as well as public material being, as noted, largely impracticable – the negative reception of an interpretative readership could and did inspire the wary poet to suppress his own work. But, of course, not all poets were as sensitive to authority – and its power over position and advancement – as the courtly Greville.

In Greville's destruction of *Antony and Cleopatra*, catalysed as it was by the warnings of his readers regarding the possibility of it being viewed as subversive in intent, one may be tempted to align him with what Burt calls the 'poet-critic': a figure who did not place the power of censorship in the hands of the state, but rather, 'as epitomised by Ben Jonson, could also perform the censor's critical function, or even be in line to serve as the Master of the Revels himself.' Certainly, there is an incontrovertible element of censorship in Greville's actions. The flaw of trying to locate Greville within such a model, however, lies in both the form of the text and the process of his actions – in other words, the creation of the closet drama, its 'performance' before its intended audience, and its destruction on the basis of audience response. Just as *Antony and Cleopatra* – as a play unintended for theatrical performance – did not lie within the remit of the Master of the Revels, neither can Greville be said to function as 'poet-critic.' The due process of the Revels Office, to edit, censor and license plays prior to performance, is certainly not in evidence here – rather, Greville's destruction of the play was entirely predicated on the reactions of his intended interpretative audience. Equally lacking is Kaplan's view of the poet as an agent operating within the slippery notion of slander and attempting to recover from the state the right to assert what is acceptable and unacceptable language.

Further complicating the notion of the closet drama as a play which, though not intended for stage performance, was nevertheless available to a limited audience in textual form, is the question of what constitutes performance. As has been noted, the laws of censorship certainly regulated stage performance. However, it will also be remembered that Elizabethan authorities also sought to keep a keen (and increasingly intrusive) grip on what could legally be said, repeated or written in the presence of others. Here laws of censorship and laws of defamation intersect.[26] Slander, as has

26 Kaplan, *The Culture of Slander*, p. 6.

been well demonstrated, constituted the speaking or writing of defamatory (or, if the victim was in high authority, seditiously) provocative words in the presence of a third party. In terms of theatrical performance, this issue is made manifestly more difficult by Elizabeth's own proclamation which held that plays touching religion and state matters must be vetted before being played before audiences of 'grave and discreet persons.' In short, one arrives at the matter of audience, or, within the legal framework of slander, the third party to whom words are read, spoken or performed.

It must be established, firstly, that reading aloud to a coterie audience was a leisure pursuit common in the period to both genders. Further, it is clear that such 'interpretative communities were made up of those who shared strategies for writing texts.' As such, Sharpe concludes that handwritten texts – and here we must include the closet drama – open up the idea of 'groups or networks in which manuscripts circulate.'[27] This notion is linked to the concept of groups of individuals (be they communities, sects or, importantly, political factions) which circulated manuscripts and nourished shared values. Here we once again arrive at scribal communities. Although, as Love notes, illicit texts ran the risk of offending authorities by being 'published outside the normal frameworks of licensing and censorship,' manuscript culture maintained vitality – perhaps due in part to censorship – and, indeed, there was a growing expectation that scribally published material (particularly lampoons) would 'traduce the great.'[28] Certainly, there is ample evidence of the networks of letter writers who corresponded (occasionally under the watchful eye of Elizabeth's spymaster, Walsingham), just as there is evidence of what Michelle O'Callaghan views as the humanist bonding of education and intellect symbolised by performance in the Inns of Court and the covert networks by which a 1588 burlesque comedy about the Earl of Leicester's ghost's arrival in Hell circulated in Catholic circles via manuscript.[29] Worth noting also is James Daybell's astute recognition that 'hundreds of manuscript copies of letters were scribally circulated from the late-Elizabethan period onwards.' Such letters

27 Sharpe, *Reading Revolutions*, p. 272.

28 Love, *Scribal Publication*, pp. v, 189–91.

29 O'Callaghan, *The English Wits*, p. 24; Raymond, *Pamphlets and Pamphleteering*, p. 22.

were, he further argues, disseminated 'in ways broadly similar to other texts such as libels.'[30] Scribal communities, therefore, may well be understood as potential sources of slander and sedition which, whilst governed by a proviso in Elizabethan slander laws, skirted official methods of censorship.[31]

Similarly, the closet drama can be defined as a grouping of like-minded individuals (such as Greville's coterie or the predominantly female audiences of the domestic sphere) which operated outside the jurisdiction of the Master of the Revels, despite the reading of drama to a private audience remaining a performative act. If, therefore, an impasse was reached between the ability of the Master of the Revels to regulate drama which was not submitted for review and the fact that closet drama was nevertheless a medium which invited a kind of performance, one must surely question the state's abilities (or, rather, attempts) to bridge the gap. It is here that the laws of slander, defamation and sedition are paramount; where the Master of the Revels could not intervene and either forbid or edit play texts (and the nature of closet dramas as manuscripts precluded this), existing laws which allowed the state to punish malfeasants found guilty of producing slanderous writings, repeating or publishing defamatory words, or sowing sedition by criticising the government remained in place to tackle even privately produced dramatic material. That Greville destroyed his work rather than risk the weight of the law falling upon him for inviting accusations of slander of the Elizabethan government attests to the fact that these laws certainly produced, to at least one closet dramatist, the need for circumspection.

It is necessary, however, not only to consider texts which themselves ran the risk of inviting accusations of sedition and slander, but those which depicted, interrogated and explored this dangerous and unstable use of language. Returning to Straznicky's recognition of the closet dramatist's ability to pass between the domestic and public spheres through print, it is useful to turn to Elizabeth Cary's *Tragedy of Mariam* (1613). A play

30 Daybell, *The Material Letter*, p. 190.

31 It will once again be remembered that libellous writing committed to the page either by pen or press precluded those arraigned for publishing it from justifying their actions on the grounds of truth.

which presents audiences (and for this, we include readers) with a vivid portrait of the effects of slander on the title character, it is noteworthy not only for its portrayal of a slanderer, but for its publication history. Firstly, it is necessary to turn to the representation of the slanderer in drama. Habermann discourses at length on the suitability of the mechanisms of slander to the dramatic form; slander plots, she argues, allow audiences to 'observe those mechanisms at a moment when, from the point of view of the characters in the play, the slander has not yet become a public event.'[32] She further recognises that 'the specific heuristic value of drama lies in its performativity, in the possibility to place human actions and their consequences in such a way that they can be examined from a point of view otherwise unavailable in real life.' That slander plots were used with some frequency leads Habermann to then conclude that 'defamation was, in the period, an important public issue.'[33] We must, however, question the nature of this importance – particularly, in the case of *The Tragedy of Mariam*, in relation to gender.

First published in 1613 (but alleged to have been written some ten years earlier), *The Tragedy of Mariam* was originally circulated in manuscript (aimed at a domestic literary circle) before being marketed (in a selective sense) to an educated public of play-readers.[34] Centring on the Biblical tale of Herod's second wife, the virtuous Mariam, and her subsequent slandering by Salome, the play explores the efficacy of sexual slander of female by female (something of a commonplace in the Elizabethan law courts), a method of defamation consistently linked in the period with incontinence of speech, and the means by which females could negotiate it. The conventional equation of female loquaciousness with promiscuity and sexual incontinence is made manifest by Cary in the opening lines of the play, as Mariam laments, 'How oft have I with public voice run on.'[35] An immediate invitation is thus made for learned readers to equate Mariam's fate – a result of the false imputations of sexual misconduct levelled by

32 Habermann, *Staging Slander and Gender*, p. 4.
33 Habermann, *Staging Slander and Gender*, p. 37.
34 Straznicky, *Privacy, Play Reading and Women's Closet Drama*, pp. 48–66.
35 Cary, *The Tragedy of Mariam*, I.I.1.

Salome – with a prejudicial view of her previous lack of moderation in speech. That the slander emanates from a female is also, to Habermann, a matter of some consequence; indeed, it invites the interpretation of slander 'both as a form of female empowerment and a potent threat to women.'[36]

Though certainly accurate in this summation, what must, however, be stressed is the very frequency of Elizabethan civil disputes involving slander between women. In representing the slandered heroine and devious slanderer through the lens of high politics, Cary engages also with defamation as an important public issue – and one which plagued the law courts. Further, Habermann, through close textual analysis of the play, makes the astute point that the character of Mariam provides for her readership an exploration of the 'moral dilemma women face in trying to live up to the complex and conflicting requirements of society.'[37] Through the presentation of a heroine who, though unjustly maligned, accepts a noble and submissive death by finally adopting a womanly silence, it is arguable that the play offers further insight into the complexities of slander. It is well established that, to the sixteenth-century sensibility, spoken utterances could have 'situation-altering effects,' with those who lacked 'temperance and moderation in language' apt to 'provoke violence, discord, unhappiness or sedition ... intensifying divisions within communities and eroding the fabric of society.' The trouble was that there were a great many people apparently willing to do just that.[38]

Whilst Salome is undoubtedly the slanderer of the play, it is surely noteworthy that she rebukes Mariam, saying, 'You durst not thus have given your tongue the rein,' before recognising, 'now stirs the tongue that is so quickly moved; / But more than once your choler I have born, / Your fumish words as sooner said than proved, / And Salome's reply is scorn.'[39] Thus, it may be argued that, rather than representing the 'slander triangle' of slanderer, victim and listener (as Habermann believes to constitute the primary paradigms of the slander plot), *The Tragedy of Mariam* serves also

36 Habermann, *Staging Slander and Gender*, p. 148.

37 Habermann, *Staging Slander and Gender*, p. 150.

38 Cressy, *Dangerous Talk*, pp. 5–6.

39 Cary, *The Tragedy of Mariam*, I.III. 13, 21–4.

to explore the slippery nature of speech and its relationship with slander, especially in the burgeoning, defamatory feuds between Elizabethan women.[40] In short, Mariam and Salome represent not simply slanderer and slandered, but two sides of a verbal feud which, as in the law courts, ends with judgement in favour of one party (whilst there is tacit criticism of the verbal machinations of both). Furthermore, given the play's initial intended audience of female domestic acquaintances, it is surely to be expected that Cary would focus her representation of slanderous activity not only on the ways in which women could and should negotiate conventional attacks on female behaviour, but on that which predominantly affected women: that which took place between them.

In her comparative reading of Webster's *The Duchess of Malfi* (1612–13) and Cary's *Mariam*, Reina Green foregrounds what she perceives as Cary's concern that 'the truth should be heard regardless of the cost … the need to determine the veracity of a speech' being paramount.[41] Naturally, this has implications for the study of the play's treatment of slander. Accepting Habermann's 'triangular constellation' of 'slanderer, listener and victim,' the play invites consideration of the position of 'listener.' Certainly, much has been made in feminist critiques of Cary's play of the gendered, sexual imagery invited by Herod's condemnation of Mariam's lack of chastity as encapsulated by her mouth being 'ope to ev'ry stranger's ear.' To Green, Cary presents unchaste behaviour as being indicated not only by women's lack of temperance in speech, 'but by their role as listeners – and receptors for – men's speech,' citing Herod's evidence of infertility against Mariam taking the form of what she has heard rather than what she has said.[42] However, in a play in which the power of speech is frequently noted and

40 A rigorous study of the rise in defamation suits fought between women can be found in Laura Gowing's *Domestic Dangers*, pp. 30–8. In late sixteenth-century England, she notes, slander litigation was on the rise in both secular and ecclesiastical courts. Particularly in London (where close quarters may have fostered tensions), women were a growing presence in the courtroom and by the early seventeenth century 'the deposition books are largely given over to the meticulous recording of the disputes about sexual insult fought largely between and about women.'

41 Green, 'Ears Prejudicate,' pp. 459–74.

42 Green, 'Ears Prejudicate,' p. 463.

the effects of its misinterpretation are explored, it is arguable that, whilst issues of contemporary femininity are indeed engaged with, it is the agent of the 'listener' (regardless of gender) in the 'process' of slander which is often overlooked – a strange omission, given that slander is merely insult, and thus undamaging, until a third party hears it.

Overarching the commonly discussed themes of chastity and the link between female speech and sexual conduct (which are, it must be made clear, present in the play) is the process of slander itself, underscored by Constabarus' assertion that the slanderous Salome's mouth 'though serpent-like,' 'never hisses, / Yet like a serpent poisons where it kisses.'[43] It is impossible not to recall the Elizabethan perception of slander as a 'poison,' as here the slanderer assumes the role of a speaker whose language is both seductive and poisonous: a particularly insidious threat. Further, the dangers of listening (and misunderstanding) are equally well illustrated in the hapless Mariam, whose downfall is in part precipitated by her willingness to listen to others. As a consequence, readers of the play are encouraged not only to recognise the dangers posed by slanderers, but by the means by which they spread their poison and the very fact that their power to subvert, damage and destroy lies not only with the slanderer on his or her own, but with a third party's willingness to listen and believe. In short, the play depicts slanderous language as being granted potency through the conduit of listeners' ears, as criticism of the slanderer is channelled into caution for prospective listeners.

The closet drama, it can be seen, represented a mode of dramatic expression which lay beyond the traditional remit of the Master of the Revels; despite his theoretical authority over all performances, his role largely confined him to liaising with playwrights who sought to have their work authorised as 'state' texts admissible for publication and performance on the public stage. As a consequence, those models of theatrical censorship which limit their scope to the latter type of dramatic material cannot account for the proliferation and circulation of manuscript plays which were (in the case of Greville) either destroyed due to the pressure of his coterie readership or simply explored slander as a dangerous and persistently

43 Cary, *The Tragedy of Mariam*, II.IV. 333–4.

troublesome linguistic mechanism which provided a familiar plot device. In the history of the closet drama, as with other forms of potentially politically subversive or otherwise inflammatory writings, it is thus necessary to recognise the importance of the laws of libel and slander in regulating privately produced dramatic material. All writing and reading activities, it must be noted, were performative. Not all can be accounted for by existing models of censorship.

CHAPTER 10

The Commercial Stage

If closet drama presents us with a method of play text circulation which was of little consequence to the Master of the Revels (and therefore largely unacknowledged by commonly posited models of censorship), drama which was produced for the public stage was the primary concern of Tilney, his predecessors and his successors. The increasing encroachment of the Master of the Revels over London (and then the kingdom's) playhouses is well established (even if his influence, activities, and acuity has been hotly debated). It is therefore no surprise that the history of the Revels Office is peppered with the Elizabethan authorities' role in suppressing and punishing playwrights for producing politically sensitive, potentially seditious, or allegedly slanderous dramas. Of course, as Janet Clare and Andrew Hadfield have demonstrated, the editorial role of the Master of the Revels is broadly untraceable, with original manuscripts often long lost. As a consequence, some of the most telling and informative moments of censorship of slanderous material are those celebrated cases which reached the stage and, due to the alleged offence or possible sedition they precipitated, caused the gears of Elizabethan authority to rumble into action. No stranger to controversy, despite his illustrious career as a court dramatist and subsequent favourite of James I, Ben Jonson provides not one but several of the most notorious instances of dramatic suppression.

As Sharpe and Lake term him a, 'courtly artist' who nevertheless held 'serious misgivings about courtiers, courtly culture and even kings,' Jonson was a stalwart proponent of the belief that 'speech is the instrument of society,' asserting that 'those who master language can refashion social relations' (a view which binds him, surely, to Kaplan's 'slander model' of censorship).[1] Of interest also is his association with the Inns of Court,

1 Sharpe and Lake, *Culture and Politics in Early Stuart England*, p. 11.

their legal culture's influence on his dramatic style, and his 'experiments with comic satires [which] gave the public stage a vital role to play in the commonwealth by turning the theatre into a law court.'[2] This notion of the collapsing of the law courts and the theatre is a particularly arresting one; Jonson was no stranger to either. In 1597, his satirical comedy (written in collaboration with Thomas Nashe), *The Isle of Dogs* was performed at the Swan Theatre and almost immediately suppressed.[3] As Ian Donaldson makes clear, the court records relating to the play are unanimous in their use of the descriptors 'seditious' and 'slanderous.'[4] Although the text is lost, the very use of the words suggests that the play made libellous reference to high-ranking court figures. Speculation abounds as to the exact figures targeted in Jonson's play, with scholarly detective work hinting at members of the Privy Council, Lord Cobham and even the Queen herself.[5]

However, regardless of the victim of the slanders, the content found its way via an informer to Elizabeth's notorious interrogator, Richard Topcliffe, who instructed the Privy Council to investigate the matter. Crucially, however, not only were Nashe and Jonson apprehended, but three of their players, charged with 'lewd and mutinous behaviour' by performing a play 'containing very seditious and scandalous matter,' with the disingenuous Nashe claiming that the actors themselves were responsible for the offensive matter.[6] Although the entire troupe were soon released for lack of evidence (Topcliffe's methods presumably having failed to yield results), a variety of questions arise from this curious case. Firstly, it must be assumed that Tilney (and his associate, Samuel Daniel), normally a proactive Master of the Revels, sanctioned the play. The reasons for this cannot be ascertained,

2 O'Callaghan, *The English Wits*, p. 35.

3 One of the amphitheatres popular amongst lower-ranking citizens, the Swan Theatre was, as Andrew Gurr (*Playgoing in Shakespeare's London*, p. 47) recognises, a site which could 'generate a high intensity of audience reaction and hubbub amongst the packed mass of understanders.' Unfortunately for Jonson, his later play, *Eastward Ho* (1605), was to cause similar problems in the more illustrious 'hall' playhouse of Blackfriars.

4 Donaldson, *Ben Jonson*, p. 117.

5 Donaldson, *Ben Jonson*, pp. 119–22.

6 Donaldson, *Ben Jonson*, p. 113.

but James Forse has not unconvincingly argued that they may be linked to a complex network of bribery and patronage.[7]

Perhaps more interestingly, in terms of contemporary legal (and moral) attitudes towards speech, repetition, and performance, however, is the question of why the actors were arrested for their 'behaviour' in performing the play. The answer here can only lie in the law. Whilst Jonson and Nashe were certainly the creators of the texts (despite Nashe's claims to the contrary), the players nevertheless spoke the slanderous and seditious words before a third party; in effect, they were viewed as active agents in the spread of sedition. We therefore arrive at a key intersection of slander and dramatic performance. As has been seen, in the annals of Elizabethan and early Jacobean legal history, one found to have republished (be it through speech, writing or print) an existing slander was considered by the law to be as culpable as its originator. The method of transmission, we can therefore conclude, was less important than the person who transmitted slander – a slanderer was apt to be anyone who contributed to the spread of defamatory material. The slanderous language itself represented the thought and intent to cause damage. Although technically statute law viewed spoken defamation as less dangerous than written defamation, due to its limited impact and lack of anonymity, it seems that theatrical performance presented an unusual anomaly in that, although it was spoken by actors, it was also written, learned, repeated and projected to wide audiences.[8] Thus, whilst Kaplan is correct in her assertion that 'the laws regarding slander were on Jonson's side more than he probably knew,' due to the more stringent regulation of printed material, the evidence suggests that dramatic actors could be not only accused of speaking slander, but implicated in its writing and as suspected of seditious behaviour as any writer.[9] Indeed, it was this recognition of the playhouse as a collaborative space in which words were communal property that Nashe used to try and deflect blame.

Despite his brush with authority, and the government's subsequent attempts to crack down on the 'lewd matters handled' on London's stages (in

7 Force, *Art Imitates Business*, p. 170.
8 Kaplan, *The Culture of Slander*, p. 65.
9 Ibid.

direct parallel to the Privy Council's reactionary attitudes to non-theatrical occasions of sedition), Jonson's chequered career continued to court controversy. Following what Michelle O'Callaghan has termed the bitter factionalism and libellous politics of the 1590s, the eminently satirical Jonson continued to employ comic satire of the type he so admired in the Inns of Court revels. Grappling with the ethics of laughter – the 'key element in the persuasive armoury of the comic satirist' – Jonson sought to negotiate between the permissible limits of speech and conduct and the Ciceronian and Quintilian precept that invective was acceptable if delivered with an urbane wit and observed decorum.[10]

Such negotiations were to come to the fore during the infamous 'War of the Theatres' (or 'Poets' War') of 1600–1: long considered a literary feud between Jonson, Dekker and Marston, the precise nature of which has been of enduring contention to scholars. Bringing a fresh perspective to a centuries-old debate, James P. Bednarz has effectively reconstituted the episode as 'a theoretical debate on the social function of drama and the standard of poetic authority that informed comical satire,' fought out mainly between Jonson, Shakespeare and Marston.[11] Comprising competing plays in which Jonson and his rivals investigated, through dramatic means, whether invective should satirise the man or his vice (or both) within the paradigms of satiric decorum (defended, albeit ingenuously, by Jonson as 'free and wholesome sharpness'), the playwrights satirised one another on-stage with gusto.[12] Crucially, the 'War of the Theatres,' and its resultant satirical plays, constitutes what O'Callaghan recognises as a pivotal Jonsonian attribute: the questioning of the ethics and liberty of speech. Furthermore, the plays did not arouse to any known degree the attention of the Master of the Revels, despite resulting in a 'flurry' of

10 O'Callaghan, *The English Wits*, p. 38.

11 Bednarz, *Shakespeare and the Poets' War*, p. 7.

12 Jonson, *The Poetaster*, V.1.95. Bednarz provides arguably one of the most convincing accounts of what he term the 'Poets' War.' In particular, his recognition of Shakespeare's role in 'the quarrel's rich vein of personal satire' and the development of literary theory he views as being paramount in the episode are particularly noteworthy. See: Bednarz, *Shakespeare and the Poets' War*, p. 5.

libels for their alleged attacks on lawyers and soldiers.[13] As a result, they represent satirical jabs in Jonson's ongoing attempts to 'master language' and indicate a model of censorship in which slander (in the guise of satirical experiment) was permissible, even reciprocal. The playwrights were at liberty to attack one another's abilities and attributes under the freedom of artistic expression, and, whatever the true nature of the feud, none of the parties involved saw fit to sue one another in the civil courts, preferring to wield their pens instead.

What therefore emerges is what Kaplan describes as a 'dissolving' of the distinction between slander and satire, as evidenced by Jonson's final entry in the 'War' series, *The Poetaster* (1601), a play which resulted in an angry disturbance from audiences. Jonson was brought before the Lord Chief Justice and ultimately defended his work in his 'Apologetical Dialogue': an appeal to authority on the merits of satire which, to Kaplan, 'served only to confirm the notion that satire, in any form, was merely slander.'[14] It is a lofty claim, but the parallels between the common metaphorical understanding of slanderous activity as actively injuring victims (in addition to its 'poisonous' nature) bears unmistakable similarity to Jonson's threats in *The Poetaster*:

> They know, I dare
> To spurne, or baffull 'hem; or squirt their eyes
> With inke, or urine; or I could doe worse,
> Arm'd with Archilochus fury, write Iambicks,
> Should make the desperate lashers hang themselves.
> Rime 'hem to death, as they doe Irish rats
> In drumming tunes. Or, living, I could stampe
> Their foreheads with those deepe, and publike brands,
> That the whole company of Barber-Surgeons
> Should not take off, with all their art, and playsters.[15]

Certainly, Jonson equates the act of writing with an act of aggression: it becomes a potent and destructive weapon. Ink itself becomes susceptible

13 Kaplan, *The Culture of Slander*, p. 85.
14 Kaplan, *The Culture of Slander*, p. 91.
15 Jonson, 'To The Reader,' 145–54.

to the author's malicious intent. It takes on the ability to destroy lives and, further, it is imbued with indelibility. With satirical jabs 'stamped on the forehead' of victims, satire, like slander, is made public. It is to be read by third parties and, once read, it cannot be erased – the reader (or viewer) cannot unread the damaging words. It is difficult not to draw parallels with one of the more barbaric methods of Elizabethan punishment – branding. A relatively popular punishment, Jonson's metaphorical engagement with the practice is noteworthy, not only due to the indelibility of branding, but for the way in which violent acts could redound on the person inflicting them.[16] Here must be recalled the punishment meted out to John Stubbs which resulted in a public recognition of the severity of the state. Further, in terms of language, Cavanagh has noted that at the beginning of Elizabeth's reign, Lord Keeper Bacon accused those indulging in inflammatory speech of being 'guilty of fomenting the very sedition they purported to oppose.'[17] Thus, one might contrast Jonson's conception of the aggressive and reciprocally damaging nature of language with Montaigne's idealised view of it as a volley and thrust between interlocutors, 'as betweene those that play at tennis.'[18] The playful 'back and forth' of speakers is, when transplanted into the realities of theatrical satire, reduced to the violent and injurious semantics associated with slander, despite Jonson's spirited apologetic. Yet to claim that slander and satire were indistinguishable under Jonson is to do him a disservice and to fall into the trap of accepting the agenda pushed by the Elizabethan state. He pushed the bounds of decorum, certainly, but, ever the literary snob, only on educated poets' terms. He did not call for free, vitriolic speech amongst the unlearned; to Jonson, slander was a an uglier, less refined beast than satire. What Jonson (and like-minded writers) sought was not simply the right to slander under the guise of satirical expression, but something artistic to call their own. Satire proving unsuccessful (given

16 Julie Crawford (*Marvelous Protestantism*, p. 22) has noted that the bodies of criminals were frequently 'mutilated with signs of infamy calibrated to reflect their crimes … faces were branded with V for vagabond, SS for sower of sedition and SL for slanderous libeller.'

17 Cavanagh, *Language and Politics in the Sixteenth-Century History Play*, p. 36.

18 Montaigne, 'Of Experience,' p. 834.

the authorities' intolerance of it as merely slanderous), 'libel' would later meet the demand, coming into its own as a separate, more witty category of language with the added boon of classical heritage.

Jonson, thus no stranger to the slanderous properties of satire (or to the dangers of offending authority with publicly performed slanderous plays) nevertheless combined the two in his 1605 play, *Eastward Ho*. Another collaborative venture, this time written in conjunction with George Chapman and John Marston, the play (unlike most successful plays of the age) was quickly released to the printers – a sign, to Joseph Quincy Adams that it had been swiftly prohibited from the stage due to the displeasure of the royal court.[19] Deftly historicizing *Eastward Ho*'s publication, Adams convincingly argues that the play's censorship was based on its performance history rather than its release in print: a notion borne out by extant letters (in manuscript) penned by Jonson following his voluntary admission to prison. According to his own declaration, Jonson was subject to the 'King's high wrath' based only on 'malicious rumour.'[20] This, to Adams, is persuasive evidence that the offence stemmed from stage performance – 'cold type' being unlikely to be described as 'rumour.' One might recall, however, the somewhat elastic English statute of *Scandalum Magnatum* (which put a firm penalty on the spread of false rumour) in order to discern in Jonson's indignant defence what Kaplan recognises as the playwright's characteristic desire to reassert poetic authority within her 'defamation model' of reciprocal accusation. Certainly, Jonson's behaviour – submitting voluntarily to the authorities and countering allegations of seditious writing with appeals to 'misreport' and 'rumour,' lend themselves well to the paradigms of Kaplan's projected model of censorship. Indeed, one might argue that it is predominantly with playwrights such as Jonson – producing works for the public, commercial stage rather than the closet – that the 'slander model' can be best supported.

19 Adams, '*Eastward Ho* and its Satire Against the Scots,' p. 689. Plays rushed to print were the early modern equivalent of direct-to-DVD films which failed at the box office.

20 Jonson, 'To an Unnamed Lady, probably the Countess of Bedford. 1605,' p. 131.

The issue of intended audience is, furthermore, one of paramount importance in the censorship of *Eastward Ho*, a comedy which features satirical representations of Scottish glitterati. Originally performed by the Children of Her Majesty's Revels at Blackfriars – a playhouse patronised by the elite of London – the play came to the attention of the Court and the newly crowned James I's raft of courtiers.[21] Noting that 'much of the play's satire is directed against the rapacity and ambition of the Jacobean parvenu,' Clare identifies play as having offended, in particular, Sir James Murray due to its containing 'something written against the Scots.'[22] Lucy Munro reinforces the point, recognising in Murray's displeasure a failure of the comedy in creating a unified audience response.[23] Nevertheless, she notes that in order for the play to be published (as it swiftly was, as was typical of those which were unsuccessful as performance pieces), offensive jokes were trimmed.[24] This raises an important issue in terms of the public perception of slander (which, it will be recalled, needed only to reach a third party of listeners). E. A. J. Honigmann's assertion that 'for Shakespeare [and here we must substitute Shakespeareans], the theatre gave the primary form of publication' is particularly relevant.[25] Simply by virtue of having been performed before (or orally published to) a third party, the play had achieved slanderous potential. Accepting Adams' contention that the play's initial performance incited James' wrath, with the manuscript's subsequent pre-publication alteration taking place during its (in no way fully traceable) journey between actors, official censor and publisher, we

21 Established in 1596 (though not without resentment amongst locals), the Blackfriars represented an 'emphatic shift up-market, from the amphitheatres serving primarily the penny-paying standers in the yard to the private or select kind of audience which expected seats and a roof over their heads' (Gurr, *Playgoing in Shakespeare's London*, p. 24). As one of the emerging 'hall' playhouses, the Blackfriars was a more expensive proposition designed to attract a higher-ranking audience.

22 Clare, *Art Made Tongue-Tied by Authority*, p. 140. Existing documentary evidence concerning the responses generated by the play make it particularly suited to Clare's methodological approach.

23 Munro, *Children of the Queen's Revels*, p. 75.

24 Munro, *Children of the Queen's Revels*, p. 80.

25 Honigmann, *The Stability of Shakespeare's Text*, p. 191.

are left with the vexing problem of ascertaining both what caused offence and how the play came to be performed in its initial state.

To address the former question is to enter into a somewhat crowded area of scholarly debate, with extant theories including the actors' mimicry of Scottish accents to the stated wishes of the play's characters that the Scots remained outside England.[26] We can, however, conclude that the outrage provoked by the play's ridicule of the Scots (in whatever guise it took) invited accusations of sedition by compromising the authority of those now in power. It will, after all, be remembered that the perceived failings of those in public office, or any other utterances or writings which brought the government into disrepute, stood in danger of being called 'seditious' by virtue of inciting a breach of the piece amongst listeners. The King's anger, therefore, may be directly linked with the Elizabethan regime's established legal tradition of retroactively responding to discrete moments of seditious or slanderous activity with punitive retribution. The latter question, however, is more easily answered – the play was not, before its initial performance, passed through the proper channels of authority, the Revels Office because, due to legal technicalities brought about by patents reissued on the accession of the new monarchy, the Master of the Revels had ceded his jurisdiction.[27] As such, whilst the Master of the Revels has been accused of contributing, however indirectly, to political instability by licensing controversial plays, here it seems his authority lapsed before the

26 Redmond, *Shakespeare, Politics, and Italy*, p. 178; Heinemann, *Puritanism and Theatre*, p. 44.

27 Dutton, 'Ben Jonson and the Master of the Revels,' p. 72. Richard Dutton's recognition of the state of flux into which the jurisdictions of censorship were thrown by the Stuart accession is worth quoting: 'Eastward Ho did not come before the Master of the Revels because it was outside his jurisdiction. In February 1604, the Children of the Chapel were re-incorporated as the Children of the Queen's (i.e. Queen Anne's) Revels; their royal patent gave them the right to perform: "Provided always that no such plays or shows shall be presented … or by them anywhere publicly acted but by the approbation and allowance of Samuel David". This was a large corollary of the fact that James' succession not only installed a new monarch but also created a second royal household, that of Queen Anne.' In essence, the Master of the Revels (now the King's man) lost control over plays which were to be licensed by the Queen's official censor.

manuscript's initial journey from author to playhouse.[28] This differs from, for example, the case of Shakespeare's *Richard II* (1597) which was likely passed for performance in 1595 and entered into the Stationers' Register for publication in 1597. The command performance organised on the eve of the Earl of Essex's abortive coup resulted in a Privy Council investigation, but the players were not punished – potentially because to do so would be to admit that the state had erred in authorising the play in the first place.

In his efforts to prove that it was the stage performance of *Eastward Ho* which was responsible for Jonson, Marston and Chapman's punishment, Adams notes that the chief manager of Blackfriars (with whom nominal responsibility for securing the formal allowance of theatrical presentation lay) was also punished.[29] It is thus tempting to envision the wheels of retribution swiftly turning against the perpetrators of a play which not only presented practitioners of sedition on-stage, but put in their mouths words actively liable to cause offence to the now ruling Scottish nobility – all without the required endorsement of the official in charge of the Children of the Queen's Revels (at the time the previously mentioned Samuel Daniel, whose period in office was marked by controversies), the Master of the Revels, or his own overseer, the Lord Chamberlain. Curiously – and perhaps crucially – such was not the case. Despite specious concerns voiced by Jonson about the King's desire to have he and Chapman's 'ears cut and noses' (Marston having fled London at the outbreak of the controversy), the pair willingly submitted themselves to prison, and after a few months were quietly released. Further, no evidence suggests that the players were punished (unlike those unfortunate enough to be embroiled in the ignominy surrounding Jonson's earlier *Isle of Dogs*), despite their publicly speaking the allegedly seditious words; and nor was the eventual publisher of the play punished following its licensing as a printed text.[30] The variant

28 Burt, 'Licensed by Authority,' p. 543.

29 Adams, '*Eastward Ho* and its Satire Against the Scots,' p. 693.

30 It is possible that the age of the actors spared them legal retribution for their part in the *Eastward Ho* affair. However, this is unlikely. Despite maintaining the troupe name, 'The Children of the Queen's Revels,' Lucy Munro (*Children of the Queen's Revels*, p. 40) has noted that, by the reopening of the theatres in 1605, 'many of the boys were well into their teens.' She further notes that 'there is no evidence to

responses exhibited by Marston, and Jonson and Chapman are worthy of consideration. On the one hand, Marston's flight suggests that he feared (and therefore anticipated) a serious form of state retribution. On the other, Jonson and Chapman saw no reason not to hand themselves in and trust that the punishment they received would not be inordinately harsh. What does this tell us about the poets' understandings of the mechanisms of the state in punishing slanderous and seditious material? Quite evidently, the suggestion is that there was no clear or assured way for those who impugned authority through language to be quite sure of the severity of the reaction which would result. Different playwrights, it seemed, held different beliefs as to what their punishment might be (and how best to approach it). What must be remembered here is the differing degrees to which the Elizabethan and early Jacobean authorities could flex their legal muscle. Whilst slanderous or seditious language might result in mutilation (as Jonson professed to fear), it might incur a spell in the pillory, a spell in the Marshalsea, or a stiff fine. At the whim of a legal system which could be relatively lax or extremely punitive, those who angered the state (or its leading citizens) evidently had no fixed penalty of which they could be sure.

It is thus necessary to question just how well this celebrated case of theatrical censorship can adequately fit any single currently accepted model. Whilst Jonson's professed and visible attempts to castigate those who accused him of sedition as being slanderers themselves – or more pointedly, spreaders of false rumour, which carried legal connotations of sedition – appears to fit well with Kaplan's conception of the public playwright attempting to wrest linguistic control from authority, there is a good deal more complexity evident in *Eastward Ho*'s censorship. For one, the nature of expediency and political circumstance – important factors in the development of legal penalties for slander and sedition – are paramount, as the very nature of the seditious material touching the new Scottish dynasty attests. The willingness of one author to flee the city in (one must assume)

suggest that actors were forced to leave the company when their voices had broken,' and that (despite being atypical) Nathan Field remained with the 'Children' until he was 25. It is thus evident that at least some of the actors in 1605's performance of *Eastward Ho* would have been socially, culturally and legally adults.

fear of the retribution of the state, whilst the remaining two entered prison voluntarily is also worthy of note, as is Jonson's continued royal patronage after the furore of the offensive performance had abated.

What this episode suggests, one might tentatively propose, is not simply a relationship between poet and censor, or even a battle of wits between playwright and state (although both are inarguably factors) but a greater and more expedient performance in which two of the playwrights were willing to work in tandem with the state to resolve an unforeseen moment of political peril caused not only by the writing of conceivably seditious words, but by a period of transition and novelty in the procurement of licence and performance before a sensitive audience. Whilst Jonson and his cohorts (well-schooled in the properties and ethics of satirical expression) are unlikely to have intended offence (and certainly not sedition), the play's performance and the anger levelled at the authors and theatre manager required the public submission of Jonson and Chapman to the law in order to shore up the system of licensing and censorship which had visibly failed. Evidently the pair were willing to play their roles; Marston was less convinced. Such a notion, certainly, is not unfamiliar to scholars of Jonson's work. In the epilogue to his 1614 *Bartholomew Fair*, for example, he appealed directly to the King in judging the play's merits:

> You know the scope of writers, and what store,
> Of leave is given them, if they take not more,
> And turn it into license. You can tell
> If we have used that leave you gave us well;
> Or whether we to rage, or license break,
> Or be profane, or make profane men speak?
> This is your power to judge, great Sir, and not
> The envy of a few.[31]

On first sight an affirmation of the supreme symbol of authority, the King's, power of judgement, Burt discerns Jonson's appeal as tacitly implying 'a set of tensions' between the King and actors who may have 'exceeded' the King's leave, in much the same way that his voluntary admission to

31 Jonson, 'Epilogue,' 1–12.

prison – though outwardly it asserted the state's ultimate authority and 'mutually authorised' poetics and politics, nevertheless exposed a general weakness in the state's ability to fully control dramatic expression.[32] At any rate, the key factors in the *Eastward Ho* affair appear to have been expediency and audience; the historical circumstance of the influx of Scottish nobility to London and the performance at Blackfriars – a playhouse likely to number many of those nobles as patrons.

It is necessary here to pause on the importance of audience in matters of state suppression of dramatic material.[33] As has been noted, the theatre was a site which invited the distaste of a swelling number of reformist (and simply moralist and anti-theatrical) polemicists. Importantly, however, much of the anxiety voiced by those who espoused anti-theatrical sentiments was predicated not primarily on the dangers of playing (although public players were held in contempt) but on those associated with public playhouses, the threat to law and order and the 'social atmosphere of theatres' as much as the content of plays themselves.[34] Philip Stubbes, for example, exempted such plays as could be seen to constitute moral edification, and Margot Heinemann has, in her study of Puritan opposition to drama, identified a majority concession that 'college or Inns of Court plays might be allowable.'[35] Although the content evidently retained a degree of

32 Burt, 'Licensed by Authority,' p. 553.

33 As Gurr (*Playgoing in Shakespeare's London*, pp. 85–6) notes, the word 'audience' harks back 'to its judicial sense of giving a case a hearing.' Recognising the unsuccessful efforts of poets to find a more fitting word to describe the 'feast of the senses which playgoing ought to provide,' Gurr further notes that Elizabethan playwrights 'rated hearing far above seeing as the vital sense for the playgoer.' Jonson, ever sensitive (if apparently not successfully anticipatory) was particularly keen that the wealthier audiences attracted to the Blackfriars would be possessed of 'learned ears' rather than the 'vulgar and adulterate brains which thronged the amphitheatres.' More important than Jonson's failure to tailor his material to his audiences, however, the importance placed on 'hearing' plays offers an interesting dimension on the judicial notion of slander. By being communicated to a third party (however learned), the opportunity for dramatic material to cause offence and invite accusations of slander was unavoidable.

34 Heinemann, *Puritanism and Theatre*, p. 27.

35 Ibid. Here one might recall Gildersleeve's (*Government Regulation of Elizabethan Drama*, p. 22) assertion that Inns of Court dramas (such as *Gorboduc*) were

importance – Stubbes, for example, lauded the 'tragedies and interludes ... being used and practised in most Christian common weals, as which contain matter (such as they may be) both of doctrine, erudition, good example, and wholesome instruction.'[36] Consequently, one might readily conclude that the dramas of the Inns of Court which, despite their revelry, could and did provide instructional and practical legal matter for attendant students were exempt from the criticism applied to the commercial stage.[37]

Similarly, closet dramas – which bypassed the Master of the Revels if publication or staging was not sought, and which relied largely on self-censorship – were not attacked. Far more importance, it seems, was attached to potential disorders attendant on fear of the 'many-headed multitude' congregating to enjoy salacious entertainments.[38] However, as Heinemann has further noted, prosecutions for performances of satirical, slanderous or seditious plays – at least in the late Elizabethan and early Jacobean period – predominantly affected such expensive, indoor theatres as Blackfriars, 'with their greater proportion of lawyers, courtiers and gentlemen up from the country.'[39] To her, this is indicative of a

---

'approved by public opinion.' Even anti-theatricalists, it seems, may have made exceptions.

36 Stubbes, *The anatomie of abuses*, p. 6.

37 The strategy adopted by Norton and Sackville in *Gorboduc* is also worth reasserting. Ruminating on the limits of counsel as well as offering the possibility of interpretation as a lesson to the Queen on the importance of marriage, the play was properly submitted for censorship prior to general publication in print.

38 Heinemann, *Puritanism and Theatre*, p. 32.

39 Heinemann (*Puritanism and Theatre*, p. 38) is correct in her identification of the wealthier patrons of the private theatres. However, her recognition of the fact that the preponderance of prosecutions for seditious plays resulted from those performed in the more hallowed 'hall' theatres is noteworthy. It will be remembered that Jonson himself hoped for a more nuanced and sensitive reception from the wealthy patrons of the 'hall' theatres due to their more discriminating minds. Evidently, his hope was in vain (as the result of *Eastward Ho*'s initial staging was to show). What might therefore be suggested is that, far from guaranteeing a positive reaction from high-ranking playgoers, staging productions in the 'hall' theatres simply opened up the possibility of greater legal retribution should plays cause offence.

'questioning of what the censor could allow: and that in turn narrowed by the growing lack of confidence by city and country in the integrity and dignity of monarch and court.'[40] Yet, whilst issues of public 'confidence' in the ruling elite undoubtedly affected the censor (indeed, the very fact that legal bans on criticism of government officials and the existing Bishops' Ban on satire against influential people existed attest to the desire to quell public discontent), it must be noted that such anxieties were not exclusive to the new King's reign. Rather, it may be posited that censorship, perhaps more than has been previously appreciated, occurred not only at moments of political crisis, but rather, as in *Eastward Ho*'s case, could cause the need for authoritarian retribution by virtue of being not simply shown, but shown to unappreciative, hostile or potentially rebellious audiences (as in the infamous case of the Earl of Essex's staging of *Richard II* on the eve of his abortive coup against Elizabeth's government). As in Star Chamber libel cases, it was the effect that mattered, or even the potential effect, more than the words.

The Jacobean Court's decision to bring all London theatrical troupes under royal patronage certainly encouraged actors and playwrights to 'align the subject matter of their plays in future to suit the tastes of their patrons and protectors in preference to that of humbler citizens' – the suggestion being that the Court sought a theatrical culture which fostered dramatists who would tailor their plays to suit their benefactors and audiences.[41] Dutton has, however, added complexity to this view, noting that whilst acting companies required patronage (granted by letters patent) from noble figures, they did not necessarily reflect or concur with the views of their patrons.[42] At any rate, the necessity of patronage did not end the 'tradition

40 Heinemann, *Puritanism and Theatre*, p. 38.

41 Wickham, *Early English Stages*, p. 94.

42 Dutton, 'Patronage, Licensing, and Censorship,' pp. 75–94. Paul Yachnin ('Reversal of Fortune,' pp. 757–86) has recognised Renaissance plays' frequent engagement with courtly culture and noble values not simply as a sop to the nobility, but as an exercise in economics. In Yachnin's view, the early modern theatre was a virtual marketplace for faux luxury goods (or 'populuxe' culture). Nevertheless, for the purposes of the present study, it must be noted that even playwrights whom Yachnin views as purveyors of 'populuxe' theatre (and he includes Shakespeare) were nevertheless constricted by the laws and regulations (as well as the unpredictability of

of radical criticism in the popular theatres,' and one cannot help but appreciate that the authorities themselves recognised the dangers of playwrights appealing to humbler audiences.[43] Just as Fulke Greville recognised the danger of his play being misread as slanderous by a private, yet powerful courtly audience; just as Elizabeth Cary's presented a cautionary tale of a slanderous female and willing listeners to edify her intended female coterie; just as the Inns of Court were largely spared criticism from moralists or interference from the Master of the Revels; and just as *Eastward Ho* was swiftly suppressed for the anti-Scottish sentiments it presented before a private audience including at least one disgruntled Scot, audiences can be seen to be an enormously important factor in the censorship of slanderous and seditious dramatic material. Hence, it is entirely possible to suggest that any model of censorship must take into account not only the form of drama – be it manuscript, print or staged – but the intended audience. Certainly, in many celebrated incidents, it was a play's reception (intended or otherwise) that resulted in suppression.

If Elizabethan and early Jacobean authorities were keen, as Kaplan has contended, to distinguish drama which threatened to 'criticise and expose' as slanderous (and such is certainly the case with the previously discussed plays by Jonson), there nevertheless remains a plethora of sanctioned plays in which the mechanisms of slander were represented on stage.[44] Jonson's contemporary, Shakespeare, for example, featured slanderers (and their

---

audiences) as those actively seeking approval from patrons. This is a view shared by Whitfield White and Westfall (*Shakespeare and Theatrical Patronage*, p. 2), who identify the need to explore the Elizabethan theatre's mediatory position 'within a web of interdependent, though often discordant, relationships crossing class and regional boundaries and involving kinship ties, political loyalties, and economic transactions.' Thus, the authorities' desire for patrons to influence their acting companies may have been there, but it was more ideal than reality as economic and artistic concerns aided resistance.

43 Heinemann, *Puritanism and Theatre*, p. 35.

44 Kaplan, *The Culture of Slander in Early Modern England*, p. 92. In effect, such depictions may be viewed as commercial, stage versions of Cary's *Mariam*: a play which was never accused of being slanderous or seditious, but instead offered a depiction (and moral lesson) on the mechanisms by which slander was deployed, and its effect on listeners and victims.

effect) in numerous plots, from tragedies to comedies to history plays.[45] In the ongoing pursuit of material evidence for her 'defamation' or 'slander model' of early modern censorship, Kaplan identifies in Shakespeare's *Measure for Measure* (1603–4) an unequivocal example of the poet's attempts to employ 'the state's own methods of exposure to censure the arbitrariness of its response to theatre and, in so doing, demonstrate that the instability of slander is just as likely to humiliate the perpetrator as his intended victim.'[46] Adroitly identifying in Duke Vincentio's admission that Lucio (ostensibly being punished for fornication) is in fact to suffer for 'slandering a prince,' Kaplan considers the play as representing seditious libellers as 'usurping' the state's own authority to deploy slander – here read as any means by which reputation is damaged – in order to 'batter the majority' of subjects into 'submission and silence.'[47] Analogous to the danger inherent in public executions and punishments – namely the risk of the audience sympathising with the condemned in his moment of humiliation – Kaplan asserts that Lucio's punishment for slander rather than fornication 'exposes and calls into question the Duke's own defamatory practices while raising questions about the punishment owing to the more dangerous slanderer.'[48] Certainly, this would have been a notion familiar to Jonson who, as has been noted, viewed slander as leaving an indelible mark akin to branding – a punishment apt to bring those who inflicted it into as much disrepute as those that stood accused.[49]

It is impossible not to draw parallels here with punishments meted out by the Elizabethan and Jacobean regimes against sowers of sedition and accused libellers. John Stubbs' loss of a hand for his *The Discoverie*, indeed, is perhaps the quintessential case of the 'audience' sympathising with the condemned slanderer and questioning the state's right and methods of censure. Further, the notion of the poet drawing attention to authority's

45 Recognising the 'curiously fraught' relationship between the playwrights, Meskill (*Ben Jonson and Envy*, p. 36) offers an interesting critique of what she recognises as envy between the pair.

46 Kaplan, *The Culture of Slander in Early Modern England*, p. 108.

47 Shakespeare, *Measure for Measure*, V.I.2969.

48 Kaplan, *The Culture of Slander in Early Modern England*, p. 106–8.

49 Jonson, 'To The Reader,' 145–54.

attempts to harness slander as its own prerogative was also one well understood and displayed by Jonson (both in his flagrant and public submission in the *Eastward Ho* controversy and in his courtly epilogue to *Bartholomew Fair*). In short, Kaplan's analysis of *Measure for Measure*'s representation of slander-on-stage as one which uses the Duke as a cipher for the state and Lucio as the ostensible slanderer who 'reveals' the hazards of that state's own malicious destruction of character is very likely correct. However, it may be further argued that despite her profitable close reading of the play, Kaplan does not fully appreciate the role of the audience. For audiences, slander against the state, as enacted by the unwitting Lucio, is played for laughs, not sympathy. Part of the humour rests on the fact that no slander technically takes place, because the slanderer spills his criticism and mockery of the Duke not, as he believes, to a third party – 'Lodowick' – but to the Duke himself. The only third party is, therefore, the audience, who are in on the joke.

The damage slander can do to private individuals, however, is played for pathos, with scurrilous stories about, for example, Mariana, slandered before the events of the play by Angelo, making her a tragic figure for much of the story. Audiences do not see Lucio's slanders as truly threatening the state – although Escalus' jittery 'slandering the state!' says much about authorities' fears – and instead see his loose tongue as indicative of a careless fool. This rather calls into question the notion of the play being transgressive (a notion which Kaplan herself posits in her reading of the play's denouement, in which she identifies Shakespeare's recognition that slander's power lies in its instability and inability to be contained whether authorised or not).[50] If there is subversiveness in the Lucio–Duke dynamic, it is ultimately laughed off, the very real horror of Lucio's potential punishment averted and turned into comic retribution against a figure of fun.

Kaplan's examination of *Measure for Measure*'s subversive qualities are understandable given that it articulates the poet-state relationship she is keen to address by means of the dramatic presentation of state versus subject slanderers. On the fact that Shakespeare's play (and the poet himself) did not fall foul of the authorities when, as she admits, Jonson – and earlier,

50 Kaplan, *The Culture of Slander in Early Modern England*, p. 110.

Edmund Spenser – faced accusations of sedition for more vociferously arguing that state criticism was libellous, she is curiously perfunctory.[51] Suggesting that Shakespeare avoided these 'pitfalls' by not accusing the state or insisting on the poet's ultimate right – as 'producer of virtuous discourse' – to determine himself what was legitimate or transgressive language, Kaplan suggests that Shakespeare's presentation of slander's 'instability,' of its slipperiness and the play's ultimate ambiguity, absolve him from state censure. The implication here is that Shakespeare was playing an elusive game with the censors, pushing the limits of criticism of authority whilst retaining a sufficient level of ambiguity to ensure that the whole might appear innocuous.

This verges on overstatement, and there is no reason to imagine Shakespeare was engaged in a battle of wits with authorities which, naturally, he won. Quite simply, the play's content, whilst it questions and interrogates power negotiations as much as any other early modern play, simply does not break the generally accepted principles which guided the actions of Jacobean censors. Drawing on the work of G. E. Bentley (1966), Margot Heinemann has recognised that particularly proscribed (as notable cases of censorship show) were:

1. Critical comments on the policies or conduct of the royal court.
2. Unfavourable representations of friendly foreign powers (including sovereigns, nobles and subjects).
3. Comment on religious controversy.
4. Profanity and oaths (from 1606).
5. Personal satire and influential people.[52]

To this list, Margot Heinemann adds 'a ban on the representation of any (living) ruling sovereign, even if favourable.' At least one of these rules can was broken (or claimed to be broken) in each of the celebrated cases of censorship we have hitherto examined. *Measure for Measure* crosses no such boundaries. It is a play interested in reputations, and in exploring

51 Ibid.

52 Heinemann, *Puritanism and Theatre*, p. 39.

how they are made and how they are broken, it was inevitable that the law, which could protect or destroy them, would play a central role.

In addition to not breaching the code of practice which informed the demonstrable actions of censors, consideration of the play's production history is also needed in order to gain a fuller picture of its presentation of slander against and by authority figures. The earliest recorded performance of the play is St Stephen's Day (26 December), 1605; *Measure for Measure* was a comedy of misrule performed during the traditional festive period of licence. It has been much argued that the licensing of commercial entertainments allowed authorities to 'harness and appropriate potentially unruly energies' and that at least some festive licence was authorised 'in order to contain subversion': that is, to keep entertainments which playfully questioned state authority within the control and under the acceptable limits licensed by the state.[53] This certainly seems to have been the view of James I who, in his *Basilikon Doron* (1603) advises on the necessity for public entertainment:

> In respect whereof, and therewith also to allure them to a common amitie among themselves, certaine days in the yeere would be appointed, for delighting the people with publike spectacles of all honest games, and exercise of armes: as also for conueening of neighbours, for entertaining friendship and heartliness, by honest feasting and merriness: For I cannot see what greater superstition can be in making playes and lawful games in Maie, and good cheere at Christmas.[54]

It is a notion further expounded by Natalie Zemon Davis, who cautions that festive licence, whilst it allowed for a measure of insubordination within state-defined parameters in the belief that this might allow discontent to be vented indirectly, was nevertheless not simply a 'safety valve' used by authority:

> It is an exaggeration to view the carnival and Misrule as merely a 'safety valve,' as merely a primitive, prepolitical form of recreation … the structure of the carnival form can evolve so that it can act both to reinforce order and to suggest alternatives to that existing order.[55]

53 Burt, 'Licensed by Authority,' p. 531.

54 James I, *Basilikon Doron*, p. 128.

55 Zemon Davis, *Society and Culture in Early Modern France*, pp. 122–3.

It is within this paradigm that we might conceivably place *Measure for Measure*'s questioning of the slandered ruler deploying his own 'slanderous' attack on the libeller by using his authority to literally 'defame' his reputation.

The 'order' reached by the end of the play is thus problematic, and merits further discussion. In a play which parodies excessively repressive laws – the criminalisation of fornication – and concludes with the official 'institutionalisation' of that law by means of marriage, we are presented with four couples at the end: of whom the accused slanderer Lucio and the unwanted Kate Keepdown are as problematic a couple as the slandered Mariana and her slanderer, Angelo (who did not wish to marry her, but who was tricked into premarital sex with her). In a sense, order is restored by the legal process of marriage imposed by the central authority, Duke Vincentio. However, as Kaplan has noted, the Duke is himself a somewhat contentious figure, and Lucio's punishment is predicated on his misuse of power to impugn: not for the ostensible crime of fornication, but for offensive speech. So too is Angelo's 'punishment' in marrying Mariana only a punishment because we know he had used slander to malign and reject her. Ultimate order, therefore, is achieved not just by the strict enforcement of law, but by the personal rule of authority to the detriment of the recalcitrant subject. What remains, then, is the visible subjection of the state-accused slanderer to punishment. Whilst, of course, authority (personified in the Duke) cannot be said to be the victor in this presentation – after all, his authority has been parodied by Angelo, he has been comically defamed, and the audience has witnessed the self-satisfying whims which dictate his use of power – that authority nevertheless holds sway. However, the contemporary audiences to which the play was performed (during periods of festive misrule or otherwise) must be taken into account. Elizabethan and early Jacobean theatregoers of even the most common kind were, as illustrated by the evidence found in legal records, no stranger to the rule of law. Many would have been aware of its occasional arbitrariness, the dangers of inviting its wrath, or the possibility of abusing it for personal gain. A litigious people well-acquainted with slander, its uses, punishments, and encroachment on the crime of sedition when uttered or written against the ruling elite, contemporary audiences may well have laughed at witty Lucio, or recognised in Vincentio a ruler bent on deploying defamation himself in the regulation of power – but such figures cannot have been novel. Nor can Lucio's fate have been unexpected, undeserved, or unamusing to those familiar with the systemic operation of absolute rule. Insofar as the play engages with slander and sedition, it is important to reiterate, at the last, that civil slanders are presented as damaging and tragic, whilst slanders against the state are comic to all but the state's governors.

It will, however, be remembered that in addition to being increasingly litigious, Elizabethans and early Jacobeans, of even the humblest origins, were not unfamiliar with the criticism of authority – much to that authority's chagrin, of course. Adam Fox has been instrumental in casting light on the complexity of social relationships which constituted early modern society and in cautioning any facile polarisation of riotous rebels and deferential plebeians. He writes:

> It has been suggested that the façade of paternalism and deference may obscure a reality of animosities, but that we 'catch sight of it only rarely'... Clearly, men and women, no matter how illiterate, were not inarticulate when it came to expressing their opinions and they could do so through a subtle and extremely powerful complex of channels.[56]

Consequently, we can conclude that *Measure for Measure* was not only a play composed to exploit the licence afforded festive misrule, but one which was tailored to a popular audience attuned both to the workings of slander and the order imposed (or insisted upon) by an authoritarian regime. Further, whilst the play certainly explored the state's role in punitively suppressing alleged slander by personal whim and counterattacks on the slanderer's reputation, its subversive nature was mitigated both by its entry in the comedic canon of 'festive license' and the fact that, unlike the verse libels, raillery, mockery, ballads and popular ridicule which attacked the government and its officials, the play offered a benign, humorous and contained exploration and parody of social and legal order as it existed in the period. If one seeks a potentially subversive reading, though, it is worth considering that, in witnessing the Duke's actions and

56 Fox, 'Ballads, Libels and Popular Ridicule,' p. 77.

attitudes, audiences are invited to consider whether laws are independent of the ruler, who is their custodian, or whether they are his playthings. One can imagine that this was a hot topic in theatrical circles with the accession of the new king.

Audiences, it has been seen, played an enormous role in the creation, dissemination and censorship of Elizabethan and early Jacobean drama. When plays were deemed slanderous, it was audiences who were the 'third party.' When slander plots were presented on-stage, however, audiences became privy to the dramatist's (and, if the play was licensed, the censor's) perception of the power and results of slander. By extension, they were invited to consider in dramatic form the ramifications of a social action with which they would have been familiar. One of the most famous slanderers in Shakespeare's canon is Iago, the antagonist of *Othello* (1603). Particularly useful is consideration of Iago's slander, and the effect of his words on Othello (as third party) and Desdemona (as victim). It is clear that Shakespeare does not simply use the process of slander as, as Ina Habermann suggests, a means to dramatise the politics of gender through the formation of the female subject.[57] Rather, the gendered dimensions of the play (primarily the attacks on Desdemona's reputation and her self-fashioning as a 'slandered heroine') are products of Shakespeare's engagement with the trope of slander as a destructive poison which draws its power from the listener's willingness to believe. Certainly, critics have long conjectured the reasons underpinning Othello's head-scratchingly quick acceptance of accusations of his wife's adultery. They include psychological discussion of Othello's subconscious distrust of the woman who had, after all, defied patriarchal authority by eloping, his jealousy of his wife's intercession on Cassio's behalf and even his 'deep rooted inferiority complex.'[58] Lisa Jardine has also convincingly argued that the privacy of Desdemona's protestations of innocence (in counterpoint to the necessary and popular method of declaring innocence of slanderous charges in the courtroom) ensures that the lingering public doubt over innocence hardened into certainty.[59]

57 Habermann, *Staging Slander and Gender in Early Modern England*, pp. 135–41.

58 Stoll, 'Slander in Drama,' pp. 434–5.

59 Jardine, *Reading Shakespeare Historically*, p. 31. In her interpretation of the play, Jardine makes use of records from the Durham ecclesiastical courts in order to

Whatever underlying reasons may be ascribed to the fictional Othello's *volte-face* from loving husband to murderous, alleged cuckold, the fact remains that early modern audiences were presented with this shift. Further, many watching, it will be recalled, would have been familiar with the spread of the most common libels hurled at men (including cuckoldry) and women (sexual incontinence).[60] That Shakespeare's slander plot relies on such commonplace libels is particularly relevant, the public theatre of the late Elizabethan and early Jacobean theatre being marked by a considerable level of social diversity.[61] Both plebeians and the middle classes flocked to public stages and, it may be argued, Shakespeare's use of 'cuckold' and 'adultress' as the base elements of Iago's slanders would have been recognisable as universal libels applicable across the social spectrum (and potentially damaging to all).[62] At any rate, as we have seen, the very nature of slander lay not only in its assault on reputation but in the unfortunate tendency on the part of listeners to believe libellous words.[63]

Othello, unlike *Measure for Measure*, depicts what would have been familiar to audiences as a civil or ecclesiastical slander. Iago falsely accuses Desdemona of adultery; yet the eventual outcome is raised to criminal effect for dramatic purposes. Whilst the denouement of the play, the bloody tableau of deceased victim and third parties, may seem an exaggeration of the effects of the slanderer's ability to destroy, it is a scene which not only

---

underscore the perceived importance of public denials of slanderous accusations. It is worth noting that her recognition of the play's engagement with this importance is well grounded. As Gowing (*Domestic Dangers*, pp. 125–9) has argued, allegations which impugned a woman's sexual morality could have considerable consequences. It is therefore unsurprising that women were increasingly willing to publicly reclaim their reputations in the courtroom.

60 Drawing on the London consistory deposition books, Gowing (*Domestic Dangers*, p. 64) provides a useful table which lists the nature of slanderous words most common between 1572 and 1594, and 1606 and 1640. Unsurprisingly, women were most likely to be accused of being 'whores, jades and queans' whilst men were likely to be accused of cuckoldry, the whoredom of their wives or other specific sex acts.

61 Coddon, 'Slander in an Allow'd Fool,' p. 311.

62 As will be seen, accusations of whoredom were even to provide useful avenues of polemical abuse for those seeking to discredit Queens.

63 Cressy, *Dangerous Talk*, p. 34.

draws power from its overt tragedy, but from its engagement with the likely hyperbolic (but nonetheless powerful) exhortations made by early seventeenth-century defendants in their pursuit of slander suits. Adam Fox recounts, for example, the 1605 Star Chamber case of Henry Cunde, of Shropshire, whose wife Joan was accused of an 'infamous lybelle' in August 1604 which destroyed her marriage and led to her taking 'such inward grief and sorrowe that she presentlye fell sicke and pyned, wasted and consumed away, and shortly afterward dyed.'[64] In presenting his audiences with the gruesome and tragic effects of slander, Shakespeare thus provides both a cautionary tale and a commonplace motif of defamation's power not only to destroy reputations, but to literally end lives.

The cautionary nature of the tale is, perhaps, worthy of further consideration. As has been noted, the play places great emphasis on the dangers associated with the unfortunate propensity of the third party to listen to and accept defamatory words. Arguably, however, in depicting an extreme case of libel's destructive power (in Habermann's slander triad both listener and victim are destroyed and the slanderer silenced – his power removed) Shakespearean audiences were invited to consider the necessity of vigilance in speech, thought and action. It is a matter of record that much of the perceived danger associated with the public stage hinged on the alleged likelihood that the 'hellish confluence of the stage' was liable to encourage audiences to emulate the vices presented than rail against them.[65] It was this form of anti-theatrical belief that Shakespeare, in presenting the vice of slander – a vice he was later to recognise as 'sharper than the sword, [whose] tongue / Outvenoms all the worms of the Nile' – was thus in a position of having to negotiate between criticisms levelled at the presentation of vice and the much-vaunted desire for plays to edify or morally instruct (as well as entertain) through dramatic means.[66]

This negotiation can be seen not only through the structure of the plot and the tragic conclusion, but in the presentation of the figures themselves. Iago, as slanderer, is presented from the outside as a poisoner – he literally

64 Fox, 'Ballads, Libels and Popular Ridicule, p. 75.

65 Anton, *Vices anotimie*, p. 47.

66 Shakespeare, *Othello*, III.4.1751–3.

breaches the peace of the Venetian night by insisting that Brabantio be roused:

> Call up her father,
> Rouse him: – make after him, poison his delight,
> Proclaim him in the streets; incense her kinsmen,
> And, though he in a fertile climate dwell,
> Plague him with flies.[67]

Immediately, Iago is established as disruptive and, in the tradition of accused slanderers, 'poisonous.'[68] In further accord with the legal (and contemporary legal writers') traditional presentation of slanderers as those who subvert established hierarchies, it is also relevant that Iago's early complaints (and the subsequent motives for his actions) include his hatred for Othello, his (military) superior. His role as a meddler in hierarchy is, of course, later converted into physical action by his Machiavellian machinations in having Cassio stripped of his rank. In short, Shakespeare is overt not only in portraying Iago as a slanderer by having him defame Desdemona, but keen to engage with contemporary characteristics of 'the slanderer' as a recognisable type. Similarly, Desdemona is, as Habermann notes, a figure fraught with what critics have often termed inconsistency, but which she herself recognises as a move on Shakespeare's part to elicit audience interest and eventually follow the 'victim pattern' of the innocent, slandered heroine.[69]

However, Desdemona's innocence and submission are not only key to her character, but to the nature of the slander plot. As the civil and ecclesiastical courts accepted the pivotal importance of truth or falsity in slander cases, audience awareness of her innocence (and ultimate death) brings into

67 Shakespeare, *Othello*, I.I.70–4.

68 Alastair Bellany ('The embarrassment of libels,' p. 151) has noted that the perception of slander as a 'poison' was an enduring trope. Commentators such as Thomas Adams were apt to consider slander as a form of oral poison, which passed through the ear and corrupted the soul. Of more pressing concern was the notion that the audience could be 'implicated in the libel's immorality.' Such certainly seems to have been the case for Othello.

69 Habermann, *Staging Slander and Gender in Early Modern England*, pp. 140–1.

stark relief Hamlet's words in Shakespeare's earlier play: 'Be thou as chaste as ice, as pure as snow, thou shalt not escape calumny.'[70] Othello himself displays with gravity the dangers of accepting the words of a slanderer: he laments 'Why he hath thus ensnared my soul and body.'[71] The caution to the audience, therefore, is of allowing slanderous words to trap those who hear them: the result being the destruction of both victim and the listener. Slander, it is shown, is an inescapable fact of early modern life. The danger inherent in the play, however, is not of slandering, but of allowing oneself to be poisoned by the slanderer. Given the prevalence of slander suits in the period – and the fact that the victims brought them forth primarily because their reputations had been defamed and their honour and credit adversely affected, it seems that, as with *Measure for Measure*, Shakespeare was well attuned to both the times and his audience; cautioning a society fraught with slander suits against slander was largely fruitless; turning a deaf ear to those who were bent on malicious destruction was, it seems, the only remedy to the tide of defamers.

One of the key concerns of the commercial stage was the negotiation not simply between playwright and censor, but between playwright, audience and censor. Play manuscripts bound for the commercial stage, it has been seen, could potentially avoid the censor, and it was when they met unreceptive or hostile audiences that some of the most famous cases of theatrical suppression are to be found. The problem was, as Jonson discovered, that audiences could be unpredictable, and even the most exclusive (or rather, expensive) playhouses were apt to result in hostile reactions from those sensitive to rank and stature.[72] Further, playwrights in the Elizabethan and early Jacobean period were increasingly encouraged to tailor their work

70 Shakespeare, *Othello*, III.I.136–7.

71 Shakespeare, *Othello*, V.II.302.

72 Paul Yachnin ('Eye to eye opposed,' p. 80) has noted that, far from being communal experiences, 'the pleasures of playgoing … had more to do with the volatile possibilities of radical individuation than with the experience of sacramamentalised collectivity.' Such a notion, whilst it accounts for the possibilities of negative response from some audience members (made doubly dangerous if they were high-ranking figures) certainly illustrates the problems faced by early modern playwrights in avoiding accusations of slander or sedition.

to the noble figures under whom they were granted patent to perform, as well as to negotiate the virulent charges against the theatre that were brought not just by Puritans, but by anti-theatrical city fathers and a government which increasingly sought to control the output of the playhouses via licence (hence, our records of censorship of the ensuing decades become more voluminous, with such well-known cases as Middleton's *A Game At Chess* [1624]).[73] Authorities increasingly tried to control not drama alone but audiences and their access to theatrical output: by patronising theatre troupes; by controlling the presses which printed play texts; by applying the same laws against printed play texts as existed against other seditious works; and by formally demanding official licence. Censorship of the commonly understood variety – that is, state suppression or editing of plays – happened not only in collaboration with the Master of the Revels before performance (as was the perceived ideal), but reactively, when libellous or seditious works greeted unreceptive or potentially rebellious audiences. In such cases, punishment against authors, the managers of playhouses and actors was the prerogative of the state, despite the voluble efforts of such writers as Ben Jonson to appropriate the right to wield language as the prerogative of the poet. A variety of models of censorship in the public theatre have, of course, attempted to explain the mechanisms by which the state licensed, censored or suppressed dramatic material, but despite each one's merits, it is ultimately impossible to explain the complex and untraceable journeys of a manuscript between poet, actors, playhouse, censor, audience and publisher with any single theory: commercial drama was too much affected by changes in political circumstance, the personalities and motivations of playwrights and officials, the degree of licence given at any one time, the nature and response of the audiences which the play originally reached and, of course, the contents of each individual play.

73 All acting companies required a noble patron (officially endorsed by letters patent from the monarch). Without one, they were deemed to be vagabonds or masterless men.

CHAPTER II

Mastering Language

Slander, when viewed through the lens of Elizabethan and early Jacobean drama, appears in two main ways – those plays which were themselves deemed slanderous or seditious (and which stirred the ire of the state) and those which represented the processes of slander on-stage. Traditionally, the study of censorship has provided the backdrop for the ways in which 'slanderous' dramas have been examined, and the resultant myriad models of the relationship between playwright and state attest to the fact that scholars have been keen to promote explanatory mechanisms by which the production and performance of plays which invited accusations of slander (and subsequent suppression or alteration) were dealt with. As has been seen, such models, whilst each boasting considerable merits, are largely unable to account for the messy, unstable and politically sensitive exigencies of censorship as it operated in practice. It is here worth acknowledging Michelle O'Callaghan's warning that 'there are dangers in completely rejecting a model of state censorship.' Doing so, she continues, can cause censorship to be 'depoliticised, reduced to the micro-level of individual interests … or deemed to be so inefficient that one is left with the impression of a state that is by default capable of tolerating all dissenting viewpoints.'[1] However, as has been seen, this is not a necessary consequence. The problem is one of terminology. 'Censorship,' and extant models of censorship, convey a sense of a recognisable and recoverable system, and the latter in particular tend to focus their scope on specific cultural sites (or suitable examples and media). This is problematic. Different cultural sites exercised different jurisdictions, and even within jurisdictions, the idiosyncratic nature of early modern governance – in many areas of life – ensured that processes were imperfectly

1 O'Callaghan, 'Publication: Print and Manuscript,' p. 92.

systematised. The best any proposed model of theatrical censorship can hope to do is suggest 'this is how regulation was ideally meant to operate in this particular area of dramatic expression.' Even then such a model will likely be excavated from evidence of the breach rather than the practice. It will struggle to take into account the breadth of dramatic production that took place across multiple sites, from the Inns of Court to the private homes of gentry and nobles to provincial innyards to the well-trodden London stages.

Whilst M. Lindsay Kaplan puts forward a persuasive case for playwrights' alleged attempts to wrest the prerogative of mastering language away from authorities, and whilst Richard Dutton's notion of censorship arising when the intermediary Master of the Revels failed to arbitrate adequately between playwright and court can certainly be recognised in certain cases, the fact remains that no single 'model' can account for all cases of state intervention in the politically charged arena of the stage. It is also necessary to recognise that, in the extant models of theatrical censorship of slanderous or seditious material, the emphasis on the poet's relationship with authority excludes the 'third party' central to the process of slander itself: the audience. The nature of early modern audiences was, quite simply, vital to both the playwright and the state: censorship, in the main, was thrust into action not when writers and players produced dangerous or inflammatory material, but when hostile or sensitive audiences were exposed to that material. This dimension to the study of slanderous drama is further underscored by the fact that playwrights themselves showed an acute awareness of the reactions of their audiences: from Fulke Greville's self-censorship following the negative reaction of his small coterie to Ben Jonson's compulsive use of marginalia to preclude the possibility of his plays being misinterpreted.

That existing models of censorship are also prone to restricting their views to the public stage is again of paramount importance. Dramatic material was not confined to the public, commercial stage but, in the late sixteenth and early seventeenth centuries, produced privately for coterie reading 'performances,' composed for performance in the semi-private arenas of the Inns of Court or the court itself, or disseminated illicitly. Naturally, each type of performance brought to the fore its own issues concerning censorship, with the closet drama relying on self-censorship based on audience reaction; the Inns of Court allowed licence by their own appointed Master of the Revels; the Court performance monitored and altered by the official Master of the Revels (and in some cases, altered for performance depending on the nature of the content and the viewers); and the illicit, scurrilous dramas circulated in manuscript governed by the same slander and libel laws which held sway over other seditious writings. Although, as Richard Burt has noticed, the seventeenth century coincided with an increasing lack of distinction between courtly and commercial art, it is clear that, early in James' reign (and throughout Elizabeth's), there existed a sensitivity to audiences which greatly informed playwrights' and authorities' cultural practices.[2]

If audiences – as the ostensible third party to putative slanders – were a key part of the operation of censorship (be it by the poet or the state) in producing material which itself invited accusations of libel or sedition, it is also true that plays which simply represented slanderers were also heavily tailored towards the understanding, recognition and edification of those before whom they were to be performed. From Elizabeth Cary's representation of the female slanderer and female victim of slander to be read by her domestic audience to Shakespeare's licensed, comedic representation of the slanders employed by servant and state (and the resultant use of arbitrary legal punishment by the state), it is abundantly clear that writers whose plays successfully portrayed slander and its effects were attuned to the expectations and cultural knowledge of their audiences. *Othello*'s Iago is a prime example of Shakespeare's deployment of the 'slanderer' figure, with its commonly held connotations of poison, destruction and the danger he poses to order and hierarchy. In short, focusing only on either the role of the censor or those moments when the relationship between poet and state broke down in the historical record of the public stage ignores the complexity of drama's relationship with slander, complicated as it was by different mediums, different audiences, different approaches and different jurisdictions. 'Slanderous' and 'seditious' were not only accusations levelled at plays to which audiences had reacted negatively or the state deemed

2 Burt, 'Licensed by Authority,' p. 543.

inflammatory; slander was a category of cultural currency which provided dramatic plots familiar to audiences increasingly acquainted with the public 'theatre' of the law courts and thus allowed dramatists to engage directly with the expectations, demands and cultural awareness of their patrons.

It must finally be noted that, however spasmodic, unpredictable and porous theatrical regulation was, the theatre and dramatic production did not provide a safe mode of criticising or mocking authority. The government well recognised that there was a thin line between making people laugh contemptuously at authority figures and making them angry enough to rise up, and satire, by its nature, straddled that line. Yet there was evidently a thirst for satirical expression and interrogation of the state, as evidenced by the attempts of poets to test the boundaries of decorous speech and writing (in addition to the perceived necessity of authoritarian attempts to stifle and punish satire). With coterie manuscripts apt to invite accusations of slander even amongst small readerships and theatrically performed and printed drama subject to censorship and/or legal reprisals, it was up to satirists to find alternative means of poetically expressing their views. The emergence of a new literary genre was to cater to this need, and lessons in the success and failure of methods of circumventing censors, indulging in criticism freely and avoiding legal retribution were to be learned from various celebrated episodes of libellous activity in the Elizabethan religious sphere.

PART III

Slander and Sedition in the Elizabethan Church

CHAPTER 12

Slander and Sedition in the Elizabethan Church

With the Elizabethan period coinciding with a veritable boom in litigation and slander suits in the secular courts, and with dramatic production engaging with discourses of slanderous language in a multitude of ways, it is now necessary to turn to one of the central institutional structures in early modern society – the Church. In doing so, we might turn for one last time to the industrious and fictional John in order to consider the various ways in which slander, sedition, and religion collided.

1. John calls his neighbour, Alice, a whore. Alice might well take him to task in the ecclesiastical courts under the jurisdiction of canon lawyers. The crime, after all, is spiritual. Lucky for John, Alice is of no particular political importance or fame, and so he has not – as he might have done had he traduced Queen Elizabeth – broken any felony statutes.
2. John calls his neighbour, Alice, a whore and a thief. Ecclesiastical and canon lawyers might well engage in a battle over whether secular or church courts have jurisdiction – and Alice herself might strongly prefer one or the other depending on the remedy she seeks.
3. John is a Catholic. His religion is either proscribed or discouraged (depending on the decade) but he spreads books he did not write which accuse the Queen and the state's governors of heresy. Whether the authors can be found and punished or not, he is liable to be prosecuted and the books banned (if they are not already). Depending on the year of his activities, the authorities in charge of printed matter will vary.

4. John is a Catholic. He spreads books accusing the Queen and the state's governors in manuscript form. He would be very unlikely to use his own name, but the book would swiftly be banned. If he were caught (whichever name he used) he would be subject to increasingly severe potential penalties under a number of statutes.
5. John is a Catholic. He spreads books calling for the return of Catholicism and defaming Protestant ministers but insists that he holds a true and faithful allegiance to the Queen and state. If caught, the alleged effects of his spreading slander will likely rouse the ire of authorities.
6. John is an extremely reformist Protestant – a Puritan. He spreads printed books or writings defaming the established Church and its leaders in print or manuscript forms. If the former, the high ecclesiastical authorities will be increasingly empowered to respond to him and, if in the latter, efforts will likewise be made to locate him and use either the breaching of licensing laws or felony statutes to bring him to task.

As we have seen, far from being the bawdy stuff of dispute, slanderous language was recognised as having perlocutionary force. It could break the reputations of the lesser or greater in society; it could influence politics; it could provoke civil unrest; and it could play a role in creating drama and providing dramatic instruction. So too could it be put to use in the fraught religious sphere, and in doing so draw on all of its rhetorical possibilities. As the state was interested in slander and sedition as legal issues (whether crimes or torts) and poets sought an ever-increasing stake in language regulation, the politico-religious nature of the times absolutely demanded the Church maintain an interest in what people were saying that they shouldn't be. Many of those who shouldn't be saying what they did were equally interested in religion. Luckily for the Church, it had a long and chequered history of arbitrating dangerous speech and writings.

Wedded (though not always harmoniously) to the state since its inception, the reformed Anglican Church followed the lead of its predecessor (the increasingly abhorred Roman Catholic Church) not only in certain (often contested) customs and beliefs, but in retaining jurisdiction over certain categories of defamatory activity.[1] Indeed, although the foundational basis of slander as a transgression in English legal history is tangled, the Catholic ecclesiastical courts of the Middle Ages had most certainly exercised judgement over all suits which did not demand civil redress – staking a claim, as Helmholz records, to jurisdiction over defamation from the thirteenth century onwards.[2]

Once considered a primarily moral offence (and therefore within the purview of the ecclesiastical courts), slander had, as we have seen, become a lucrative source of income for civil lawyers (and the successful recipients of damage suits) by the age of Elizabeth. Nevertheless, throughout the period the church retained judicial power over moral misdemeanours, and hence the power to try slanderers who accused their victims not of temporal crimes, but of 'sins.'[3] As a consequence, the records of the English ecclesiastical courts (also known as the 'courts spiritual' or, more colourfully, the 'bawdy courts') are filled with defamation suits ('defamation' being the ecclesiastical counterpart of secular 'slander' and 'libel' in legal parlance) brought against those falsely accusing neighbours and acquaintances of moral crimes.[4] Defamation cases, therefore, are rife in the records of the spiritual courts, proceeding as they did alongside more mundane breaches

1 One might legitimately question how useful is the term 'Anglican,' given that it is, as Collinson (*The Elizabethan Puritan Movement*, pp. 26–7) notes, anachronistic. A better term, probably, would be 'conformist.' This study will follow Collinson's use of the term, which acknowledges its usefulness for the scholar in differentiating the established, conservative Church of England from 'the hotter sort' of Protestantism. For thorough discussion on the birth of Anglicanism and Puritanism in the period, see Collinson's *Richard Bancroft and Elizabethan Anti-Puritanism* (2013).

2 Helmholz, *Select Cases*, p. lii.

3 In a useful and comprehensive overview of the early modern ecclesiastical courts, Martin Ingram ('Religion, communities and moral discipline,' p. 3) notes the quirks in Elizabethan terminology. 'Sin and crime,' he argues, 'were not clearly differentiated.' Hence, one finds accusations of 'moral crimes' such as adultery and fornication (and, hence, defamatory accusations of the same).

4 Defamation suits in the ecclesiastical courts were dealt with as suits between opposing litigants – rather like civil actions in the secular courts. See: Ingram, 'Religion, communities and moral discipline,' p. 3.

of canon law – from whoredom and marriage without the requisite banns to playing football in the churchyard at the time of evening prayer and, quite remarkably, 'casting things at the maides in sermon tyme and sticking feathers on a maides wastcoate.'[5]

In his study of the Elizabethan legal system using records from Essex as evidence, F. G. Emmison elaborates on the criteria that determined which court should properly have jurisdiction in cases of defamation, concluding that 'only if slanderous speech bore on the moral character of the plaintiff could the Church courts prosecute; though it was asserted, but not always maintained, that they had cognizance in all cases when a minister was defamed.'[6] Further, if the slander contained both moral and temporal offences, the action lay in the secular courts, although, as expected, a plethora of exceptions and curious distinctions litter the legal record. At any rate, the result of a stricter adherence to the punishment of slanderers whose words pertained to spiritual offences was, as Helmholz has noted, the disappearance from the Church courts of causes involving slanderous imputations of crimes punishable by the secular courts.

However, despite the spirited proposals of radical reformers who wished to strip the ecclesiastical courts of all jurisdiction over defamation, litigation within the church flourished. Indeed, the remedy offered by the ecclesiastical courts broadened, as the sixteenth century witnessed the Church's increased jurisdiction over cases which not only tended towards the false accusation of moral offences, but which included merely abusive language. It is therefore unsurprising to find cases (although in a relative minority) from the Church court records in which accusations of

5 Hair, *Before the Bawdy Courts*, p. 87.

6 Emmison, *Morals and the Church Courts*, p. 48. Questions here arise as to the representativeness of Emmison's sample. Drawing on Ingram's discussion of the Diocese of York and the Consistory Court of Chester (as well as his own study of the records of Wiltshire and Salisbury), however, it is clear that defamation suits increased (to varying degrees) in regions across the country (Ingram, 'Religion, communities and moral discipline,' p. 299). Furthermore, whilst the numbers of suits and the discipline of clerics fluctuated regionally, the courts' focus on moral lapses remained the same. See: Ingram, 'Religion, communities and moral discipline,' p. 13; Marchant, *The Church Under the Law*, pp. 230–1.

'hypocrisy,' 'drunkness' and 'crafty knavery' were brought before judges.[7] Though defamation was never destined to provide the principle source of litigation in the Church courts, actions against the speakers of defamatory words thus remain a not unfamiliar sight in the legal record of the period.

Certainly, such cases have provided a rich source of material for scholarly endeavours. Tracing the language of insult in early modern London, Laura Gowing has identified amongst the records of London's primary ecclesiastical court, the Consistory court, hundreds of defamation cases and, in so doing, has recognised the preponderance of gendered insults (with cases often fought between women).[8] The Church courts, certainly, held a monopoly on defamation suits dealing with accusations of female sexual misconduct. Gowing's work has provided a much-needed analysis of the ways in which gender – and gendered insult – were crucial in the construction of reputation and the means by which defamation could undermine it and shame others into conformity.[9] This raises the issue of whether defamatory speech, particularly when it attacked reputation through allegations of spiritual crime, was considered a feminine mode of expression, and thus words (particularly anonymous written ones) which alleged sexual misconduct of religious or political figures might have involved women as collaborators or writers. The possibility of women providing grist for male writers bent on satirising and slandering religious and secular authorities will certainly offer scholars room for consideration in future studies.

Yet much remains to be considered within the wider framework of the Church courts and their relationship with defamation. Through the analysis of records from the Consistory courts as well as those of the Archdeaconry, it is possible not only to examine the variant ways in which the Church courts treated defamation suits in comparison to their civil counterparts, but to account for differences in the remedies provided and assess the likely

7 Helmholz, *Select Cases*, p. xlv.

8 Gowing, *Domestic Dangers*, p. 1.

9 Ingram ('Religion, communities and moral discipline,' p. 3) notes that, whilst the Church courts' ostensible aim was to reform culprits, punishments often amounted to 'a deeply humiliating experience designed to deter others and give satisfaction to the congregation for the affront of public sin.'

reasons underpinning the bawdy courts' perennially popular role in defining (and exercising authority over) certain categories of defamatory language.

The relationship between slander and the church is a complex one due to the convoluted and labyrinthine means by which the ecclesiastical authority of the Middle Ages gradually shifted towards the limited jurisdiction over defamation exercised by the Elizabethan 'bawdy courts.' Before and throughout the early modern age, the established church (be it the Catholic church of the pre-Reformation years or the reformed church in its various guises) posited itself as the true, state-sanctioned Church of England.[10] Slander, therefore, provided a useful tool in the arsenal of the state church, which could, and did, engage various voices and media in an attempt to denigrate its equally vituperative enemies. Compelled to fight fire with fire, the Elizabethan government engaged with an enemy prepared to flout the law in drastic and vitriolic ways: in the 1580s, one enterprising Catholic recusant even managed to set up an illicit press within the walls of London's Clink prison.[11] Here, a concession was likely being made to an established tradition of religious invective. Where once the most vocal adherents of Catholicism had courted favour in tracts denouncing heretical reformist beliefs (often, as in the case of Thomas More's writings against Luther, including vitriolic personal attacks), by the late sixteenth century, religious authority in England had swung from Catholic to Protestant. Hence, it is no surprise to find a slew of slanderous invectives between

10 Whilst the ecclesiastical courts under Elizabeth sought communal unity and operated on the presumption that the English Church 'embraced the whole of the nation,' it is necessary to note that 'adherents of the Catholic faith implicitly rejected this notion.' It was only in the later years of Elizabeth that the courts were to find themselves in a 'much more stable religious environment' (Ingram, 'Religion, communities and moral discipline,' p. 84–5). Ralph Houlbrooke (*Church Courts and the People*, pp. 4–6) has also noted the important difference in regional ecclesiastical operation, with vigorous Protestantism in East Anglia ensuring a greater degree of acceptance of the Church courts whilst regions such as Winchester (thinly populated and possessed of poor lines of communication) was to become a hotbed of Catholic recusancy. Further, certain parishes were known to have radical or Catholic sympathies, which Houlbrooke (p. 166) discusses with reference to their finances.

11 Lake, 'The Politics of Popularity,' p. 68; Cooper, *The Queen's Agent*, p. 186.

Catholic and Anglican (as well as against and from various sects of the latter) which are consistently marked by the positing of the writer as arbiter of truth and the victim as false heretic. To Catholics, Elizabeth herself provided a popular target of opprobrium in matters religious, whilst the Pope remained inimical to Protestants of varying factions; yet whatever the source or target, the cutting pens of religious fanatics invariably found defamatory language (of the kind usually punishable by either civil or Church courts) a reliable and effective bulwark to theological argument. The scurrility of the former, it seems, was absolved by the truth of the latter.

However, the slanderous activity of factional Protestants and Catholics was not combatted simply by governmental censorship. On the contrary, government officials themselves were to provide a range of anti-extremist discourses which were themselves quite capable of descending into slanderous invective. In fact, Alastair Bellany notes that 'Popery, in its foreignness and otherness, threatened, and hence, of course, helped to constitute, an essentially Protestant England.'[12] The result was, as will later be seen, a jostling for control of public opinion, with a regime 'happy to do so through a variety of media – printed pamphlets, ballads, the planting and circulation of news and rumour – a fairly straightforward trail which led straight back to the Privy Council and its agents.'[13] Catholic agents tried a number of strategies: the importation of books defaming the Queen and high-profile members of her Council; the spread of false news (such as the strength of support amongst the downtrodden Catholic laity for Spanish invasion); and even songs accusing high-profile 'hate figures' in the government. All were anathema, and whispers of any had to be investigated with what resources were available. A ballad sung against the Queen's secretary, Robert Cecil, accusing him of engineering the death of the Earl of Essex might be no more than disgruntlement amongst Londoners, or it might be the beginning of a more successful coup. Insulting words daubed on the gates of the secretary's townhouse might be the work of Catholics breeding popular discontent with a supposed *regnum cecilianum*, or mere words of abuse. The Privy Council could never be sure. The result, therefore, was a

12 Bellany, 'The embarrassment of libels,' p. 60.

13 Lake, 'The Politics of Popularity,' p. 68.

series of campaigns throughout the Elizabethan period which pitted the official might of authority (in various guises and through various secretly sanctioned intermediaries) with unlicensed enemies beholden of illicit presses and apt to be besmirched as the heretical, anti-Christian other.

The material which issued from illicit presses is further of note. The control of the High Commission – the supreme ecclesiastical court in England from the Reformation until its abolition in 1641 – over print was to have enormous repercussions for the ways in which this particular arm of state authority was caparisoned in legitimacy.[14] Further, it was a legitimacy which it could extend to licit, printed religious discourses whilst tacitly defaming the writers of unlicensed, non-conformist or Catholic texts and tracts as criminal malfeasants. Thus, the nature of the Church's relationship with slander is bound up not simply with ecclesiastical authority over false accusations of moral crime, but with a wider struggle against Catholicism and non-conformity, as the established Church fought to secure its authority over illicit language by espousing truth and legitimacy and counter-slandering attacks from Catholics and non-conformists alike.

14 Unfortunately, the legal records of the London High Commission have been lost.

CHAPTER 13

Defamation in the Ecclesiastical Courts

Defamation (the legal term especially associated with slanderous speech and writing in the Church courts) remained a staple in the various ecclesiastical courts of England throughout the Elizabethan and early Jacobean period. Like the royal and common law courts, the ecclesiastical courts comprised a hierarchical network of jurisdictions, from the Archdeaconry courts (which dealt primarily with local matters) to the Bishops' or Consistory courts (which encompassed the Bishops' dioceses and could be subdivided into smaller, Commissary courts) and the prerogative courts of the English Archbishops. Symbolising the link between sovereign and church was also the inquisitorial court of High Commission (a by-product of the Reformation), convened at the will of the sovereign and possessing significant power over both civil and religious matters. In sum, the jurisdiction of the ecclesiastical courts extended to, as Ingram suggests, 'some of the most intimate aspects of the personal life of the population as a whole.'[1]

Dealing with a range of moral offences from adultery, heresy, prostitution, recusancy and, of course, defamation, the role of the Church courts (the most active Archdeaconry and Consistory courts bearing the unenviable appellation, 'the Bawdy Courts') in the post-Reformation period was one of contestation. Radical proposals to strip the Church of all jurisdiction over defamation, in particular, were debated in sixteenth-century legal tracts and it was only after the Elizabethan Settlement (1559) that the remit of the Anglican Church courts stabilised (although attacks continued from the common lawyers who plied their trade in a rival concern).[2] Writing in 1583, Thomas Smith recognises the ecclesiastical courts as being the domain of

1 Ingram, 'Religion, communities and moral discipline,' p. 1.

2 Helmholz, *Select Cases*, p. xlv.

> the Archbishops and Bishops [who] have a certaine peculiar jurisdiction unto them especially in foure manner of causes: Testamentes and legations, marriage and adulterie or fornication, and also of such things as appertaine to orders amongest themselves and matters concerning religion ... So those matters be ordered in their Courts, and after the fashion and maner of the lawe civil or rather common by citation, libel.[3]

By this time, libel and slander suits had emerged as blossoming sources of litigation in the secular courts. It is therefore no surprise to find 'libel' somewhat of an afterthought in Smith's assessment of the Church courts, with the majority of his writing on the 'court which is called spirituall' focusing on the idealised boundaries between civil and ecclesiastical law. At any rate, it is impossible to ignore the attempt made to neatly demarcate the correct powers of each type of court in a manner which almost certainly did not mirror the actual means by which litigant sought justice and redress.

Crucially, for the legal development of defamation (and unlike in the slander suits familiar in the common law courts) the ecclesiastical courts did not subscribe wholeheartedly to the ancient, canon law of *Auctoritate dei patris*, which had, since the inception of English defamation law in 1222, held that defamation took place 'when a crime was maliciously imputed ... for the sake of hatred, profit, or favour, or for whatever other cause ... to any person who is not of ill fame among good and substantial persons.'[4] Whilst the Common Pleas, especially, increasingly demanded the false imputation of a punishable crime under the rule of *Mitior Sensus* (which sought to stem the flow of personal suits between rowing neighbours), the Church courts exercised a far greater degree of laxity in accepting actions for defamation. As a direct consequence, the records of the ecclesiastical

3 Smith, *De Republica Anglorum*, p. 61.

4 Ecclesiastical law in the Elizabethan and early Stuart periods was based mainly on pre-Reformation ecclesiastical law, which derived from the following three sources: the *Corpus juris canonia*, the *corpus juris civilis*, and ecclesiastical common law. However, Habermann (*Staging Slander and Gender*, p. 43) notes that the application of *auctoritate dei patris* was 'narrower than the Roman law concept of *iniuria*, where any abuse that damaged a person's good name was actionable. Hence, if it could be proven that the alleged words were actually spoken, the defendant would claim to have spoken in anger or jest, but not maliciously.'

courts (which are, unfortunately, often incomplete and usually comprise only the 'presentment,' or preliminary accusation) are replete with charges amounting to what Emmison terms 'abuse rather than defamation.'[5] Arising from the 'ubiquitous welter of parochial gossip and intrigue,' it is common to find amongst the extant records cases in which suits against slanderers who had allegedly made accusations of knavery were heard in tandem with those who had falsely imputed whoredom and cuckoldry.[6]

Further, accusations of defamation encompassed wordless behaviour. It is not uncommon to find a reputed slanderer brought before the Church courts accused of having attached horns to the house of a married man – the joking symbol of having an unfaithful wife. Such intolerance of the physical actions of the defamer in the Church courts, coupled with the overwhelming preponderance of suits brought for slanderous utterances, serve to remind us that the writing of libellous words between the lower orders (a relatively rare phenomenon in itself) tended to fall under the common law rather than canon law. Evidently, it seems, the Church courts provided a readier ear for warring neighbours involved in local and domestic disputes of the verbal and symbolic variety than did the civil courts. However, the hanging of 'cuckold's horns' is worthy of further consideration – not least for the glimpse it offers into the practice of non-verbal slanderous activity. Although suits involving sexual slander were predominantly fought between those of middling rank, the Church courts remained popular sites for various plebeian (and thus not necessarily literate) litigants.[7]

5 Emmison, *Morals and the Church Courts*, p. 48.

6 Ibid.

7 Ingram, *Church Courts, Sex and Marriage in England*, p. 319. Ingram ('Religion, communities and moral discipline,' pp. 177–93) also provides a useful account of the diversity of litigants who sought justice in the Church courts. Noting the 'different kinds' of plebeian litigant, he recognises that 'even within economically or topographically distinct regions, there was considerable diversity of economic and social development at the parochial level.' We must not, therefore, entirely assume that those hanging horns on the doors of neighbours were illiterate, but it certainly possible.

Whether those who hung horns on their neighbours' doors were literate or not, the action itself suggests another dimension of slander. Slanderers, it seems, did not have to be vocal or literate in order to tear at the social fabric. They could sow discord in the community through covert, symbolic action. The interception and defacement of private property is of particular importance. As Andrew Gordon has argued, the casting of written libels through and above doorways 'appropriated thresholds' and served to 'reconfigure radically the relationship between space and authority, challenging control over both the security and the significance of the civic topography.'[8] Here, the libel is non-written and non-verbal, and on a domestic scale; nevertheless, the principle remains the same. By affixing horns to the doorway of a dwelling, the slanderer exhibited an ability not only to disrupt communal harmony non-verbally, but to expose the vulnerability of the domestic sphere. Not only did his or her actions covertly impute the moral failings of a man's wife (and hence his inability to control her), but they demonstrated before the community his inability to protect his own home.

Given the Church courts' common adherence, however, to the letter of canon law, it may seem somewhat paradoxical that their willingness to tolerate a wider range of actions for defamation grew. The answer probably lies in the perceived weakening in the jurisdiction of the courts by both reformers and rival courts and the subsequent need of the Church courts to retain relevance in people's daily lives. It is entirely possible that, in order to maintain authority over defamation and ensure steady business, the Church courts were compelled to offer litigious parishioners a ready means of bringing a wide variety of suits – although, admittedly, the suggestion is somewhat speculative. The demand in which the Church courts found themselves may also be attributed to such varied reasons as the cheaper costs of litigation; the desire of litigants to receive apologies and penitential satisfaction (rather than financially crippling) their neighbours; the power of the Church to bestow good reputation on parishioners; or the willingness of the Church courts to play a mediatory role in disputes.[9]

8 Gordon, 'The Act of Libel,' p. 386.

9 Gowing and Crawford (*Women's Worlds in Seventeenth-Century England*, pp. 10–11) note that 'central courts such as the Star Chamber and King's Bench

Ecclesiastical courts were not second-rate; they wielded real power in communities. Further, the willingness to adjudicate in cases of simple abuse and pejorative words was frequently tempered, in legal procedure, by an almost fanatical observance of canon principles.

As noted, the incomplete nature of the majority of Church court records has ensured that the full processes and outcomes of many cases are unavailable. Nevertheless, the basic procedures involved in suing at the ecclesiastical level are well recorded. Paul Hair, in his compilation of Archdeaconry court records, provides a useful overview of the process by which litigation in the Church courts proceeded.[10] In a manner not dissimilar to the methods of the civil courts, the familiar course of action was the presentment of a charge, answer, evidence, decision, penalty and response. Typically, the presentment would be made by either churchwardens or clergymen at a 'visitation' to the district or parish by an Archdeacon or Bishop (such visitations occurring, at the minimum, annually). Such presentments then formed the basis of cases in the Church courts, presided over, in the main, by Vicar Generals, Chancellors, Commissary General Auditors or other clergy to whom the task was often delegated by the Bishop or Archdeacon. The general method of proceeding was, it will be noted, broadly similar throughout the country – although naturally defamation suit levels and the diligence of those involved in the process differed regionally.[11] Of key interest to the scholar, however, is not the process of

---

tended to deal with richer litigants and cases on appeal. Ingram (*Church Courts, Sex and Marriage in England*, pp. 317–18) makes the point that, whilst defamation suits increased in the Church courts, they never got out of hand. He attributes this, in part, to the length of the process which saw suits often settled or discontinued 'when rancour evaporated or money ran out.' The ecclesiastical courts, it seems, served to play an important role as a release valve for parochial tensions.

10 Hair, *Before the Bawdy Courts*, pp. 18–19.

11 Using the Dioceses of Norwich and Winchester, Ralph Houlbrooke (*Church Courts and the People*, pp. 38–54) provides an excellent delineation of the procedures of the two regions' ecclesiastical courts. In so doing, he recognises that 'every system of judicial procedure is open to abuse,' with much depending on the calibre of those who operate in it and the spirit in which they approach their work. Norwich, in particular, he notes, was the victim of a 'loosening of judicial control over inferior scribes and lawyers.' Further, the levels of punishment varied from

Church courts, but rather the wealth of indirect oral evidence recorded by churchwardens, registrars and scribes of the courts. Indeed, the surviving records are fruitful in their documentation of phrases and epithets spoken by those charged with 'defaming laymen and abusing clerics.'[12] As a consequence, it is possible to trace the types of language which proved of interest to the Church and the general means by which Church lawyers (often proctors or advocates) presented the victims of defamation in order to win favour with the court.

A scant year after the accession of Elizabeth I, the Consistory court in the diocese of Exeter heard a defamation case brought by one John Kingwell against his neighbour, Robert Taylor, of which the presentment survives. Opening in the typical rhetoric of the ecclesiastical courts, the framing of the charge begins:

> In the name of God Amen. Before you, the venerable and eminent M. John Blaxton, B.Cn.L., vicar general in spiritualities of his lordship the reverend in Christ, James, by divine permission lord bishop of Exeter, and official principal of his Episcopal consistory of Exeter, or other judge competent in this matter whomsoever, the honourable John Kingwell complainant asserts, alleges and in this writing proposes judicially in articles against and in opposition to Robert Taylor of Morton, of the diocese of Exeter.[13]

court to court, with 'social offences more severely punished than church offences in the Archdeaconry courts.' For the purposes of this study, Houlbrooke's assertion must be borne in mind – in the case of Kingwell and Taylor, presiding Bishop James Turbeville had reason to approach his duties in stout spirit.

12 Emmison, *Morals and the Church Courts*, p. xii. A note of caution has been expressed by Gowing and Crawford (*Women's Worlds in Seventeenth-Century England*, p. 10) concerning the reliability of scribes in accurately transcribing the words of obloquy spoken by litigants. They note that Church court records 'record, in English, the responses of witnesses, accusers or accused to questions by JPs. They are mostly, but not always, written in the third person … [but] their fidelity to the spoken word cannot be assumed; there is always some mediation by the JP, questioning, and the clerk, writing down a form of the answer. Nevertheless, they represent a version of how women and men told [their] stories.'

13 Helmholz, *Select Cases*, p. 16.

Conventional though the language of the law is, it is necessary to look through the formal, legal verbiage in order to uncover the ways in which such rigorous attention to the estate, status and hierarchy of the early Elizabethan Church sought to cement its authority and position. Emphasis, most certainly, is placed upon the 'divine permission' granted the Bishop in his office in addition to the 'official' sanction of his role in the Church. The incumbent in this case, James Turberville, was to be deprived of his office within a year, having declined the Oath of Supremacy: he being a noted opponent of the Elizabethan Settlement and a leading Marian Bishop.[14] Certainly, the early years of Elizabeth were marked by religious uncertainty. The Queen herself entertained petitions that sought gradual abasement of those who had stood in high favour in the reign of her late sister, had opposed the transference of wealth from church to crown, and who had shown opposition to the desire to carry reform further.[15] Turberville it seems was ingloriously associated with all three. It is therefore not inconceivable that the explicit references to Turberville's divine and official standing (which, even by the standards of later and earlier ecclesiastical court records, are prodigious) represent an example of the ways in which the Church courts could be used as a political arena.[16] Here, the formulaic language appears to have provided a useful tool in shoring up the authority of a weakened officiating figure.

Interestingly, the preamble includes also a pointed reference to the necessity of the imputation of a crime:

> Imprimis to wit, that there was and is a certain constitution of the PROVINCE of Canterbury which begins *Auctoritate dei patris omnipotentis etc.*, in which it is provided and established that each and all members and subjects of the province of Canterbury who for the sake of hatred, profit, or favour, or for any other cause,

14 Oliver, *Lives of the Bishops of Exeter*, pp. 136–7.

15 Whiting, *The Blind Devotion of the People*, p. 231; Hurst, 'The Elizabethan Settlement,' p. 679.

16 For comparable court records which show the differing styles of language employed regarding religious authorities, see Helmolz, *Select Cases*, pp. 2–26. Of the thirty records relating to ecclesiastical courts, which include a range of regions including York, Norwich and Stopham (from 1290 to 1593), none grant the same level of overt respect for the office of the officiating cleric.

> maliciously impute a crime to any person whereby he is defamed among good and substantial persons, by reason of which purgation at least is awarded to him or he is harmed in some other manner were and are by the culpability bound *ipso facto* by the sentence of major excommunication promulgated in the said constitution of the province of Canterbury.[17]

As has been established, the constitution of *Auctoritate dei patris* was one not strictly adhered to in the Church courts. Several conclusions may be drawn here, the likelihood being that a combination of all may explain the concise summary of the fundamental values of the constitution.

Firstly, it may be argued that, in the middling years of the sixteenth century, the laxity for which the courts were to be known in their handling of suits which crossed the boundary from defamation into abuse was not yet fully established. Perhaps more convincingly, however, is the notion that rules and constitutional dogmas were practised with differing rigor according to region. This is a view well recognised by historians such as Ralph Houlbrooke, whose work on the ecclesiastical court records of Norwich prompts him to recognise a diocese in which things 'went badly wrong.'[18] Similarly, Martin Ingram has recognised the regional variation present in the 'disciplinary machine for the supervision of moral and religious behaviour' as it operated in sites such as York, Wiltshire and Salisbury.[19] Certainly, the overt and frequent references to the 'province of Canterbury' are indicative of an acceptance of local variation; and as E. R. Brinkworth persuasively alleged in his history of the antiquarian study of Church court records, local ecclesiastical courts could and did vary greatly in efficiency and just dealing.[20] We might therefore identify a link between the somewhat chaotic development (and treatment) of slander in the common law courts – which were often hampered by overlapping jurisdictions and pragmatically opportune interpretations of the law – with the Church's acceptance of the vagaries of interpreting canon law. It is a point well grounded, as 'the

17 Helmholz, *Select Cases*, p. 16.
18 Houlbrooke, *Church Courts and the People*, pp. 43–53.
19 Ingram, *Church Courts, Sex and Marriage in England*, pp. 13, 22.
20 Brinkworth, 'The Study and Use of Archdeacons,' p. 107.

two court systems … travelled a parallel road.'[21] A winding and rather broken road it was.

The presentment continues with a useful – if prolix – definition of defamation as it pertains to ecclesiastical jurisdiction: namely, the (proclaimed) 'abuse, vituperation or calumnious, opprobrious, injurious, contumelious, disparaging, slanderous and defamatory words or other words whatsoever against public morals sounding or tending to the defamation, denigration, derogation or depreciation of the good fame of any person.' The emphasis, it will be noted, is on the damage (or injury) caused by slanderous words not on the business of a man, but on his 'good fame.'[22] This notion is to provide an especially useful defence of the plaintiff in the presentment as, after the typically characterised 'false, wicked and malicious' accusations of witchcraft are described (taking place, as was common, 'before neighbours'), considerable pains are taken to establish the previous good fame of the slandered Kingwell. He was, as the record asserts, 'previously in no way defamed,' and yet the utterance of the abusive and defamatory words did 'grievously injure and diminish the status and good fame of the same John Kingwell, and good and substantial persons have ascribed and given the same less faith and favour by reason of the aforegoing.' If the vehement references to the prior fame of the plaintiff seem a conventional means of establishing the previous good character of Kingwell, it is no accident. Under the dictates of canon law, the notion of *infamia* was one which undoubtedly helped shaped the English remedy. English cases required that the plaintiff be of good fame prior to the imputation of a crime, and it was not uncommon for the representatives of those bringing defamation suits to make manifest their previously pristine reputations in words culled directly from sections of the canonical texts dealing with *infamia*.[23] Similarly, the 'good and substantial' persons before whom Kingwell was accused of

21 Helmholz, *Select Cases*, p. xlvii.

22 It is useful here to note Laura Gowing's discussion of the effects of slander; 'in a largely oral world,' she argues, 'people were what they said.' This may be linked to attitudes found in statute and common law – namely, the importance placed not on the content of what was said, but the intended and actual effects of language. See: Gowing, *Domestic Dangers*, pp. 125–33.

23 Helmholz, *Select Cases*, p. xxi.

witchcraft are so described in order to meet the principle of *cum infamatus non sit apud bonos et graves*: that is, in order to give rise to remedial harm, the words must have been spoken before persons whose good opinion was worth having.

As such, the vernacular of the presentment provides a useful textual artefact which illustrates the judicial strategy favoured by ecclesiastical lawyers in framing suits according to canon law and precedent. The highly formulaic use of language may also, it must be stressed, represent not only a skilled lawyer's exhibition of legal knowledge, but a highly literate acknowledgement of the Church's provenance in matters of canon law and authority over defamation. It is, further, a timely attempt to bolster the status of the Church, emerging as it does from a period of religious uncertainty in which a nascent core of highly placed Protestant laymen were vociferously expounding the importance of expelling the clergy from the political stage and 'reshaping the ecclesiastical structure to that of the state ... conceiving of the advancement of religion in terms of an international power struggle.'[24] It is here worth noting, also, the relatively recent reappraisal of the status and usage of the canon law in the post-Reformation Church court. Long held to have met an unceremonious end with the Reformation, the practice of canon law has, as the revisionist work of Helmholz has shown, proven that ecclesiastical lawyers kept continental canon law a 'living law' until its eventual overhaul in the seventeenth century's 'Long Parliament.'[25] As a consequence, the much-hoped for reforms in ecclesiastical court proceedings, which had been touted since 1534, remained largely the contentious pleas of such ardent reformers such Robert Beale, who engaged in vituperative criticism of the 'Romish' precepts of the existing canon law.[26] Instead, the ecclesiastical courts bowed only to reformist pressure in acceding to the

24 MacCaffrey, 'Elizabethan Politics: The First Decade,' p. 32. The Church, of course, had many critics. Richard Cosin was to pen *An Apologie of and for sundrie proceedings by jurisdiction ecclesiastical* in 1591 in response to the trenchant criticisms of the Anglican Church. Nevertheless, one cannot escape the sense of a Church riven by competing discourses – from recalcitrant Catholics to eager Protestants desirous of radical reform.

25 Carlson, 'Review of *Roman Canon Law in Reformation England*,' p. 365.

26 Guy, *The Reign of Elizabeth I*, p. 137.

enforcement of parliamentary statutes, which acknowledged the Church courts as one manifestation of the sovereign's responsibility for justice in his or her kingdom.[27] This was an inevitable result of the Reformation's instatement of the ecclesiastical courts' *de facto* position as royal courts. In daily practice, however, ecclesiastical lawyers endeavoured to maintain the law they knew: the canon law. In such a climate, it is unsurprising to find the traditional and historical foundations of Church authority demonstrated in appropriately customary terms in its judicial processes.

Although the outcome of the case is lost, the possible remedy is nevertheless alluded to, as the presentment makes explicit reference to the canonical punishment allowed by law. Defamers will, it is stated, 'be canonically corrected and punished by the canonical sanctions salutarily provided and established in this behalf and are to be canonically required and compelled wholly and entirely to abstain and desist in the future from such abuse and other unlawful and dishonourable words.' Bypassing the repetitive displays of pervasive canon authority, the nature of the possible punishment is itself noteworthy. Whilst the demands for financial redress were, of course, irrelevant in ecclesiastical tribunals –the recovery of damages lying outside canon law – a range of 'spiritual remedies' lay within the remit of the Church courts. Such condign punishments ranged from purgation and public penance to, as mentioned in the case of Kingwell versus Taylor, an order imposing silence on the defamer. Crucially, the remedies offered by the ecclesiastical courts are alike in their attempts to restore public order and prevent further abuse of language, and likewise limited in inflicting 'spiritual' penalties. The goal of the ecclesiastical courts in defamation cases was, most certainly, the restoration of reputation and the extinction of *infamia*.[28]

This was to be the primary objective of the courts throughout the reign of Elizabeth and beyond, and the cases for which we have the extant record of outcomes illustrates the sundry means by which the 'bawdy courts' attempted to expunge the moral crimes of slanderers. One might turn, for example, to the 1575 case of Lawrence Boyden, found guilty of 'scoffinge &

27 Carlson, 'Review of *Roman Canon Law in Reformation England*,' p. 362.

28 Helmholz, *Select Cases*, p. xxxix.

uncomely rimes in the church' in Fobbing, Essex (although, unfortunately, it is unknown whether the rhymes were written or merely composed and uttered, the remaining record being fragmentary). For Lawrence's actions, 'John Boyden, father of Lawrence, appeared and undertook to punish his son with a thrashing, in the church in front of the wardens and parishioners.'[29] Such a punishment is remarkable for a variety of reasons, not least of which is the inclusion of public humiliation, which took place in tandem with penance and punishment. Combined, they provided a powerful tool in instilling fear of like embarrassment amongst members of the congregation similarly inclined to break canon law. Further, the fact that the physical aspect of that punishment – the 'thrashing' – was carried out by the offender's father indicates a certain degree of elasticity and arbitration in the meting out of chastisement. One can only assume that the willingness of John Boyden to publicly beat his son was a boon to the court's judges, unable as they were to exert physical penalties on guilty parties.

Not all decisions were quite so severe. In a presumably less strict courtroom in Oxfordshire in 1584, one Anna Wrigglesworth of Islipp

> appeared and denied the charge that ever she made any ryme, but said a certeyne ryme, and for goodwill she told the same to goodwife Willyams and her daughter and to the goodwife Cadman and her daughter because she thought it as made to there discreditt, and she hard it as she came to the market to Oxforde ... last of one Robert Nevell who did sing it by the way, and the ryme is this, viz. If I had as faire a face as John Williams his daughter Elizabeth hass, then wold I were [wear] a taudrie lace [necklace] as goodman Boltes daughter Marie dosse, And if I had as mutche money in my purse as Cadman's daughter Margaret hasse, then wold I have a bastard less then Butlers mayde Helen hasse.[30]

Clearly, Wrigglesworth's rhyme falls more under the aegis of local gossip – the allegation of bastardy notwithstanding. The case thus stands as compelling evidence for Emmison's assertion that 'less substantial people were often the objective of neighbours' recriminations, righteously offended on moral grounds, or the butt of acquaintances' rough humour; and

29 Hair, *Before the Bawdy Courts*, p. 168.
30 Hair, *Before the Bawdy Courts*, p. 74.

ballads, more or less obscene, probably circulated at one time or another in many towns.'[31] Clearly, this was not a phenomenon confined to Essex.

The record of the case, however, is notable not for the inflammatory slander repeated, but rather for the strategy used in Wrigglesworth's defence. Unlike those found in the common law and the more powerful, prerogative courts, in which even the repetition of slander (especially against magnates) was roundly punished, her defence couples a lack of authorship with an even more germane lack of intent to cause harm. Following the principle as set out in the case of Kingwell and Taylor (namely, that the words be spoken maliciously, 'for the sake of hatred, profit, or favour, or for any other cause'), Wigglesworth's defence hinges on her repetition of the rhyme for the 'goodwill' of the subjects therein maligned, 'because she thought it as made to there discreditt.' Such a claim thus counters one of the key tenets of slander as it was defined in canon law; it attempts to establish the absence of malice. We might here locate the means of Wrigglesworth's defence in binary opposition to the presentment brought by Kingwell. Whilst the latter was eager to confirm the 'wicked, malicious' intent of Taylor, here Wrigglesworth is equally eager to refute malice as a motivation and instead substitute that particularly pervasive and corrupt attribute of the slanderer with pure and honest intent. Certainly, it seems, the elaborate and formalised strategies by which accusations of defamation could be deflected were well known to some litigants. Such strategies, further, rested on the manipulation of language. For every appeal to the canon law's requirement of *maliciose*, a lexicon of 'goodwill' and honesty provided the defendant with a ready and typical script for enacting the drama of the courtroom. Taking advantage of the ambiguity of language and the potentially innocent gloss with which even the most barbed of comments could be varnished, was, it seems, a potential prerogative of defendants. At any rate, her defence was a success. Unlike the hapless Lawrence Boyden, Anna Wrigglesworth was dismissed with a warning.

The importance attached to the ostensibly malicious intent of the defamer and the good reputation and standing of the defamed were to remain hallmarks of the ecclesiastical presentment throughout the Elizabethan

31 Emmison, *Elizabethan Life Vol 1*, p. 78.

period. Rarely are they more rigidly and characteristically displayed than in the 1593 case of Ingram versus Knowles, brought before the Consistory court in the diocese of York. Alleging the defamation of his character, the incensed Richard Ingram asserted himself

> an honest man, chaste and never joined in matrimony, of good fame and of honest conversation and life, not implicated, defamed or in any way incriminated of any crime, at least in public notoriety … And for such and such as he was and is commonly spoken, taken, held, named and reputed openly, publicly and notoriously.[32]

Central to his presentation are Ingram's good fame (as might be expected) and, interestingly, his previous lack of defamation and freedom from the implication of any previous crime (to his neighbours' knowledge). As we have seen in the earlier case of Kingwell and Taylor, the prior good fame of the plaintiff was a necessity under the principle of *infamia*. Stress on the lack of any previous imputation of a crime, however, served the dual purpose of establishing (as is customary) his good name and meeting one curious criterion of ecclesiastical defamation law: that *Auctoritate dei patris* (with its focus on malicious accusations of crime) did not apply if the plaintiff had been previously accused of the same trespass.[33]

Thus qualifying his right to bring the case to court, Ingram goes on to allege that one Elizabeth Knowles

> within the parish or chapelry of Hedon and other neighbouring places, maliciously and with the intent to defame, did defame the same Richard Ingram and did say, speak, utter and proclaim to the same Richard Ingram, or of him, many opprobrious, injurious, abusive, reproachful and defamatory words and especially these following words in English … 'The said Liz Knowles alias Simson alias Pearson did call the said Richard Ingram whoremaster, whoremongering harlot, and did say (though falsely) that he the said Richard did lie in bed with another man's wife or another man's maid,' meaning that he did commit adultery … He propounds that the said Elizabeth, before trustworthy witnesses … often, outside and repeated times … has openly, publicly and notoriously confessed and acknowledged that she spoke, said, uttered and proclaimed these defamatory words.[34]

32 Helmholz, *Select Cases*, p. 18.
33 Helmholz, *Select Cases*, p. xxxv.
34 Helmholz, *Select Cases*, p. 16.

Claims of slanderous imputations of the spiritual crimes of whoremastery (a favourite term of opprobrium) and harlotry were no stranger to the ecclesiastical courts, although the latter was prevalent, in the main, between female litigants.[35] A key fact of Ingram's presentment, however, is the claim that Knowles defamed him not only (as is common) before a neighbour or neighbours, but repeatedly and across various parishes. The notion of the words spreading regionally through the conduit of a serial slanderer is arresting, and forms an important link to the canonical demand that one's prior fame must be public and held as the opinion of trustworthy persons (good fame resting, of course, on the good opinion of an honest and upright social network). As a direct result, however, of Knowles' loose and malicious tongue, Ingram contends that

> by reason of the utterance of these defamatory words, the status, good fame and reputation of Richard Ingram are greatly and grievously injured and lessened among good and substantial men with whom he had been of good fame and reputation, and in all likelihood they will be injured in the future … He propounds and alleges that of and upon each and all of the aforesaid there was and is public voice and fame in the said parish … and in other neighbouring places … [and he] prays that right and justice may be executed and that the said Elizabeth Knowles … may be ecclesiastically corrected and punished.[36]

We might linger here briefly on the nature of Ingram's good fame, as well as the way in which his counsel presented their plaintiff as a previously well-reputed individual within a wider, honest populace. It is a strategy which sought to accomplish the twin purpose of bolstering Ingram's suit and asserting the Church's place in affirming a supposedly well-ordered society.

Reputation and fame, we have seen, were of pivotal importance in defamation law dating back to the canon remedies instituted in the thirteenth century, with classical antecedents stretching back still further. By the

35 Ingram (*Church Courts, Sex and Marriage*, p. 301) usefully tabulates the most popular defamatory words sued over in the ecclesiastical courts of York, Wiltshire and Ely. In all three, allegations of adultery, fornication and the birth of illegitimate children prove to have been the most widely used.

36 Helmholz, *Select Cases*, p. 16.

Elizabethan period, however, the necessity of good fame and reputation had become a sensitive issue for men and woman at all levels of society.[37] Recognising that although the concept of 'honour' was one peculiar to disagreements between equals, 'reputation' was at stake with everyone, Anthony Fletcher has argued at length that 'disrespect and defamation by countrymen were constant threats to the effective exercise of local government.'[38] Somewhat constrained by a focus on the danger posed by defamation to the reputations of office-holders, gentry and administrators of justice, however, his brief study is apt to neglect the complex influence of the Church in arbitrating between more plebeian litigants in defamation suits.

Whilst slander in the common law courts was reckoned to result in the loss of earnings or trade amongst the lower orders, the *infamia* caused by the false imputation of moral failure was believed to result in the loss of one's standing in the community. More pointedly, this could result in public infamy which, in the extreme, could bar *infames* from certain public acts; for example, those tainted by *infamia* could not serve as an advocate or testify in criminal trials.[39] The purpose of the English law of defamation was, therefore, to permit the removal of unjustly incurred *infamia*. Ecclesiastical courts, it may therefore be understood, provided a forum in which the unjustly defamed could make manifest the injustices perpetrated by slanderers against their previous good fame and seek the Church's aid in the restoration of their reputations. In that regard, the repeated references to the 'good fame and reputation' once enjoyed by Ingram become obvious: his counsel merely followed a pattern of extolling the injustice – and the metaphysical injury – done to him in the eyes of his reputable peers.

It may be further argued that the Church's ability to 'restore' good fame to unfairly maligned individuals worked not only in the interests of the individuals themselves, but of the Church. As has been seen, the common law and parliamentary statutes played an enormous role in defining (and punishing those wont to spread) unacceptable language. From the Common Pleas to the King's Bench and Star Chamber, the administration of justice

37 Fletcher, 'Honour, Reputation, and Local Officeholding,' p. 92.
38 Fletcher, 'Honour, Reputation, and Local Officeholding,' p. 110.
39 Helmholz, *Select Cases*, p. xxi.

was a potent means of ensuring the state's authority over language. The Church – an increasingly contested site towards the end of the Elizabethan era – had, however, long staked a judicial claim over defamatory language. Although the result was a complex network of litigation between the courts, with jurisdiction dependent primarily on the nature of the slanderous words spoken (or written), the popularity of the Church courts amongst the litigious certainly attest to their continued association with the regulation of language. Furthermore, the remedies offered by ecclesiastical judges remain worthy of consideration. The 'ecclesiastical correction and punishment' desired by Ingram could have taken a number of forms. In addition to the public penances and apologies previously mentioned, the extreme penalty of which the ecclesiastical courts were capable was excommunication: a very public removal from the Church, with the discretion of judges left to dictate the means by which the sentence could be lifted. Such a remedy had the combined effect of removing individuals from religious life – a penalty of some enormity – and inflicting a not inconsiderable degree of public shame and humiliation. Parochial ostracism and subsequent social sanctions, then as now, must certainly have been viewed as powerful incitements to refrain from provocative behaviour.

But where does this leave us in the case of Ingram and Knowles? The language deployed throughout Ingram's presentment serves to fortify an image of the Church's ecclesiastical authority both in 'correcting' and 'punishing' abusers of language, in addition to making plain the central role of the Church courts in what is presented as a society comprised of upstanding parishes and parishioners. Further, the very nature of the presentment as a text delivered in the public forum of the court reinforced the palliative role of the Church in restoring communal harmony. The metaphysical power to remove *infamia* and restore members of society to their previous, spotless reputations also carried with it not a small amount of social and cultural capital. As such, one can discern in the records of the ecclesiastical courts an ongoing attempt to confirm and maintain authority over language, even as religious figures – and the Anglican Church itself, as will be seen – were being traduced by the slanderer's tongue, the satirist's cutting pen and attacks from ardent reformers.

That the Church courts had the power to try those accused of calumnious activity against their neighbours tending to the unjust infliction of *infamia* is a matter of record. So too, however, is the authority of the Church over those who voiced dissatisfaction with the morality or behaviour of its ministers. Here we arrive at a phenomenon which had its likely beginnings in the shifting view of the clergy catalysed by the early days of the Reformation. Tracing the dominant views of Christian leadership in Elizabethan England, Richard Greaves has argued that 'the nature and function of the ministry were redefined [in the Reformation], so that the emphasis was on the clergy as teachers and exemplars of God's will for man, rather than as agents of the miracle in the mass or the dispensation of grace in the sacraments.'[40] As a consequence, the moral and spiritual worth of ministers became of paramount importance to churchgoers. Contemporary writings, certainly, point to the perceived qualities necessary in the reformed clergy, from Tyndale's 1534 prologue in his *New Testament* (which set forth the qualities that bishops and lower clergy ought to possess) to the 1537 *Matthew Bible*'s condemnation of the covetousness of prelates and priests. Yet people seldom live up to ideals and given the fact that iconoclastic criticism of clergymen of the old faith had been encouraged during the reformation, it was axiomatic that criticism of episcopal polity, too, would blossom throughout the later sixteenth century. The genie was out of the bottle. Nor is it unsurprising either that the lower orders showed a willingness to slander unpopular ministers, or that the Church courts were empowered to root out and punish those who reviled ministers and churchwardens.

Collating a series of court charges typical of Essex in the period, Emmison's brief synopsis of the abundance of attacks which comprised the slanderer of prelates' almanac is worth quoting:

> An indictment in 1572 lay against John Gray and Peter Gray of Wivenhoe, who being 'reproved for not coming to church reviled the churchwardens calling them drunks and churls.' They were commanded to confess before the congregation and to reconcile themselves with the wardens. A woman called her churchwardens 'knaves in doing their office,' adding that they were 'officers for a dog'; others were merely

40 Greaves, *Society and Religion*, p. 33.

> accorded the term knave, or they 'were gotten in a knave's office.' 'Railing on the churchwardens doing their office' and 'abusing the churchwardens with beastly speeches on being reproved' are not uncommon entries. One warden was called 'a liar'; a second, 'whoremaster'; a third, 'busy merchant' [fellow]. A rector had been earlier a 'mender of saddles and panels' (an abusive appellation).[41]

The language deployed against churchwardens is typical enough, but rather more interesting is the high incidence of raillery against those whose job it was to ensure that the legally prescribed attendance (established by the 1559 Act of Uniformity) at church services was adhered to by Essex parishioners.[42] Certainly, the endeavours of the Church courts here indicate a persistent desire to curtail the visible breaches in religious uniformity exhibited by those who flouted the state's insistence on attendance at sermons. In this way we might again view the Church courts as operating as a judicial arm of the state. Given the contrariety of religious interests and beliefs which would only increase in number and proliferation throughout the early modern period, the need for the ecclesiastical courts to perform a unifying role in restoring the fame of its upholders and returning malfeasants to the fold is certainly understandable. It was not only for the Church courts to ensure order between sharp-tongued neighbours, but as the very polity of the Church's hierarchy came under attack from ever more ardent reformers, it became crucial to maintain uniformity amongst the lower orders, lest, as Archbishop Whitgift cautioned, disorder follow on the heels of challenge to the episcopacy.

Attempts to stem the tide of the slander of minor church figures (as it followed those figures' attempts to stamp out non-conformity) were discernibly common. However, the Church's purgation and punishment of the 'common slanderers' who spat epithets at those who desired their presence at church were arguably of lesser import than the more direct aspersions cast on senior Church officials. Recovering the importance of the voices of the

41 Emmison, *Morals and the Church Courts*, p. 63.

42 Essex was not unique. As Houlbrooke (*Church Courts and the People*, p. 44) attests, churchwardens were unpopular figures as far afield as Winchester and Norwich – due in no small part to their 'enforcement of sometimes unpopular official demands.'

'inarticulate' in Elizabethan Essex, Joel Samaha recognises the unbreakable link between religion and politics in early modern England, noting that attacks on religion were considered tantamount to assaults on the peace and security of the realm (falling as they did within the realms of sedition).[43] Familiar as we are with the statute of *Scandalum Magnatum*, which forbade the seditious slandering of the Queen's subordinates, it becomes clear that ecclesiastical authority (fronted as it was by the Queen's deputies) here met with criminal jurisdiction, as malicious or inflammatory attacks on the leading figures of the state Church invited the full machinery of criminal law. In this vein, we must view the Church court's authority over certain types of defamatory language as working in conjunction with the criminal and civil courts as, whilst the practitioners of law within each might have wrangled over jurisdictions, each separate branch of the state was, in theory, to work together in providing as all-encompassing a bridle as possible over inadmissible, disruptive, slanderous or seditious language across the social, domestic, and political spheres. Nevertheless, polemicists and slanderers of the Church and its figures from the top downwards flourished in a period of religious intolerance, just as the secular slanderer's tongue continued to wag and the slanderous dramatist's inkpot was drained only haphazardly. Whilst the Church courts' control of slander focused mainly on the defamation suits brought by litigants as a means of maintaining its historical, regulatory, and proprietary authority over language at a time in which both the structure of the Church and its judicial remit were being questioned, this was far from the only way in which slander, sedition and the Church intersected. As will be seen the avowed 'true' Church of England met its critics and defamers with a veritable arsenal of legal, symbolic, and literary counterblasts.

43 Samaha, 'Gleanings from Local Criminal Court Records,' p. 70.

CHAPTER 14

The High Commission and the Catholic Threat

By now familiar with the arguments advanced by M. Lindsay Kaplan in her influential *Culture of Slander in Early Modern England*, the notion of state-authorised slander (and counter-slander) is not a strange one. However, with Kaplan's study focusing analysis on the power relations between poets and theatrical censor, the Church's role as state slanderer is unfortunately overlooked. Whilst it is inarguable that the Revels Office provided an important means of regulating language, the Church courts and religious authorities were likewise engaged in an attempt to develop an increasingly systematic process of supervision and control over the printed, handwritten and spoken word.

As we have seen, the ecclesiastical courts had the power to grant, remove and restore public fame to those who had been maligned. In effect, they posited themselves as the metaphysical arbiter in cases in which reputation had been unfairly tarnished by slanderers – and they could, in turn, bring the slanderer himself into communal disrepute. Thus carrying the implicit threat of religious exclusion in order to ensure conformity, the Church undoubtedly played a societal role as governor of public fame. Coupled with its traditional social control over language, as evidenced by its judicial authority over local defamation (when no temporal crime was imputed), it is therefore no surprise to find that the religious divisions of the sixteenth century proceeded in tandem not only with an increase in ecclesiastical litigation, but the inception in 1559 of a new and powerful court: that of the High Commission.[1] Armed with powers unavailable to other Church courts (such as the ability to fine or imprison), the commissioners, chosen

1 Known officially as the Commissioners for Causes Ecclesiastical (Helmholz, *Roman Canon Law in Reformation England*, p. 46).

by the Queen, were charged with enforcing Elizabeth's Act of Uniformity and, consequently, putting down

> all and singular heretical opinions, seditious books, contempts, conspiracies, false rumours, tales, seditions, misbehaviours, slanderous words or showings, published, invented or set forth ... by any person or persons against us, or contrary or against ... the quiet government and rule of our people and subjects, in any county, city, borough or other place or places within this our realm of England.[2]

The overlapping of jurisdictions is obvious; the quorum of six commissioners, which included the incumbent Archbishop of Canterbury, Matthew Parker, and former Marian exile, William Grindal (Bishop of London) were given prerogative power over matters which were, ostensibly, within the purview of the criminal and civil courts. Divided into diocesan branches, these powers were exercised with varying degrees of zeal – and yet the wide royal commission which they were granted nevertheless ensured that contemporaries were displeased with the resultant intrusiveness and authority of the court.[3]

As the reign of Elizabeth proceeded, the court of High Commission was to increase in power and in the number of clergymen it comprised as it strove to bridle the dissidence of unorthodox ministers and other religious non-conformists. McCabe, in particular, notes the set of ordinances set forth in 1566 by the Privy Council for 'reformation of divers disorders in pryntyng and utterying of Bookes' at the request of the High Commission. The first ordinance, it will be noted, stipulated that

> no person shall print, or cause to be printed, nor shall bring, or cause, or procure to be brought into this Realme imprinted, any Booke or copye agaynst the fourme and meanyng of any ordinaunce, prohibition or commaundement, conteyned, or to be conteyned in any the statutes or lawes of this Realme, or in any Iniunctions, Letters patentes, or ordinaunces, passed or set forth, or to be passed or set forth, by the Queenes most excellent Maiesties graunt, commission, or aucthoritie.[4]

2 Elton *The Tudor Constitution*, p. 227.
3 Helmholz, *Roman Canon Law in Reformation England*, p. 47.
4 McCabe, 'Right Puisante and Terrible Priests,' p. 79; Rivington (ed.), *A Transcript of the Registers of the Company of Stationers of London*, p. 145.

Further, it was declared that any caught in violation of the ordinance would forfeit all books and copies to be 'destroyed or made waste paper.' One might stop to consider the implications of such edicts, not only for the anxieties they betray on behalf of the Privy Council, but for the way in which they present the High Commission as a religious adjunct to the body politic.

The state's concern with stability and its desire to curtail threats can be seen to cross the jurisdictions of its institutional components. Slanderous and inflammatory material at home and from abroad, in handwritten or printed form, was anathema to the state as a nominally united body. It is hence possible to detect the impossibility of establishing any model of censorship predicated on a single cultural site. The Elizabethan state relied on a network of authority figures overseeing various sites (from theatres to booksellers) and is perhaps best perceived as an internally variegated group of bureaucratic hierarchies. Within each hierarchy, authority figures (whether Masters of the Revels or Archbishops) shared and delegated authority to varying degrees and with varying effects. Additionally, the nature of the ordinance is worthy of comment. Under the authority of the 'Queenes most excellent Maiesties graunt commission, or aucthoritie,' the legitimacy of state authorship is placed in contradistinction to illicit, prohibited material worthy only of destruction. Book burnings and the destruction of manuscripts – however haphazardly policed – were to provide a visual dimension to the exercise of authority as the Church attempted to cement its role as a state regulator of language and arbiter of truth against slanderous and false heretics.[5]

5 David Cressy ('Book Burning in Tudor and Stuart England,' pp. 359–74) provides a useful and persuasive account of the destruction of books as such events operated in Tudor and Stuart England. Ultimately, he suggests that attempts by the state to expunge texts from the kingdom were not only unsuccessful (as evidenced by the fact that many survive), but counterproductive. Rather than removing works from public view, autocratic attempts to destroy them simply brought them to the attention of the public. This notion is supported by Alastair Bellany ('The embarrassment of libels,' p. 149), who has further argued that not only destruction, but prosecution of offensive material may even have given libels extra publicity.

The success of this early injunction is a matter of lively debate. It is generally accepted, however, that whilst on the surface an autocratic and monolithic diktat, in practice a degree of liberty was available to those who produced or possessed unlicensed but inoffensive texts.[6] One might recall Cyndia Clegg's perception of the ways in which slanderous printed material was repressed being suggestive of a government which responded to events rather than pre-emptively sought to control them: her proposed *ad hoc* model of press censorship. It is here worth dwelling on the notion of censorship as a process, which has now crossed from theatrical performance to press output. The plethora of conflicting (and, less often, complementary) models of censorship espoused by various scholars in recent decades are each useful in pursuing certain aspects and incidents of state intervention in textual production, and yet any concise and all-encompassing model remains elusive.

In terms of press censorship – which fell increasingly under the control of Bishops and their underlings – the issue is made still murkier by the lack of a central official operating as censor. Unlike the Revels Office's circumscribed authority over dramatic material (as exercised by its Master and his deputies) control over printing presses was undertaken more messily. From the outset of Elizabeth's reign, control over the presses was provided by the Stationers' Company, which was chartered under Mary I in 1557, and thereafter operated its own licensing procedure over the printed word.[7] In 1560, the Stationers' Company also became a Liveried Company of the City of London, which 'consolidated their control over printing in England … [serving] the Crown's interest in regulation and surveillance' via 'the right to search anywhere, anytime for printing equipment.'[8] In 1586 (in response to the proliferation of printing presses) the Star Chamber set forth ordinances which reaffirmed the monopoly of the Stationers' Company and demanded that anyone involved in the printing of books first register with

6 Raymond, *Pamphlets and Pamphleteering*, p. 67.

7 The Stationer's Company operated its own licensing procedure over the printed word. Joad Raymond (*Pamphlets and Pamphleteering*, pp. 67–70) provides a useful description of the ways in which these licensing procedures operated, and the interests which they served.

8 Halasz, *The Marketplace of Print*, p. 23.

the Company's warden and master.[9] Evidently, however, the privileging of the Stationers' Company did not provide Elizabethan authorities with as comprehensive a system of press regulation as they desired; thus, in 1587, the nominal control of Archbishop of Canterbury and his various ecclesiastical cohorts. It is therefore best to refrain from overlaying censorship models on incidents of press censorship (different models, as we have seen, applying with varying value to different historical moments and certainly different genres). Instead, we may recognise in all moments in which the machinery of state swung into action evidence of a larger concern with improper or dangerous language and the parties to whom it was exposed. In short, one must consider the perceived danger of slander as a method of using written or spoken language in ways which might have potentially destabilised an insecure social order. Despite bearing a superficial and mechanistic similarity to Kaplan's 'slander' or 'defamation' model, emphasis on the processes of language regulation cannot neglect the audiences exposed to disruptive language. What did they make, if anything, of the rules, licensing laws, regulations, and official bodies instituted by the state in these early, quixotic attempts to organise and centralise language regulation? And can we be certain that readers made any distinction between a satirical poem or play, a printed book which slandered a state governor, and a defamatory libel aimed at a prelate? Whether readers (or hearers) gave much thought to who should have prevented it, such exposure to (and consequent spreading of) unsanctioned religious doctrine was to the detriment of established and authorised modes of worship.

Citing a letter sent over the Queen's signature in January 1565/6 to Lord Treasurer Winchester, which stressed the need to search ships in English ports for 'lewde and slanderous books,' Clegg has argued that the ordinances of 1566 were a direct response to the influx of illegal books which had been making their way from the continent's Catholic presses and English exiles in Europe.[10] Catholicism and Catholic recusants were to be a thorn in the side of the Elizabethan body politic throughout the

9 Clegg (*Press Censorship in Elizabethan England*, p. 29) provides comprehensive discussion of the nine items issuing from this decree.

10 Clegg, *Press Censorship in Elizabethan England*, p. 45.

Queen's reign. Whilst the early years of the Elizabethan era were marked by a grudging tolerance of Catholicism (with occasional sharp reminders of its fallen status), the identification and subsequent persecution of Catholics as sowers of sedition was an inescapable result of the abortive Northern Rebellion and Rome's Papal Bull of 1570, which excommunicated Elizabeth and absolved of divine punishment any Catholic who brought about her death. The Treasons Act (1571) followed, making explicit that it was a capital crime to deny Elizabeth's right to the throne by speech, word, or deed. Coupled with the 1571 statutory law against writing on the succession and the parliamentary Act against reconciliation which prohibited the import of Catholic religious objects, Clegg has recognised the shift in Elizabethan policy as resulting from the threat now posed by those whose allegiance was to Rome:

> Catholic texts were [now] illegal, and Elizabeth's government relentlessly sought out Catholic presses and suppressed Catholic texts. Commands existed to burn popish books and paraphernalia. Searches, midnight raids, patrols of English ports, spies and counterspies at home and abroad sought to stifle the thought and faith of man.[11]

The tide had turned. Where once religion had been largely a matter of personal faith as long as an outward show of conformity was made, the battle lines were now drawn and – in England – the Anglican Church had the weight of the law on its side. Further, what the common law and ecclesiastical laws did not address, the rumour and sedition statutes did.[12] As we have seen, the Marian statute against rumour and libel was extended by Elizabeth and, further, anyone found guilty of writing anything 'containing anie false matter, clause or sentence of slaunder, reproach and dishonour of the [Queens] Majesty would … have his or their right hand stricken off.' In 1581, and as a possible response to the controversy surrounding Stubbs' *Discoverie of a Gaping Gvlf*, this statute was replaced with one mandating the death penalty for anyone found guilty of 'devising, writing, printing or setting forth [or] procuring or publishing false, seditious, and slanderous matter to the defamation of the Queenes

11 Clegg, *Press Censorship in Elizabethan England*, p. 79.
12 Clegg, *Press Censorship in Elizabethan England*, p. 32.

Majesty.' Naturally, criticism or denial of the Queen's spiritual role fell under the umbrella of seditious slander.

The power to define slander and sedition in Elizabethan England lay, most certainly, in the (several) hands of the English government and its established Church, with those texts which flouted the law losing the cultural and legal currency of legitimacy. It is necessary, however, to examine the ways in which texts, both Catholic and Anglican, sought to manipulate law, language, and the importance of truth in defence – or offence – of their religious and doctrinal bases. With the Church's authority over printing, writing, and publishing manifest (if of arguable efficacy) and its similar power to remove and award 'fame' according to ecclesiastical custom, the strategies by which it could disseminate its own propaganda by means of censure or the punishment of malefactors remains to be seen. One might turn, for example, to the writings of John Leslie, Bishop of Ross: a Catholic adherent to the regal rights of Mary Stuart. Having penned *A defence of the honour of the right highe, mightye and noble princesse Marie quene of Scotlande* (1569), Leslie incurred the displeasure of the English government by attempting to restore the fame of the Scottish Queen (she having been brought into disrepute by the death of her husband, her subsequent remarriage to the Earl of Bothwell and her flight to England) and discuss the succession – a contentious subject, albeit one about which discussion was not to become illegal until 1571. Writing two years after the publication of the book, Burghley recalled it as having defended the Queen of Scots 'for her title to the crown and for the murder of her husband Lord Darnley, and [that it] contained a great number of manifest untruths, and namely to the prejudice of her majesty's right.'[13]

13 Burghley's jaundiced view of the *Defence* is understandable. Not only was he then involved in a pitched battle for public opinion, in which his Catholic opponents were using Marian polemic as a weapon, but his opinion of the book came immediately after Charles Bally, a servant of Leslie, had been found smuggling illicit copies of the text into Dover. Bally was imprisoned in the Marshalsea; unrepentant, he and Leslie continued to communicate in ciphered letters. A fuller account of the doings of Burghley, Bally and Leslie can be found in the *Calendar of State Papers Relating to Scotland and Mary, Queen of Scots* – Vol. IV.

Quite evident in Burghley's mistrust of the Bishop of Ross's motives – and apparent in his *Defence* – are those 'manifest untruths' which harmed his own sovereign. What seems obvious here is the emphasis placed not only on Elizabeth's right to rule – itself not touched upon in Leslie's text – but the truth of the Protestant cause in the battle against 'manifest untruths.' The language here is that of the courtroom, as Burghley adopts the role of plaintiff to Leslie's untruthful slanderer. It is therefore interesting to note the Bishop of Ross's subsequently penned defence of his original work. Answering charges that his book advanced Mary as the 'right heir of the realm,' Leslie pleaded that he was

> very sorry from his heart that the Queen's majesty should 'tak ony evill opinione thairof,' considering that nothing was intended but a defence of her honour against so many blasphemous 'treteis' and 'pamflettis' as have been set abroad both in England and Scotland, which are printed at London … If the same might have given any occasion to offend the Queen's majesty in any sort, it should not have been printed, and although it had been printed, the same did not comprehend so manifest untruth as is reported.[14]

Particularly noteworthy is Leslie's claim that his *Defence* sought only to redeem the reputation of his fallen mistress, which had been unjustly maligned in both Scotland and England via pamphlets and treatises. He therefore contends that his work had been not a slander of nor a seditious attack upon Elizabeth, but a necessary response to the slander of Mary. This, in itself, offers us the suggestion that, whilst attempts to recover the honour of the Scottish Queen were apt to arouse the suspicions of the English government, slanderous attacks on Mary's character were admissible according to English authorities – either tacitly or with furtive encouragement. Indeed, in tracing Mary's reputation, John D. Staines reaches the pointed conclusion that

> the strategy employed [was] a favourite tactic of Cecil, who appears to have acted without the Queen's knowledge [in allowing the publication of tracts detrimental to Mary's character]. Indeed, Cecil seems to have been working against the Queen. Elizabeth, though, seems not to have looked too carefully at the sources of these

14 *CSP, Relating to Scotland and Mary, Queen of Scots* – Vol. IV.

> pamphlets when it was in her interest. Elizabeth and her council began a policy of plausible deniability: Cecil, Walsingham, and their agents printed and distributed propaganda against Mary, while Elizabeth and her representatives publicly insisted that such works were forbidden. They made no attempt to suppress, for instance, *Salutem in Christo*, a work probably by Richard Grafton that accuses Mary of actively fomenting rebellion against Elizabeth.[15]

The state, it seems, allowed the slander of its enemies, yet labelled those who dared to advance the reclamation of those enemies' reputations as themselves seditious. Not actively or intentionally seditious, the *Defence* offers us, therefore, a window into the ways in which polemicists sought to advance their arguments through the high-ranking individuals who provided the visible figureheads of their cause. However, whilst Leslie maintained an outward show of deference to Elizabeth's majesty, others were to be more vocal in their criticism of the English Queen's person.

Whilst Mary Queen of Scots lived, she proved a troublesome rallying figure for Catholic malcontents as well as a useful focal point for English, state-authorised slander: a foreign folk devil who could be used by the state to blacken the names of all Catholics. As Louis Montrose notes, the spirited and flagrant abuse of Mary was to provide a steady stream of anti-Catholic sentiment. In a parliamentary speech, Peter Wentworth, when cautioned for having called Mary a Jezebel, replied, 'Did I not publish her openly in the last parlment to be the most notorious whore in all the world? And wherefore should I be afraid to call her soe nowe againe?'[16] In advancing his biting slander of Mary in parliament, Wentworth was demonstrably exercising the liberty of parliamentary privilege, which would have safeguarded him from charges of slander and sedition.[17] To Lake, the early

15 Staines, *The Tragic Histories of Mary, Queen of Scots*, p. 35.

16 Montrose, *The Subject of Elizabeth*, p. 195.

17 Something of a renegade, Wentworth was to push Elizabethan acceptance of parliamentary free speech too far in 1576, when he was arrested in the House of Commons for speaking of the Queen's 'great faults' in refusing bills against Mary (Mack, *Elizabethan Rhetoric*, pp. 241–2). His arrest came despite his apparent belief in the inviolable right of parliament to counsel the monarch. One can therefore identify in the episode another example of the lack of safety inherent in adopting the rhetoric of counsel (even in a privileged site).

modern parliament was a 'privileged sounding board or arena were things unsayable in public could elsewhere be uttered in a context likely to garner them the rapt attention of a very generously defined political nation.'[18] Nevertheless, it seems he took particular advantage of that privilege by not just advising the House (and hence the Queen) of Mary's faults, but attacking her person, morals and reputation. In the cultural sphere, the English defamation of Mary as a whore was to find expression in Edmund Spenser's 1596 epic, *The Faerie Queene* – described by Shuger as 'the only piece of Elizabethan religious literature by a layman' – which portrayed Mary in allegorical guise as the duplicitous Duessa. As a result, James VI called for a ban on the poem and Spenser earned Elizabeth's favour.[19]

Such attacks were typical, and invariably placed the Queens at odds in a religious and political power struggle whilst foregrounding the politics of the personal. Mary represented thousands of Catholics, as Elizabeth did Protestants – whether either sovereign wished it or not. Unremarkably, therefore, the slew of personal invectives levelled at Mary brought about equally virulent defences, which, not unlike the *Defence*, provide historic examples of the English government's strategy in condemning and answering slanders against the state.

The cultural construction of a 'good Queen' in opposition to a 'bad Queen' (by both sides of the Catholic–Protestant divide) was, as McLaren argues, deeply rooted in discourses of gender.[20] This is a view explored at length by Helen Hackett, who recognises the attempts of English artists and Protestants to construct in Elizabeth a 'figurehead of militant nationalistic Protestantism.'[21] The notion is persuasive, though one might question the interdependence of the images of the Queens. Clearly, gender played an important role, as both Catholic and Protestant sought to stake a claim in presenting the opposing monarch in as negative a light as possible. Mary's reputation, it may be argued, could best be redeemed by reinforcing Elizabeth's bastardy and alleged whoredom (as declared in 1572 by William

18 Lake, 'The Politics of Popularity,' p. 78.

19 Shuger, 'A Protesting Catholic Puritan,' p. 630.

20 McLaren, 'Gender, Religion, and Early Modern Nationalism,' pp. 739–67.

21 Hackett, *Virgin, Mother, Maiden Queen*, p. 237.

Allen) whilst Elizabeth's reputation was equally well served by trumpeting Mary's sexual incontinence, allegedly murderous history, and ill-defined tyranny.[22] Further, to Catholics Mary was a good monarch because she had performed the necessary function of her office – the begetting of an heir – whilst Elizabeth had not.[23] To Protestants, Elizabeth was a good monarch because she lacked the frailty of her sex, being 'more than a man, and in truth, less than a woman.'[24] The spread of slanderous oppositional religious treatises and pamphlets which were to repeatedly reconfigure the two as virtuous paragons and sinful demons was to be a recurring feature of Mary's captivity in England.

Circulated in print and manuscript – testament, surely, to the impotence of authorities in preventing outbreaks of dissidence – *A Treatise of Treasons Against Q. Elizabeth and the Croune of England* (1572), like the *Defence*, proclaimed itself a response to the *Salutem in Christo*. Also dubiously attributed to John Leslie, the *Treatise* followed the *Defence*'s lead in defending the reputation of Mary Stuart (and the Duke of Norfolk, who was to be executed that year for complicity in a Catholic plot to marry Mary and oust Elizabeth) and advancing the Stuart claim to the throne. Central to the means by which the *Treatise* launches its diatribe against the corrupt officials in England – two nameless ministers, popularly accepted to be Nicholas Bacon and Burghley, being its primary targets – is the claim that the text set out to 'confuteth the false accusations and slanderous infamies printed in certain nameless and infamous libels against the Q.['s] Majesty of Scotland, heir apparent to the crown of England, and against Thomas, Duke of Norfolk, Earl Marshall of the same realm.'[25] One cannot help but be instantly reminded of the back-and-forth nature of

22 McLaren, 'Gender, Religion, and Early Modern Nationalism,' p. 752.

23 Susan Doran ('Why Did Elizabeth Not Marry?,' pp. 30–53) provides an interesting overview of the ways in which Elizabeth successfully managed attacks on her refusal to marry and subsequent lack of fecundity. In addition, she recounts some of the scurrilous rumours concerning the begetting of bastards which dogged the Queen, and provide further examples of familiar slanders being aimed at great personages of state.

24 Levin, *The Heart and Stomach of a King*, p. 147.

25 Leslie, *A treatise of treasons*, p. 2.

slander suits as they operated in the courtroom, as here we have what may be termed in legal parlance a public demur, or answer, to a 'false charge.' Almost acting as Mary's counsel, the author of the *Treatise* is careful to make clear her innocence of the charges set forth in previous pamphlets, in addition to drawing attention to the dubious authority of those charges. It will be remembered, after all, that anti-Marian pamphlets were illegal if not actively suppressed.

Thus affecting legal rectitude, the *Treatise* goes on to accuse those who have spread libels of labouring to 'defame and discredit that virtuous Lady the Queen's Majesty of Scotland … [and] to slander and deface that noble prince the Duke of Norfolk' with marginalia protesting – rather ingenuously – that the author's intent is 'not to impugn authority.' Instead, it is contended that only two chief ministers of the Crown are at fault, as the author defends his good character and standing as a long-term witness to England's prosperity:

> when I use any term that may seem to touch authority … I mean none other authority than of them two only, who (by craft and circumvention) have obtained that authority that whatsoever impugneth their pestilent private purpose (the end whereof I verily believe your Q. seeth not) must be taken and published for traitorous, slanderous, seditious, rebellious, & whatsoever else can be thought more odious, be it never so well meant, and tend it never so evidently to the security of your Q., to the benefit of your realm, and to the honour of your nobility.[26]

In order to forestall the common accusation of malice commonly made against slanderers, the writer makes an overt appeal to the lack of malicious intent allegedly exhibited by the pamphlet. Indeed, the author claims an anxious and well-meaning concern for the good of Elizabeth and England in the revelation of her ministers' infamy. Nevertheless, there remains prevalent throughout the text a sharp and stinging condemnation of the inability of English subjects to voice concerns about their governance. Defending the right of a foreigner to pen words which may be deemed opprobrious to authority, the author laments the natives'

26 Leslie, *A treatise of treasons*, p. 8.

> thrall, state and servitude … having (by severe searches, by suborned accusations, by sudden arrests, by sharp imprisonments, by fraudulent examinations and penalties) their hands bound from writing, sending, or receiving, their eyes closed from reading or beholding, their ears stopped from hearing, their mouths and tongues tied up from speaking, yea, their very hearts and minds restrained from thinking.[27]

The flagrant criticism of the thraldom in which the English live – which was, of course, an exaggeration – represents one of several attacks on the state's government veiled by the allegedly honest intentions of the author.

Particularly notable is the attempt on the part of the writer to deploy the rhetoric of counsel in his provision of 'honest' advice. He does not attack the Queen; instead, he seeks to offer her advice for the good maintenance of the realm. Here, one may draw parallels with Stubbs' *The Discoverie*. Stubbs couched his criticism of the Alençon match in the ostensible need for a subject to publicly appeal to a monarch failed by self-serving ministers; and so too does the writer of the *Treatise* frame his need to defend Mary.[28] It is, he claims, his duty to do so in order to 'benefit' the realm. Like Stubbs, however, the public mode of expression deployed in conjunction with espousing the rhetoric of counsel was unsuccessful. Whilst Guy recognises the language of counsel as being predicated on the friendly offer of advice that the monarch was duty-bound to take in good part, it is once again clear that it was by no means a safe rhetorical strategy nor a warrant to speak or write with licence.[29] As Lake and Pincus note, 'there were emerging protocols to be observed when having recourse to the politics of popularity, but they remained hazy and ill defined, and it was always horribly easy to fall over the edge into sedition.'[30] Given that 'sedition' was as yet hazy and undefined (being whatever authorities decided it was

27 Ibid.

28 Peter Lake ('The Politics of Popularity,' pp. 59–89) provides an excellent reading of the *Treatise of Treasons* with particular focus on the ways in which the author's language follows the framework of traditional counsel. For the purposes of the present study, interest is not focused on the appropriation of rhetorical discourse, but the ways in which that appropriation was deployed as an (unsuccessful) means of combatting charges of slander and sedition.

29 Guy, 'The rhetoric of counsel,' p. 294.

30 Lake and Pincus, *The Politics of the Public Sphere*, p. 7.

in any given case), this is not surprising. Such was certainly the case with both the *Treatise* and *The Discoverie*. Appropriating the rhetoric of counsel (however disingenuously) could easily become slander, sedition or libel when it came from those who had no business dictating to the monarch, and – more dangerously – when aspiring 'counsellors' dared to air their grievances before an indiscriminate audience.

The issue of the *Treatise*'s anonymity is also worthy of note. As we have seen, the anonymity of libels proved to be a vexatious problem for Elizabethan authorities – the law was habitually plagued by unattributed verses pinned on doors or repeated vocally, and the result was the 'severe searches' and 'sharp imprisonments' recognised by our nameless pamphleteer. As Marcy North recognises, anonymity was a 'necessary and effective protective device that allowed for … broad dissemination, and the particularly unobtrusive form of anonymity used by most libel authors focused attention away from the author and onto the libel's victim.'[31] The author of the *Treatise* evidently made full use of this slipperiness, adopting anonymity in his own writing and castigating it in others.' Having initially denounced the 'nameless and infamous libels' circulated about Mary, a neat legal dodge is then used to defend the anonymity under which the *Treatise* was produced. Making the bold claim that only 'railing rascal parasites' set forth slanderous libels in order to 'destroy and not edify the honour and good name of any person of account before due and orderly conviction,' the author forbears to reveal his own name because he 'comes not to accuse any person by name that is in disgrace.' Instead, he alleges, he seeks to tell no 'strange or hidden thing,' but rather to 'lay forth open known facts and manifest deeds known to all men, without the blame of any person by name now in estate to take harm thereby.'[32] Once again, we have a swerve which is so familiar to the courtroom that it can only betray a popular perception of how accusations of slander might be mitigated. The calumnies alleged are unspecific, with the allegations offered to the reader for judgement. He is most assuredly not, as Lake would have it, 'broaching

31 North, 'Anonymity in Early Modern Manuscript Culture,' p. 15.
32 Leslie, *A treatise of treasons*, p. 31.

the secrets of the *arcana imperii* before the people.'[33] The author, therefore, aligns himself only with the defence of the Scottish Queen and goodwill towards the realm of England, adroitly placing suspicion in the minds of his readers and inciting them to slander authority by linking his own claims of the Council's slanderous activity and corruption to two individuals. Always he is careful to profess the lack of actionability of his claims; yet those claims could only have sought to bring the entire government into disrepute. To that end, the two ministers are inveighed against as the source of every disturbance felt in England, from foreign wars, faction at home, the abuse of Catholics, perversion of the succession, slanders against the Spanish King, and the encouragement of atheism.

If one is to accept that the *Treatise* constituted a defence against alleged slanders by aping the due processes of slander lawsuits, then the paradoxical nature of an unlicensed tract which castigated the government – an activity strictly forbidden by law – manipulating the process of law must be addressed. Calling for an investigation of Elizabeth's Council and railing against the corruption of her ministers, as we know, directly contravened laws against bringing the Queen's government into infamy; and yet the *Treatise* does so whilst being vocal in its appeal to justice and its recognition of sedition and slander as operated by the state and its authorities. It may consequently be argued that implicit in the *Treatise*'s rhetorical stratagem is an appropriation not just of the language of counsel, but of the apparatus of state – the implication being that when the state is dogged by corrupt men, the private individual might, indeed must, assume the role of authority. A direct threat to the government, this was not merely slander – it was sedition. Recognising the supposed fissures and cracks in the Elizabethan regime's use of power, the text adopts an outward gloss of reason, honest counsel and deference to the English Queen's authority whilst undermining it by exposing the supposed corruption in her governors, the oppression of her subjects, the slanderous activity of her government, and the falsity of her ecclesiastical authority. Further, the manipulation of the law and

33 Lake, 'The Politics of Popularity,' p. 74. The *arcana imperii* [mysteries of state] was a Tacitean concept invoked by Elizabeth, who used it to stress the limits of counsel and advice which could be given to a prince, particularly by parliament.

the indignant accusations of slander (accusations which were the prerogative of the state) raise the text, intermittently, to the level of satire, as the foreign-born author usurps the language and privileges of the authority it seeks to discredit. Such a notion finds further confirmation in the layout of the text itself. Engaging directly with the practical conventions of legitimate, authorised contemporary texts, the *Treatise* makes copious use of marginalia, with summations of the various points of law and order germane to its assuredly illegal case neatly filling the margins and, arguably, emphasising the text's misuse of the formalities of expression familiarly associated with legal treatises.

The response to the *Treatise of Treasons* was draconian: a proclamation of suppression was issued which ordered the book's destruction. It was, however, to be largely ineffectual, as the text made its way from the continent in another form, and circulated for several more years.[34] The inability of the royal proclamation to eradicate the contentious text's dissemination illustrates not only the practical difficulties of suppression, but also a key means by which the state operated as the judge and supreme arbiter of what was and was not slanderous. Whilst our anonymous author claimed wholeheartedly that his work was a defence against slander, the machinery of the state, in banning his book, sought to bestow legitimacy on its own position and render false, illicit and defamatory the alleged 'truths' posited in the *Treatise*. Much as the permitting of the anonymous anti-Marian tracts conferred a degree of unofficial state authorisation, the proclamation issued in reaction to the *Treatise* rendered it slanderous and seditious, particularly due to its having reached audiences and achieved its slanderous potential. In essence, the act of granting a licence and the attempted suppression of unlicensed religious texts is, therefore, best understood as a power struggle in the politico-religious arena between the state Church and its enemies, with Catholic pen and illicit press pitted against England's laws, statutes and licensed slanders. The defamation of key figures in each faith proved a useful tool in the war of religion, and each faction assured itself of the right to win by virtue of higher truth.

34 Clegg, *Press Censorship in Elizabethan England*, p. 90.

If the *Treatise of Treasons* maintained a pretence of respect for Elizabeth's position (instead calling into question the actions of her government), it was by no means typical. Scurrilous writing against the Queen's person, fame and reputation was, as has been noted, as real a danger to the English Queen as it was to the Queen of Scots. The 1587 execution of Mary Stuart led both Catholic recusants and Protestant writers to widen their search for target figures in the war of words which embroiled the rival religions, with Elizabethan state papers outlining a stream of intelligence regarding manuscripts and books which advanced one Catholic line or another to the detriment of James VI – by then a committed Protestant.[35] Whilst hard-line Jesuits circulated material advancing the case for the right of the Spanish infanta, the Catholic presses at home and on the continent proceeded with renewed vigour in producing vituperative attacks on Elizabeth.[36]

Reacting to Mary's death, Cardinal William Allen produced *An Admonition to the Nobility and People of England and Ireland* (1588), an appeal to the English Catholic nobility to support an upcoming invasion. Replete with declarations of Elizabeth's crimes against true religion (truth, again being a useful means of warding off accusations of mere slander), the text openly flouted a surfeit of felony statutes designed to preserve the Queen's fame and authority. Unlike Leslie, Allen evidently saw no need to affect the language of counsel to forestall accusations of slander – or perhaps he recognised the futility of doing so. On the contrary, his work called Elizabeth's position into question by describing her as a 'pretended Queen,' and her moral reputation was defamed by her depiction as a 'wicked Jesabell.' Similarly, her religious role was openly denied by Allen's claim that she was 'Antichristian' and responsible for an 'unnaturall proude challenge of supremacy.'[37] Here is no subtle mask of deference under which lies a carefully organised attack: the *Admonition to the Nobility and People* was an unfettered call-to-arms resulting from political and religious circumstance (the Armada then arming) which was, nevertheless, to provide the

35 Clegg, *Press Censorship in Elizabethan England*, p. 85.
36 Shuger, 'A Protesting Catholic Puritan,' p. 590.
37 Allen, *An Admonition to the Nobility and People*, p. 8.

Elizabethan government with a further means of denouncing the illegitimate and slanderous Catholic threat.

The language of obloquy used by Allen – and frequently echoed in court records of cases in which the Queen was the subject of verbal attack – is of particular interest in any consideration of the ways in which Elizabeth, as Supreme Governor of the Church of England, provided Catholic recusants with a target.[38] Just as Mary Stuart's moral character granted her enemies ample avenues for defamation, so too did Elizabeth's detractors make full use of her femininity, her position in the Church, and her background in their attempts to publicly defame her. Allen's seditious activities are of particular note; he accuses Elizabeth of the spiritual crimes of whoredom and bastardy, bolstering his charge with her alleged falsity and pride. It was a popular mode at that moment. In retaliation for Mary Queen of Scots' execution, libels were reported to be circulated in Edinburgh which read, 'To Jesabell that English whore / Receive this Scottish chain / As presages of her great malheur / For murdering of our queen.' King James and his Anglophile, Protestant ministers were incensed, particularly as an example of the libellers' work (in the form of a hemp cord with the writing attached, which had been affixed to the gate of Robert Carlyle) was sent south to Elizabeth's spymaster, Walsingham.[39] The English Queen was as vulnerable to accusations of spiritual crime – whoredom – as Mary had been in life. Yet the back-and-forth slanders made by supporters of each Queen was not simply sixteenth-century soap opera, but rather an extension of a phenomenon which was plaguing wider society north and south of the border.

38 Susan Doran ('Why Did Elizabeth Not Marry?,' p. 52) provides a selection of similar spoken slanders against Elizabeth emanating from various sources, both foreign and domestic. Henry of Anjou was to label the Queen a 'whore' in 1571; eight years later, the papal nuncio in Paris was to accuse her of having borne Leicester's bastards; and in 1590 two Essex villagers declared that she had stuffed her illegitimate offspring up a chimney. Additionally, Carol Levin ('Gender, Monarchy and the Power of Words,' pp. 80–91) recounts rumours of Elizabeth's pregnancies, the supposed immorality of her sexual behaviour, scatological references to her person and allegations of whoredom.

39 May and Bryson, *Verse Libel in Renaissance England and Scotland*, p. 110.

Such accusations, though here made against a sovereign, are familiar – the Church courts records abound with slanderous discourses of whoredom against women. As such, one cannot fail to note that gender provided a ready means of defamation across the social spectrum. The defamation of women, evidently, centred on sexual morality regardless of rank. In making accusations of spiritual crime, Allen sought to undermine Elizabeth's religious position by affirming her guilty of the very crimes which were of concern to her Church and which evidenced a wider social trend in the denigration of women. In the vulnerable position of a woman in stewardship of the Church, Elizabeth was subsequently open to the animadversions of sexual slander which threatened all women in the period. It is therefore necessary to linger briefly on the ways in which the Elizabethan regime countered personal invectives.

Firstly, in the case of the *Admonition to the Nobility*, the book was outlawed and those found in ownership liable for punishment as malefactors. After all, possession of the offensive book more than qualified as a breach of security and was a direct rejection of legal statutes against defamation of the Queen's character. It may be further argued, however, that the state responded to both the malicious, gendered attack on Elizabeth and the aspersions cast upon her governorship of the Anglican Church in a number of subtler ways. It has long been claimed that there existed in the latter years of the sixteenth century a 'cult of Elizabeth': that is, widespread expression of adulation towards the Queen, with poets and artists celebrating the ageing monarch as an eternally youthful virgin. Suggesting a tentative link between the cult of the Virgin Mary – recognised as one of the key abuses of the Catholic Church – Frances Yates has claimed that Elizabeth, though not directly attempting to replace the Madonna figure, sought to 'draw to herself' a similarly mysterious tradition.[40]

Challenging any notion of Elizabeth becoming 'a sort of Protestant substitute for the Virgin Mary, filling a post-Reformation gap in the psyche of the masses, who craved a symbolic mother-figure,' Helen Hackett has instead argued that specific political circumstances dictated changes in iconography.[41] Further problematising the issue, Susan Doran has questioned

40 Yates, *Astraea*, pp. 79–80.

41 Hackett, *Virgin, Mother, Maiden Queen*, pp. 7, 11.

the existence of any systematic 'cult' of Elizabeth which comprised the Queen's own, organised process of Virginal image-building. Alluding to the wealth of imagery and literary panegyric which portrayed the Queen, Doran concludes that, whilst no evidence of an orchestrated campaign exists, it remains certain that courtiers, authors, counsellors and prominent citizens loyal to the state nevertheless sought to please Elizabeth with flattering depictions within certain proscribed limits.[42] As such, one need not look far to find the Queen celebrated as Astraea, in Thomas Dekker's *Old Fortunatus* (1599), as (amongst others) the virginal Belphoebe in *The Faerie Queene* (1596), and in possession of a host of tokens signifying the virgin state in portraiture. Protestant emblems, too, abound in the various images of Elizabeth, from the pelican and phoenix to the regal, scholarly and occasionally allegorical images included in the frontispieces to various Anglican texts – each of which draw unabashed attention to the chastity and virtue of Elizabeth, her divine right to rule, or her ecclesiastical authority.

Regardless of the reasons for these depictions, the political messages are undeniable. It is therefore possible to argue that surviving portrayals (the Queen notoriously ordering unapproved visual images destroyed in the absence an official, artistic censor) allow a glimpse into the means by which the state authorised – if it did not commission – cultural artefacts which contrasted sharply with the epithets and calumnies poured out by Catholic recusants in their unlicensed tracts. As a result, any 'cult of Elizabeth,' whether deliberate or incidental, may be better understood as an artistic, visual, and literary response by adherents of the English church and state to anti-Elizabethan slanders. Whilst Catholic malcontents such as Allen used Elizabeth as a lens through which anti-Protestant sentiment could be focalised, English Protestants responded by celebrating their head of Church and State in precisely the opposite terms. With the susceptibility of a female, Protestant ruler to attacks on chastity and Church authority, it is entirely reasonable to assume that the public image of Elizabeth was a calculated, if not strictly or carefully organised, method of legitimising the Queen's rule and bolstering her public fame.

42 Doran, *The Myth of Elizabeth*, p. 192.

Disaffected Catholics produced unauthorised texts challenging the Anglican Church ranging from the broadly satirical to the uncomfortably personal. Allying themselves with the 'true' Church of Rome and the righteousness of their consciences, Catholics appropriated the language of authority in portraying their religion and its figureheads as the truly slandered. By either attacking the 'usurping heretic' Elizabeth or appealing for her return to the Catholic fold, texts poured in from the continent and required ever more rigorous penalties, proclamations and statutes as the state Church sought to assert its own authority over press control against the threat from without. Crucially, the popular means by which Catholic polemicists plied their trade included the slander and counter-slander of key figures in the Elizabethan establishment, and the establishment, in turn, used its power to cast high-ranking Catholic figures into infamy. With the libellous battles between Catholic and Protestant so often encroaching on personal slander between famous personages, the notion of the Anglican Church waging a war on one front is tempting; and, indeed, the varying voices of Protestantism did, on occasion, unite in order to take up the cudgels against Rome.[43] The tumultuous years of the Reformation, the Act of Uniformity, and the dissatisfaction with the Elizabethan Settlement, however, ensured that the High Commission and the Anglican Church itself faced internecine conflict with increasingly militant Puritans in addition to the problem of continental and home-grown Catholic sympathisers.

43 Lake, *Moderate Puritans and the Elizabethan Church*, p. 66.

CHAPTER 15

The Problem of Non-conformity

Whilst slanderous and seditious Catholic texts proved to be a perennial source of trouble for the High Commission and Privy Council, matters were certainly not helped by growing intolerance of the Settlement established in 1559. In turn, the establishment was forced to turn the arsenal of state not only on the threat from the Papacy, but on that posed by its own non-conformist subjects. Just as Edmund Tilney's accession to the role of Master of the Revels represented a general shift towards a more active Revels Office, the investiture of John Whitgift as Archbishop of Canterbury in 1583 (following the tenures of Parker and Grindal, respectively) heralded an increased lack of tolerance towards the ever more querulous voices of reformist dissidents. Having clipped the wings of popular Puritan churchman Thomas Cartwright prior to his accession to the Archbishopric of Canterbury, Whitgift was no stranger to the methods by which Protestant divines loyal to the established Church could best serve the state by responding to Puritan appeals through official and unofficial channels. Indeed, he had gained first-hand experience during the Puritans' earliest attempts to subvert the Anglican Church's authority.

1572's *Admonition to the Parliament* (likely authored by London clergymen John Field and Thomas Wilcox) marked the first of several coordinated Puritan 'manifestos,' in which the perceived faults in Elizabethan Church doctrine and practice were laid down and widely circulated.[1] Described by Patrick Collinson as a 'public polemic in the guise of an address to parliament,' the *Admonition* became the first shot in a protracted, pitched battle of heavy paper cannonballs which would last for the

1 Pierce, *An Historical Introduction to the Marprelate Tracts*, p. 36.

remainder of the sixteenth century.[2] Thus, although speciously addressed to the parliament, the text was actually aimed at wider audiences – a fact which suggests its dangerous blurring of the line between a privileged site of counsel and debate and a wider, potentially unlimited public which had no business in matters of state. Such threats to the episcopal polity were, it will be seen, to typically invite charges of slander and libel from the Anglican hierarchy. A visible breach in the uniformity which the High Commission was charged with ensuring, the *Admonition* makes stark reference to the inability of Anglican ministers to attain the spiritual heights called for by the Scriptures:

> Then as God gave utterance they preached the worde onely: now they read homilies, articles, injunctions, etc. Then it was paineful: now gaineful. Then poore and ignominious, now rich & glorious. And therfore titles, livings, and offices by Antichrist devised are geven to them, as Metropolitane, Archbishoppe, Lordes grace, Lorde Bishop, Suffragan, Deane, Archdeacon, Prelate of the garter, Earle, Countie Palatine, Honor, High commissioners, Justices of peace and Quorum, etc. All which, together with their offices, as they are strange & unheard of in Chrystes church, nay playnelye in Gods word forbidden … These, and a great manie other abuses are in the ministerie remainyng, which unlesse they be removed and the truth brought in, not onely Gods justice shal be powred forth, but also Gods church in this realme shall never be builded.[3]

Chief amongst the deficiencies identified in the Church is the hierarchy associated with Rome. Not content, however, with finding fault in the episcopacy, Field and Wilcox go on to lament the injustices perpetrated by the ecclesiastical courts (which, one will recall, had already met with similar criticism from their secular counterparts):

2 Collinson, *The Elizabethan Puritan Movement*, p. 118. That the text posited itself as an address to parliament recalls the parliamentary privilege assumed by Wentworth. Clearly, there was some recognition of the sites in which speech and writing should be employed safely, even if the necessity (on Cartwright's part) of the need for subterfuge alludes to the fact that in reality that 'safety' was highly problematic.

3 Field and Wilcox, *An Admonition to the Parliament*, p. 3.

> The chieffest parte and last punishment of this discipline is excommunication, by the consent of the church determined, if the offender be obstinate, which how miserably it hath ben by the Popes proctours, and is by our new Canonists abused, who seeth not? In the primative church it was in a many mennes handes: now one alone excommunicateth. In those days it was the last censure of the church, and never went forth but for notorious crimes: Now it is pronounced for every light trifle. Then excommunication was greatly regarded and feared. Now because it is a money matter, no whit at al estemed. Then for great sinnes, severe punishment, and for small offences, little censures. Now great sinnes eyther not at al punished, as blasphemy, usury, etc, or else sleightly passed over with pricking in a blanket, or pinning in a sheet, as adulterie, whoredome, drunkennes, etc.[4]

The *Admonition* closes in a vein of religious righteousness with a Godly appeal to the Scriptures:

> The God of all glorie so open your eyes to see his truth, that
> you may not onely be inflamed with a love thereof, but with
> a continuall care seeke to promote, plant, and place the same
> amongst us, that we the English people, and our posteritie, enjoyeng
> the sinceritie of Gods gospel for ever, may say alwayes: The
> Lorde be praysed. To whome with Chryst Jesus his sonne our
> onely saviour, & the Holy gost our alone comfortor, be honour,
> prayse, and glorie, for ever and ever. Amen.[5]

Both the rhetoric and content of the *Admonition* are worthy of comment, not least for the response the text generated. Incumbent Archbishop of Canterbury Matthew Parker, incensed at the temerity of text's authors, wrote to Burghley:

> As for the puritans I understand how throughout all the realm, among such as profess themselves protestants, how the matter is taken: they highly justified, and we judged to be extreme persecutors. I have seen this seven year how the matter hath been handled on all parts. If the sincerity of the gospel shall end in such judgements, I fear you will have more ado than you shall be able to overcome. They slander us with infamous books and libels, lying they care not how deep they go.[6]

4 Field and Wilcox, *An Admonition to the Parliament*, p. 7.
5 Field and Wilcox, *An Admonition to the Parliament*, p. 8.
6 Price, *The History of Protestant Non-conformity*, p. 280.

Familiar as we now are with the strict, legal definition of slander, over which lawyers furiously paralogised in the courtroom, Parker's opinion of the *Admonition* – which was to receive an officially sanctioned *Answer to a Certen Libel Intituled An Admonition to the Parliament* (swiftly penned by Whitgift in 1572) – raises some important issues surrounding the authorities' conception of 'slanderous' and 'libellous' activity.

We might begin with the difficulties in reading the text as slanderous in the legal sense. No individuals, it will be noted, are either falsely or truthfully imputed to have committed crimes punishable at the common law. Nevertheless, the notion of 'truth' plays a key role in the *Admonition*'s rhetoric. Following an initial appeal to the derogation of 'truth' at the expense of remnant Catholic structures visible in the contemporary Church, the text closes with a fervid and pious exhortation to the reader to 'open his eyes' to God's truth. As we have seen, the importance of truth was a matter expounded with equal religious rectitude in the slanderous tracts of Catholic and Protestant – so here does its association also illustrate a carefully deployed tactic in the game of one-upmanship against the state's authorised 'true' Church.

If making a case for the text's 'slanderous' status is problematised by its disingenuous desire for 'truth' and the lack of individual figures accused of temporal crimes, then we might further consider its defamatory possibilities. The Church, of course, had a stake in governing defamation. It could award fame to and remove it from parishioners via ecclesiastical court proceedings. It is therefore interesting to note that the *Admonition* seeks to bring the Church into disrepute through association with Catholic (and, hence, to Protestant readers, anti-Christian) practices as well as questioning the clerical positions of its ministers. Here one is met with a curious problem: could 'slander,' when applied to institutions and public roles, be defined as condemnation of the role itself rather than the individual incumbent? In Parker's usage, this certainly seems to be the case: the text 'slanders us' (that is, the upholders of the Elizabethan Settlement) collectively. It defamed the Church by attempting to defrock its ministers and, crucially, held the potential to compromise those in authority by inciting unlicensed reform or revolt against established structures by a third-party readership.

The difficulties, therefore, in aligning Parker's exasperated assessment of the text as 'slanderous' (and Whitgift's subsequent *Answer to a Certen Libel*) with slander in the legal vernacular may lead us toward another conclusion. 'Slander' had become an elastic term which could be used by the state to denote any inflammatory attacks (literary, verbal or printed) on its leading personages and institutions.[7] No crime need be imputed by the slanderer – the Church had jurisdiction over merely abusive language – and it may therefore be argued that in castigating the *Admonition* as libellous in Whitgift's officially sanctioned *Answer*, the state sought to exercise its own authority in judging and remedying defamatory attacks. Furthermore, the very condemnation of the *Admonition* as slanderous (both privately and publicly) inextricably linked it with a widely known and derided category of dangerous language (the courts being filled with slander suits and the theatres using the process of slander as a rich vein of dramatic material) which could only have compromised the integrity of the text. With 'libel' and 'slander' still very much collapsible terms of opprobrium useful in de-legitimising language, the association of the *Admonition* with dangerous, illicit and potentially seditious language was entirely functional.

If Parker inclined towards the *Admonition* being slanderous and Whitgift certainly tackled it as a libel, it most certainly attracted accusations of sedition; and its production and dispersal was, above all, criminal in both intent and practice. As has been seen, criminal suits in the secular courts were no stranger to Elizabethans, and the authority of the High Commission over printed matter is well established. The ordinances of 1566 introduced strictures forbidding the publication of any adverse criticism of any law or statute, or any edict or injunction issued by royal authority. Further refined in 1586, the ordinances were to see offending printers lose their licence and to be imprisoned 'without bail or mainprise.'[8] The strictness of the injunctions and their overt attempt to control the printing presses sought, of course, to stifle (amongst other things) further Church

7 Here will be recalled Ina Habermann's recognition that in matters criminal, the state decreed on what was slanderous – umbuing all acts it wished to proscribe with illocutionary force. See: Habermann. *Staging Slander and Gender*, p. 48.

8 Pierce, *An Historical Introduction to the Marprelate Tracts*, pp. 22–3.

reform. As a consequence, the authors of the *Admonition*, despite their specious defence of the scrupulous and principled reasoning behind the text, and the public approbation they sought from the Godly, undoubtedly thumbed their noses at authority.

What the publication of the text, however, reveals, is the procedural inefficiency of the early Elizabethan government's system of licensing and regulation. As Parker was to go on to lament in his letter to Burghley, 'we have sought as diligently as we can for the press of the Puritans but we cannot possibly find it. The more they write, the more they shame our religion.'[9] The vexatious problem of the illicit press (and neither the press or printer behind the *Admonition* were ever identified) is one which was compounded by the physical nature of its offspring. The *Admonition* was small.[10] Lacking the bulk of a quarto or folio, the text was easily transferable, and marked the embryonic years of a political culture of prohibited pamphleteering. The very circulation of the text and its subsequent popularity (despite the activity of censor and pursuivant, it was reissued whilst its authors were in Newgate) attests to the fact that it obtained a measurable degree of cultural currency.[11] It is a fact which was to further stir the ire of committed conformist divines and lead to still greater powers of censorship being awarded to the Church. However, secret presses were not just problematic in 'opening up relatively stable and restricted patterns of consumption'; they exposed the inability of the state in maintaining authority over print.[12] Worse, they made a mockery of that supposed authority. In so doing, they became sources of potential outbreaks of slander and sedition anywhere (and at any time) in the kingdom.

Prior to the publication of Whitgift's *Answer to a Certen Libel*, the secret presses were again in action. When *A Second Admonition to Parliament* – likely penned by Whitgift's former adversary at Cambridge, Thomas Cartwright – reached audiences towards the end of 1572, the

9 Parker, 'Archbishop Parker to Lord Burghley,' p. 410.
10 Pierce, *An Historical Introduction to the Marprelate Tracts*, p. 40.
11 Pierce, *An Historical Introduction to the Marprelate Tracts*, p. 42.
12 Halasz, *The Marketplace of Print*, p. 19.

search intensified.[13] Again, the elusiveness of the illicit presses proved a humiliating challenge for authorities, with an anonymous open letter addressed to the prelates asking:

> Is plain speech and vehement words so evill? The old prophets, if now living, would have been cast by the Bishops into the Marshalsea // the White Lion // the Kings Benche // the Gatehouse // or other prisons: yea (and rather than they should be unprisoned), to Newgate with them as they can trotte.[14]

Once again, the libellers, in a clear rejection of authority, espoused their cause to religious righteousness – stretching their provenance back to the 'old prophets' – and directly challenged the established Church's jurisdiction in defining and regulating the limits of acceptable, or 'plain' speech.[15] Indeed, the very tools of state retribution are roundly condemned as anti-Christian, as prisons and courtrooms alike are castigated as an oppressive means of keeping down the devout and Godly. The unidentified author of the open letter went on to ask, rather pointedly, 'why should not the Prelates be criticised?'[16]

To Whitgift, the vehemence, tenacity and temerity of the non-conformists was no less than scandalous. As Parker had complained about the authors of the *Admonition*, so did Whitgift voice concerns about the slanderous nature of ensuing attacks. The Puritans, he complained, may 'think it a heinous offence to wear a cap or a surplice; but in slandering or back-biting their brethren ... in disquieting the church and state, they have no conscience.'[17] An important juncture in the breach between conformists

13 Patrick Collinson (*The Elizabethan Puritan Movement*, pp. 132–3) provides an account of the text's considerable support amongst men of influence, Whitgift's exasperated assertion that it sought to create religious schism, and Cartwright's subsequent defence on the grounds that it sought to bind the Church together rather than effect separation.

14 Frere and Douglass, *Puritan Manifestos*, pp. 59–9.

15 Marcy North (*The Anonymous Renaissance*, pp. 134–5) provides further discussion of the ways in which the authors defended their anonymity. In particular, she argues, they cite the authoritarian attempts of the Bishops to suppress all Puritan literature, including books better than their own humble appeal.

16 Pierce, *An Historical Introduction to the Marprelate Tracts*, p. 43.

17 Whitgift, *The Defence of the Answer*, p. 522.

and non-conformists, it is here worth noting that despite Whitgift's displeasure with the authors behind the secret presses, they are nevertheless still 'brethren,' though regrettably slanderous and viciously biting in their attempts to reform the Church. Nevertheless, the suspicion and potential for disruption perceived in the actions of dissidents is palpable. Furthermore, they were suspicions well founded, for the insidious and seductive power of anti-Anglican slanders were to hit, quite literally, closer to home. Not content with harnessing the power of the hidden press, Whitgift's *Answer to a Certen Libel* resulted in 'scandalous libels' secretly set up against him on the doors of Cambridge.[18] Yet to become inextricably associated with the semiotics of political dissidence, as in the latter years of the sixteenth century (and throughout the seventeenth), the pinning of written libels to the doors of prominent citizens provides us with an invaluable means of assessing the personal nature of political discourse in the period.[19] Invariably anonymous, such easily distributed invectives achieved the twin goal of voicing opposition without attracting punishment and ensuring a climate of distrust within communities. Already a hotbed of religious and theological debate and ferment, the secret libellers of Cambridge likely raised questions about the university's allegiance to the established Church.[20]

That anonymous, anti-clerical writings were to dog Whitgift is worthy of consideration. As Andrew Gordon has noted, the pinning of libellous material onto the thresholds of public figures sought to 'reconfigure radically the relationship between place and authority.'[21] As a consequence, it may be argued that Whitgift's control was challenged not only by what was written against him, but by the fact that the security of his professional

18 Brook, *Whitgift and the English Church*, p. 48.

19 For a particularly useful insight into the personal nature of political libels, see James Knowles' discussion of the attacks on such public figures as Francis Bacon and the Duke of Buckingham (Knowles, 'To Scourge the Arse,' pp. 74–92).

20 Collinson (*The Elizabethan Puritan Movement*, pp. 122–30) provides a useful discussion of the ways in which Cambridge (and other English universities) served as virtual breeding grounds for religious reformers. Rebellious attitudes, he contends, were 'contracted in [an] academic war of the generations [which] would transfer themselves far beyond Cambridge.'

21 Gordon, 'The Act of Libel,' p. 386.

position was compromised from within. Whilst Marcy North has cautioned that the 'flexibility of anonymity and the multiplicity of meanings that it evokes make it difficult to interpret,' what remains clear is the insecurity of the conformist position as exposed by its invasion by non-conformist malcontents.[22] Furthermore, such a method of exposing the weakness of authority was, as Pauline Croft has suggested, to develop beyond its 'Puritan flavour,' with the proliferation of libels increasing in frequency at different moments in the Elizabethan and Jacobean periods.[23] Evidently, appeals to parliament were not entirely successful and, as Catholic antagonists discovered, neither was the adoption of the rhetoric of counsel a guaranteed method of affecting freedom from allegations of slander and sedition. What does seem to have been effective is the guise of anonymity, which allowed for the criticism of authority and resulted in the law securing convictions mainly on luck. Given what has thus far been seen of the legal dangers inherent in public writing and appeals to both parliament and monarch, it is unsurprising that anonymous libels, which could make polemical arguments whilst exposing (by their spread and conscription of public space) the flaws of authority, were to increase in popularity. Indeed, they were ultimately to create a 'new vogue for satire,' which was to grow into the 'popular verse libel.'[24] This new mode of illicit expression was to develop, it may be argued, out of the various crises of free expression, the authoritarian attempts of Elizabethan authorities to police the printing presses, and the relative success of such anonymous, untraceable writings (either handwritten or secretly printed) as that used to compromise the authority of traditionalists like Whitgift.

With internal division blossoming within the Protestant brethren, presses both licit and illicit were to remain hard at work throughout the early 1570s. It is perhaps to be expected (given what is known of the nature of slander suits and counteraccusations) that Whitgift's *Answer*, too, was met with a secretly printed reply in the form of Cartwright's *Reply to the Answer*, which issued from the press in April 1573. As with familiar cases of

22 North, *The Anonymous Renaissance*, p. 14.
23 Croft, 'Libels, popular literacy and public opinion,' pp. 268–9.
24 Croft, 'Libels, popular literacy and public opinion,' pp. 272–3.

non-religious, inflammatory publications and dramatic material, the government was galvanised into action. A rather unsuccessful royal proclamation ordering the surrender of all copies of the original *Admonition* and all books defending or agreeable to it, followed by the High Commission's commandment for his arrest, caused Cartwright's flight abroad, but had little other effect.[25] In addition, Whitgift took up the gauntlet with a further *Defence of the Answer* against Cartwright's *Reply*. The very titles of the antagonistic works are difficult to ignore. Here, once again, were our conformists and non-conformists reverting to the processes of law and the unvarying, formalised to and fro of answer, replication, rejoinder and surrejoinder. Seeking the higher ground of truth and attempting to back up their competing positions through the overt display of impressive theological debate, Cartwright and Whitgift engaged in a battle of wills as well as words, and the notion of slander was to play a pivotal role.

Countering the latter's accusations of 'back-biting slander,' for example, Cartwright's *Reply* was to provide an arch-defence in that

> they which speake slanderously of them that offend not, of and not to those that serve God in their doing, which call them rebels and affect seditious, which are faithfull subjects to God & their Prince, which either wrest mennes words, or falsefie them, what deserve they? God forgive them that, and far worse matters, for his Christes sake, and give them better mindes towardes his true churche & a right reformation ... And yet for as much as we heare they will answere us, this I say, if they wil keepe them to the truth it selfe, the worde of God, then will the maters shortly come to a good issue, but if they draw us to other trials, there will prove craft in dawbing (as they say) for that hath beene the craft of the papistes, to rigge up all corners, and to finde all the shiftes they can, to have scope enough to varie a lye: to say much nothing to the profe, and yet to amase the people with shewe of authorities.[26]

In countering Whitgift's charge of slander with an indictment of slander itself, one cannot help but recall Kaplan's conception of state-authorised

25 Brook, *Whitgift and the English Church*, p. 44.
26 Cartwright, *A Second Admonition to Parliament*, p. 85.

accusations of slander against poets, and her notion of the poet attempting (rather unsuccessfully) to wrest the power of language from its traditional locus. Here, it may be argued, was not the poet exercising a self-identified and deserved right to language, but the religious radical. Here, that right was not predicated on the poet's muse, but on 'the truth it selfe, the worde of God.' In claiming stewardship of that truth and attempting to appropriate authority over language – Cartwright here presents himself in contradistinction to the Anglicans who 'wrest mennes words, or falsefie them' – we are therefore met with both a direct assault on the Church's foundation of truth and the state's ability to judge language as slanderous 'through shewe of authorities.' In turning state accusations of slander into slanders themselves, the Puritan pamphleteers were, in effect, attempting to destabilise not only existing categories of permissible speech and slander (by espousing truth), but authority itself.

That non-conformists fought their critics with appeals to the latter's 'slanderous' claims of slander and misuse of authority is of especial interest. Given the necessary anonymity sought by reformers and the subsequent illegality of their literary output, their status as criminals was undeniable. In short, it lay within the power of the established Church, as an arm of state, to criminalise texts. With authority over defamation granted to the Church and authority over criminal slander vested in the secular courts, the upper hand in the judgement of admissible language and acceptable, textual material is not difficult to detect. One might recall Ben Jonson's assertion that 'he who masters language refashions social relations'; to the Church and state, the underpinning notion was that he who legally governed language and had the power of state apparatus to back that authority up was, perforce, the master – albeit, a master undermined by those who questioned his temporal power by professing a greater, spiritual truth. The fact that illicit texts were to remain popular, however, suggests that the Church's ostensibly overarching authority to criminalise unlicensed writings served also to give them piquancy. It will, after all, be noted that Cartwright enjoyed the support of 'men of influence' and his *Reply* was to enjoy two editions within the year.[27] Of the thousand copies produced

27 Collinson, *The Elizabethan Puritan Movement*, p. 132–3.

of the second edition, only thirty-four were to fall into the eager hands of the Bishops.[28]

Such unsettling attempts to topple the edifice of state power were, of course, intolerable to the Elizabethan regime. It was, however, bolstered by more than the sum of its written answers to anonymous attacks; once again, accusations of slander – which Cartwright and his fellows neatly turned on their accusers – were to be of central importance. Though Puritans were eager to defend their reputations and counter accusations of slander as themselves slanderous and unjust, the undeniable fact was, as has been noted, that their texts were illegal according to statute law and the authority of the state. As such, the Church's labelling of anonymous malcontents as 'slanderers' was to allude merely to the inherent infamy of law-breaking by conferring otherness on these vocal yet seditious non-conformists. This implicit power of the state was, further, a familiar sight in early modern eyes – 'slanderer' was an epithet often used as an adjunct in lawsuits involving other matters, with the action of slander a state-defined category of illicit speech which connoted subversiveness, criminality, and attacks on stable hierarchies. As a consequence, the Puritans could rest their case only on perceived spiritual truth pouring from confoundingly elusive presses. The Church, meanwhile, counted licence, authorised counter-texts, the state's legal power, royal authority, and a still popular tradition of jurisdiction over language and public fame amongst its armoury. The result was an imperfect system of balances. The English government, weighted with religious, traditional, and legal authority, proved a wieldy Goliath to a weakened yet querulous and persistent David. The inability of the former to completely eradicate the latter was to be a sticking point which remained into the succeeding century.

It was, further, an act of balance familiar to sixteenth-century society. One need look no further than the Shakespearean oeuvre to find ratification of the notion. It is surely no coincidence that Malvolio – that most hypocritical of Puritans – was to find himself humiliated, in part, at the

28 Collinson, *The Elizabethan Puritan Movement*, p. 140. Collinson further notes that 'the ensuing movements of the Puritan press and of the printers is indicative of the widening influence of the Presbyterian movement.'

hands of Feste, in whom slander was 'allow'd' by the state by virtue of the season.[29] Yet Malvolio was to leave the stage vehemently vowing revenge, a humiliated yet unsilenced malcontent. One might also recall that the instrumental figure in recognising – and resolving – Hero's loss of reputation as a defamatory slander was *Much Ado About Nothing*'s sole religious official. Similarly, the Puritanical misuse of power by Angelo and the slanders voiced by Lucio were upset by the Friar-Duke Vincentio as the untruthful former was, again, humiliated by the combined might of an embodied government. Vincentio's restoration of order (if not harmony) suggests the perceived importance of religious and civil authorities in countering slanderous attacks on official institutions and figures. Throughout, audiences cannot fail to have recognised the power of the state and established religion in playing a traditionally palliative and conciliatory role in cases of defamation whilst thwarting the defamatory activities of Puritans (with the latter nevertheless remaining frequently obdurate in their own loss of reputation and prestige).

The idea that the heavily theatrical Marprelate controversy gave rise to the appearance on the popular stage of the stock figure of the 'stage Puritan' is nothing new. Tracing the invention of Puritanism, Collinson provides compelling evidence that 'audiences and readers either learned what a Puritan was from the torrent of fictions released by Martin Marprelate; or that these fictions helped them to identify, label and hate the Puritan who had been all the time in their midst.'[30] Whichever means by which Elizabethans discovered and identified the figure of the Puritan, however, one characteristic remains prevalent – his words could not be trusted whether due to his flagrant use of slanderous language or (on the stage) his comic hypocrisy and ultimate defeat. Therefore, Collinson makes a persuasive point in suggesting that the non-comformist controversies of the 1570s

29 Paul Yachnin ('Reversal of Fortune,' pp. 757–86) compares the portrayal of Malvolio to Nicholas in Middleton's *The Puritan Widow*, particularly noting the hypocrisy which is exposed when 'the smooth functioning of rank meets quite another agenda.'

30 Collinson, *The Elizabethan Puritan Movement*, p. 169. The writings of Martin Marprelate, the pseudonym adopted by a likely collaboration of aggressive Puritan writers in 1588–9, will be investigated in the following chapter.

and 1580s gave rise to the popular conception of the Puritan in the 'nasty nineties' as well as aiding the growth of the 'new genre of formal satire.'[31] Nevertheless, it is important not to lose sight of the fact that, whilst the satirised stage Puritan was a figure of fun born in response to the resistance of non-conformists, playwrights retained a fundamental awareness of the role of the Church in deflating the pretensions of such characters, even if it was unlikely to be done with any sense of finality.

Whilst the original *Admonition to the Parliament* launched the Puritan controversy and established a counterculture of disaffected Protestant writers and pamphleteers, it was also to have serious repercussions for the ways in which authorities reacted to and sought to forestall such politico-religious crises. Experienced in the literary methods by which dissenters voiced their aims, and having been at the heart of state counter-attacks during the tenures of his two predecessors, it is little surprise that John Whitgift – on ascending to the Archbishopric – was to pursue a still more sanguine course in promoting the established Church and silencing its detractors. Whitgift's star had been in the ascendant throughout Elizabeth's reign – he had risen to the position of royal chaplain and the Archbishopric following an equally meteoric rise through Cambridge; eventually she gave him the affectionate nickname of her 'little black husband.' One of the 'new men' who rose to prominence during the reign, he was, as has been seen, scrupulous in his dedication to the state and well versed in framing official responses to unlicensed religious polemics.[32] Under Whitgift's premiership,

31 Collinson, *The Elizabethan Puritan Movement*, pp. 168–70. For more on the libellous politics of the 1590s, see Michelle O'Callaghan's *The English Wits* (2007) and Andrew McRae's *The Culture of Early Stuart Libelling* (2004).

32 Collinson (*The Elizabethan Puritan Movement*, pp. 122–30) traces Whitgift's ascendance, in particular coining the phrase, 'the new men.' It refers, in Collinson's usage, to those who sought to 'correct the dangers of the old constitution.' Although Whitgift was in opposition to men who were hotter for reform, he was nevertheless known as a 'sympathiser with the younger, Puritan dons and their pupils' and he enjoyed a considerable following. It is likely due to these leanings that Cecil, 'surveying the university for reliable men of promise, and within a year of Whitgift's conformity … arranged that he should preach before the Queen and be advanced rapidly to the Regius professorship, a royal chaplaincy, and the mastership in quick succession of Pembroke Hall and Trinity.'

it was decreed that 'no book, work, reaffirming, coppye, matter, of any other thinge' was to be printed without being 'first seen and perused by the Archbishop of Canterbury and Bishop of London.'[33] The formal appointment of Whitgift and John Aylmer as *de facto* press regulators indicates that the publication of illicit material remained as pressing a problem under Whitgift's Archbishopric as it had under Parker's and Grindal's.

Whilst the actual influence of the Archbishop in the passing of the 1586 Star Chamber decrees which granted him hitherto unknown powers of censorship are contentious (Clegg, for example, notes the necessity of regulating print as a trade, whilst McCabe recognises such considerations as proceeding in tandem with the need to secure the medium of print), the result was the same: a further draconian attempt to regulate, control and censor printed material was launched.[34] Representing a watershed moment in the history of copyright, the 1586 decrees are remarkable also for the increasing power they bestowed upon religious luminaries in the enforcement of censorship. With Whitgift thus at the heart of a system which insisted on the strict control of printing presses – only London, Oxford and Cambridge were to house them – it was perhaps inevitable that, in the ensuing years of his administration, he was to find himself the primary victim of illicitly printed slanders. Censorship, it may be argued, had rather the opposite than the intended effect – rather than curbing defamatory material, it produced it. Further, it aimed it at one of the central figures involved in that censorship. The fact that high-ranking and public figures were more likely to be victims of libellous attack is well recognised, but here was a figure not only open to obloquy due to his entrenched religious position, but due to the political currency that could be gained by undermining his role as one of the state's primary censors.[35]

We have thus far noted the elastic nature of the Church's condemnation of illicit texts. The animadversions of those who impugned authority and established doctrine were routinely castigated – though not without

33 Wagner, *Voices of Shakespeare's England*, p. 60.

34 Clegg, *Press Censorship in Elizabethan England*, p. 46; McCabe, 'Right Puisante and Terrible Priests,' pp. 78–9.

35 Croft 'Libels, popular literacy and public opinion,' pp. 280, 284.

oppositional rejoinder – as 'slanderous, seditious libels' by the state. Further, the legal definition of slander was at the mercy of the state; 'slander' was, as has been seen, an accusation which was, in effect, deployed at the will of the Church and its ministers in their capacity as custodians of permissible religious speech. One must ask, however, precisely how the Church reacted to attacks which conformed to the more familiar, legal definition of slander, which insisted on the false (or seditious) imputation of a crime made against specific individuals before a third party. Interestingly enough, just such a method of attack was to emerge in one of the most notorious outbreaks of religious disagreement in the late Elizabethan period. It was, of course, the curious exchange of slanderous invective which was to pass between the anonymous collaboration which hid behind the pseudonym Martin Marprelate and the Anglican Church in 1588/9.

CHAPTER 16

Martin Marprelate and the Slanderous Press

The Puritan arguments against the established Church – which had their literary roots in the *Admonition* series of tracts and counter-tracts – were to continue throughout the 1570s and 1580s. Finally exhausting the convoluted argument and counter-argument surrounding matters of doctrine in 1587, Dean of Lincoln John Bridges' weighty *Defence of the Government Established in the Church of Englande* was, in the view of Cyndia Clegg, to herald a new form of religious debate. Whilst the Puritans' anonymous assaults on the polity of the established Church had become a familiar sight to authorities, the resultant counter-texts and accusations of slander and sedition had largely focused on the willing debating of Protestant dogma. From 1572's *Admonition to the Parliament* onwards, the Anglican Church had proved a curiously responsive – if exasperated – interlocutor attempting to exercise its role as state-authorised custodian of public fame and protector of official religious policy.

By 1588, however, the plethora of theologically argued illegal and authorised texts which had passed between Puritan and conservative Protestant had reached a point of stalemate rather than continuing to advance the argument into new territory. It was small wonder that, in such a climate, a new voice – in rhetorical terms – sought to refresh the dispute. The first manifestation of this contentious and troublesome new style of argument was to appear in October of that year. Commonly entitled *An Epistle*, the pithy publication was pseudonymously ascribed to one Martin Marprelate: the author (or, more likely, the team of authors) who was to go on to provide the Anglican Church and its leading figures with one of their most notorious slanderers. The accusation of slander itself was anticipated, as Martin was to pre-empt it by stating:

> You will go about I know to proue my booke to be a
> libell but I haue preuented you of that aduantage in lawe

> both in bringing in nothing but matters of fact whiche may easily be prooued if you dare denie them: and also in setting my name to my booke.[1]

Not only did Martin forestall accusations of libel by presenting his writings as factually accurate (conveniently flouting the fact that libellous writings were apt to be considered so regardless of veracity), but he plays also with the idea of his identity. As Marcy North notes, 'the Marprelate controversy marked a transformation in the use and tolerance of anonymity … it became not simply a protective device [but] a weapon.'[2] Such certainly seems to be the case, as the pseudonymous Martin assuredly knew that, despite giving his name to authorities willingly, no Martin Marprelate could be found to prosecute. Underscoring that point, North makes the important point that 'Martin confronted the relationship between libel and anonymity explicitly. Rather than allowing the Bishops to make this equation, he pulls the definition of libel into the text … within the boundaries of the text, the *Epistle* cannot be a libel. Outside of the text, no Martin can be found to accuse of libel.'[3]

Quite what made the emergence of Martin Marprelate, his peripatetic press, and his selection of pamphlets (of which seven survive) of such note has long been a matter of interest to scholars. Joad Raymond views the Marprelate controversy as a watershed in the history of pamphleteering, in which the pamphlet as a political semiotic achieved its earliest degree of popular recognition.[4] Holden, however, had earlier taken a somewhat wider view, arguing that similar satirical attacks on the Roman Catholic Church had existed prior to the Martinist material, with Marprelate simply breathing fresh life into the stagnant Puritan controversy.[5] To an extent,

1 Marprelate, *An Epistle*, p. 36.
2 North, *The Anonymous Renaissance*, p. 133.
3 North (*The Anonymous Renaissance*, p. 148) also notes Martin's playfulness with these categories, insisting as he does on the corporeality of 'Martin Marprelate' by shifting in his later works to insistence on the 'eternal nature and collaboration' of authorship.
4 Raymond, *Pamphlets and Pamphleteering*, p. 38.
5 Holden, *Anti-Puritan Satire*, p. 49.

both are correct. Whilst Marprelate consciously sought to appropriate a place in an established tradition of aggressive, Protestant writing, the tracts produced under the pseudonym nevertheless marked a rise in scurrilous – and populist – religious discourse. Such material sought not only to question established hierarchies, but appealed to the public and, crucially, attacked not simply offices and institutions, but individuals. Indeed, taking full advantage of his pseudonym, Marprelate's *Epistle* immediately sought to mar the names of England's leading prelates as 'petty popes and antichrists.'[6] That Marprelate focused much of his output on personal invective against high-ranking figures is of enormous importance – both for the ways in which it forced authorities to respond and for the effect it had on moderate Puritans uneasy with the flagrant and unflinching deployment of slander.

The slander of religious figures, it will be remembered, was a phenomenon not unfamiliar to the Anglican Church. In addition to recounting various cases brought before the ecclesiastical courts which dealt with immoderate speech against churchwardens, Emmison has recognised the frequency of punishments meted out for cases of 'slanderous speech' against local clerics.[7] In 1579, three Essex ministers were slandered, each by parishioners; one labelled a 'saucy jack'; another, a 'knave'; and the final, 'an arrant knave.' In 1584, as many as nine ministers received 'slanderous and reproachful words,' whilst in 1585, one Lancelot Ellis was charged with publicly calling the curate of Great Sampford a 'sauce box, against the form of the statute.'[8] Incontinent and inflammatory speech against clerics was, quite obviously, no particular novelty. Yet, it is in such accounts that we might find at least one source for the popularity of the Marprelate project: a popularity of which contemporaries were unanimous in their recognition.[9]

With criticism of Church figures so common a sight, it is hardly surprising that one anonymous account of the time remarked somewhat disdainfully that Martin's 'seditious libels made easy way into the hartes of

6 Marprelate, *An Epistle*, p. 5.

7 Emmison, *Morals and the Church Courts*, pp. 205–7.

8 Emmison, *Morals and the Church Courts*, p. 211.

9 Black, *The Martin Marprelate Tracts*, p. xxxii.

the vulgar [because such people] were apt to entertaine matter of Noveltie especiallie if it have a show of restraining the authoritie of their Superiours.'[10] As evidenced by the vigorous governmental attempts to respond to and unmask 'Martin,' however, the Marprelate texts evidently represented a more insidious and dangerous problem than the vitriolic speech of identifiable malcontents. It was a problem which stemmed not simply from what Marprelate said, but how he said it – the content (or 'matter') being as problematic as the public and frustratingly furtive 'manner' in which it was delivered. As a consequence, it is necessary to examine the ways in which the Marprelate canon combined a pseudonymous mode with personal slander, accessible language, and a covert means of production which, like the anonymous printers of the 1570s, eluded – and mocked – the stringent laws and searches of authority. Martin's use of print, a method of production which Harold Love claims was governed by a certain expectation of formality and decorum, demonstrated the ways in which that decorum could be flouted.[11] Eschewing the problematic approach of rhetorical counsel and appealing directly to the public rather than (disingenuously) to parliament or the monarch, Martin evidently recognised the failure of affecting wise counsel as a method of seeking change. Instead, he revelled in notoriety, indulging shamelessly in gossip and slander.

In addition to launching personal attacks on the various English Bishops – those 'popelings,' to whom the *Epistle* so irreverently referred – another key facet of the Marprelate texts is their vocal appeal to the virtues of plain speech. In the month following the *Epistle*, Martin's second tract, the *Epitome*, reached circulation. Building on his criticism of Whitgift, he asked,

> for may I not say, that John of Canterbury is a pettie pope, seing he is so? You must then beare with my ingramnesse. I am plaine, I must needs call a Spade a Spade, a Pope a Pope.[12]

10 Ibid.

11 Love, *Scribal Publication*, p. 189.

12 Marprelate, *An epitome*, p. 2.

Given that the *Epistle* had previously aligned Martinist texts in direct contradistinction to the 'flowers of error, popish and others,' which had 'stuffed the bookes' of his enemies, the rhetorical strategy is a powerful one. In a manner not dissimilar to the way in which Cartwright and his earlier cohorts had attempted to wrest authority over 'spiritual truth' from Protestant divines, here Martin visibly sought to appropriate 'plaine English' from the Protestant Church. It was a radical move undoubtedly calculated to form an historic link with the Reformation, of which one of the guiding principles was the availability of the Bible in English.[13] It was thus the prerogative of Martin to highlight the idea that religious reform had stalled, with theological debates remaining the preserve of the learned and religious elite. Furthermore, in identifying himself as 'plaine,' Martin sought to firmly establish the acceptability of his use of print for scurrilous purposes. Love makes the point that those writing for print were compelled to maintain the standards of their rank, lest they 'lose caste in the eyes of social inferiors.'[14] By positing himself as a plain and honest man, there is little need for Martin to maintain decorum – he, like the audiences for which he writes, is straightforward. As one of the people, Martin Marprelate attempted to wrest control over religious matters from the state and place it in the hands of the multitude.

That Martin attempted to destabilise the authority of the state Church is, further, borne out not only by his witty criticism of the Church's defenders (the *Epistle* having denounced 'lerned brother Bridges' as 'a man [who] might almost run himselfe out of breath before he could come to a full point') but by similarly humorous criticisms of the very institutions which sought to silence him. Adroitly mocking the apparatus of state, Martin's *Epistle* had directly addressed Whitgift, asking:

> Doth your grace remember what the Jesuit at Newgate said of you, namely, that my Lord of Canterbury should surely be a cardinal, if ever popery did come again unto England (yea, and what a brave cardinal too)? What a knave was this Jesuit! Believe

13 Mack (*Elizabethan Rhetoric*, pp. 253–79) discusses at length the variations in the rhetorical style of preaching across the country in period, in addition to providing a useful overview of the disputes about language and English Biblical interpretation.

14 Love, *Scribal Publication*, p. 189.

> me, I would not say thus much of my Lord of Canterbury for a thousand pound, lest a *scandalum magnatum* should be had against me. But well fare him that said thought is free.[15]

The mocking tone of Marprelate – which allowed him to simultaneously question and demean – owes obvious credit to his conversational use of language, and the flippant reference to the statutory law (which the text flouted by its very publication) is as difficult to miss now as it must have been to contemporary readers. As such, it is clear that Martin's prose – pithy, frequently rhetorical in punctuation and self-assuredly witty – represented a conscious attempt to blend style with substance. By setting the voice of Marprelate up as a minatory yet inherently succinct and piquant alternative to the declamatory (and tiresomely grandiloquent) tracts of the religious elite, Martin encouraged his readership to delight in the texts' artful interplay between the dressing down of stuffy and overly verbose prelates and refreshingly unadorned language. The effect, in short, was an engaging dialogue which, though scurrilous in nature, was indicative of a presumably welcome change from the didactic sermonising of more traditional religious polemic.

Marprelate's satirical tone, though it proved popular, was nevertheless to provide his critics with ample ammunition in the deconstruction of the authors' position. The streak of crudity which provided such a change in style from the tireless efforts of the Cartwrights and Whitgifts of previous decades was, therefore, to invite comparisons with similarly poorly regarded forms of speech. As Black records, Martin's 'popularising gestures' led contemporary critics to 'associate the tracts with other disreputable cultural sites that targeted popular taste with colloquial language and irreverent scurrility,' with Francis Bacon likening the cultural turn instituted by Martin as debasing matters of religion to the extent that they were 'handled in the style of the stage.'[16] Similarly, Martin's approach to the debate was condemned as 'fit for a vice in a play,' whilst the persona invoked was

15 Marprelate, *An Epistle*, p. 22.

16 Black, *The Martin Marprelate Tracts*, p. xxvi; Bacon, 'An Advertisement,' p. 413.

compared with the 'direct audience address, racy insinuations, taunting personal attacks and extensive wordplay' of popular clown Richard Tarleton.[17]

Contemporary attitudes towards Martin's style notwithstanding, it is important to note, as Patrick Collinson has done, that Martin had an 'affinity to the rather different but complementary tradition of composing mocking and libellous rhymes and libels, a form of Elizabethan culture which on the face of it appears as amateur and grass-rootish as Tarleton's world was professional and metropolitan.'[18] Shared by both, however, was rhetorical power in 'both oral and written forms.' That rhetorical power, of course, lay in the ability of the tracts to spread their slanders amongst the illiterate and literate by infecting the ears of listeners and infecting communities by covert passage from person to person. Part of the efficacy of Martin's strategy (if not his argument) lay in his manipulation of contemporary cultural modes of expression. It is here worth noting Collinson's claim that the tracts were intimately connected with the 'ritual of defamatory ballading ... [which accidentally served] to fix in imperishable print an otherwise more ephemeral and localised polemic, part oral, part written down, flourishing primarily in the word spoken and sung, secondarily in handwritten form, and only exceptionally printed, for an exceptional reason.'[19] What therefore becomes apparent is that Martin found the press a useful tool in maintaining an anonymous mode, whilst circulating demotic Elizabethan libels to a wider audience. The pedigree of his style might have been that of the defamatory ballad; the medium he chose for its expression and circulation was not.

That Martin attempted to capitalise on the possibility of his texts' orality is obvious; as Kristen Poole recognises, the Marprelate tracts were 'inherently theatrical, full of dialogue, scene changes and asides to the audience.'[20] However, the appeal of the strategy offers us a useful insight

17 The death of Tarleton on 3 September 1588 (shortly before the publication of the first Marprelate tract) was, as Patrick Collinson ('Religious satire and the invention of puritanism,' p. 159) notes, not lost on contemporaries, 'who identified Martin as a fool or vice filling the vacant, Tarleton-shaped space.'

18 Collinson, 'Religious satire and the invention of puritanism,' p. 159–60.

19 Collinson, 'Religious satire and the invention of puritanism,' p. 163.

20 Poole, *Radical Religion*, p. 29.

into the largely oral society into which the Marprelate tracts were released. A cursory look at the linguistic style of the texts illustrates clearly that, as Poole contends, they were inherently performable. The 'voice' of Martin, as the author himself attested, was public – the day that Martin was hanged, he claimed in his fourth tract, *Hay Any Worke For Cooper*, 'assure yourselves there will be twenty Martins spring in my place.'[21] The challenge was unmistakable; in adopting the voice and style of the libel and utilising direct oral address, Martin transferred religious debate from the traditional loci of the Commons, the universities and the court to the public spheres of tavern, marketplace and home – a fact which will recall his attempt in the *Epistle* to take the monopoly on religious discourse out of the hands of the episcopacy and place it in the hands of his fellow 'plain speakers.'[22] In so doing, it has been argued that the pamphlets enacted a 'grotesque breaking of the boundaries of the text and of conventional ecclesiastical discourse.'[23] This view, however, is problematic. Whilst the division may have been grotesque to authorities, to the Martinist project the breakdown of ecclesiastical discourse was less grotesque than it was necessary, with pseudonymous print allowing the authors to both symbolically and safely spread their denigration of the episcopacy and champion the use of plain English. More startlingly, there is a suggestion in Martin's colloquial and idiomatic style of a subtle attempt to undermine the power of the ecclesiastical courts (and, hence, the Church itself). One might recall, for example, the heavily scripted and formulaic language utilised in the Archdeaconry court records of the Marian Bishop, James Turberville, in

21 Marprelate, *Hay any worke*, p. 20.

22 Furthermore, Martin's shifting of religious debate to such public spaces as taverns and alehouses brought it into what Adam Fox ('Ballads, Libels and Popular Ridicule,' p. 145) recognises as sites which 'offered a sanctuary for relative freedom of speech … it provided the chance to ridicule in private those whom it was an offence to challenge in public.' The place of the libel in the development of free speech is itself a source of interest for David Colclough, who argues that libels provided 'a liminal space whose instability was evinced in the dual implications of the words "liberty" and "license/licence" in the period' (Colclough, 'Of the alleadging of authors,' p. 107.

23 Poole, *Radical Religion*, p. 31.

order to buttress the authority of the court despite its controversial representative. With aureate language thus a political and rhetorical tool prized by the Church, it was unquestionably the perquisite of Martin Marprelate to reclaim religious dialectic for a non-elite audience and undercut the authority and power vested in the euphuistic style of his enemies. Martin's orality was not that of the preacher; nor was it that of the parliamentarian, the professional actor or the rhetorician.[24] Rather, it was that of the gossipy, parochial slanderer writ large and laid down in print, in defiance of common, statutory, and ecclesiastical laws and courtrooms which usually disciplined such erstwhile troublemakers.

The oral recitations made possible by Martin, as suggested by both his style and his claims (and the print runs of up to a thousand, sold covertly for sixpence apiece) virtually ensured the state's accusations of slander. After all, unlike the *Admonition* series, the *ad hominem* thrust of the Marprelate texts was overt in the texts' imputations of the alleged moral and spiritual crimes carried out by specific Bishops. However, the pseudonymity of Martin Marprelate presented unique difficulties in terms of punishment and state response. Attempting to follow a course of action broadly similar to the ways in which the 1572 *Admonition* and its successors had been challenged, Thomas Cooper (then Bishop of Winchester and one of those targeted in the *Epistle*) produced – somewhat predictably – a state-authorised response to Martin's scurrilous charges. *An Admonition to the People of England: Wherein are Answered, Not Onely the Slaunderous Untruethes, Reprochfully Uttrd by Martin the Libeller, but Also Many Other Crimes by Some of his Broode* (1589) represented an attempt to discredit the 'scoffing, mocking, rayling, and depraving [of] the lives and doings of Bishoppes.' Yet the 250-page response, which was very much in the vein of previous weighty, forensic rebuttals, merely served to provide Martin with fresh grist for his ever-grinding mill of opprobrium.

Indeed, it was the production of Cooper's work that provided the basis for *Hay Any Worke* (March 1589), a fifty-seven-page verbal attack on

24 Peter Mack provides a comprehensive discussion of the various rules of decorum which governed various types of public rhetoric and speech – from the political to the religious spheres – in his *Elizabethan Rhetoric* (2002).

Cooper, which contemptuously referred to the Bishop as 'father Thomas Tubtrimmer of Winchester.'[25] Continuing in the demotic style pioneered in the *Epistle*, the fact that Cooper's response to the earlier tracts was forced, by virtue of Martin's lack of fixed identity, to condemn only 'scoffers' and 'slanderous pamphlets,' whilst Martin himself could respond with scathing, personal invective, is central to our understanding of the state's impotence in the Marprelate controversy. Cyndia Clegg provides a particularly useful summation of the frustration engendered by Martin:

> By naming the bishops and their victims, Martin lends considerable credibility to his claim of 'matters of fact.' But whether these are indeed factual matters rather than libels – and the accusations of popery the bishops certainly regarded as libels – could only be determined by law. Martin here extended a double false dilemma. The first rests in 'the peace': the bishops can deny their own authority and allow Presbyterian polity to emerge, or they can maintain their authority only to have it marred by Martin's slanders. The second rests in their legal recourse: if they opt for his slanders, and seek to prosecute him in court for libel, the libels will be proven true. The only genuine option … [was] for the bishops to proceed in a libel trial and have him proven a libeller … but he cannot be prosecuted unless he can be found.[26]

Clegg's convincing abridgement raises a number of issues critical to the understanding of slander and sedition as they operated within the Elizabethan Church. Firstly, the challenge extended by Martin was a difficulty which had not been prevalent during the activity of early reformers. As has been seen, the Church, though condemnatory of 'slanderers' who questioned the offices of episcopacy, was nevertheless armed with the tools to respond in kind: Biblical allusions, the interpretations of Scripture, the justification of truth – all were available to the state Church (through its extensive libraries and expert theologians) when the 'broad' slanders of the *Admonition*-era Puritans were countered. Even when the presses which issued the works popularly ascribed to Cartwright, Field, and Wilcox proved elusive, the Church was capable of entering – quite willingly – into religious debate. By eschewing complex theological issues and focusing instead on the slander of living individuals, however,

25 Marprelate, *Hay any worke*, p. 3.

26 Clegg, *Press Censorship in Elizabethan England*, p. 189.

Martin Marprelate played a trump card. The Church, faced with the visible failure of the traditional legal remedy of a prosecution (as it could mete out in the more minor cases of defamation recounted by Emmison) was confronted with vitriolic personal attacks for which no specific figure could be held to account. Simply, the anti-Martinists 'could not see the fox they were chasing.'[27]

Thus hamstrung by Martin's intolerable taunting not simply of the prelates but of the very institution of law, the Anglican Church was forced to fall back on a strategy which had served – not entirely successfully – in previous religious disputes. As in the 1570s, the High Commissioners were quick to condemn Martinist material as seditious and dangerous, and officials were authorised to conduct a campaign of searches, questioning and seizure. The prelates, however, were placed in the unenviable position of having to clear their names before an upstart clown – a fact which must certainly have undermined their divine authority over language at the same time as it underscored the sensitivity of fame (and infamy) across all social levels. Cooper's own *Admonition to the People of England* (1589) was to be instrumental in displaying the constraints under which the bishops were placed. Including responses from five of his colleagues, the text was engineered with the twin purpose of denouncing Martin's slanders as potentially treasonous and restoring the good names of those libelled. Once again, however, the authorities were caught in a difficult position. Unable to employ due process of law (either ecclesiastical or secular) in proceeding against Martin in the courts and similarly ineffectual in stemming the flow of scurrilous tracts, the Church was forced to frame its own responses to the same audiences. Since Martin had reconfigured the terms of the debate by popularising the genre of the chapbook-style pamphlet, rich in invective and possessed of an eminently readable (and recitable) charm, authorised texts following Cooper's *Admonition* attempted to appropriate Martin's own polemical mode and medium. Unfortunately, this led contemporaries to the uneasy conclusion that such officially sanctioned responses helped

27 Holden, *Anti-Puritan Satire*, p. 51. This is a view also taken by Marcy North (*The Anonymous Renaissance*, p. 142), who provides a textual analysis not only of the state's impotence, but of Martin's engagement with it.

legitimise rather than suppress Martinist discursive freedom. Elizabethan print culture, it must be noted, was then 'sufficiently small scale that some authority was lent to any printed text.'[28] Furthermore, one might reconsider Harold Love's assertion that the medium of print demanded a level of decorum predicated on the social standing of the author. Whilst Martin could write with alacrity as a plain-speaking man of the people, Church-authorised texts written in the same style could serve only to cause authorities to 'lose caste in the eyes of social inferiors.'[29]

Typically, further response therefore included reactive legal manoeuvring. A few weeks after Cooper's *Admonition*, a united front against Martin was illustrated by the Queen's issuing of *A Proclamation against Certaine Seditious and Schismatical Bookes and Libels* – a further sign, to Joseph Black, that 'all authority was conceived as interdependent' with 'a threat to one form of authority threatening the entire network.'[30] Black is certainly correct in his assertion, as borne out by the various ways in which we have now witnessed separate branches of the state (from the Revels Office to the law courts to the Church) work in concert in an attempt to regulate and control slanderous and seditious language. Elizabeth's proclamation, however, provides also a useful marker in the ongoing process by which the state negotiated the relatively new phenomenon of print. Accepting Black's claim that novelty ensured all printed texts a certain degree of legitimacy, the denunciatory proclamation must represent, in part, a concerted governmental effort to assert control over the printed word.[31] Texts sanctioned by the state, it seems, were to be the only ones granted legitimacy. In contrast, the Marprelate tracts, and any others which incurred the displeasure of the Queen, were to be publicly censured.

28 Black, *The Martin Marprelate Tracts*, pp. lvii–lix.

29 Love, *Scribal Publication*, p. 189.

30 Black, *The Martin Marprelate Tracts*, pp. lviii). Kristen Poole (*Radical Religion*, p. 5–6) takes this idea further, remarking that sectarians such as Marprelate were viewed as corrupting the vision of corporate perfection … [making] the body of the Church a confused deformity.'

31 Arguably, it is also evidence of what Halasz (*The Marketplace of Print*, p. 15) recognises as a perception that printed texts 'offered the possibility of widened access to discourses that have enduring cultural value and offer topical information.'

Official printed responses to Martin were, interestingly, not unique. Although orchestrated anti-Martinist campaigns were sanctioned (albeit, according to Black, difficult to track down), there also emerged an unofficial anti-Martinist voice. Opposition to Martin was to be issued from secret presses (without, apparently, stirring the ire of searchers), and manuscripts which aped Martin's style but picked up the gauntlet against his religious position were even presented to the Queen.[32] Similarly, anonymous rhymesters were keen to turn on the Puritanical yet slanderous Martin, with John Lyly and Thomas Nashe popularly implicated in the production of *A Whip for an Ape: or Martin Displaied*, also published as *Rhymes Against Martin Marre-prelate* (1589), and at least six prose satires aimed at Martin appeared in 1589–90. Nor was independent opposition to the Marprelate tracts confined to the pen or press. Defying existing bans on the theatrical treatment of religious themes on the stage, anti-Martinist theatre flourished in the summer of 1589.[33] Making 'plain jests' and putting him 'cleane out of countenance,' the Queen's Men, the Lord Strange's Men, the Lord Admiral's Men, and Paul's Boys all appear to have been active in a theatrical campaign. Eventually banned in their own right in November 1589, for 'treating matters unfytt and undecent to be handled in playes, both for Divinitie and State,' the brief interlude in which these productions flourished offer us a particularly useful insight into the cultural phenomenon instigated by Martin.

Firstly, that the theatre was deemed a suitable site in the dissemination of the anti-Martinist message suggests the widespread public knowledge of the Marprelate tracts; audiences must certainly have been familiar with the war of words being waged between this mysterious slanderer and the state. Perhaps more interestingly, the theatrical response to Martin lends further support to the notion that the theatricality (and orality) of the canonical Marprelate texts was, indeed, both critical and successful in widening the parameters of ecclesiological debate – to an extent deemed inappropriate by both contemporary commentators and the Elizabethan government. Martin, it seems, also provided satirists and playwrights of the day not

32 Black, *The Martin Marprelate Tracts*, p. lxii.

33 Black, *The Martin Marprelate Tracts*, p. lxv.

merely with religious disputation, but with ready means of constructing the recognisable, cultural figure of the Puritan. Gaining currency in the 1590s, the stock figure of the Puritan was developed, due in no small part, to Martin Marprelate's ubiquity and vocal defence of the Puritan cause. Echoing the work of Patrick Collinson, Kristen Poole identifies the category of 'Puritan' as a potentially problematic one which itself defied the rigid categorisation demanded by religious uniformity.[34] In his hypocritical deployment of personal, vitriolic slander whilst simultaneously accusing the Church of being a slanderous institution, Martin arguably provided the cultural sphere with a ready attribute which could form the basis of a clownish, theatrical figure.

Despite Martin's inarguable success in engaging with print culture, taunting existing laws, and deploying slander at the same time as denying his victims judicial recourse, it is important that one not consider his rejuvenation of the Puritan versus Anglican debate a victory for the former. Indeed, the wealth of anti-Martinist sentiment (especially that which bears no traces of official instigation) demonstrates with some gravity the extent to which Martin's message (and his raillery) – though popular and of concern to the state – was met with hostility. Critics were quick to express their disapproval not only of Martin, but of the ways in which his pseudonymous, slanderous methods forced the Church to respond in kind, derogating the terms of the debate. To Francis Bacon, the episode represented a particular crisis of theology, as he lamented, 'whatsoever be pretended, the people is no meet judge nor arbitrator, but rather the quiet, moderate, and private assemblies and conferences of the learned.'[35] It was, as has been noted, just such grave assemblies from which Martin attempted to wrest the progress of religious reform.

As such, it is understandable that even many Puritan sympathisers sought to disassociate themselves from the Marprelate texts. Moderate Puritans, in particular, were keen to voice disapproval of the prevailing wind to which, though blown by Martin, the state Church had trimmed

34 Collinson, *The Elizabethan Puritan Movement*, pp. 150–70; Poole, *Radical Religion*, pp. 16–45.

35 Bacon 'On the Controversies of the Church,' p. 94.

its sail. The anonymous *Plaine Percevall the Peace Maker of England* (1590) attempted a middle-ground approach, calling for reconciliation between Marprelate and the Church. Leonard Wright's *A Friendly Admonition to Martine Marprelate and His Mates* (1590) was to prove a similarly weak criticism of the extremists of both persuasions. Citing the 'lack of wit, spirit and knowledge' of the neutral tracts, Holden considers the textual output of those who adopted a moderate position a failure.[36] However, that such a position is evident at all suggests an undercurrent of contemporary distaste for the Marprelate project and the resultant debasement of religious discussion, which threatened the reputations of reformers and conservative Anglicans alike. Indeed, it is undoubtedly in response to the Marprelate episode that, as Patrick Collinson notes, 'puritanism [in the 1590s] ceased to be a political campaign and underwent a double internalisation, in localised communities and especially households, and in individuals.'[37] To Collinson, Martin's achievement was not the intended one of further religious reform, but rather the creation of a firmer, unified Anglicanism and the reinvention of Puritanism as a term to be used as a 'polemical and political weapon.'[38]

Attempting to address the question of why many Puritans of a more moderate complexion were alienated by the literary output of Martin Marprelate, Cyndia Clegg has concluded that

> [Martin's] subversive discourse was not really the issue. Nor was it that Elizabeth could brook no criticism of her church. Naming prelates and peers and taunting the institution of law, however, violated the government's basic assumptions about English institutions ... in violating libel laws, flaunting legal process, and seeking reformation by extortion, Martin had proven what most reformers had taken great pains to deny; radical religious reform endangered the state.[39]

There is a considerable degree of accuracy in Clegg's claim. Much of the danger in Marprelate's texts, to those who still sought reform of the

36 Holden, *Anti-Puritan Satire*, p. 49.
37 Collinson, *The Elizabethan Puritan Movement*, p. 152.
38 Collinson, *The Elizabethan Puritan Movement*, p. 154–5.
39 Clegg, *Press Censorship in Elizabethan England*, p. 197.

Anglican Church, lay in Martin's exposé of the weakness and potentially ineffectual nature of law and order. However, it may be further argued that the threat posed by Martin hinged, in no small part, on the nature of slander (and the state's mechanisms in dealing with it), which underpinned those 'libel laws.'

The authority of the Church and state over defamation, slander and libel are, by now, familiar. Not only did the Church posit itself as a guardian and arbiter in regulating public fame, but it exercised a traditional (if contested) role in defining and punishing defamation, as well as acting as a state regulator in the legitimisation of printed material. Martin, quite visibly, was an unrepentant enemy to all such state apparatus. Furthermore, he was an inveterate slanderer who used the pseudonymous mode as a means of exposing the weak points in the armour of the established Church – a tactic equally as likely to bring it down as to lead to reform. Martin's slanders not only brought the Church into disrepute, but Martin himself could not be openly denounced in court, and the Anglicans were forced into the humiliating position of having to clear their own names from the allegations and popular libels which poured from Martin's press. It was a strategy which can only have served to display the ineffectuality of their vaunted authority over public fame and print censorship.

It is necessary also to consider the nature of the press and its output in light of the Marprelate controversy. As has been noted, the small-scale of print culture in the period (aided, with some irony, by the attempts of the state to limit it) ensured that all printed texts – licit or otherwise – were likely to be invested with a measure of authority.[40] However, this view has been somewhat problematised by Joad Raymond, who contends that 'print would, for decades to come, continue to be stigmatised as an unrespectable, sullied means of speech, socially inferior to manuscript circulation.'[41] The two views are, nevertheless, reconcilable; and it may be argued that, once again, Marprelate – and the use of slander – played a role. If one accepts that the Marprelate texts – which marked a well-recognised shift in religious debate from theology and doctrine to personally slanderous and seditious

40 Black, *The Martin Marprelate Tracts*, pp. lvii–lix.

41 Raymond, *Pamphlets and Pamphleteering*, p. 57.

pamphleteering – coincided with a residual sense of the authority felt to reside in all print, then the government's increasing attempts to control the presses and censor illicit output can be linked to the alleged 'stigma' of print. In simple terms, disapproval of print was a matter which was either consciously or unconsciously in the interests of the state. By adopting anonymous print as his method for spreading pseudonymous and vitriolic libel, Martin (whether purposefully or accidentally) brought the printed word into a degree of disrepute.

Furthermore, the early modern period stimulated debates specifically concerning the divisions in legitimacy between the printed and the handwritten word. Noting the differing attitudes towards the two between writers, Harold Love contends that tensions about the sense of presence and familiarity fostered by manuscripts (in opposition to mass-produced print) ensured that contemporary attitudes were unfixed.[42] Both mediums had their advantages and disadvantages – although traditionally manuscripts lent themselves to the evasion of censorship and the covert, anonymous transmission of libel. Martin, however, blurred the lines between the two. That his medium was print, and that his language and strategies were direct refutations of accepted decorum concerning press output, is a rather obvious point; so too must it have been to his contemporaries. It is, however, possible to argue that print might have been viewed with a more pacific disposition had not Martin (and other illicit printers) misused the press as a tool for mass-producing slander. However, the derisive view of print suggested by Raymond, whilst undoubtedly exacerbated by the Marprelate project, was built upon pre-existing cultural notions. Like Harold Love, Cathy Shrank recounts the perceived intimacy associated in the period with manuscript transmission, due to its apparent proximity to speech and, as Walter Ong would have it, the greater degree of 'presence' possessed by the handwritten over the printed word.[43] Early moderns, she argues, subscribed to a 'rhetoric of presence' which was made manifest in the development, perpetuation and manipulation of the written word. It is,

42 In particular, Love (*Scribal Publication*, pp. 141–8) compares the attitudes towards manuscript and print shown by Shakespeare and Jonson, and Donne and Spenser.

43 Shrank, 'These fewe scribbled rules,' pp. 295–6.

certainly, a notion borne out by contemporary proponents of linguistic and orthographic theory: Thomas Smith's *De recta emendata linguae Anglicae scriptione, dialogus* (1568) recognised writing as a 'picture of the voice' and the prevailing view of writing as a purer, more mimetic representation of speech than print was to retain a high level of cultural currency into the seventeenth century – although, as Jonathan Hope has demonstrated, it was not unproblematic: the pen was yet 'dull, dumb and gross' in comparison to the breath of the voice.[44]

Nevertheless, being still further deferred from speech, the output of the press failed, perforce, to capture even the intimacy and value of the handwritten letter. Although, as Shrank illustrates, concerted efforts were made by printers to appropriate the style, structure and rhetoric of epistles, the immediacy and presence which formed a cultural bond between speech and writing were lacking. As we have seen, however, the Martin Marprelate tracts were overt in deployment of oral conventions, albeit the conventions of the gossipy and irreverent slanderer. Thus, it may be argued that despite the predominant view of print as twice removed from speech – a 'sullied means of speech, inferior to manuscript circulation' – Martin engaged directly with contemporary concerns about the status of print as an emerging and maligned medium. In using the vernacular in print, Martin provided a provocative challenge to deeply held convictions which prized the primacy of manuscript and its closer associations with speech. Yet by employing direct, scurrilous and non-esoteric language, Martin brought not only brought presence, but pseudonymity and brazen libel to print. In so doing, he helped emphasise the status of the press as a weapon which could produce slander in quantities exceeding the smaller scale of scribal production, whilst exposing the deficiencies of the state's press laws, ordinances and regulations.

Naturally, Martin's use of print had other, more easily recognisable benefits. One might consider, for example, the practical power of printed material over manuscripts. The moveable press employed by the

44 Hudson, *Writing and European Thought*, p. 93; Hope, *Shakespeare and Language*, p. 38.

Marprelate authors (housed, at various times, in the homes of reformist sympathisers) allowed for the mass production of slanderous material without the need to make use of scribes or the comparatively small increments of production associated with scribal publication. Rather, the press allowed for the 'explosive provision of copies' and, when used with the stealth of Martin, allowed for publication outside the acceptable frameworks of state licensing and censorship. Yet presses were far from perfect, with even the portable ones still bulky and vulnerable to searches. As such, manuscripts continued to provide a means of distributing slander (Catholic manuscripts slandering the Earl of Leicester and his relationship with the Queen circulated also in 1588), albeit in smaller increments of production.[45] Indeed, it will be noted that manuscript libels were to blossom in subsequent decades, eventually acquiring literary status as press control continued to tighten, the rhetoric of counsel continued to fail, and satirists became increasingly interested in exploring the boundaries of slander and satire.[46] At any rate, the Marprelate canon's utilisation both of considerable print runs and demotic English ensured that the debate was apt to reach audiences sufficiently wide that even the anti-Catholic spy network instituted by Walsingham would have found it difficult to find useful informants.

One must here return to the issues which were of such vital importance in the censorship of dramatic material – the potential audience. As has been noted, stage dramas were apt to incur the displeasure of the state when they treated on matters (or deployed language deemed slanderous) before audiences likely to take offence. In terms of the Marprelate tracts,

45 Despite the smaller increments of production noted by Love (*Scribal Publication*, pp. 37–8), it must be noted that a particular danger of handwritten material lay in its ability to form scribal communities, defy definite authorship and enjoy uncontrollable afterlives. Given that slander was felt to be a poisonous force, it is to be expected that early modern authorities would show anxiety about the potential of illicit manuscripts to poison groups amongst which they covertly circulated, as well as other third parties who may have co-opted them into collected miscellanies.

46 Croft, 'Libels, popular literacy and public opinion,' p. 272. Martin, very possibly, played a role in the continued tightening of press controls even if he himself recognised the fruitlessness of adopting the rhetoric of counsel.

the slanders which peppered Martin's invectives had the potential to reach unlimited audiences, and the victims of the slander were the very officials charged with maintaining the peace of the state. Further, the quixotic efforts of the Church in responding to Martin with similarly slanderous rebukes – in essence, attempting to assert its own primacy over language and role as judge in matters of defamation – which were of such concern to Bacon, can only have suggested the corrupting influence of print. As such, the use of the press as a tool in the production of slander, and the weaknesses which printed slander exposed in the state, confirmed and cemented the press's place as a dangerous and potentially anarchic medium. Adding considerable weight to the notion, of course, was the government's failure in tracking down the authors. Whilst 1589 saw the seizure of the press in Manchester (with incriminating tracts awaiting circulation), popular suspect John Penry – who volubly denied being Martin Marprelate – escaped, and the final tract, *The Protestation of Martin Marprelate* (1589), appeared several months later.

The Marprelate controversy continues to enjoy a level of notoriety unrivalled by its fellow Elizabethan reformist debates for a number of reasons. In addition to raising issues surrounding the perceived necessity for plain speech in religious debate, the episode invites study of the merits and dangers of print (as Martin's favoured medium) and the weaknesses in the Church and state's governance of censorship and libel. At root, Marprelate challenged and refreshed a religious debate which had previously subscribed to decorum and affected the frameworks and traditions of counsel. Whilst the 1572 *Admonition* had been denounced – virtually routinely – as 'slanderous' by a Church which was armed with the necessary theological weapons to respond, Martin slandered individuals without compunction, revelling in the knowledge that his pseudonymity ensured that the state was unable to respond in kind. Emerging from the Marprelate episode, it may be argued, were several key developments. The popularity of slanderous discourse as a polemical mode was confirmed, as was the relative success of anonymous libel in comparison to affectations of confessional counsel and parliamentary advice and appeal. Only the confiscation of his final press in 1589 stopped Martin – but by then his railing style and pseudonymity had proved a successful means of circumventing both censors and the law.[47] Thus, embracing covert, anonymous, written libel was visibly demonstrated to be safer than trying to forestall accusations of slander and sedition. Arguably, therefore, the handwritten verse libel, which was to blossom in ensuing decades had learned an object lesson from Martin Marprelate's activities: whilst presses could be confiscated, anonymity and shameless libelling were an effective mode of voicing disaffection.[48] As if to underscore the dangers of being identified, it was only a few years after the Marprelate affair, in 1593, that the non-conformist John Penry was discovered at Ratcliff, having returned to England following his flight to Scotland when first accused of being Martin. Penry had been operating his own press in 1588 which certainly played a role in circulating Martin's tracts. When he was identified the spring of 1593, he was arrested whilst searches were made, and ultimately convicted and hanged for the ostensible crime of writing a petition to Parliament full of vituperative language. This was a pretext. Penry went to the gallows because he was identified as a trouble-maker, with the actual text – the petition – a fig-leaf for the execution of rough justice of which the frustrated government (in both its religious and legal arms) was occasionally capable. Unsurprisingly, Penry was accused of slandering the Queen and government.[49] If the authorities could find you and they were out for blood, they would often have it. 'Slander,' as ever, provided a neat means of blackening the name of the caught.

If identification was dangerous, though, pseudonymity was not entirely successful either. 'Martin Marprelate' provided future generations with another important lesson. Although the pseudonym precluded the state from taking legal recourse in punishing him as a slanderer – in giving him a day in court – it was partly responsible for the ultimate failure of the campaign. Recalling Marcy North's recognition that 'anonymity … focused

47 North, *The Anonymous Renaissance*, p. 157.

48 For ratification of this notion, one may return to the previously discussed Star Chamber case of Lewis Pickering, prosecuted for writing a libel against Whitgift. Though Pickering was unfortunate enough to be caught, it is clear that he was indulging in a strategy similar to Martin's. The unlucky Whitgift was not only to face the latter's calumny whilst alive, but the animadversions of libellers like Pickering even when dead.

49 Waddington, *John Penry, the Pilgrim Martyr*, p. 116.

attention away from the author and onto the libel's victim,' it is clear that pseudonymity had rather the opposite effect. Although attempting to bring about reform by denigrating leading churchmen, Martin Marprelate, in modern parlance, instead became the story. It is probably safe to say that, today, scholars and history enthusiasts are more familiar with the figure whose false name has been given to the episode than with, for example, Thomas Cooper, one of the hapless victims. The success of the tracts in building a larger-than-life persona was, ironically, deeply problematic in that the persona was more memorable than the real-life figures it targeted. Authorities could not locate and punish a pseudonym, but that pseudonym could well prove useful in drawing attention away from the people it was trying to target and mock.

Nevertheless, whilst our understanding of slander as transgressive language which compromised reputations in the eyes of a third party, and the state's authority in defining and punishing it offers us critical insight into the whole episode, one cannot lose sight of the ultimate failure of the Martinist campaign in achieving its goal of religious reform. In addition to causing the Church to involve itself in the debasement of hitherto sacred and 'grave' debates, Marprelate alienated many reformers and, through the cross-cultural efforts of theatrical, lyricist and literary anti-Martinists, initiated a cultural blossoming of politico-religious pamphleteering and helped crystallise the popular image of the Puritan. One may therefore argue that the production of the Martin Marprelate tracts – and the vitriolic, personal slander contained therein – succeeded in both widening the debate, breaching entrenched notions of decorum, and positing anonymous if not pseudonymous libel as a polemical alternative to disingenuous attempts to counsel and appeal to authority. Though the inefficacy of the Church and state in mobilising censorship and punishing Martin was temporarily exposed, his use of libel – a category of language which, though prevalent and gaining cultural ground, was viewed with official disdain across all genres – ensured that his message was drowned out in the cacophony of disagreement and, ironically, the infamy which it caused.

CHAPTER 17

The Crises of Church Control

Clearly, the relationship between the Elizabethan Church and slanderous discourse is complex and multi-faceted. Manifesting itself not only in the traditional role of the ecclesiastical courts in exercising judicial authority over defamation – an authority which was widened rather than curtailed by the Reformation – it also became incumbent on the state's religious dignitaries to exert, or at least attempt to exert, increasing controls over the production of printed material. Slander was to prove an infinitely malleable category of language which could be broadened at the whim of the state. Furthermore, this elasticity is to be found at virtually every intersection of the Church and slanderous language: the ecclesiastical courts bolstered their cultural position as custodians of admissible speech by widening the legal remedy to include abusive words in addition to false imputations of spiritual trespass, and the leading figures of the Church were similarly willing to label any unauthorised text which, upon reaching a third party, threatened the episcopal polity as 'slanderous,' 'seditious' and 'libellous' – whether individuals or offices were accused of spiritual crime or not.

In applying such terms to any supposedly injurious or inflammatory text which was perceived as compromising the reputation and authority of established structures (or which accused the state of being unfit or comprising spiritually unsound representatives) the Elizabethan government betrayed not only a deep antipathy toward dissent, but a uniform policy of casting dissenters as criminals beholden of opprobrious tongues, poisonous pens and unlicensed presses. In so doing, however, it exposed not only an anxiety over the effect which transgressive language might have on a third party, but the necessity of preserving the good opinion of that third party by maintaining the reputation of the established Church. As a result, one can readily find a host of 'slanderers' tried in the Consistory and

Archdeaconry Courts for defaming neighbours and prelates, in addition to virulent attacks on theological dissenters as 'slanderous libellers,' intent on subverting the state. 'Slander,' it may be argued, was a term so ingrained in contemporary legal and literary culture (as, consequently, was the need to espouse truth and defend reputations) that state accusations provided an official view of the transgressor: in essence, the Church's accusations of libel and sedition could not, despite the counter-accusations of many reformers, themselves be slanderous, as the state defined categories of language and held the whip hand in social exclusion and punishment. In short, language deemed slanderous to the Church may have had the potential to disrupt state authority, but the power to categorise it as such proved a useful arrow in the Elizabethan regime's quiver in terms of destabilising the cultural value of texts and unauthorised language.

In making such accusations, the Church, as a powerful arm of the body politic, can be seen to have worked in much the same manner as the secular courts and the Revels Office. The intended appearance was that of a united front against slanderous and seditious language. In addition to the routine accusations of 'slander' and 'sedition,' myriad other methods of shoring up the Anglican Church against its attackers were developed – from the deployment of state-authorised counter-slanders and fervent theological argument, to the tightening up of measures aimed at controlling press output and the exercise of injunction, ordinance and statute. The result was, as has been seen, a responsive Church which sought to exercise its ancient prerogative of authority over defamation and language. This was exercised in tandem, though occasionally in competition, with secular state apparatus, as the Church showed a willingness to respond to its critics in mutual terms. Reasoned argument was countered with scripturally drawn counterargument, illegality was fought with legality and slanderous attacks were met with polemic sanctioned by the government. All such tactics, however, were problematic. Particularly, the Church was viewed as displaying complicity in the abasement of religious argument via its acknowledgement and legitimisation of incendiary texts. The Martin Marprelate controversy thus provides an invaluable snapshot of both the unity presented by the state (the High Commission, Bishops, and popular lyricists working together in a haphazard campaign to quash and de-legitimise the Martinist threat) and the difficulties inherent in government policy. In particular, it demonstrates both the problems faced by authorities in attempting to legally counter (and punish) anonymous libel, and the popularity of ridicule, defamation and slander as modes of political expression. Martin's populist polemical style, especially, was to consequences in the succeeding century, which had learned from previous Church controversies the potential dangers of a subject espousing truth, parliamentary freedom and honest counsel against an institution fond of slander accusations and armed with theological argument, the control of the press and a popular reputation for language-governance. Martin, however, underlined the relative success of railing mockery in advancing argument, as well as inadvertently providing a warning than anonymity trumped pseudonymity if one wished the argument and object of the text to shine more brightly than the messenger.

Multi-pronged as the Church's approach to slanderous language was, what seems beyond question is the impossibility of imposing any specific 'model' of censorship on the Anglican response to provocative texts, be they Catholic or Puritan. Despite the multiplicity of strategies by which texts that 'slandered' the Church or its high-ranking figures were fought, all were variously undermined. From the inefficacy of increasingly repressive laws in stifling the voice of Martin Marprelate to the perennial slanders aimed at local ministers by disgruntled parishioners, it seems clear that the Elizabethan regime was engaged not in a successful campaign of repression, but a delicate balancing act which rested, in no small part, on the imagined hegemony of an ostensibly united, divinely appointed, and legally justified state. Nevertheless, whilst censorship becomes a difficult process to identify, the study of defamation and slanderous religious material opens up a significant number of issues surrounding the history of print culture and its relationship to manuscript, in addition to raising questions about the regulation and governance of language and the links between various arms of the state. The various 'slanderous' outbreaks which plagued the Elizabethan Church were, furthermore, to sow the seeds of a burgeoning culture of political and religious pamphleteering that was to grow to problematic proportions in ensuing reigns – with the controls of authority (the flaws of which having been exposed) to be exercised with equal difficult in the seventeenth century.

CONCLUSION

The Stuart Verse Libel: Years in the Making

In any study of early modern slander and sedition, it is axiomatic that one must draw together such variant strands as the legal status of the terms, dramatic slander and censorship (with the added complications of private and public material) and the contentious role of the Church in judging defamation and producing state-authorised defamatory texts. It is therefore somewhat surprising that, in the main, scholarship has focused on specific institutions of state – be they the Church, the theatre, the law courts or even the press – with a considerable degree of exclusivity. As has been seen, such an approach can give only a restricted and incomplete view of the complicated, overlapping and, in many ways, unclear procedures by which slanderous discourses entered the public sphere of Elizabethan and early Jacobean England.

It is more fruitful to begin with the processes by which slander – broad and catch-all term though it undoubtedly was – was recognised as a wider cultural phenomenon. Here we might begin with a brief reconsideration of the ways in which the state has been seen to define slander and sedition. The secular law courts, certainly, were keen to extol the legal definition of slander – from application of the rule of *Mitior Sensus* and the identification of malicious intent in the civil courts, it is clear that authorities were keen to stem the flow of litigious subjects waging wars of words against their neighbours. In such cases, false defamation of character before a third party which resulted in demonstrable financial damage was a key requirement of a successful slander suit. Throughout the period, the criminal courts showed a marked decrease in such cavilling – not only were slanders considered potentially seditious, but, by the beginning of the Jacobean period, the truth of a malicious accusation ceased to be a defence. Simultaneously, the ecclesiastical courts began to show a considerable amount of leeway in what might be considered defamation. When once the false imputation of a spiritual crime was required, Elizabethan Church courts were quite willing to accept cases in which pure insult had been demonstrated.

What seems clear is that the protean nature of slander as it was applied by the state (which was apt to denounce any unlicensed or illicit text or writing as 'slanderous') served a particularly useful purpose. In attempting to exercise a legal and cultural hegemony over permissible and illicit speech, the accusation of slander played a central role. With the courts (ecclesiastical, civil and criminal) each acting as arbiters in various categories of language (insulting, libellous and seditious) grouped together under the weighty adjective of 'slanderous,' the Elizabethan state governed what Shuger might term a dominant 'cultural sensibility' based on a consensually accepted understanding of civil expression and legal protection between subject and state. Nevertheless, it is clear that slander was a dangerous and potentially destructive form of language. As Kaplan has noted, an accusation of slander could redound on the accuser, even if that accuser was the state. Such certainly seems to have been the case in several recognisable moments in the historical record. One might turn, for example, to the *Admonition to the Parliament* controversy of 1572. Not only were the Puritan dissenters keen to turn accusations of slander back on the state but defended their original treatise as founded in truth – a neat legal swerve which destabilised the state's claim that the *Admonition* was slanderous.

Crucially, the means by which the authorities themselves countered unlicensed texts was not necessarily suppression. On the contrary, the *Admonition* (like several Catholic texts) was not outlawed, and nor were the writers or circulators punished with any severity. Instead, since the procedural censorship intended by the official licensing system had failed, the state reverted to the outward procedures of the law court, albeit it a case fought in the court of public opinion. Answering the charges made by the Puritans, the Anglican Church produced tract after tract of counteraccusation, surrejoinder and counter-charge. When official methods of censorship (such as that represented by the High Commission and the nominal control of all printing presses by the Bishops) failed, Elizabethan England's variegated defamation laws, familiarly put to use in the various English courts and ostensibly aimed at providing state protection of subjects, remained a template by which the slandered state could adopt the role of plaintiff and publicly argue its case.

That is not to say that the authorities of the Elizabethan and early Jacobean regime were always willing to provide an officially licensed (and therefore legitimate) public response to texts deemed illegitimate by virtue of their avoiding licensing laws and censors and attacking the state and its leading figures. Although relatively rare, there remain several celebrated cases in which the state did, indeed, crack down with sometimes baffling severity. Although, as Shuger notes, it is almost impossible to reconstruct the historical moments at which certain texts were deemed so subversive even ownership could result in arrest, a cursory look at those banned by proclamation (rather than refuted in print) is illuminating.[1] In such cases it is notable that anonymity played a key role. Confounded by an inability to either catch the author or return accusations, authorities could not engage in quite the same public, back-and-forth mirror of formalised legal procedures because their defendant was entirely elusive and persisted in personal invective with alacrity. Nevertheless, it is arguable that the attempted crackdown on texts banned by royal proclamation did reflect a semblance of legal procedure. However, it was not that of the civil courts, in which plaintiff and defendant were allowed to argue their cases; banned texts of unknown authorship were instead treated in a manner more akin to the criminal proceedings of a felony case, being labelled seditious and slanderous as a matter of course, with those found distributing them punished. For it is certainly in courts like the Star Chamber that we find anxiety about the words of those tried (without the benefit of a defence) being repeated; we have certainly seen cases in which slanderous words were 'stricken from the record' by Privy Counsellors.[2] It is thus possible to argue that, even when a day in court was impossible, the relatively rare banning of certain texts followed a line of legal thinking recognisable from the royal prerogative court, just as the more tolerant attitude shown to tracts which could be roundly denounced by the state's learned elite followed the paradigms of civil suits. That legal process provided frameworks for the ways in which

1 Shuger, *Censorship and Cultural Regulation*, pp. 2, 3, 7.

2 Hawarde, *Reportes*, p. 55.

illicit texts could be handled by the state (regardless of success) is, almost certainly, evidence of the deeply entrenched understanding of how slander and sedition ought to be treated both in and out of the courtroom in early modern England.

With frameworks in place for dealing with slanderous language – and here we must be clear that defamation laws could apply only when such language reached a third party via speech, writing or print – it is necessary to reflect on another area in which slander played a key role: censorship. As has been seen, a variety of models of censorship have been proposed by critics, from the now outmoded 'authoritarian' model first proposed by Christopher Hill to the 'slander' model of M. Lindsay Kaplan and Debora Shuger's notion of a protective defamation law underpinning a mutually beneficial relationship between subject and state whilst also providing the basis for Tudor-Stuart language regulation. Shuger's model is highly convincing – indeed, she is almost undoubtedly correct – in fusing cultural and legal perceptions of slander. As an example, one might consider the curious case of Ben Jonson's *Eastward Ho* in order to see the ways in which the law operated in governing civil language. It will be recalled that the play itself bypassed the Master of the Revels, and yet, by virtue of the third party – a bevy of newly arrived Scottish lords – to whom it evidently caused offence, Jonson submitted himself to the law, and was later quietly released. In terms of Shuger's conception of a society versed in the rules of proper and permissible speech, what seems clear is that the play reached the stage due to a disruption in the procedural system of theatrical censorship, which resulted in the rules and values which governed acceptable speech being compromised. Evidently in acceptance of this breakdown, Jonson and Chapman recognised the law's need to (once again) pick up the slack left by an imperfect system of censorship and re-assert, at least visibly, authority over permissible speech in an ever-changing political landscape. In essence, when the basic mechanisms of state censorship broke down and a text reached its slanderous potential, the law stepped in (with the consent, in this case, of Jonson and Chapman – but not Marston) to re-establish the hegemony maintained by a dominant 'cultural sensibility' rooted in the legal protection of subjects from slanderous words.

Although Shuger's model is persuasive, there remain certain flaws in her argument. For one thing, although an increasing number of Elizabethans were inclined to go to the law for remedy when slanderous and seditious speech and writing troubled them, this does not necessarily imply a populace fully conversant in the law, but rather one in constant need of legal guidance over what was and was not permissible. Shuger's recognition of the Roman foundational principles of *iniuria*, too, is well taken; yet it is at least fair to argue that the stuttering development of the common law, which was constantly being written and rewritten, meant that the concept of verbal assault as tantamount to physical assault rode at the back of a rather wobbly tandem piloted by ever-shifting precedent. Physical abuse – stabbing or punching – was a fairly clear transgression. Saying things was more dubious and, over the years, the authorities and courts in charge of prosecuting malefactors changed. The penalties inflicted on those found guilty likewise varied wildly.

Additionally, Shuger's model downplays the lack of procedural censorship in favour of the legal and cultural acceptance of slander as a transgressive mode of expression. Whilst it most certainly was roundly denounced as such (again, still loosely conceptualised as a form of verbal assault), it is clear that defamation law was not the only way in which censorship operated. From the haphazard efforts of various Revels Masters, to the vacillating attempts by the High Commission and English Bishops to prevent the spread of unlicensed material, to the evidently avoidable system of gaining official licence, censorship of slanderous material appears to have been as beholden to human error and physical limitations as to a culturally and legally accepted value system. Also notable is Shuger's dismissal of handwritten material, which she claims to have been unregulated.[3] This seems a curious omission as, despite press output being subject to the most stringent crackdowns and counter-tracts, it is clear that a certain degree of self-regulation took place amongst at least some prolific manuscript writers. In addition to the previously noted legal scribes being advised to strike slanderous material from the Star Chamber records, the case of Fulke Greville's immolation of his *Antony and Cleopatra* illustrates the ways in which the

3 Shuger, *Censorship and Cultural Regulation*, p. 4.

negative reception of a third party could lead an author to censor his own privately written work. Questions therefore arise as to what constitutes regulation – indeed, it seems clear that legal and governmental intrusion was not strictly necessary. Instead, it may be claimed that Shuger's notion of the cultural power of slander and weight of defamation law was perhaps so ingrained that it could encroach on the private writings of subjects and their coteries – but the extent to which this was true is impossible to gauge: Greville might simply have been unusually sensitive. Yet far from being unregulated, it is clear that scribally published material was subject to the same laws, rules and cultural values which governed speech – and, as has been seen in the case of verse libels, treated with less tolerance and recourse to the defence of truth than spoken slander. Under the law, it will be recalled, written slander could never be defended as true – a curious distinction which reached its peak in the early years of the Jacobean period and offers a particular insight into the heightened dangers associated with writing over the supposedly less crude medium of speech.

Given the profusion of disparate models of censorship championed by scholars (each of which has been shown to contain considerable merits and drawbacks), and although Shuger has convincingly demonstrated that slander and defamation law played a key role in Elizabethan censorship, it is arguable that an all-encompassing model of censorship is an academic impossibility. Rather than the proposition of one 'model' (be it based on specific cases, usual or unusual procedures, shared cultural and legal values, or power relationships), it is perhaps more fruitful to consider censorship not simply as the result of early modern English fears of slander, but as a multifaceted set of legal and cultural principles, beliefs and processes, which often broke down and required the application of defamation law in order to shore up the gaps exposed by the understandable weakness and lack of resources available to the agents of censorship. In short, 'censorship' – a loaded term indicative of a recoverable process – is one which no longer seems suitable in historicising events and outbreaks of transgressive language which can comprise the destruction by authors of their own work; the judicial trials of slanderous malefactors; the unknown excisions of texts by government officials; the conscious or unconscious regulation of spoken, written and printed language by those living in a litigious society;

the state licensing (or non-licensing) of texts; and a slew of other procedural, cultural and legal processes.

The study of Elizabethan slander and sedition is not, of course, limited to the examination of censorship. Rather, it acts as a particularly useful key in unlocking some of the vast complexities of press regulation; theatrical regulation; legal practice and training; the vagaries of truth and falsity in speech, print and writing; the perceived differences in the illocutionary and perlocutionary force of early modern speech (as represented by the legal battles between alleged slanderers claiming innocent intent versus the damages sought by plaintiffs); state security; the importance of honour and reputation across the social spectrum; and the development of religious dispute. The deployment of slander – and accusations of slander – by Church, state, subject and playwright provide scholars with the means to examine and better understand not just legal history, but cultural, social, and literary history. It is no understatement to say that slander and sedition, as such categories of language can be traced through surviving texts, plays and legal records, provide one of the foundation stones in understanding Elizabethan language.

It is therefore worth returning to the poem considered at the outset of this study: the boldly named 'Libell upon William Lord, Archbishop of Canterbury, in Parliament-time' (1640). We are now better placed to draw conclusions about the reasons underlying the production of a poem which was not only libellous, but proudly so. As has been seen, censorship and precedent-based common law were, in the late sixteenth century, ever-changing and unfixed. Poets, critics, and those who sought to use transgressive language learned from the slipperiness of the law; the insecurity of adopting the rhetoric of counsel; the classical provenance of satire; the porous nature of censorship; the difficulty of maintaining illicit presses; and the danger of hostile audiences and the relative success of adopting anonymity. In the face of a regime which deployed accusations of slander arbitrarily, it is therefore unsurprising that writers recognised the evasive power of the anonymous, handwritten verse libel. Verse libels had existed for centuries (if not millennia) and therefore had the armour of classical provenance which encouraged artistic creativity, but more importantly they were anonymous, populist, repeatable, and bound up with criticism.

Hence, libels became a 'method of social protest' in the Stuart period.[4] Although not a new mode of expression even for Tudor protesters and writers – Bellany recognises the use of libels against figures such as Cardinal Wolsey – they were not only to gain in popularity in the seventeenth century, but to enjoy a certain literary appreciation.[5] It is therefore possible to argue that one can find in the various failings and successes of the deployment of Elizabethan slanderous and seditious language the reasons for the oppositional appropriation of verse libels. There was no great or planned path to the proliferation of the verse libel; quite simply, they had proven to be one of the few successful means of voicing social and political dissent, with anonymity making capture and prosecution less likely and the circulation of manuscripts subject to regulation only by means of espionage, searches and an awareness of the law's lack of tolerance of the truth of handwritten material. Certainly, by the mid-seventeenth century, the state's collapsing of the terms 'slander' and 'libel' was no longer tenable, as the latter had become inextricably linked with a mode of expression simultaneously lewd, pithy, popular and virtually uncontainable in an increasingly politicised public sphere. The 1602 assertion of the Queen's Attorney that '[libel] is a growing vice, and there are more infamous libels [now] within a few days than ever there were in the ages last past' is therefore of particular interest.[6] Slander continued to belong to the state, whereas libel was being increasingly appropriated by its critics. The problem was that the state made little or no distinction between slander and libel, viewing the rise of verse libels as seditious manifestations of slander, which continued to be a negative mode of discourse because it endangered the reputations of people across the social spectrum. Containment of libellous language was evidently problematic, and it was due to the inherent difficulties in policing, regulating and vilifying all illicit language as 'slanderous' and 'libellous' that transgressive texts were to find their *milieu*. We should

4 McRae 'The verse libel,' p. 59.

5 Sharpe and Lake, *Culture and Politics*, p. 287. Bellany ('The embarrassment of libels,' p. 156) recognises John Donne's appreciation of the form when handled correctly. Further, Croft ('Libels, popular literacy,' p. 272) notes that the work of classical satirists was beginning to circulate around literary London.

6 Hawarde, *Reportes*, p. 143.

therefore not be surprised to find in the seventeenth century anonymous, slanderous language pinned to doorways and public places, being sung and preserved in manuscript collections, allowing critical poets (of wildly differing talents) to engage in the emerging vogue for satirical expression, and visibly exposing the inefficiency of authorities in maintaining control over the written word. The controversies, regulations, legal machinations, and covert slanderers of the Elizabethan age had paved the way.

Bibliography

Primary Manuscript Sources

STAC 4/3/2. Plaintiff: Andrew Revett (Ryvett) and William Bygott. Defendant: Richard Veer. Place or Subject: Forgery of treasonable correspondence between plaintiffs (2 suits). County: Suffolk.

STAC 5/A10/13. Attorney General v. Smith and Fysher.

STAC 7/6/9. Paintiff: Tyringham, Thomas. Defendant: Richard Ardis and Edward Ardis. Place or Subject: Sherrington: Unlawful entries, slander, conspiracy, etc. County: Bucks.

Primary Printed Sources

Allen, W. 1588. *An Admonition to the Nobility and People of England and Ireland Concerninge the Present Warres Made for the Execution of His Holines Sentence, by the Highe and Mightie Kinge Catholike of Spaine. By the CARDINAL of Englande.Ao. M. D. LXXXVIII.* Antwerp: A. Coninncx.

Anton, R. 1617. *Vices anotimie, scourged and corrected, in new satirs. Lately written by R.A. of Magdalen Colledge in Cambridge.* London: Barnard Alsop for Roger Jackson.

Bacon, F. 1841 [1589]. 'An Advertisement Touching the Controversies in the Church of England' in B. Montagu (ed.), *The Works of Francis Bacon, Lord Chancellor of England: A New Edition With a Life of the Author, Volume II.* Philadelphia, PA: Carey and Hart.

Bacon, F. 1862 [1589]. 'On the Controversies of the Church' in J. Spedding, R. L. Ellis and D. D. Heath (eds), *The Works of Sir Francis Bacon, Vol. VIII.* London: Longman, Green, Longman and Roberts.

Burton, R. 1863 [1621]. *The Anatomy of Melancholy, What it is: With all the Kinds, Causes, Symptomes, Prognostickes, and Several Cures of it. In Three Maine Partitions with their several Sections, Members, and Subsections. Philosophically, Medicinally, Historically, Opened and Cut Up.* London: William Tegg.

Calendar of State Papers, Domestic series, of the reigns of Edward VI, Mary, Elizabeth, 1547–[1625], Vol. 2. 1581–1590 [1865]. Mary Anne Everett Green (ed.). London: Longman, Brown, Green, Longman and Roberts.

Calendar of State Papers, Elizabeth, Relating to Scotland and Mary, Queen of Scots. 1547–1603. Vol. 4. 1571–1574. [1905]. William K. Boyd (ed.). Ann Arbor: University of Michigan.

Cartwright, T. 1907 [1572]. *A Second Admonition to Parliament* in W. H. Frere and C. E. Douglass (eds), *Puritan Manifestoes: A Study of the Origin of the Puritan Revolt*. London: Society for Promoting Christian Knowledge.

Coke, E. 1826 [1605]. 'De Libellis Famosis' in J. H. Thomas and J. F. Fraser (eds), *The Reports of Sir Edward Coke, Knt, Vol. III*. London: Peter Butterworth and son.

Crompton, R. 1641. *Star-Chamber cases Shewing what causes properly belong to the cognizance of that court. Collected for the most part out of Mr. Crompton, his booke, entitled The iuristiction of divers courts*. London: John Grove.

Field, J., and Wilcox, T. 1907 [1572]. *An Admonition to the Parliament* in W. H. Frere and C. E. Douglas (eds), *A Study of the Origin of the Puritan Revolt*. London: Society for Promoting Christian Knowledge.

Gosson, S. 1579. *The schoole of abuse conteining a plesaunt invective against poets, pipers, plaiers, iesters and such like caterpillars of a commonwealth; setting vp the hagge of defiance to their mischievous exercise, and overthrowing their bulwarkes, by prophane writers, naturall reason, and common experience: a discourse as pleasaunt for gentlemen that favour learning, as profitable for all that wyll follow virtue*. London: Thomas Woodcocke.

Gosson, S. 1582. *Playes confuted in five actions proving that they are not to be suffered in a Christian common weale, by the waye both the cavils of Thomas Lodge, and the play of playes, written in their defence, and other obiections of players frendes, are truly set downe and directlye aunsweared*. London: Thomas Gosson.

Greville, F. 1986 [1625]. *A Dedication to Sir Philip Sidney* in J. Gouws (ed.), *The Prose Works of Fulke Greville, Lord Brooke*. Oxford: Clarendon Press.

Helmholz, R. H. 1985. *Select Cases on Defamation to 1600*. London: Selden Society.

James I. 1996 [1603]. *Basilikon Doron* in D. Fischlin and M. Fortier (eds), *The True Law of Free Monarchies and Basilikon Doron*. Toronto: CRRS Publications.

Jonson, B. 1640 [1614]. *Bartholomew Fair*. London: Richard Meighen.

Jonson, B. 1905 [1601]. *The Poetaster*. New York: Henry Holt and Company.

Jonson, B. 1994 [1605]. 'To an Unnamed Lady, probably the Countess of Bedford. 1605,' in C. G. Petter (ed.), *Eastward H*. London: A & C Black.

Jonson, B., Chapman, G., and Marston, J. 1994 [1605]. *Eastward Ho*. London: A & C Black.

Leslie, J. 1572. *A treatise of treasons against Q. Elizabeth, and the croune of England diuided into two partes: whereof, the first parte answereth certaine treasons parte answereth certaine treasons pretended, that neuer were intended: and the second, discouereth greater treasons committed, that are by few perceiued: as more largely appeareth in the page following*. Louvain: John Fowler.

Marprelate, M. 1588. *Oh read over Doctor John Bridges, for it is worthy work: Or an epitome of the first book of that right worshipful volume written against the Puritans in the defence of the noble clergy by as worshipful a priest, John Bridges, presbyter, priest or elder, Doctor of Divility, and Dean of Sarum, wherein the arguments of the Puritans are wisely prevented [in] that, when they come to answer Master Doctor, they must needs say something that hath been spoken*. England: Robert Waldegrave.

Marprelate, M. 1589. *Hay any worke for Cooper: OR, A BRIEFE PISTLE DIRECTED BY WAY OF an Publication to the Reverend Byshops, counselling them if they will needes bee Barrelled up, for feare of smelling in the nostrills of his Majesty, and the state, that they would use the advise of Reverend Martin, for the providing of their Cooper, because the Reverend T. C. (by which mysticall Letters is understood, either the bounsing Parson of East|meane, or Tom Coakes his Chaplaine) to be an unskilfull and a Deceitfull Tub-trimmer. WHEREIN WORTHY MARTIN QVITS Himselfe like a Man I warrant you, in the modest defence of his selfe and his learned Pistles, and maketh the Coo|pers hoopes to flye off, and the Bishops Tubs to leake out of all cry, Penned and Compiled by MARTIN the METROPOLITAN, Printed in Europe, not farre from some of the Bounsing Priests*. England: Robert Waldegrave.

Marprelate, M. 1895 [1588]. 'An Epistle to the right puisante, and terrible Priests, my cleargie masters of the Confocation-house, whether fickers generall, worshipful Paltripolitans, or any other of the holy league of subscription & this I recommend unto them with all my heart, with a desire to see them all to provided for one day, as I would wish, which I promise them shall not be at all to their hurt' in E. Arber (ed.), *The Epistle*. Westminster: Archibald Constable & Co.

Montaigne, M. 1958 [1588]. 'Of Experience,' in D. Frame (ed. and trans.), *The Complete Essays of Montaigne*. Stanford, CA: Stanford University Press.

Nelson, A. H., and Elliott, J. R., Jr (eds). 2011. *Inns of Court: Records of Early English Drama, 3 Vols*. Cambridge: D. S. Brewer.

Norton, T., and Sackville, T. 1958 [1561]. *Gorboduc*. London: Aldine Press.

Parker, M. 1853 [1572]. 'Archbishop Parker to Lord Burghley' in J. Bruce and T. Thomason Perowne (eds), *Correspondence of Matthew Parker, D.D. Archbishop of Canterbury, Comprising letters written by and to him, from A.D. 1535 to his death, A.D. 1575*. Cambridge: Cambridge University Press.

Parsons, R. 1596. *A conference about the next succession to the crown of England divided into two parts: the first containeth the discourse of a civil lawyer, how and in what manner propinquity of bloud is to be preferred: the second containeth the speech of a temporal lawyer about the particular titles of all such as do, or may, pretend (within England or without) to the next succession: whereunto is also added a new and perfect arbor and genealogy of the descents of all the kings and princes of England, from the Conquest to the present day, whereby each mans pretence is made more plain*. N.: R. Doleman.

Price, T. 1838. *The History of Protestant Non-conformity in England From the Reformation Under Henry VIII: Vol. I*. London: William Ball.

Proclamations. 1559. *By the Quene. Forasmuche as the tyme wherein common interludes in the Englishe tongue are wont usually to be played*, 15 May. London.

Shakespeare, W. 1955 [1611]. *Cymbeline*. London: Methuen.

Shakespeare, W. 1971 [1603]. *Othello*. London: Edward Arnold.

Shakespeare, W. 1991 [1603–4]. *Measure for Measure*. Oxford: Clarendon Press.

Shakespeare, W. 2006 [1602]. *Hamlet*. London: Arden Shakespeare.

Sidney, P. 1829 [1580]. 'Sir Philip Sidney to Queen Elizabeth, Anno 1580, Dissuading Her From Marrying the Duke of Anjou' in W. Grey (ed.), *The Miscellaneous Works of Sir Philip Sidney, Knt: With a Life of the Author*. Oxford: D. A. Talboys.

Smith, T. 1583. *De republica Anglorum. The maner of gouernement or policie of the realme of England, compiled by the honourable man Thomas Smyth, Doctor of the ciuil lawes, knight, and principall secretarie vnto the two most worthie princes, King Edwarde the sixt, and Queene Elizabeth, Seene and allowed*. London: Henrie Midleton.

Stubbes, P. 1583. *The anatomie of abuses contayning a discoverie, or briefe summarie of such notable vices and imperfections, as now raigne in many Christian countreyes of the worlde: but (especiallie) in a verie famous ilande called Ailgna: together, with most fearefull examples of Gods iudgementes, executed vpon the wicked for the same, aswell in Ailgna of late, as in other places, elsewhere. Verie godly, to be read of all true Christians, everie where: but most needefull, to be regarded in Englande. Made dialogue-wise, by Phillip Stubbes. Seene and allowed, according to order*. London: Richard Jones.

Stubbs, J. 1968 [1579]. *The Discoverie of a Gaping Gvlf VVhereinto England is Like to Be Swallovved By An Other French Mariage, if The Lord Forbid Not the Banes, by Letting Her Maiestie See the Sin and Punishment Thereof* in L. E. Berry (ed.), *John Stubbs's Gaping Gulf With Letters and Other Relevant Documents*. Charlottesville: Virginia University Press.

Whitgift, J. 1853. *The Defence of the Answer* in J. Ayre (ed.), *The Works of John Whitgift: Volume 3*. Cambridge: Cambridge University Press.

Wroth. M. 1996 [*c*. 1620]. *Love's Victory* in S. P. Cerasano and M. Wynn-Davies (eds), *Renaissance Drama by Women: Texts and Documents*. London: Routledge.

Vaughan, W. 1630. *The arraignment of slander perjury blasphemy, and other malicious sinnes shewing sundry examples of Gods iujdgements against the offenders. As well by the testimony of the Scriptures, and of the fathers of the primatiue church as likewise out of the reportes of Sir Edward Dier, Sir Edward Cooke, and other famous lawyers of this kingdome. Published by Sir William Vaughan knight.* London: Francis Constable.

Secondary Printed Sources

Adams, J. Q. 1931. '*Eastward Ho* and its Satire Against the Scots,' *Studies in Philology*, 28 (4), pp. 689–701.

Archer, J. E., Goldring, E., and Knight, S. (eds). 2011. *The Intellectual and Cultural World of the Early Modern Inns of Court*. Manchester: Manchester University Press.

Axton, M. 1977. *The Queen's Two Bodies: Drama and the Elizabethan Succession*. London: Royal Historical Society.

Baker, J. H. 1978. *Legal Records and the Historian*. London: Swift.

Baker, J. H. 2002. *An Introduction to Legal History, 4th Edition*. Edinburgh: Butterworths.

Baker, J. H. 2003. *The Oxford History of the Laws of England Volume VI: 1483–1558*. Oxford: Oxford University Press.

Barnes, T. G. 1961. 'Star Chamber Mythology,' *The American Journal of Legal History*, 5 (1), pp. 1–11.

Batho, G. R. 1958. 'Payment and Mitigation of a Star Chamber Fine,' *Historical Journal*, 1, pp. 40–51.

Bawcutt, N. W. 1992. 'Review of *Art Made Tongue-Tied by Authority: Elizabethan and Jacobean Dramatic Censorship* by Janet Clare,' *The Review of English Studies*, 43 (172), pp. 545–46.

Beal, P. 1998. *In Praise of Scribes*. Oxford: Oxford University Press.

Beattie, J. M. 1991. 'Scales of Justice: Defense Counsel and the English. Criminal Trial in the Eighteenth and Nineteenth Centuries,' *Law and History Review*, 9 (2), pp. 221–67.

Bednarz, J. P. 2001. *Shakespeare and the Poets' War*. New York: Columbia University Press.

Bell, I. 1998. 'Elizabeth, Stubbs, and the Gaping Gulf' in J. M. Walker (ed.), *Dissing Elizabeth: Negative Representations of Gloriana*. London: Duke University Press.

Bellamy, J. 2013. *The Tudor Law of Treason (Routledge Revivals): An Introduction.* London: Routledge.

Bellany, A. 1995. 'A Poem on the Archbishop's Hearse: Puritanism, Libel, and Sedition after the Hampton Court Conference,' *Journal of British Studies*, 34 (2), pp. 137–54.

Bellany, A. 2007a. 'Railing Rhymes Revisited: Libels, Scandals, and Early Stuart Politics,' *History Compass*, 5/4, pp. 1136–79.

Bellany, A. 2007b. 'The embarrassment of libels: perceptions and representations of verse libelling in early Stuart England' in P. Lake and S. Pincus (eds), *The Politics of the Public Sphere in Early Modern England.* Manchester: Manchester University Press.

Bentley, G. E. 1966. *The Jacobean and Caroline Stage: Plays and Playwrights.* Oxford: Clarendon Press.

Berry, L. E. (ed.). 1968. *John Stubbs's Gaping Gulf With Letters and Other Relevant Documents.* Charlottesville: Virginia University Press.

Bird, W. 2016. *Press and Speech Under Assault: The Early Supreme Court Justices, the Sedition Act of 1798, and the Campaign Against Dissent.* Oxford: Oxford University Press.

Black, J. L. (ed.). 2008. *The Martin Marprelate Tracts: A Modernised and Annotated Edition.* Cambridge: Cambridge University Press.

Boyer, A. D. 2003. *Sir Edward Coke and the Elizabethan Age.* Stanford, CA: Stanford University Press.

Brinkworth, E. R. 1942. 'The Study and Use of Archdeacons' Court Records: Illustrated from the Oxford Records,' *Transactions of the Historical Society*, 25 (4), pp. 93–119.

Bristol, M. 1985. *Carnival and Theatre: Plebeian Culture and the Structure of Authority in Renaissance England.* London: Routledge.

Brook, V. J. K. 1964. *Whitgift and the English Church.* London: Hodder and Stoughton.

Brooks, C. W. 1986. *Pettyfoggers and Vipers of the Commonwealth: The 'Lower Branch' of the Legal Profession in Early Modern England.* Cambridge: Cambridge University Press.

Brooks, C. W. 1998. *Lawyers, Litigation and English Society Since 1450.* London: Hambledon Press.

Brooks, C. W., and Lobban, M. 1998. *Communities and Courts in Britain, 1150–1900.* London: Hambledon Press.

Bryson, A. 2016. 'Elizabethan Verse Libel' in R. M. Smuts (ed.), *The Oxford Handbook of the Age of Shakespeare.* Oxford: Oxford University Press.

Bucknell, C. 2016. 'Verse Satire from the Renaissance to the Romantic Period' in A. Hadfield (ed.), *Oxford Bibliographies in British and Irish Literature.* New York:

Oxford University Press. <https://www.oxfordbibliographies.com/view/document/obo-9780199846719/obo-9780199846719-0123.xml>. Accessed 21 May 2019.

Burke, P. 1987. *The Social History of Language*. Cambridge: Cambridge University Press.

Burt, R. 1987. '"Licensed by Authority": Ben Jonson and the Politics of Early Stuart Theater,' *ELH*, 54 (3), pp. 529–60.

Burt, R. 1998. '(Un)Censoring in Detail: The Fetish of Censorship in the Early Modern Past and the Postmodern Present' in R. C. Post (ed.), *Censorship and Silencing: Practices of Cultural Regulation*. Los Angeles, CA: Getty Research Institute.

Burt, R. 2001. 'Doing the Queen: Gender, Sexuality and the Censorship of Elizabeth I's Royal Image from Renaissance Portraiture to Twentieth-century Mass Media' in A. Hadfield (ed.), *Literature and Censorship in Renaissance England*. Houndmills: Palgrave.

Capua, J. V. 1977. 'The Early History of Martial Law in England from the Fourteenth Century to the Petition of Right,' *Cambridge Law Journal*, 36 (1), pp. 152–73.

Carlson, E. J. 2001. 'Review of *Roman Canon Law in Reformation England* by R. H. Helmholz,' *Journal of Law and Religion*, 16 (2), pp. 361–5.

Cary, E. 1996 [1613]. *The Tragedy of Mariam* in S. P. Cerasano and M. Wynn-Davies (eds), *Renaissance Drama by Women: Texts and Documents*. London: Routledge.

Cavanagh, D. 2003. *Language and Politics in the Sixteenth-Century History Play*. Basingstoke: Palgrave Macmillan.

Cerasano, S. P., and Wynn-Davies, M. 1998. *Readings in renaissance women's drama: criticism, history, and performance, 1594–1998*. London: Routledge.

Chaudhuri, S. 2013. 'Review of *The Intellectual and Cultural Worlds of the Early Modern Inns of Court* by Jayne Elisabeth Archer, Elizabeth Goldring and Sarah Knight (Eds.),' *Spenser Review*, 43.1.9.

Cheyney, E. P. 1913. 'The Court of Star Chamber,' *The American Historical Review*, 18 (4), pp. 727–50.

Clare, J. 1999. *Art Made Tongue-Tied by Authority: Elizabethan and Jacobean Dramatic Censorship*. Manchester: Manchester University Press.

Clegg, C. S. 2004. *Press Censorship in Elizabethan England*. Cambridge: Cambridge University Press.

Coddon, K. S. 1993. 'Slander in an Allow'd Fool: *Twelfth Night*'s Crisis of the Aristocracy,' *Studies in English Literature, 1500–1900*, 33 (2), pp. 309–25.

Colclough, D. 1996. '"Of the alleadging of authors": The Construction and Reception of Textual Authority in English Prose, c. 1600–1630: With Special

Reference to the Writings of Francis Bacon, John Hoskyns, and John Donne.' DPhil diss., Oxford University.
Colclough, D. 2004. *Freedom of Speech in Early Stuart England*. Cambridge: Cambridge University Press.
Colclough, D. 2006. 'Verse Libels and the Epideictic Tradition in Early Stuart England,' in A. McRae (ed.), *'Railing Rhymes': Politics and Poetry in Early Stuart England*. Berkeley: University of California Press.
Collinson, P. 1967. *The Elizabethan Puritan Movement*. London: Jonathan Cape.
Collinson, P. 1995. 'Religious satire and the invention of puritanism' in J. Guy (ed.), *The Reign of Elizabeth I: Court and Culture in the Last Decade*. Cambridge: Cambridge University Press.
Collinson, P. 2013. *Richard Bancroft and Elizabethan Anti-Puritanism*. Cambridge: Cambridge University Press.
Cooper, J. 2011. *The Queen's Agent: Francis Walsingham at the Court of Elizabeth I*. London: Faber and Faber.
Crawford, J. 2005. *Marvelous Protestantism: Monstrous Births in Post-Reformation England*. Baltimore, MD: Johns Hopkins University Press.
Cressy, D. 2005. 'Book Burning in Tudor and Stuart England,' *The Sixteenth Century Journal*, 36 (2), pp. 359–74.
Cressy, D. 2010. *Dangerous Talk: Scandalous, Seditious and Treasonable Speech in Pre-Modern England*. Oxford: Oxford University Press.
Croft, P. 1991. 'The Reputation of Robert Cecil: Libels, Political Opinion and Popular Awareness in the Early Seventeenth Century,' *Transactions of the Royal Historical Society*, 6 (1), pp. 43–69.
Croft, P. 1995. 'Libels, popular literacy and public opinion in early modern England,' *Historical Research*, 167 (68), pp. 266–85.
Daybell, J. 2011. *The Material Letter in Early Modern England*. Basingstoke: Palgrave Macmillan.
Davenport, A. 1951. *The Whipper Pamphlets: The whipping of the satyre, by John Weever*. Liverpool: Liverpool University Press.
Davis, N. Z. 1975. *Society and Culture in Early Modern France: Eight Essays*. Stanford, CA: Stanford University Press.
Dean, D. 1996. *Law Making and Society in Elizabethan England: The Parliament of England, 1584–1601*. Cambridge: Cambridge University Press.
Donaldson, I. 2012. *Ben Jonson: A Life*. Oxford: Oxford University Press.
Doran, S. 1998. 'Why Did Elizabeth Not Marry?' in J. M. Walker (ed.), *Dissing Elizabeth: Negative Representations of Gloriana*. London: Duke University Press.
Doran, S. 2003. *The Myth of Elizabeth*. Basingstoke: Palgrave.

Durant, D. N. 1999. *Bess of Hardwick: Portrait of an Elizabethan Dynast*. London: Peter Owen.

Dutton, R. 1991. *Mastering the Revels: The Regulation and Censorship of English Renaissance Drama*. Basingstoke: Macmillan.

Dutton, R. 1993. 'Ben Jonson and the Master of the Revels,' in J. R. Mulryne and M. Shewring (eds), *Theatre and Government Under the Early Stuarts*. Cambridge: Cambridge University Press.

Dutton, R. 2006. 'Patronage, Licensing, and Censorship' in D. B. Hamilton (ed.), *A Concise Companion to English Renaissance Literature*. Oxford: Blackwell.

Elton, G. R. 1982. *The Tudor Constitution: Documents and Commentary*. Cambridge: Cambridge University Press.

Elton, G. R. 1985. *Policy and Police: The Enforcement of the Reformation in the Age of Thomas Cromwell*. Cambridge: Cambridge University Press.

Emmison, F. G. 1970. *Elizabethan Life Vol 1: Disorder: Mainly From Essex Sessions and Assize Records*. Chelmsford: Essex Record Office.

Emmison, F. G. 1973. *Elizabethan Life Vol 2: Morals and the Church Courts: Mainly From Essex Archdeaconal Records*. Chelmsford: Essex Record Office.

Fletcher, A. 1985. 'Honour, Reputation, and Local Officeholding in Elizabethan and Stuart England,' in A. Fletcher and J. Stevenson (eds), *Order and Disorder in Early Modern England*. Cambridge: Cambridge University Press.

Forse, J. 1993. *Art Imitates Business: Commercial and Political Influences in Elizabethan Theatre*. Bowling Green, OH: Bowling Green State University Press.

Fox, A. 1994. 'Ballads, Libels and Popular Ridicule in Jacobean England,' *Past & Present*, 145, pp. 47–83.

Fox, A. 2000. *Oral and Literate Culture in England, 1500–1700*. Oxford: Oxford University Press.

Freeman, A. 1973. 'Marlowe, Kyd, and the Dutch Church Libel,' *Studies in Renaissance Drama*, 3 (1), pp. 44–52.

French, H. R. 2000. 'The Search for the "middle sort" of People in England, 1600–1800,' *The Historical Journal*, 43 (1), pp. 277–93.

Frere, W. H., and Douglass, C. E. (eds). 1907. *Puritan Manifestoes: A Study of the Origin of the Puritan Revolt*. New York: E. S. Gorham.

Georgecink, S. H. 2003. 'Review of *Dramatic Difference: Gender, Class and Genre in the Early Modern Closet Drama* by Karen Raber,' *The Sixteenth Century Journal*, 34 (2), pp. 597–99.

Gibson, J. 2000. 'Letters' in M. Hattaway (ed.), *A Companion to English Renaissance Literature and Culture*. Oxford: Blackwell.

Gildersleeve, V. C. 1908. *Government Regulation of Elizabethan Drama*. New York: Columbia University Press.

Goodbody, A. 2002. *The Spoken Word: Oral Culture in Britain, 1500–1850*. Manchester: Manchester University Press.

Gordon, A. 2002. 'The Act of Libel: Conscripting Civic Space in Early Modern England,' *Journal of Mediaeval and Renaissance Studies*, 32, pp. 375–97.

Gowing, L. 1993. 'Gender and the Language of Insult in Early Modern London,' *History Workshop*, 5, pp. 1–21.

Gowing, L. 1996. *Domestic Dangers: Women, Words and Sex in Early Modern London*. Oxford: Clarendon Press.

Gowing, L., and Crawford, P. 2000. *Women's Worlds in Seventeenth-Century England: A Sourcebook*. London: Routledge.

Greaves, R. 1981. *Society and Religion in Elizabethan England*. Minneapolis: University of Minnesota Press.

Green, R. 2003. '"Ears Prejudicate" in *Mariam* and *Duchess of Malfi*,' *Studies in English Literature, 1500–1900*, 43 (2), pp. 459–74.

Gurr, A. 1987. *Playgoing in Shakespeare's London*. Cambridge: Cambridge University Press.

Gurr, A. 1992. *The Shakespearean Stage*. Cambridge: Cambridge University Press.

Guy, J. A. 1985. *The Court of Star Chamber and its Records to the Reign of Elizabeth I*. London: HM Stationary Office.

Guy, J. A. 1995a. 'The rhetoric of counsel in early modern England' in D. Hoak (ed.), *Tudor Political Culture*. Cambridge: Cambridge University Press.

Guy, J. A. 1995b. *The Reign of Elizabeth I: Court and Culture in the Last Decade*. Cambridge: Cambridge University Press.

Habermann, I. 2003. *Staging Slander and Gender in Early Modern England*. Aldershot: Ashgate.

Hackett, H. 1995. *Virgin, Mother, Maiden Queen*. Basingstoke: Palgrave Macmillan.

Hadfield, A. 2001. *Literature and Censorship in Renaissance England*. Basingstoke: Palgrave Macmillan.

Hair, P. 1972. *Before the Bawdy Courts: Selections From Church Court and Other Records Relating to the Correction of Moral Offences in England, Scotland, and New England, 1300–1800*. London: Elek.

Halasz, A. 1997. *The Marketplace of Print: Pamphlets and the Public Sphere in Early Modern England*. Cambridge: Cambridge University Press.

Hamburger, P. 1985. 'The Development of the Law of Seditious Libel and the Control of the Press,' *Stanford Law Review*, 37 (1984/5), pp. 661–765.

Hammer, P. E. J. 1999. *The Polarisation of Elizabethan Politics: The Political Career of Robert Devereux, 2nd Earl of Essex, 1585–1597*. Cambridge: Cambridge University Press.

Harding, A. 1973. *A Social History of English Law*. London: Pelican.

Harmes, M., and Colclough, G. 2015. 'Proverbs and Princes in Post-Reformation England' in F. G. Gentry (ed.), *Spoken Word and Social Practice: Orality in Europe, 1400–1700*. Boston, MA: Brill.

Hawarde, J. 1894. *Les Reportes Del Cases in Camera Stellata, 1593–1609. From the Original Ms. of John Hawarde.* William Paley Baildon (ed.). London: Spottiswoode & co.

Heinemann, M. 1982. *Puritanism and Theatre: Thomas Middleton and Opposition Drama Under the Early Stuarts*. Cambridge: Cambridge University Press.

Helmholz, R. H. 1985. 'Introduction' in R. H. Helmholz (ed.), *Select Cases on Defamation to 1600*. London: Selden Society.

Helmholz, R. H. 2004. *Roman Canon Law in Reformation England.* Cambridge: Cambridge University Press.

Hickson, O., and Carter-Ruck, P. F. 1953. *The Law of Libel and Slander*. London: Faber and Faber.

Hill, C. 1985. *The Collected Essays of Christopher Hill, Volume One: Writing and Revolution in 17th Century England.* Whistable: Whistable Litho, Ltd.

Hiscock, A. 2013. '"Achilles alter": the heroic lives and afterlives of Robert Devereux, 2nd Earl of Essex' in L. Hopkins and A. Connolly (eds), *Essex: The Cultural Impact of an Elizabethan Courtier*. Manchester: Manchester University Press.

Holden, W. P. 1954. *Anti-Puritan Satire, 1572–1642*. London: Oxford University Press.

Honigmann, E. A. J. 1965. *The Stability of Shakespeare's Text*. London: Edward Arnold.

Hope, J. 2010. *Shakespeare and Language: Reason, Eloquence and Artifice in the Renaissance*. London: Arden Shakespeare.

Houlbrooke, R. 1979. *Church Courts and the People during the English Reformation, 1520–1570*. Oxford: Oxford University Press.

Hudson, N. 1994. *Writing and European Thought, 1600–1830*. Cambridge: Cambridge University Press.

Hudson, W. 1621. *A Treatise on the Court of Star Chamber*. London: E. and R. Brooke.

Hurst, J. F. 1899. 'The Elizabethan Settlement of the Church of England,' *The American Journal of Theology*, 3 (4), pp. 679–94.

Hutson, L. 2007. *The Invention of Suspicion: Law and Mimesis in Shakespeare and Renaissance Drama*. New York: Oxford University Press.

Hutton, R. 1996. *The Stations of the Sun: A History of the Ritual Year in Britain.* Oxford: Oxford University Press.

Ingram, M. 1984. 'Religion, communities and moral discipline in late sixteenth- and early seventeenth-century England: case studies,' in K. Von Greyerz (ed.), *Religion and Society in Early Modern Europe, 1500–1800*. London: Allen & Unwin.

Ingram, M. 1987. *Church Courts, Sex and Marriage in England, 1570–1640*. Cambridge: Cambridge University Press.

Jardine, L. 1996. *Reading Shakespeare Historically*. London: Routledge.

Kaplan, M. L. 1997. *The Culture of Slander in Early Modern England*. Cambridge: Cambridge University Press.

Kermode, L. E. 2009. *Aliens and Englishness in Elizabethan Drama*. Cambridge: Cambridge University Press.

Knowles, J. 2000. '"To Scourge the Arse / Jove's Marrow so had Wasted": Scurrility and the Subversion of Sodomy' in D. Cavanagh and T. Kirk (eds), *Language and Politics in the Sixteenth-Century History Play*. Basingstoke: Palgrave Macmillan.

Lake, P. 1982. *Moderate Puritans and the Elizabethan Church*. Cambridge: Cambridge University Press.

Lake, P. 2007. 'The Politics of Popularity' in P. Lake and S. Pincus (eds), *The Politics of the Public Sphere in Early Modern England*. Manchester: Manchester University Press.

Lake, P. 2016. *Bad Queen Bess? Libels, Secret Histories, and the Politics of Publicity in the Reign of Queen Elizabeth I*. Oxford: Oxford University Press.

Lake, P., and Pincus, S. (eds). 2007. *The Politics of the Public Sphere in Early Modern England*. Manchester: Manchester University Press.

Lassiter, J. C. 1978, 'Defamation of Peers: The Rise and Decline of the Action for *Scandalum Magnatum*, 1497–1773,' *American Journal of Legal History*, 22 (1978), pp. 216–36.

Levin, C. 1998. 'Gender, Monarchy and the Power of Words' in J. M. Walker (ed.), *Dissing Elizabeth: Negative Representations of Gloriana*. London: Duke University Press.

Levin, C. 2013. *The Heart and Stomach of a King: Elizabeth I and the Politics of Sex and Power*. Philadelphia: University of Pennsylvania Press.

Loades, D. M. 1974. 'The Theory and Practice of Censorship in Sixteenth-Century England,' *Transactions of the Royal Historical Society*, 5 (24), pp. 141–57.

Love, H. 1993. *Scribal Publication in Seventeenth-Century England*. Oxford: Clarendon Press.

McCabe, R. A. 2001. 'Right Puisante and Terrible Priests: the Role of the Anglican Church in Elizabethan State Censorship' in A. Hadfield (ed.), *Literature and Censorship in Renaissance England*. Houndmills: Palgrave.

MacCaffrey, W. T. 1963. 'Elizabethan Politics: The First Decade, 1558–1569,' *Past and Present*, 24, pp. 25–42.

Mack, P. 2002. *Elizabethan Rhetoric: Theory and Practice*. Cambridge: Cambridge University Press.

McLaren, A. 2002. 'Gender, Religion, and Early Modern Nationalism: Elizabeth I, Mary Queen of Scots, and the Genesis of English Anti-Catholicism,' *The American Historical Review*, 107 (3), pp. 739–67.

McRae, A. 2000. 'The verse libel: popular satire in early modern England' in D. Cavanagh and Tim Kirk (eds), *Subversion and Scurrility: Popular Discourse in Europe from 1500 to the Present*. Aldershot: Ashgate.

McRae, A. 2004a. *Literature, Satire and the Early Stuart State*. Cambridge: Cambridge University Press.

McRae, A. 2004b. *The Culture of Early Stuart Libelling*. Cambridge: Cambridge University Press.

Manning, R. B. 1980. 'The Origins of the Doctrine of Sedition,' *Albion: A Quarterly Journal Concerned With British Studies*, 12 (2), pp. 99–121.

Marchant, R. A. *The Church Under the Law: Justice Administration and Discipline in the Diocese of York, 1560–1640*. London: Cambridge University Press.

Marotti, A. 1995. *Manuscript, Print and the English Renaissance Lyric*. Ithaca, NY: Cornell University Press.

Marshall, P. 2017. *Heretics and Believers: A History of the English Reformation*. New Haven, CT: Yale University Press.

Matthews, B. 1908. 'The Legitimacy of the Closet Drama,' *The North American Review*, 187 (627), pp. 213–23.

May, S., and Bryson, A. 2016. *Verse Libel in Renaissance England and Scotland*. Oxford: Oxford University Press.

Mears, N. 2001. 'Counsel, public debate and queenship: John Stubbs' "The Discoverie of a Gaping Gulf", 1579,' *Historical Journal*, 44 (3), pp. 629–50.

Mears, N. 2003. 'Courts, Courtiers and Culture in Tudor England,' *The Historical Journal*, 46 (3), pp. 703–22.

Meskill, L. S. 2009. *Ben Jonson and Envy*. Cambridge: Cambridge University Press.

Milson, S. F. C. 1981. *Historical Foundations of the Common Law*. London: Butterworths.

Montrose, L. 2006. *The Subject of Elizabeth: Authority, Gender and Representation*. Chicago: University of Chicago Press.

Mortimer, I. 2013. *The Time Traveller's Guide to Elizabethan England*. London: Vintage.

Mukherji, S. 2006. *Law and Representation in Early Modern Drama*. Cambridge: Cambridge University Press.

Munro, L. 2005. *Children of the Queen's Revels: A Jacobean Theatre Repertory*. Cambridge: Cambridge University Press.

Neale, J. E. 1971. *Elizabeth I*. London: Penguin.

Norbrook, D. 2002. *Poetry and Politics in the English Renaissance*. Oxford: Oxford University Press.

North, M. L. 2003. *The Anonymous Renaissance: Cultures of Discretion in Tudor-Stuart England.* Chicago: University of Chicago Press.

North, M. L. 2011. 'Anonymity in Early Modern Manuscript Culture: Finding a Purposeful Convention in a Ubiquitous Condition' in J. Wright Starner and B. Howard Traister (eds), *Anonymity in Early Modern England: What's in a Name?* Farnham: Ashgate Publishing Limited.

O'Callaghan, M. 2000. 'Publication: Print and Manuscript' in M. Hattaway (ed.), *A Companion to English Renaissance Literature and Culture.* Oxford: Blackwell.

O'Callaghan, M. 2007. *The English Wits: Literature and Sociability in Early Modern England.* Cambridge: Cambridge University Press.

Oliver, G. 1861. *Lives of the Bishops of Exeter and a History of the Cathedral.* Exeter: William Roberts.

Orwell, G., and Reynolds, R. 1948. *British Pamphleteers, Vol. I: From the Sixteenth Century to the French Revolution.* London: Wingate.

Questier, M. 2008. *Catholicism and Community in Early Modern England: Politics, Aristocratic Patronage and Religion, C.1550–1640.* Cambridge: Cambridge University Press.

Painter, W. H. 1961. 'Republication Problems in the Law of Defamation,' *Virginia Law Review*, 47 (7), pp. 1131–63.

Pierce, W. 1908. *An Historical Introduction to the Marprelate Tracts: a Chapter in the Evolution of Religious and Civil Liberty in England.* London: Constable.

Poole, K. 2000. *Radical Religion From Shakespeare to Milton: Figures of Non-conformity in Early Modern England.* Cambridge: Cambridge University Press.

Prest, W. 1972. *The Inns of Court under Elizabeth I and the Early Stuarts, 1590–1640.* London: Longman.

Raber, K. 2001. *Dramatic Difference: Gender, Class, and Genre in the Early Modern Closet Drama.* London: Associated University Presses.

Raymond, J. 2003. *Pamphlets and Pamphleteering in Early Modern Britain.* Cambridge: Cambridge University Press.

Raymond, J. 2007. 'Review of *Censorship and Cultural Sensibility: The Regulation of Language in Tudor-Stuart England* by Deborah Shuger,' *The American Historical Review*, 112 (5), pp. 1604–06.

Redmond, M. J. 2009. *Shakespeare, Politics, and Italy: Intertextuality on the Jacobean Stage.* Farnham: Ashgate.

Rivington, C. R. (ed.). 1967. *A Transcript of the Registers of the Company of Stationers of London, 1554–1640.* Gloucester: Peter Smith.

Samaha, J. B. 1975. 'Gleanings from Local Criminal Court Records: Sedition Amongst the Inarticulate in Elizabethan Essex,' *Journal of Social History*, 8 (4), pp. 61–79.

Schott Syme, H. 2012. *Theatre and Testimony in Shakespeare's England: A Culture of Mediation*. Cambridge: Cambridge University Press.
Sharpe, K., and Lake, P. (eds). 1994. *Culture and Politics in Early Stuart England*. Houndmills: Macmillan.
Sharpe, K. M. 2000a. *Remapping Early Modern England: The Culture of Seventeenth-Century Politics*. Cambridge: Cambridge University Press.
Sharpe, K. M. 2000b. *Reading Revolutions: The Politics of Reading in Early Modern England*. New Haven, CT: Yale University Press.
Shrank, C. 2004. '"These fewe scribbled rules": Representing Scribal Intimacy in Early Modern Print,' *Huntingdon Library Quarterly*, 67 (2), pp. 295–314.
Shuger, D. 2006. *Censorship & Cultural Sensibility: The Regulation of Language in Tudor-Stuart England*. Philadelphia: University of Pennsylvania Press.
Shuger, D. 2009. 'A Protesting Catholic Puritan in Elizabethan England,' *Journal of British Studies*, 48 (3), pp. 587–630.
Southerden Burn, J. 1870. *The Star Chamber: Notices of the Court and its Proceedings; With a Few Additional Notes of the High Commission*. London: J Russell Smith.
Staines, J. D. 2009. *The Tragic Histories of Mary, Queen of Scots: 1560–1690*. Farnham: Ashgate.
Stoll, E. E. 1953. 'Slander in Drama,' *Shakespeare Quarterly*, 4 (4), pp. 433–50.
Stone, L. 1966. 'Social Mobility in England, 1500–1700,' *Past & Present*. 33 (1966), pp. 16–55.
Straznicky, M. 2004. *Privacy, Play Reading and Women's Closet Drama, 1550–1700*. Cambridge: Cambridge University Press.
Stretton, T. 1998. *Women Waging Law in Elizabethan England*. Cambridge: Cambridge University Press.
Tillyard, E. M. W. 1943. *The Elizabethan World Picture*. London: Chatto & Windus.
van Patten, J. K. 1983. 'Magic, Prophecy, and the Law of Treason in Reformation England,' *American Journal of Legal History*, 27 (1), pp. 1–32.
Veerapen, S. 2017. 'Slanderisation and Censure-ship: When Good Texts Went Bad in Early Modern England,' *Journal of the Northern Renaissance*, Issue 9 (2017).
Wagner, J. A. 2010. *Voices of Shakespeare's England: Contemporary Accounts of Elizabethan Daily Life*. Santa Barbara, CA: Greenwood Publishing Group.
Walker, G. 2000. 'Courtship and Counsel: John Lyly's *Campaspe*' in M. Hattaway (ed.), *A Companion to English Renaissance Literature and Culture*. Oxford: Blackwell.
Walker, G., and James, H. 1995. 'The Politics of Gorboduc,' *The English Historical Review*, 110 (435), pp. 109–21.
Watson, S. 1939. 'Gorboduc and the Theory of Tyrannicide,' *The Modern Language Review*, 34 (3), pp. 355–66.

Whitelock, A. 2013. *Elizabeth's Bedfellows: An Intimate History of the Queen's Court*. London: Bloomsbury.

Whitfield White, P., and Westfall, S. R. (eds). 2002. *Shakespeare and Theatrical Patronage in Early Modern England*. Cambridge: Cambridge University Press.

Whiting, R. 1989. *The Blind Devotion of the People: Popular Religion and the English Reformation*. Cambridge: Cambridge University Press.

Wickham, G. 1963. *Early English Stages, 1300–1660 II: 1576–1660*. London: Routledge and Paul.

Wickham, G., Berry, H., and Ingram, W. (eds). 2000. *English Professional Theatre, 1530–1660*. Cambridge: Cambridge University Press.

Wickins, P. L. 2012. *Victorian Protestantism and Bloody Mary: The Legacy of Religious Persecution in Tudor England*. Bury St Edmunds: Arena Books.

Wigfall Green, A. 1931. *The Inns of Court and Early English Drama*. London: Oxford University Press.

Winston, J. 2005. 'Expanding the Political Nation: Gorboduc at the Inns of Court and Succession Revisited,' *Early Theatre*, 8 (1), pp. 11–34.

Woodhuysen, H. R. 1996. *Sir Philip Sidney and the Circulation of Manuscripts, 1558–1640*. Oxford: Oxford University Press.

Wright, T. 1859. *Political Poems and Songs Relating to English History: Composed During the Period from the Accession of Edward III to that of Richard III, Volume II*. London: Longman, Green, Longman, and Roberts.

Yachnin, P. 2001. 'Eye to eye opposed' in P. Yachnin and A. B. Dawson (eds), *The Culture of Playgoing in Shakespeare's England: A Collaborative Debate*. Cambridge: Cambridge University Press.

Yachnin, P. 2003. 'Reversal of Fortune: Shakespeare, Middleton, and the Puritans,' *English Literary History*, 70 (3), pp. 757–86.

Yates, F. A. 1975. *Astraea: The Imperial Theme in the Sixteenth Century*. London: Routledge and Kegan Paul.

Index

www.ingramcontent.com/pod-product-compliance
Ingram Content Group UK Ltd.
Pitfield, Milton Keynes, MK11 3LW, UK
UKHW021845100926
8556IPUK00019B/1066

9 781789 976731